THE DESIGN IN THE WAX

The William and Katherine Devers Series
in Dante Studies

THEODORE J. CACHEY, JR., AND CHRISTIAN MOEVS, EDITORS

THE
DESIGN
IN THE
WAX

The Structure of the
Divine Comedy *and Its Meaning*

MARC COGAN

UNIVERSITY OF NOTRE DAME PRESS

Notre Dame   London

University of Notre Dame Press

Copyright © 1999 by University of Notre Dame
Notre Dame, IN 46556
undpress.nd.edu

Published in the United States of America

Reprinted in 2007

Library of Congress Cataloging-in-Publication Data
Cogan, Marc.
      The design in the wax : the structure of the Divine comedy
and its meaning / Marc Cogan.
      p. cm. — (The William and Katherine Devers series in Dante
studies ; 3)
   Includes bibliographical references and index.
   ISBN-13: 978-0-268-00887-1 (pbk. : alk. paper)
   ISBN-10: 0-268-00887-6 (pbk. : alk. paper)
   I. Dante Alighieri, 1265–1321. Divina commedia. I. Title.
   II. Series.
   PQ4390.C68 1999
   851'.l—dc21   98-54915

For SARAH
It was really all her fault.

Contents

2

Purgatorio 77

3

Paradiso 149

Contents

CONTENTS

Preface

The William and Katherine Devers Program in Dante Studies at the University of Notre Dame supports rare book acquisitions in the university's John A. Zahm Dante collection, funds an annual visiting professorship in Dante studies, and supports electronic and print publication of scholarly research in the field. In collaboration with the Medieval Institute at the university, the Devers program has initiated a series dedicated to the publication of the most significant current scholarship in the field of Dante studies.

In keeping with the spirit that inspired the creation of the Devers program, the series takes Dante as a focal point that draws together the many disciplines and forms of inquiry that constitute a cultural tradition without fixed boundaries. Accordingly, the series hopes to illuminate Dante's position at the center of contemporary critical debates in the humanities by reflecting both the highest quality of scholarly achievement and the greatest diversity of critical perspectives.

The series publishes works on Dante from a wide variety of disciplinary viewpoints and in diverse scholarly genres, including critical studies, commentaries, editions, translations, and conference proceedings of exceptional importance. The series is supervised by an international advisory board composed of distinguished Dante scholars and is published regularly by the University of Notre Dame Press.

The Dolphin and Anchor device that appears on publications of the Devers series was used by the great humanist, grammarian, editor, and typographer, Aldus Manutius (1449–1515), in whose 1502 edition of Dante (second issue) and all subsequent editions it appeared. The device illustrates the ancient proverb *Festina lente*, "Hurry up slowly."

THEODORE J. CACHEY, JR.,
AND CHRISTIAN MOEVS
EDITORS

Acknowledgments

This was a long project, and the debts I have incurred are many. I would like to thank the following people.

My wife, Sarah, first of all and beyond all others, for her support, patience, love, and good humor all this long time.

My friends and colleagues at Wayne State University and elsewhere, next, who helped me more perhaps than they knew: Michael Murrin and Raffaele De Benedictis, and especially Andrea diTommaso, who encouraged me throughout this project with his knowledge and his questions, and who, year after year, was willing to lend me his students so I could have new listeners to this argument. Then, my dear friends, first at Monteith College, then in the Department, later Program, of Humanities, who created the rich interdisciplinary environment (now, alas, almost entirely gone) in which it was possible to pursue an inquiry such as this one: the late Ramón Betanzos, Louise Dezur, Martin Herman, Sara Leopold, Sandra McCoy, Linda Speck, Richard Studing, and Jay Vogelbaum. Then, Theodore Cachey and Christian Moevs for their belief in this book and their wise advice. Finally, a departed and sorely missed friend, Michael Vollen, who showed me where to find the last piece of the puzzle.

Abbreviations

Certain works are cited frequently enough in this essay to warrant having a shorter form for their citation. They are the following:

CH   Pseudo-Dionysius, *Celestial Hierarchy.* The text is the Latin translation by John Scotus Eriugena in *PL*, 122, 1035b–1070c.

Conv.   Dante Alighieri, *Convivio*, ed. Cesare Vasoli, in *Opere minori,* vol. 1, part 2 (Milano and Napoli: Riccardo Ricciardi, 1988).

DDP   Dartmouth Dante Project. This on-line source (at lib. dartmouth.edu on the Internet) has been used to consult the many commentaries to the *Commedia* stored in its database.

de An.   Aristotle, *On the Soul.* The text used is the Latin translation by William of Moerbeke reprinted in the Marietti edition of Thomas Aquinas, *In Aristotelis Librum de Anima commentarium* (see below). Divisions into books and chapters follow the Marietti text. Parallel references are also given to the page numbers in Bekker's Berlin edition of Aristotle's complete works.

de Trin.   Augustine, *de Trinitate*, ed. W. J. Mountain (Turnholt: Brepols, 1968).

Div. nom.   Pseudo-Dionysius, *On the Divine Names.* The text is the Latin translation by John Scotus Eriugena in *PL*, 122, 1111c–1172b.

EH   Pseudo-Dionysius, *Ecclesiastical Hierarchy.* The text is the Latin translation by John Scotus Eriugena in *PL*, 122, 1069d–1112c.

EN   Aristotle, *Nicomachean Ethics.* The text used is the Latin translation by William of Moerbeke reprinted in the Marietti edition of Thomas Aquinas, *In decem libros Ethicorum Aristotelis ad Nicomachum expositio* (see below). Divisions into books and chapters follow the Marietti text. Parallel references are also given to the page numbers in Bekker's Berlin edition of Aristotle's complete works.

Ep. xiii   Dante Alighieri, *Letter to Can Grande della Scala*, in *Epistole*, ed. A. Frugoni and G. Brugnoli, in *Opere minori*, vol. 2 (Milano and Napoli: Riccardo Ricciardi, 1979). Earlier editions of the letters number this letter as *Ep. x.*

In de An. Thomas Aquinas, *In Aristotelis Librum de Anima commentarium,* 4th ed., ed. A. M. Pirotta, O.P. (Torino: Marietti, 1959). The English translation, *Aristotle's de Anima in the Version of William of Moerbeke and the Commentary of St. Thomas Aquinas,* trans. Kenelm Foster, O.P., and Silvester Humphries, O.P. (New Haven: Yale University Press, 1951), follows the Marietti edition's numbering of the sections of Aquinas' commentary.

In Ethica Thomas Aquinas, *In decem libros Ethicorum Aristotelis ad Nicomachum expositio,* ed. R. M. Spiazzi, O.P. (Torino and Roma: Marietti, 1949). The English translation, *St. Thomas Aquinas, Commentary on the Nicomachean Ethics,* trans. C. I. Litzinger, O.P. (Chicago: Henry Regnery, 1964), follows the Marietti edition's numbering of the sections of Aquinas' commentary.

In Metaphys. Thomas Aquinas, *In duodecim libros Metaphysicorum Aristotelis expositio,* ed. M.-R. Cathala, O.P., and R. M. Spiazzi, O.P. (Torino and Roma: Marietti, 1950). The English translation, *St. Thomas Aquinas, Commentary on the Metaphysics of Aristotle,* trans. John P. Rowan (Chicago: Henry Regnery, 1961), follows the Marietti edition's numbering of the sections of Aquinas' commentary.

In Sent. Thomas Aquinas, *Commenta in libris Sententiarum,* in *Opera omnia,* vols. 7–10, ed. S. E. Fretté and P. Maré (Paris: Vivès, 1873).

Malo Thomas Aquinas, *de Malo,* ed. P. Bazzi and M. Pession, in *Quæstiones disputatæ,* vol. 2, 9th ed. (Torino and Roma: Marietti, 1953).

Metaphys. Aristotle, *Metaphysics.* The text used is the Latin translation by William of Moerbeke reprinted in the Marietti edition of Thomas Aquinas, *In duodecim libros Metaphysicorum Aristotelis expositio* (see above). Divisions into books and chapters follow the Marietti text. Parallel references are also given to the page numbers in Bekker's Berlin edition of Aristotle's complete works.

Myst. Theol. Pseudo-Dionysius, *Mystical Theology.* The text is the Latin translation by John Scotus Eriugena in *PL,* 122, 1171b–1176d.

Phys. Aristotle, *Physics.* The text used is the Latin translation by William of Moerbeke reprinted in *de Physico auditu* in Thomas Aquinas, *Opera omnia,* vol. 22, ed. S. E. Fretté (Paris: Vivès, 1875).

Abbreviations

PL   *Patrologiæ cursus completus* (Latin), gen. ed. J.-P. Migne (Paris: Migne, then Garnier, 1844–).

SCG Thomas Aquinas, *Summa de veritate catholicæ fidei contra gentiles* in *Opera omnia*, vol. 12, ed. S. E. Fretté (Paris: Vivès, 1874).

Sent. Magistri Petri Lombardi (Peter Lombard), *Sententiæ in IV Libris distinctæ, ed. PP. Collegii S. Bonaventuræ ad Claras Aquas,* t. 1, 3d ed. (Grottaferrata [Rome]: Editiones Collegii S. Bonaventuræ ad Claras Aquas, 1971) [Spicilegium Bonaventurianum 4] and *Sententiæ in IV Libris distinctæ, ed. PP. Collegii S. Bonaventuræ ad Claras Aquas,* t. 2, 3d ed. (Grottaferrata [Rome]: Editiones Collegii S. Bonaventuræ ad Claras Aquas, 1981) [Spicilegium Bonaventurianum 5].

Singleton Charles Singleton, *The Divine Comedy,* translated with a commentary, 3 vols. (Princeton: Princeton University Press, Bollingen Series 80, 1970–75).

ST   Thomas Aquinas, *Summa theologica.*

The text of the *Commedia* is that edited by Giuseppe Vandelli from Scartazzini's earlier edition, 21st ed. (Milano: Ulrico Hoepli, 1988).

Introduction

ANOTHER BOOK ON THE
STRUCTURE OF THE *COMMEDIA*?

Even to myself, writing a book about the structure of the *Divine Comedy* seems a very old-fashioned, if not positively reactionary, thing to do. There was a time when books were written on this subject, for the most part in the early years of this century. Nowadays, if the subject is treated at all, it is as a brief note to those few places in the *Commedia* where the structure of a *cantica* is discussed explicitly. As a separate subject, the poem's structure seems to have been exhausted, or discredited. There are only two things I can say in my defense: first, that I too had not originally intended to do an overall examination of the subject. Dealing with what was once a much more modest and circumscribed issue in the poem, I discovered that to confirm the conclusions I had reached required situating them in the context of the structure, first, of the *Inferno,* and then of the poem as a whole. It was the argument that forced me to make the inquiry you have before you.

My second defense is that however old-fashioned the subject may seem to be, there remains no more important subject for our understanding of the poem, or for any other inquiries we might wish to make into it. All of our most sophisticated interpretations of the narrative depend on its subtle and erudite structure. For that matter, it would not be that great an exaggeration to say that everything we discover in the poem begins from one most simple and most intuitive structural principle regarding the order in which we encounter events in the narrative: down is worse; upward is better. No matter how rudimentary, even simple-minded, this axiom may seem, we should stop to consider how fundamentally important it is—so important that Dante makes sure to have Virgil confirm it explicitly—both to Dante writing the *Commedia,* and to us reading it. Let us suppose, for example, that we had only the poetic details of the *Inferno* from which to determine Dante's view of the natures and the seriousness of the sins we encounter. We naturally assume that justice demands that worse sins be punished more severely. Yet anyone who has ever discussed the punishments of the *Inferno* with friends, colleagues, or students has discovered that no two people are repelled or horrified by the same punishments. So, if all we had to rely on were our own estimations of the severity of the punishments as they are described, we would find that our interpretations of Dante's intentions regarding sin would be similarly diverse, subjective, and contradictory.

The problem, of course, is not restricted to the *Inferno.* Throughout the poem Dante is working to fulfill three goals simultaneously: to indicate through its incidents something of the underlying natures of sin, redemption, and blessedness; to indicate the graduated seriousness of sins and vices, and the similarly graduated levels of blessedness; and to indicate the principles by which different species of sin and vice and different kinds of blessedness are related to one another—all of this with a view to our understanding both the common origin of all actions, sinful or pious, and the sacred principles by which we distinguish and judge them. To accomplish all three goals in the events of the narrative alone is impossible. Poetic details, like all concrete particulars, are by their nature ambiguous, and at every stage we would find ourselves facing the same irreconcilable diversity of personal opinion regarding the meaning of these particulars.

Knowing this, Dante relies on the structure of the poem and its parts to embody and reveal the principles that enable us to reduce this ambiguity to clarity. Some of the embodiment of the narrative—I mean the overall shape of each realm through which Dante passes, and the order in which events occur within the narrative—is embodiment not of individual persons or individual sins, but of more universal philosophical and theological principles and distinctions in the light of which the other details of the narrative can be meaningfully interpreted. We encounter these abstract principles also in the narrative, and they create the contexts in which individual events occur and acquire meaning.

Leaving the structure of the narrative to carry its fundamental philosophical doctrines was poetically liberating for Dante. Structural relations could indicate both the gradations of sin, redemption, and blessedness, and also the affinities and distinctions that may exist between groups of sins, vices, or blessed activities. The structures made it possible for him to concentrate, in the characters and descriptions and events of the narrative, on throwing the clearest light on the natures of the actions that we see in the poem. But it is still with the structure that all interpretation begins, since we can be confident that we have properly understood the details of the narrative only when we are sure that we can place them in the structure of each *cantica* and of the poem as a whole.

We might have thought that after so many years the question of the structure of the poem and its parts had been resolved, all the more so since any inquiry into the structure begins from an explicit statement in the *Commedia* itself regarding the structure of its first part, the *Inferno*. Indeed, our understanding of the allegorical significance of the incidents of the *Inferno* would be lamentably, maybe fatally, defective if we did not possess the explanation of the organization of Hell that Dante has Virgil provide in canto xi. Until that moment, while it has been clear to the reader that distinctions were being made as Dante and Virgil moved from one circle of Hell to the next, we neither knew the principle of the distinctions nor did we know that we would ever know it. But when Virgil informs us that the organization of Hell not only separates one sin from another, but also groups related sins with one another in geographical proximity, principles are made explicit that explain why certain sins are distinguished from one another, why some sins are more serious than others, and how sins of different gravities are related to one another. Only the structure of Hell as it is described by Virgil—which is also the organization of the narrative of the *Inferno*—reduces the ambiguity of the details of the narrative and makes us believe that it is possible to reach a univocal statement of the meaning of the incidents reported in the poem.

Unfortunately, that most important explicit statement as to the organization of Hell has been repeatedly misunderstood. Virgil's description of the structure of Hell explains its distinctions by reference to Aristotle's *Nicomachean Ethics*. If we take Virgil at his word, we must conclude either that Dante did not understand Aristotle, or that despite using Aristotle, he contradicts him in the details of the narrative at almost every turn. For if the Aristotelian distinctions that Virgil employs are taken as we would currently understand Aristotle, they cannot be consistently applied to the souls and sins we encounter in the

Inferno. The fault is ours, however, not Dante's. The Aristotle of the *Commedia* is not our Aristotle, he is the Aristotle the Middle Ages would have understood. Trying to make Dante's distinctions fit Aristotle as Aristotle is now interpreted, previous writers on the structure of the *Inferno* failed, and in attempting to reconcile two irreconcilable systems ran into two other errors. On the one hand, of course, they misunderstood crucial aspects of both the doctrine and the poetry of the *Inferno*. On the other, they also missed the opportunity to discover the relation of the structure of the *Inferno* to the structures of the other two *cantiche*. When we read Virgil's references to Aristotle, taking account of the semantic shifts the Middle Ages made in their interpretations of Aristotle, we discover that the contradictions between Aristotle and the incidents of the poem disappear, and we discover more completely the significance of those incidents.

Nor is this reinterpretation relevant only to the *Inferno*. When Dante gave the *Inferno* an explicit philosophical structure, he also created the expectation that the other realms of the poem would have their own structures too, and that those structures would be equally important in understanding the significance of the poetic details of the following two *cantiche*. It is that expectation that directs us to consider the question of structure in the *Commedia* generally. When Virgil provides an equivalent account of the structure of Purgatory in canto xvii of the *Purgatorio*, our expectation is confirmed; and while there is no explicit description by Beatrice of the structure of Heaven in the *Paradiso*, we remain convinced that it too most likely has a structure, whose discovery would be an aid to the understanding of that *cantica*.

Finally, when we have recovered the proper principle of the structure of the *Inferno*, we find we are able to recognize that that same principle operates in all of the realms of the *Commedia*. Since the field of the *Commedia* is ethics, as Dante explicitly states in the *Letter to Can Grande* (*Ep.* xiii, 16), the principle Dante finds in Aristotle to organize the *Inferno*, and the other *cantiche*, is an eminently ethical one. As we will discover, the three sinful states that Virgil identifies in canto xi would have been associated in the Middle Ages with the three human appetites, in which, for Aristotle and medieval Aristotelians, all action begins. Thus every action, sinful or blessed, can be characterized by its relations to the appetites, and Dante can use the appetites as the common ground that relates the subjects of each of the *cantiche* to each other, and by which their doctrines can be bound together and organized. It is love, after all, that moves *il sole e l'altre stelle* (*Par.* xxxiii, 145), and in the variations on love that we see in the three *cantiche* Dante constructs the single plot and single allegory that is the *Commedia*.

DANTE AND AQUINAS

Before beginning, I should clarify one aspect of the strategy of this inquiry. The reader will soon discover the heavy use I have made of the works of Thomas Aquinas. A comment is needed to make clear the way in which they have been used, and to avoid misunderstanding regarding the question of Dante's dependence, or not, on Thomistic doctrines.

Trying to determine Dante's sources is a daunting task, as all students of Dante recognize. He was eclectic in his reading, quick to put a wide array of authorities to his own uses (without worrying overly about their consistency with other texts he might be using), and also perfectly capable of making purely idiosyncratic interpretations of common texts and doctrines. Earlier in this century a heated controversy was joined in which studies were written arguing, on the one side, that Dante was an orthodox and devoted Thomist (Busnelli), and, on the other, that Dante overlooked Aquinas altogether in favor of other medieval theologians (Nardi).

The bitterness with which this controversy was pursued led both participants to make quite intemperate statements. We can now easily recognize the futility of their more extreme positions. On the one hand, it is absurd to argue that Dante faithfully, or slavishly, follows Aquinas, when so many of his most fundamental, most manifest, and most immediately encountered assertions regarding the gravity of diverse sins, for example, differ so markedly from Aquinas'. On the other hand, it is equally absurd to say that Dante did not admire Aquinas and did not often incorporate many of his doctrines in the poem. On two matters critically important to the principle of the *Commedia* as a whole and to the organization of the *Inferno* and the *Purgatorio* in particular—first, on regarding justice as a virtue of the will; second, on the details of the process of appetition or love—Dante enunciates positions that can be found before him only in the works of Aquinas. More generally, despite Nardi's efforts to convince us that Albert the Great was Dante's preferred philosophical source, it is Aquinas whom

Dante chooses as the principal spokesman for theology in the *Paradiso*, not Albert or any other theologian.

Were this essay a study of Dante's sources, it obviously could not be appropriate to use Aquinas until the question of Dante's adherence to his doctrines was settled. But this is not an inquiry into sources, and, as the reader will see, I have not used Aquinas in that way. Rather, I have used Aquinas, and especially his two *summæ*, precisely as *summæ*: as summaries of known medieval positions regarding theological and ethical matters. They are used to provide a sort of background against which Dante's positions are thrown better into relief. In most cases, it would have been possible to amass a dense set of citations from other medieval authors arguing positions identical or similar to Aquinas'. From time to time I have done so, but most frequently it was far more convenient to rely on the terse statements of the *summæ*. I do not believe that there is ever a moment in which I argue that what Dante says must be so because Aquinas had said something like it. In fact, it is more frequently the case that citations from Aquinas are used to show that Dante's position is divergent and novel. But when an issue appears in Aquinas, we can at least be sure that the issue was alive and under consideration among medieval theologians or at least among medieval Aristotelians. Thus, Aquinas can be used to confirm the likelihood of Dante's interest in the issue, and to suggest avenues the poet would have considered in coming to his own determination. It is in this way, and this way only, that I have used Aquinas throughout this study. It is, I believe, a harmless use, and one that leaves open more detailed inquiry into the ultimate sources of Dante's doctrines.

1

Inferno

PART I

THE PRINCIPLE OF THE STRUCTURE OF HELL

Virgil's Description of Hell and Its Anomalies

The moral significance of the physical structure of Hell is itself an explicit subject of the narrative of the poem. The Hell that Dante describes to us is not only a collection of separate circles in which individually distinguishable sins are punished; those individual circles are themselves organized into larger "geographical" regions that, explicitly, collect sins that possess a common fundamental nature, and simultaneously, of course, distinguish the "genus" of sin collected in the one region from other genera of sins that have essentially different natures, and that are therefore situated in a physically distinct location. It is Virgil who explains this to us in a conversation he initiates with Dante in canto xi of the *Inferno*. As Virgil describes to Dante the sinners they will soon encounter and those they have already encountered, his explanation links the different natures of groups of sin to the different locations in which they are punished.

Given Virgil's explicit statement of the linkage between the physical structure of Hell and fundamental moral distinctions, we might expect that any questions regarding the significance of the structure of Hell must be beyond dispute. Unfortunately, they are not. While no reader can deny, given Virgil's explanation, that there exist distinct regions (in addition to individual circles) in Hell, and every reader must also accept the names of the genera of sin Virgil associates with each region, controversies among readers arise regarding how to interpret the natures of the genera of sin Virgil has named, and therefore how to understand the natures of the individual sins included under each genus. Moreover, since we are convinced that Dante intended the poetic details of the narrative as a means of fleshing out (literally as well as metaphorically) his philosophical descriptions of the sins, disagreement regarding their natures leads inevitably to disagreement regarding the interpretation of individual incidents and descriptions in the poem. It is for this reason that we cannot avoid addressing this issue.

Virgil's explanation of the structure of Hell is based on a familiar passage from the beginning of the seventh book of Aristotle's *Ethics*—Virgil himself gives the citation—in which three different blameworthy dispositions, vice, incontinence, and bestiality are distinguished.

> Non ti rimembra di quelle parole
>   con le quai la tua Etica pertratta
>   le tre disposizion che 'l ciel non vole,
> incontinenza, malizia e la matta
>   bestialitade?
>
> (*Inf.* xi, 79–83)

The sins of upper Hell, whose punishments he and Dante have just witnessed, are located in upper Hell, Virgil says, because incontinence is less hated than vice:

> . . . e come incontinenza
>   men Dio offende e men biasimo accatta?
> Se tu riguardi ben questa sentenza,
>   e rechiti alla mente chi son quelli
>   che su di fuor sostegnon penitenza,
> tu vedrai ben perchè da questi felli
>   sien dipartiti, e perchè men crucciata
>   la divina vendetta li martelli.
>
> (*Inf.* xi, 83–90)

By implication, Virgil is stating that all of the sins of upper Hell form one group or genus of sin because all are sins of incontinence. The sins punished in Hell below where Dante and Virgil are sitting during this discussion are all sins of malice, Virgil explains, and the sins contained in these three lower circles fall into two further subcategories: violently malicious sins and fraudulently malicious sins.

> «Figliuol mio, dentro da cotesti sassi»
>   cominciò poi a dir «son tre cerchietti
>   di grado in grado, come que' che lassi.
> Tutti son pien di spirti maladetti;
>   ma perchè poi ti basti pur la vista,

intendi come e perchè son costretti.
D' ogni malizia, ch' odio in cielo acquista,
   ingiuria è 'l fine, ed ogni fin cotale
   o con forza o con frode altrui contrista.
Ma perchè frode è dell'uom proprio male,
   più spiace a Dio; e però stan di sutto
   li frodolenti e più dolor li assale.»
                                    (*Inf.* xi, 16–27)

According to this explanation, then, there are three primary genera of sin—sins of incontinence, of violence, and of fraud—and these genera, in keeping with poetry's fundamental principle of concretely representing abstract states, are described as being punished in appropriately distinct regions of Hell, their geographical separations presumably reflecting philosophical distinctions between their natures.[1]

This very reference to a single, well-known philosophical source is paradoxically the origin of controversy regarding the structure of the *Inferno*. For as many previous readers have grappled with, the distinctions made by Aristotle in that passage from the *Ethics* simply will not work properly to explain what is seen in the events of the voyage through Hell. When Dante has Virgil use Aristotle's distinction to discriminate regions of Hell and their associated sins he is using the terms *malizia* and *incontinenza* in senses that are at once too narrow and too broad to be orthodoxly Aristotelian. At verse 22, Virgil restricts *malizia* to sins of lower Hell. In verse 82, he characterizes all of the sins of upper Hell as instances of incontinence. Yet in a properly Aristotelian use of these terms, neither identification could be made, and, indeed, the examples Dante provides of sinners in these regions frequently challenge the association of the regions with Aristotle's dispositions as Aristotle would have defined them, as we will consider in the next section.

The source of our confusion, and resulting controversy, is that Dante's understanding of Aristotle is not precisely Aristotelian, at least as we currently interpret Aristotle. Rather, Dante understood Aristotle as Aristotle was interpreted and articulated by medieval commentators, and to their interpretations he added further reinterpretations of his own. It is likely that Dante believed that his own interpretations were perfectly Aristotelian; we can see that they were not. When we try to match Dante's distribution of sins to Aristotle's distinctions according to the way *we* understand Aristotle, we encounter problems almost immediately. But if we can recover the meanings that *Dante* assigned to the distinctions, problems of the distribution of sins disappear. Thus, our first task will be to determine how Dante diverges from Aristotle's intentions; our second will be to recover the specifically Dantean meanings assigned to the three terms that appeared in Aristotle's distinctions. Only at that point can we confidently proceed to interpret the significance of the structure of Hell (and through it of sin) that Dante proposes.

Dante's Divergence from Aristotle

We can best reveal the semantic alterations implicit in Dante's use of Aristotle by examining the meanings of the two key terms used by Virgil, *incontinence* and *malice*. *Malizia* (*malitia,* in the Latin philosophical texts and translations that Dante would have been using) has both common and technical meanings. Most generally, it refers to any qualities that render an act evil rather than good; more strictly, it refers to certain specific qualities that render an action *deliberately* evil. But in technical Aristotelian discussions of ethics, it has a further, special meaning. *Malitia* is the Latin term for vice, and it is in this latter sense that the term is used in the passage from book seven of the *Ethics* to which Virgil alludes in verse 82. The passage constitutes the initial statement of book seven, introducing, according to Aristotle, "another beginning" within his inquiry.

> After these matters, making another beginning, it should be said that the dispositions [*mores*] to be avoided are of three species: vice [*malitia*], incontinence, and bestiality. (*EN*, vii, 1; 1145a15)[2]

Aristotle calls this a new beginning in order to distinguish the states of virtue and vice (to which Aristotle had restricted his inquiry in books two through six of the *Ethics*) from two other states of character or "dispositions" (and their opposites) with which virtue and vice could be confused—that is, continence and incontinence, heroic virtue and bestiality. Although this distinction has a profound ethical significance, it is literally correct to call it an afterthought in the *Ethics,* since the need for such a distinction could only arise after the specific determination Aristotle had made of the natures of virtue and vice. To much of Greek philosophy (in Plato, for example), what Aristotle called continence *was* virtue, and thus there was neither purpose nor matter on which to distinguish the two terms. For Plato, not only

4

could you not distinguish virtue from continence, but what Aristotle was calling incontinence was impossible, or a contradiction in terms. Yet for Aristotle, in the context of the inquiry that organizes the *Ethics*—happiness insofar as it is within the power of humans to achieve—this distinction at the beginning of book seven was fundamental. By demonstrating how the continent person, while conventionally considered virtuous, could not be considered happy (while the truly virtuous person, in his terms, was), Aristotle could fashion a concluding proof of the greater value and robustness of his solution to the question of virtue.

To Aristotle it was straightforward that virtue and vice should be distinguished from continence and incontinence. For reasons we shall consider shortly, however, the distinction is problematic in a Christian context, and Dante's divergence from Aristotle is largely in order to circumvent these problems. But to understand Dante's solutions to these new problems posed by writing about ethics with a view to salvation, we must first recognize the purpose of Aristotle's original distinction.

The actual subject of the *Ethics*, we recall, is not virtue, but happiness. Virtue is a subject of the book only because Aristotle defines happiness as a certain operation in accordance with complete virtue (*EN*, i, 13; 1102a4). Since the human soul performs generically distinguishable functions (nutrition, appetition, thought), the virtues—those dispositions that perfect the operation of its functioning "parts"—must also be plural (*EN*, i, 13; 1102a25–32; see also *EN*, i, 6; 1098a15). With respect to the first part of the soul (the nutritive, or vegetative), there are no virtues, as we usually use the term, since its operation is not within our control. A healthy nature is all that is needed for its perfect operation. But since the other two parts of the soul are wholly or partially under our rational control, virtues exist to perfect the operation of each. While the appetitive part of the soul is not rational in itself, it is said to be amenable to reason, being both controllable and malleable (*EN*, i, 13; 1102b1–10 and 1102b12–35). The intellectual part of the soul is obviously by its nature under rational control. For the appetitive and intellectual parts of the soul, therefore, Aristotle concludes that there will be as many virtues as there are different functions these parts perform. For the intellectual part there are intellectual virtues, acquired, for the most part, by experience, or inquiry, or teaching. For the appetitive part, there are virtues inculcated by habit, and which therefore receive the name ethical (or in Latin, moral) virtues (*EN*, i, 13–ii, 1; 1103a3–25).

For Aristotle, a virtuous life, properly speaking, requires more than merely the performance of virtuous acts; it requires that such acts be performed as a virtuous person would perform them: that is, consistently and autonomously, since no one would call virtuous someone who was only fitfully virtuous in action, nor someone who acted virtuously only under the direction of another person, nor, again, someone who was intellectually unable to determine what the virtuous course was under differing circumstances. According to Aristotle, the consistent performance of virtuous actions depends on habit, and so the moral virtues are defined as habits of acting in appropriate ways relative to the objects of the appetites. Discovering those habits is the subject of books two through five of the *Ethics*.

The autonomous possession of these habits, however, and the ability to exercise and maintain them in the manifold circumstances of an active life depend not on habit, but on the possession of intellectual standards and capacities by which actions can be judged and courses of action set. Book six therefore examines the intellectual virtues generally, and especially prudence, the specific intellectual virtue ordered to action. It is prudence that knows what the standard of virtuous action is with respect to each of the objects of the appetites, and it is prudence that considers what the virtuous course of action is in a given situation.

As virtue demands not only the performance of virtuous acts but also their performance in the manner of a virtuous person, so vice, for Aristotle, is more than simply the performance of vicious acts. It, similarly, is their performance in a vicious way. The vicious person is not intermittently vicious, nor accidentally so. Vicious acts, properly speaking, are the result of both bad moral habit and bad thinking. The vicious person, first of all, has appetites uncontrolled by good habits (which appetites, therefore, tend to improper actions); but, secondly, the vicious person also pursues actions based on those appetites in such a way that the intellect not only makes no attempt to control them, but abets their tendencies. For Aristotle, the truly vicious intellect, inasmuch as it lacks knowledge of the proper standards of virtuous action, sees nothing unfit in the evil tendencies of its bad habits. Since the vicious intellect will cooperate in the accomplishment of vicious desires, and since habit, good or bad, is inculcated and consolidated by repetition, the actions undertaken by the vicious intellect will in their turn reinforce the bad habits of the appetites. For Aristotle, vice is as durable and self-sufficient a state of character as virtue.[3]

It is only at this stage that Aristotle could, or would want to, distinguish virtue and vice from continence and incontinence (and bestiality), in order to draw two novel ethical conclusions that complement the results of books one through six: first, that the continent person, while conventionally considered virtuous, is not virtuous in fact; and second, therefore, that neither is the continent person happy.

For Aristotle, the properly habituated appetites of a truly virtuous person propose worthy ends to the intellect for accomplishment, and the intellect, properly trained in prudence, discovers virtuous ways in which to accomplish them. In a continent person, however, the situation is poignantly different. While the intellect fully knows the standards of virtuous action and the appropriate courses to follow in practical situations, it must struggle continually with badly habituated and disordered appetites.[4] Insofar as the person is continent and is able to control the appetites, good actions result—but not, properly speaking, virtuous ones, for the right actions have not been performed in the right way. (The conflict of reason and appetite is no characteristic of virtue for Aristotle.) In the incontinent person the appetites overpower the intellect, and evil acts result—but again not, properly speaking, vicious ones, for while vicious actions have occurred, they have not been performed as a vicious person would. Unlike the truly vicious intellect, the intellect of the incontinent person knows what the right actions should have been, and the same conflict between reason and appetite that exists in the continent exists also in the incontinent, with this sole difference: that since the intellect of the incontinent person is too weak to resist the appetites, the conflict plays out to an evil, rather than good, conclusion.[5]

Incontinence is to be avoided, obviously, since its results are evil. But just as clearly it is less blameworthy than vice, since only the appetites of the incontinent person are evil, not the intellect.[6] Continence is to be sought, one supposes, but only if virtue is not an alternative. For the life of the continent person is manifestly unhappy: unlike the tranquillity of the virtuous whose appetites are orderly and never propose shameful desires, the life of continence is one of unceasing, and therefore painful, struggle. For that matter, a life of incontinence is also painful. Knowing the good but being unable to perform it, the incontinent person is wracked by shame and cannot even take the unqualified pleasure in satisfying wrong desires that the truly vicious do. Virtue exhibits strength and fitness both of appetite and of intellect; continence displays only strength of intellect.[7]

It is in the context of our understanding of these Aristotelian distinctions that we can recognize the problems in applying them to the sins and sinners of the *Inferno*. On the one hand, beginning with our very first introduction to the sinners of Hell, it is easy to find instances in which it is clear that Virgil's restriction of *malizia* to lower Hell takes the term in a much narrower sense than Aristotle intended by *vice* in book seven. In Aristotle's distinction, vice covers a whole panoply of actions and objects regarding which one may develop bad habits, and about which one may make evil choices. And there are many in upper Hell—as well as in lower Hell—who exhibit vice and not mere incontinence. One of the particular vices treated by Aristotle in the *Ethics* is intemperance, within which would be included actions that Dante identifies as lustful and gluttonous.[8] For Aristotle, the viciously lustful and gluttonous can, and must, be distinguished from the incontinently lustful and gluttonous. The latter recognize their bad habits with respect to the objects of lust and gluttony, but are incapable of controlling those habits. The viciously lustful and gluttonous have intellects that are in a certain sense morally blind to the evilness of their habits. Without the shame felt by the incontinent, they cheerfully follow the urgings of these habits, mistakenly believing them worthy of fulfillment. But in precisely this regard, we can see that many of the souls whom Dante classes among the incontinent would not be considered incontinent by Aristotle, but intemperate; that is, vicious and exhibiting *malizia* (if *malizia* is taken in its technical sense). Surely, this is how we should understand the lives of Semiramis and Cleopatra among the lustful (*Inf.* v, 52–63),[9] and Ciacco among the gluttons (*Inf.* vi, 49–57).[10] The deliberateness with which they pursued their sinful lives, as well as what appears to be their utter lack of shame in pursuing them, is the best evidence to us that their actions were actions of intemperance (that is, of vice or *malitia* in a properly Aristotelian sense) rather than incontinence.[11] They pursued their disordered desires not because they could not control them, but because they *chose* to pursue them.

On the other hand, Dante also shows us incidents that suggest that Virgil's attribution of *malizia* to all the sinners of lower Hell uses the term in a sense much broader than Aristotle intended. Vice, for Aristotle, requires the cooperation of two evil properties: not only a corrupted intellect, but also *settled habits* tending to evil which consistently propose evil ends to the intellect for fulfillment. Yet in many cases of the most notable sinners in the lowest circles of Hell, it is hard to find the second of these conditions. In all the sinners of the lowest circles (specifically circles eight and nine), we can see the operation of a corrupt intellect. But in many instances Dante seems to draw attention to the exceptional quality of the act for which they have been damned. As far as we know, for example, neither Bertram de Born's arousing of discord between Henry II and his son (*Inf.* xxviii, 133–41) nor Ugolino della Gherardesca's betrayal of Pisa (*Inf.* xxxiii, 79–87) was anything other than an exceptional incident in each sinner's life. Nothing in their lives suggests settled habits of this kind of action. These are terrible acts, to be sure, but we must recognize, nonetheless, that they are not truly vicious acts, in Aristotle's terms, because they were not performed in the way that vicious acts are. As departures from the sinners' habitual character, indeed, they are actually closer to the pattern of incontinence. Even an example such as Vanni Fucci challenges his location among those exhibiting *malizia*. There was vice in him, without doubt: he spent a life in bestial and violent actions (*Inf.* xxiv, 122–39), actions that therefore must have been habitual. But he is not damned to where he is for his violent habits, but for a single act of theft.[12] Finally, it is perhaps appropriate to point out that even the worst instance of the worst of human sins, Judas' betrayal of Jesus, can only be understood as a singular action, not as the result of a depraved habit or habits.

In the face of such serious and widespread inconsistencies, it is obvious that Virgil is not using Aristotle's terms correctly, at least as we would understand them. Either Dante did not understand Aristotle, or he understood Aristotle's distinctions differently from the way we do. The latter explanation is the case, and those readers who have tried to apply Aristotle's distinctions without taking into account Dante's semantic adaptations of the distinctions have inevitably run into new anomalies and contradictions. Dante, in fact, was acting under two conflicting motives, which made it, on the one hand, impossible for him to take Aristotle's distinctions in their original sense, while, on the other, desirable to retain Aristotle as his authority for the structure of Hell. To deal with this conflict Dante turned to a specific medieval interpretation of this text, and it is that interpretation—which Dante is very likely to have believed was orthodoxly Aristotelian, even if we do not—that we see embodied in his distribution of sinners.

The first motive, the one that drove Dante in a different direction from Aristotle, arose from a real conflict that exists between Aristotle's ends and Dante's. Were Dante to have tried to understand and explain the nature of sin by means of the distinction of book seven of the *Ethics,* taking its terms in their properly Aristotelian senses, he would have encountered almost insuperable theological difficulties. For book seven's distinction of three states of character under the influence of which an act is committed (three "dispositions," to use their conventional medieval translation), however significant to Aristotle, must be either irrelevant or positively damaging to Christian determinations of sin and estimations of its gravity. (Indeed, the importance of Aristotle for Dante can be measured by the lengths to which he goes to find a way to reinterpret the terms of the *Ethics* so that he can use them in his Christian context.)

First, virtue and vice, in Aristotelian terms, are fundamentally irrelevant to the question of salvation or damnation. Both virtue and vice depend on habit, but salvation and damnation do not. In Aristotle, one does not judge a person virtuous or vicious on the basis of any individual action, but on the basis of a settled character, as embodied and exhibited in habits and habitual choices. Habit can be the result only of repeated similar actions, though individual actions may be undertaken at the direction of habit or against habit, since habits do not determine actions by necessity. But sin, even mortal sin, does not depend on habit. Christian concentration on the freedom of the will renders each individual act potentially decisive, whether shaped by habit or not. Can one be judged to have committed a mortal sin even with a single act? Absolutely.[13] (As, for that matter, it is possible to be saved by a single, "uncharacteristic" act.)[14] Thus, the primary reason for which Aristotle distinguished incontinence from vice—to indicate the greater seriousness of vice—becomes insignificant and potentially misleading from the standpoint of determining someone's salvation or damnation.

A strict Aristotelian understanding of vice poses a second, even more troubling problem. Since vice depends not only on evil habits, but also on the agreement of a corrupted intellect in the objects of the habits, it can be said that a truly vicious person is fundamentally unconscious of his or her vice.[15] In the virtuous person, the intellect measures possible actions against a rational standard. But so, in a sense, does the vicious person. Objectively, we can judge that that standard is incorrect, yet to the vicious person the standard and its consequent action appear not only desirable, but even reasonable insofar as wholly consistent with and adapted to the evil desires. Theologically, this poses an impossible situation: How could one argue that a certain category of sinners, presumably the worst, were actually unconscious of the fact they had committed a sin? Certainly, no soul that Dante encounters in Hell is unaware that its action was wrong, nor in any doubt that the wrong in fact constituted a mortal sin. But for Aristotle, this sort of awareness of the proper standard in the midst of committing a wrong action is characteristic only of those who act wrongly through incontinence, not vice. For theological reasons, therefore, all the sins we see in the *Inferno* must be treated as if they had been actions based on incontinence (in Aristotelian terms) rather than attributed to vice.

Yet if these two theological problems demanded abandoning what we see as Aristotle's intentions in the *Ethics*, a quite different, but perhaps equally significant theological motive suggested to Dante that despite the problems Aristotle posed, some system like his ought to be used to provide the structure for Hell and its sins. A fundamental axiom is that the damned be damned according to principles of justice. But in order for any condemnation to be justly applied, those same principles must be known to the condemned. Since many of the damned are pagans who lived before the time of Christ, justice therefore also demands that the nature of sin be comprehensible in terms that do not depend upon Christian revelation, but are instead natural or philosophical. Were it impossible to understand sin apart from Christianity, it would be unjust to condemn pagans for sins they could not perforce recognize they were committing. Poetically, insofar as we believe that Dante's geographical organization of Hell is meant to furnish a metaphorical reflection of the nature of sin and its genera, justice demands that the principles Dante uses for articulating that organization correspond to some naturally understandable definition of sin. A realm wholly restricted to Christians could be justly organized by specifically Christian doctrine, as Purgatory is organized by the seven deadly sins. But such would not be just for a realm in which sinful pagans are damned side by side sinful Christians. This explains Dante's need for Aristotle (a need important enough, as we have said, to make it worthwhile taking an unorthodox interpretation of him to avoid the theological problems already cited), since in Aristotle, evil actions are defined by reference to human nature, its faculties, and the rational standards by which their operation should be ruled. Thus, the

11

range and character of good and evil as we encounter it through the *Ethics* could be apparent to any human being at any moment in history, and the damnation of non-Christians could not be overturned by counterpleas of ignorance. Any other pagan philosophy based on human nature would also serve, of course, but the issue here is not between Aristotle and some other pagan. Aristotle, for Dante, was the master of human reason, "lo maestro de l'umana ragione" (*Conv.* iv, ii, 16). The issue is: Is it proper to use a pagan philosopher at all in the organization of Hell? And Dante's answer is that it would be unjust not to. To use Aristotle, however, required that he be adapted.

Dante's Reinterpretation of Aristotle

What were the adapted senses in which Dante used Aristotle's terms and distinctions? The key to Dante's idiosyncratic reading overall of the *Ethics* can be found in Virgil's first statement about *malizia*, for the semantic shift we find in that use of the central term in the Aristotelian distinction reveals a general transformation in the interpretation of the *Ethics*.

> D'ogni malizia,...
> ingiuria è 'l fine.
>
> (*Inf.* xi, 22–23)

In Dante, perhaps, but not in Aristotle. In Aristotle, as we have indicated above, *malizia*, taken as a translation for vice, would cover a wide range of vices, many of which (for example, intemperance, illiberality, even cowardice) would not have injury as their end. In this regard, then, not only is Virgil's restriction of *malizia* to the lowest three circles of Hell un-Aristotelian, so is his very definition of it.[16] Indeed, Virgil can restrict *malizia* to the lowest three circles only because he has first restricted the meaning of the term. At the same time, as several commentators have recognized, while the sins of the lowest three circles do not exhaust the full range of vices treated in the *Ethics*, they do substantially correspond to one particular Aristotelian vice, injustice[17]—to which, we notice, a linguistic reference is made in the definition—at least as injustice would have been understood by medieval Aristotelians. What Dante has done, in effect, is to take a term, *malizia*, which in Aristotle refers to vice generally, and to restrict it to one specific sort of vice, injustice. (We should perhaps better say that Dante has restricted *malizia* to a specific sort of action—unjust acts, whether properly vicious or not—since, as we have considered, it was desirable to sidestep the issue of habitual versus individual action.) As we come to understand the grounds according to which he made this restriction, the special meanings he attributed to the other terms of the Aristotelian distinction will in turn become explicable.

Despite the peculiarity of choosing to restrict a general Aristotelian term to a single vice, it is clear that all of the sins of the lowest three circles of Hell share with what Aristotle calls acts of injustice in the *Ethics* one fundamental and essential characteristic: they are actions committed against other people. When Virgil calls all of these sins *malizia,* because they have injury as an end, it is this interpersonal dimension that specifies what it means to have injury as an end: "ogni fin cotale . . . *altrui* contrista" (*Inf.* xi, 22–24). And it is precisely this characteristic that identifies *malizia* with injustice, for, according to Aristotle, the subject matter of justice and injustice (and of just and unjust actions, whether they are the results of the virtue or vice or not) is action directed toward other people.[18] This is the primary differentiating characteristic of action related to justice and injustice (as distinct from other virtues and vices), since it is often the case that actions that ordinarily would be within the purview of other virtues or vices become just or unjust when placed in a social or interpersonal context. Thus, while cowardice is initially considered in the *Ethics* as a strictly personal vice, regarding only the individual's response to situations of danger, cowardice on the battlefield becomes, according to Aristotle, a form of injustice, and receives separate treatment.[19] It even gets a new name to reflect its new quality. Cowardice on the battlefield is not called cowardice simply; it is called desertion. Similarly, intemperance with respect to sexual passion, which is lust in the context of the individual, may become adultery in a social context, and thereby become an instance of injustice rather than mere intemperance.[20] Shifting the context in which action occurs is not a casual or incidental change. It alters the real character of the action. As Aristotle points out, there are individuals capable of acting virtuously with respect to the simply personal, whose virtue breaks down in their actions with other people, and it is for this reason that these new situations call for the acquisition of a new moral virtue (or corresponding vice).[21]

Because the primary distinction of the subject of justice and injustice is the context of the action rather than the physical event itself, acts of injustice often appear confusingly similar to actions more properly

attributed not to injustice, but to other vices or to incontinence, insofar as they occasionally share physical attributes, or, one might say,
subject matter, with those actions. Aristotle makes a point of such
examples in the *Ethics*, and we can find a multiplicity of examples in
the *Inferno*, especially in the eighth circle. Indeed, the apparent reappearance in the lower circles of Hell of sins seen in earlier circles is
itself one of the significant confirmations of Dante's identification of
malizia with injustice, for this doubling occurs for just the same reason
as it does with injustice in the *Ethics:* the transfer of the action from a
personal to an interpersonal context.

But we cannot simply say that Dante has merely substituted the
term *malizia* where Aristotle would have spoken of the vice injustice,
since Virgil does seem markedly to depart from Aristotle in including
among sins of malice a whole category of actions that Aristotle would
not strictly consider acts of injustice. When he introduces the lower
three circles of Hell, Virgil distinguishes between malicious actions
committed by violence and those committed by fraud.

> D'ogni malizia, ch'odio in cielo acquista,
>   ingiuria è 'l fine, ed ogni fin cotale
>   o con forza o con frode altrui contrista.
>   (*Inf.* xi, 22–24)

If *malizia* is intended to be identical to injustice, then Virgil is associating certain acts of violence with injustice which, as we will soon
see, Aristotle would exclude. But there is an even more immediate
problem raised by this distinction. That Dante wants this distinction
taken seriously is clear, since it is meant to furnish a principle for assigning sinners to different circles in Hell.[22] But given that function, we
discover ourselves confronted with the problem of finding an explanation for how little the distinction corresponds to what we actually
encounter in the lower circles of Hell. On first reading, Virgil seems to
be saying that all sins involving violence are punished in the seventh
circle of Hell, the final two circles being reserved for sins committed by
fraud, as distinct from violence. But the events of the narrative compel
us to find a somewhat different interpretation to the statement, for it is
most definitely *not* the case that none of the sins of circles eight and
nine (the circles of fraud) is accompanied or actualized by violence.
Either through Dante's explicit reminder, or from what we know from
sources outside the poem of the histories of the individuals encoun-

tered in the eighth and ninth circles (the circles of fraud, that is, not of violence, according to Virgil), we are confronted again and again with sinners punished for fraud in incidents connected to violence. In some cases, such as the simony of Pope Nicholas III (see especially *Inf.* xix, 97–99) or the evil counsel of Ulysses (*Inf.* xxvi, 58–60) or of Guido da Montefeltro (*Inf.* xxvii, 108–11), the violence is only consequent to their sinful actions. But in other cases, the sinful act itself is an act of violence, whether the murder of Buondelmonte de' Buondelmonti by Mosca de' Lamberti (*Inf.* xxviii, 106–8), which begins the civil strife in Florence, or a host of murders through which the betrayals punished in the ninth circle were accomplished. The first two souls in the ninth circle to whom Dante turns his attention are there for having murdered one another (Alessandro and Napoleone degli Alberti; *Inf.* xxxii, 55–57); the third is also there for murder (Sassol Mascheroni; *Inf.* xxxii, 64–66).[23] Murder is the action through which their treachery was expressed also for Frate Alberigo (*Inf.* xxxiii, 118–20) and Branca d'Oria (*Inf.* xxxiii, 136–38).[24] Indeed, the connection to violence runs down to the lowest point of Hell, for Brutus' and Cassius' sin, punished in the very jaws of Satan (*Inf.* xxxiv, 64–67), was also practiced by murder.

Since it is manifestly not the case that all acts of violence are confined to the seventh circle, what is the real nature of the distinction that Virgil is making?[25] All of the acts of the eighth and ninth circles, whether violent or not, do share one common characteristic: the motive for all of them is some calculated profit, advantage, or gain. Among the murderers, the degli Alberti and Sassol Mascheroni committed their crimes to gain inheritances.[26] Brutus and Cassius committed theirs for power (as would also have been the case for Nicholas III, Ulysses, and Guido da Montefeltro). Mosca de' Lamberti and Frate Alberigo committed theirs for honor.[27] It is, indeed, on just this basis— that the sinners of circles eight and nine were explicitly motivated by gain—that it is possible to distinguish their violent actions from those of the sinners of circle seven. And in using this as the basis for his distinction, Dante is actually following Aristotle quite closely, even when the terms in which he has Virgil express it are not in themselves Aristotelian. For Aristotle, it was important to be careful in two kinds of situations where it was possible to be confused as to whether an action was an injustice or not. On the one hand, certain actions that were injustices could appear to be the results of vices of other sorts. In these cases, the actions could be distinguished from their "doubles" by consideration of motive.

> And so, if one man commits adultery for the sake of gain, and receives it, while another commits adultery because of concupiscence, and expends money to do it, and in fact suffers a loss, the latter man would seem to be lustful; the former, rather, would appear greedy. The first man, indeed, is unjust, while the lustful man is not. (That the first is unjust is obvious, since he did this for gain.) . . . Particular justice [the term used in medieval translations of Aristotle for the virtue we usually call justice simply] is concerned with honor or money or security, or whatever else we might include of this sort. It is also concerned with the pleasure that comes from possession. (*EN*, v, 4; 1130a25–b5)

In such cases, the "physical event," as it were, of the action appears to be an act normally associated with another vice, but the event becomes an act of injustice because its end is gain rather than the usual end of the other vice. In these cases, an act that initially appears not to be an injustice in fact is an injustice. On the other hand, certain other actions can be mistakenly identified with injustice though they are not properly acts of injustice. Aristotle recognizes that there are certain actions that normally would be associated with injustice, but which under certain circumstances ought actually to be distinguished from it. These actions are indisputably injuries, but injuries committed for motives other than gain. Injurious actions—which, therefore, seem to be injustices— can also be committed, according to Aristotle, under the influence of passion. While such acts can be called unjust, they are not properly identified as acts of injustice, because their difference in origin alters their natures. Someone acting in the grip of anger, for example, is not acting in the same calculated and deliberate way that someone coolly pursuing advantage is. The results for their victims may well be identical. But the acts through which the victims were injured are of significantly different characters, and moreover—and of signal importance to Dante—are of significantly different degrees of blameworthiness. Being impelled to an action by passion reduces the degree to which someone can be considered to be responsible for the action and thereby diminishes the guilt.

> When [an injury is committed] knowingly but without premeditation, it is an unjust act. This is how we should consider anything done because of anger or of any of the other passions which occur necessarily or naturally in men. Those injuring others and sinning in this way commit

unjust acts and are acting unjustly. But they are not unjust [persons] on this account, nor evil, since the injury they did was not the result of vice *[malitia]*. But when the injury is by choice, then the person is unjust and evil. (*EN*, v, 10; 1135b20–25)

As Aquinas explains this passage in his commentary, persons committing unjust actions because of passion do not exhibit the vice of injustice:

> Those who injure others because of the aforesaid passions sin and commit an unjust act, and the activity itself is an unjust activity. Nevertheless, this does not make them unjust or evil [persons], since they did not intend the injury because of vice *[malitia]*, but because of passion. Such persons are said to sin through weakness. (*In Ethica*, §1044)

As we have noted, the inclusion of sinners who make use of acts of violence in the circles that Dante reserved for sins of "fraud," rather than "force," demands that we find a somewhat more complicated sense to the distinction between the circles of force and fraud. As *malizia* was an ambiguous term, so too is *ingiuria*. It could mean "injury," simply, some damage done a victim; or it could be used to identify a specific kind of injury, an "injustice." And in fact, the distinction Aristotle makes in the *Ethics* to reduce that ambiguity and to discriminate injustice properly so called from other vices seems usefully to match and to make sense of the two kinds of malicious acts Virgil distinguishes in lower Hell. The sinners of circles eight and nine commit sins that not only damage their victims (injury in the common sense), but are intended to damage them for a purpose—gain—which gives these injuries the specific character of injustices.[28] On the other hand, the sinners of circle seven, while they undoubtedly injure their victims, do not necessarily do so in pursuit of gain, and therefore, while malicious in Virgil's terms, are not unjust in Aristotle's. We will consider more fully below why it is appropriate to consider that the violent of circle seven are violent for different motives than the violent among the fraudulent, but we can find a first hint that Dante intends such an interpretation in the poetic descriptions of the circumstances in which these sinners are punished. Insofar as the details of the poem taken figuratively provide clues as to the nature of actions we witness, the pervasive use of poetic descriptions of fire and heat in circle seven suggests a passionate source (especially the passion anger) for the violent actions of that circle. These sins, then, would be intended to correspond to the actions Aristotle recognizes as superficially like acts of injustice inasmuch as they result in injury, but not properly injustice in that they arise from impulses other than gain.

Given that we find violence accompanying injuries in all the circles of lower Hell, I believe that it would be best to consider Virgil's distribution of malice into two species, of "force" and "fraud," as the effective equivalent of Aristotle's distinction between injustice properly so called and acts apparently unjust, yet originating in states of mind different from the vice of injustice.[29] All of the actions punished in circles eight and nine, violent or not, took their origins in calculations of gain, whether of money, or power, or honor. For this reason they truly are acts of injustice. But since Dante has Virgil distinguish them from the actions of circle seven, it is manifest that he is trying to indicate that they have a different character and origin. I believe we should probably conclude that *con forza* effectively means "not for gain only, but with some other—indeed, some more violent—impulse." Later in this chapter we will discover the nature of that impulse and its appropriate kinship to *forza*. Indeed, for Dante to call the sins of circle seven *malizia* along with the sins of circles eight and nine would in fact faithfully preserve two important aspects of Aristotle's discussion of injustice in the *Ethics:* first, that considered from the standpoint of the results of the action, all of these actions seem of the same sort, and in the end can be distinguished from one another only by considering the different mental states that are their origins; second, that it is these different origins that determine the relative gravity of the actions—a judgment reflected in Dante's location of the sins of "fraud" in a circle lower in Hell than those of "force," a judgment with which Aristotle effectively concurs.

We began this chapter by exploring seeming inconsistencies in Virgil's use of Aristotle's distinction of *malizia* from *incontinenza* and *bestialitade*. We discovered that while his use of the terms would not fit orthodox Aristotelian interpretations, there was a consistency to the inconsistencies. Dante's linking of the sins of the eighth and ninth circles to one specific vice, injustice, and his distinguishing them from similar actions in the seventh circle on the basis of a specific difference in motive, recasts the discussion of sin in terms that consistently echo a medieval reinterpretation of Aristotle's psychological and ethical doctrines. If we examine the medieval theories that suggested these identifications and distinctions to Dante, we can discover the principle that underlies and informs his distribution of sins and understanding of their natures.

Action, Passion, and Appetite in Medieval Psychology

Dante's distinction between acts whose motive is gain and all other acts is fundamentally a distinction between acts undertaken by calculation, and thus essentially passion-free, and those driven by some passion. Now, the passions, for medieval philosophers and theologians, were a subject to be dealt with in psychology, in connection with the mental faculties called appetites. Since for Aristotle and his medieval commentators, and for Dante too, at least with respect to this subject, all motion—and therefore all purposive action, and the virtues and vices by which action is conditioned—begins in the appetites, distinctions regarding the operation of the appetites not only discriminated the physiological bases of action, but also furnished grounds for distinguishing acts of different moral characters. When Dante distinguishes the sins of circle seven from those of circles eight and nine on the basis of the presence or absence of passion, he draws on an extensive philosophical discussion regarding the appetites. We must now quickly review this discussion, not only to understand how Dante would have distinguished one form of violence from another, but also because the same discussion provides explanations of his location of those sins that appear in upper Hell.

What distinguishes animals (including human beings) from plants is their ability to move. In the *de Anima*, after establishing that the internal principle of movement for animals cannot be the soul's vegetative power or even its sensitive or rational powers in themselves, Aristotle concludes that the internal principle of movement must be an appetitive power, a power dependent on, but distinct from, the sensitive.[30] Aquinas puts this pointedly in his commentary on the *de Anima*:

> It is manifest, therefore, that the power of the soul which is called the appetite is the moving cause. . . . If moving causes are considered formally and according to their species, there will be a single moving cause—that is, either the object of appetite or the appetitive power. (*In de An.*, §§827, 830)[31]

For rational beings, both appetite and thought can be said to be principles of movement, but Aristotle declares that thought cannot itself cause motion if separate from appetite. The rational function that can be the cause of movement—what Aristotle calls "wish," and the medieval commentators "will"—is itself also an appetite.[32]

> The intellect is not found as a cause of motion without the appetite, for the will *[voluntas]* (through which the intellect causes movement) is an appetite. (*In de An.,* §824)

Appetite, for Aristotle and his commentators, is the inclination of a soul toward an external object.[33] It is by this inclination *toward* something external that appetite can cause movement, and so this inclination is what distinguishes appetite from apprehension, the other operation of the senses and the intellect.[34] The appetitive powers move the soul *toward* an object; the apprehensive powers work in the opposite direction, bringing the object *into* the soul.[35] The senses and intellect in their proper operations merely apprehend objects as actual or true, without moving to action; the appetites, however, by regarding objects as goods or evils, move the organism to their pursuit or avoidance.

> Something that can be both an object of apprehension and an object of appetite is the same as subject (that is, materially) but differs in the principle that makes it an object. For it is apprehended insofar as it is a sensible or intelligible entity; but it is an object of appetite insofar as it is suitable or good. Indeed, it is this diversity in the principles that make things objects (and not material diversity) that demands diversity of powers. (*ST,* 1a 80, 1 ad 2)

Since powers exist for the sake of their objects and operations, given that appetible objects and operations are different from the objects of apprehension, appetite must constitute a distinct power from the apprehensive power.[36]

Starting from relatively brief Aristotelian statements regarding the appetites, medieval commentators on Aristotle articulated a much more elaborate doctrine concerning appetites, their operations and objects, and the relations between and order among them. Since appetite was an operation dependent on the prior operation of an apprehensive faculty, appetitive faculties and functions were described coordinate with apprehensive functions, and so two genera of appetite came to be distinguished by medieval writers to correspond to the division of apprehension between the senses and the intellect. A sensitive appetite was identified, whose objects were objects of sense perceived as goods. Similarly, an intellectual appetite was identified, whose objects, though also perceived as goods, were objects of intellect and not of sense.

Powers are distinguished from one another insofar as there exist significant differences in their objects, and so a further distinction among the appetitive powers was made corresponding to a distinction made in the natures of things perceived as goods, that is, in the natures of appetible objects. Medieval commentators discriminated two different kinds of good with respect to *sensitive* goods: objects that were simply good or evil, and therefore simply to be pursued or avoided; and objects that were called "arduous" goods or evils—goods or evils that either were difficult to attain or avoid, or that might not be good in themselves, but were desirable for the sake of other goods. As an example of the latter sort of goods, and of the inclination (that is, genuine appetite) of animals and persons to pursue them, Aquinas regularly used the readiness of animals to fight for food or reproduction.[37] The appetite for things simply good (and avoidance of simple evils) was named the concupiscible appetite; the appetite for arduous goods was named the irascible appetite, from its most notable emotional manifestation, anger.[38] These two appetites together composed the "sensitive" appetite: appetites for goods apprehended by the senses. Differences in object not only made it possible to distinguish these faculties, they also established an ordered relation between them. Since the pursuit of arduous goods (or avoidance of arduous evils) is ultimately for the sake of simple goods and pleasures, all irascible appetite is for the sake of, and terminates in, as Aquinas says, the concupiscible.[39]

While medieval commentators distinguished two sensitive appetites on the basis of the distinction of arduous and simple goods, they recognized only a single intellectual appetite. Goods apprehended by the intellect were said to be apprehended as simply good in general, without further discrimination into simple or difficult goods. The will—the intellectual appetite according to medieval Aristotelians— was not, therefore, further divided. Thus, within the medieval redaction of Aristotle there existed, in total, three appetites.[40]

> The sensitive appetite does not regard the common principle of the good, for no sense apprehends the universal. Therefore, the parts of the sensitive appetite are distinguished according to the different principles (or characters) of particular goods. For the concupiscible appetite regards the proper principle of a good, namely, insofar as it is delightful to the senses and suitable to one's nature. The irascible, however, regards that principle of a good by which something repels and combats something that would be harmful. But the will regards the good under its

common principle: and so no other appetitive powers are distinguished in the intellectual appetite, such as an irascible power in the intellectual appetite or a concupiscible. (*ST,* 1a 82, 5)[41]

The principle that all action begins in appetite could be used to recast ethical discussions, including the discussion of those habits of action that are virtues and vices, in terms of the appetites of which they were the habits. A given action would be said to have a specific appetite as its subject, or substrate, and this appetite would give the action a certain character. Similarly, since virtues and vices are habits that dispose powers to good and bad operation, there must be virtues and vices that are dispositions of these appetitive powers.[42] In medieval Aristotelian discussions of ethics, moral virtues came to be distributed among the three appetites (as the sources of all actions) according to perceived affinities between the operation of the individual appetites and the virtues. In making these assignments, one critical distinction made by medieval authors was between virtues and vices that were dispositions with regard to passions, and those that were not. This distinction was specifically drawn (and here is the relevance to the *Inferno* of our lengthy exploration of Aristotelian interpretations) in regard to justice and injustice. In commenting on the beginning of Aristotle's discussion of justice in book five of the *Ethics,* Aquinas asserts that all other virtues and vices (treated in the books that precede book five) concern the proper regulation of the *passions.* He distinguishes justice and injustice from the other virtues by claiming they concern actions, rather than passions. More to the point, for our purposes, he says that justice and injustice have no concern with passion:

> After the Philosopher completed his treatment of the moral virtues concerning passions, here he treats of the virtue of justice, which concerns actions. . . . The virtues and vices previously discussed were virtues and vices in regard to passions; so with respect to these we principally consider how a man is affected *internally* by the passions, and we do not consider what he does externally, except secondarily. . . . But with respect to justice and injustice, we pay principal attention to what a man does *externally.* Nor do we consider how he is affected internally, except secondarily. (*In Ethica,* §885–86)[43]

According to Aquinas and other medieval sources, the sensitive appetites, because of their linkage to the senses, and therefore the body, inevitably have passions associated with their operation.[44] Moral virtues and vices that are dispositions in regard to passions, then, can be understood as dispositions of the sensitive appetite, and that, indeed, is how Aquinas regards the moral virtues and vices discussed by Aristotle in books three and four of the *Ethics*.

> All virtues which concern passions must reside in the sensitive appetite. Thus, fortitude concerns the passions of fear and daring which are in the irascible appetite; temperance, on the other hand, is about pleasures and pains, which are in the concupiscible. Therefore, fortitude itself is in the irascible appetite, but temperance is in the concupiscible. (*In Ethica*, §596)

But justice and injustice, as dispositions to action, must also be dispositions of an appetite, though if they are concerned with action apart from passion, they must have as their subject an appetite that operates (or can be considered in its operation) apart from passions, if such an appetite exists: that is, they must be dispositions of an appetite that can initiate action, yet do so apart from the influence of any bodily passion. Aquinas finds precisely such a faculty in the will—the "intellectual," rather than "sensitive," appetite. It is appetitive, without doubt, but since it necessitates no bodily alteration during its operation, as those appetites connected with passion do, it can be said to be appetitive without passion.[45] And so, Aquinas concludes, justice and injustice have the will as their subject, and are habits of the will in the same way that, for example, temperance is a habit of what the Middle Ages called the concupiscible appetite.

> [Aristotle] appropriately distinguished justice by reference to the will, in which there are no passions, but which is nevertheless the principle of external actions. Therefore, it is the proper subject of justice, since justice is not concerned with passions. (*In Ethica*, §889)[46]

As I have already suggested, this interpretation is not, strictly speaking, Aristotelian.[47] Yet, even if Aquinas' interpretation was more an extension of Aristotle than strict Aristotle, it was sure to have been widely accepted as Aristotelian, since it was based on a distinction between justice and the other moral virtues which was itself widely accepted as Aristotelian. More to the point, this interpretation was known to Dante. He echoes the attribution of justice to the will in the *Convivio*:

> To the extent that its goodness is more proper [to us], something is that much more beloved, whence it comes that while every virtue is desirable in men, that one is most loved in him which is most human, and that virtue is justice, which is solely of the rational or, really, intellectual part, that is, of the will. (*Conv.*, i, xii, 9)[48]

Since justice is the virtue most to be loved, injustice is the vice most to be hated, as Dante continues in the *Convivio*—"and so injustice is far and away the most hated" ("la ingiustizia massimamente è odiata" [*Conv.*, i, xii, 10])—and for the same reason: that injustice is the vice most "proper" to human beings. In one sense, of course, justice and injustice are no more proper to human beings than any other virtue or vice. For both Aristotle and Aquinas, all virtues and vices are purely human, because they all depend on choice, a uniquely human operation. Animals cannot be said to possess virtues or vices. Justice and injustice are no more human than any other of these moral states. When Dante declares that justice is the most properly human virtue, he is so characterizing it simply because justice is the virtue of a faculty that is proper to humans, rather than one common to humans and other animals: that is, the will, the intellectual appetite. While animals may not properly be said to possess virtues, they do share with human beings the two sensitive appetites, the subjects of the moral virtues other than justice. But humans, as distinct from animals, also possess an intellectual appetite, and so, Dante concludes, its virtue is more properly human, and for this reason more worthy of being loved.

Now, we have already noticed that the same principle was used by Virgil to explain why sins of fraud constitute the worst category of sin. They are worst because most hated by God, and most hated because they are sins proper to human beings.

> Ma perchè frode è dell'uom proprio male,
> più spiace a Dio; e però stan di sutto
> li frodolenti e più dolor li assale.
> (*Inf.* xi, 25–27)

There is nothing casual in Dante's saying, in one place, that injustice, and in another, that fraud is most hateful and also most proper to human beings. For Dante, actions of these two descriptions—that is, unjust actions and fraudulent actions—were identical. For Dante, fraud is *ingiuria* in a technical sense: injuries that are also injustices. And indeed, when Dante in the *Convivio* lists the contraries of justice (which he calls sins, *peccati*, rather than vices), the list that he gives is in a general sense identical to the actions that appear in the eighth and ninth circles of Hell, and very different from the list of injustices given by Aristotle in the *Ethics* (*EN*, v, 5; 1131a1–10). (The one injustice in Dante's list that does not appear in either circle eight or nine, *rapina*, robbery, may be intended in the *Convivio* in a somewhat different sense than as it appears in the *Inferno*.)

> Injustice is far and away the most hated, as are betrayal, ingratitude, falseness, theft, robbery, fraud, and anything like them. (*Conv.*, i, xii, 10)

What properly characterizes both injustice in Aristotle and fraud in Dante is having gain as one's object, whether one's acts include violence or not. Having gain as the object also identifies both injustice and fraud as dispositions of the intellectual appetite, the will. It is this connection of fraud to the will that is most important to the structure of the *Inferno*, for making that connection to the will makes it possible for Dante to distinguish sins of fraud from other sins, including other violent sins, in ways that avoid the potential theological problems we have also identified.

Associating the sins of the eighth and ninth circles with a particular appetite enabled Dante to explain the nature of these sins and their gravity without having to be concerned with the question of whether the acts arise from a settled habit of mind—a vice—or not. For Aristotle, only acts of injustice committed from such a settled habit are properly speaking called acts *of* injustice; and such acts are the worse for having the vice as their source. But, we reflected, for Dante all acts of a given sort, whether habitual or unique, must be equally culpable, and even unique acts of injustice must be punished in the same way as habitual acts of injustice when they remain unforgiven. Since he could not use the habitual character of an act (as Aristotle would have) to discriminate between actions, Dante needed a different criterion. By making use of Aquinas' conclusion that injustice is a vice of a particular appetite, the will, Dante could determine what were acts of injustice, or, more appropriately, sins of fraud, by identifying the faculty from which they originated, whether they were single events or habitual acts. The act would receive its special character from the properties of the appetite that initiated it; its gravity would be determined from the appetite that directed it.[49]

The common characteristics of the actions of the eighth and ninth circles which they possess as acts of will—first, that they are pursued free from passion, because the will operates without passion; and second, that they embody a certain calculation of advantage—also furnish an explanation for the "doubling" of sins that we see in the *Inferno*. (Specific examples will be more fully discussed below, as we consider the particular circles of Hell and their sins.) Certain of the actions punished in the circles of fraud are similar to actions punished in higher circles; to the uninstructed onlooker, they may appear identical. Why is schismatism distinguished from heresy? Why is seduction separated from lust? We can now recognize that the distinction turns on the coexistence, or not, of passion with the commission of the sin. Any act might be committed with passion, or without.[50] The sinners of the eighth and ninth circles committed sins whose pursuit of gain bespeaks the intellectual action of the will. For the will acts with reason, not by passion, and these sinners acted deliberately and calculatedly, rather than passionately, in pursuing gain. But similar actions might be committed passionately rather than deliberately, and we should therefore conclude that the "doubled" sins we discover in locations higher in Hell than the last two circles, while similar in action to their fraudulent doubles, were initiated, or were accompanied in their execution, by one or another passion, rather than by deliberation. Their having been committed in the grip of passion altered the character of the actions, and diminished their culpability, though it did not, of course, absolve the sinners from punishment.

We can go further. Since all action originates in appetite, any actions that do not originate in the will must originate in one of the two "sensitive" appetites, either concupiscence or irascibility. Thus, any of the sins in Hell located in circles higher than eight and nine can be attributed to one or the other of these appetites. These two appetites are called sensitive because their objects are objects first apprehended by the senses. The two appetites are thus intimately connected to the body, and because of that, in the pursuit of or flight from their objects, physiological and psychological changes occur in the body in response to these objects. These changes are what we recognize as the passions associated with these appetites. Because human beings are composites of body and intellect, we are strongly moved by the passions, and those of our actions that are affected by them are to that extent less rational. To the extent that we commit sins under the influence of passions, those sins can be said to be less blameworthy because less rational. Thus, sins initiated by the will are not only more hateful because the will is a properly human faculty, they are also more hateful because the will operates independently of passion.[51] Sins occasioned by passion are found higher in Hell.

The two sensitive appetites have their own special objects distinct from one another, and have associated with them passions appropriate to these distinct objects. As we consider the nature of these objects and their associated passions more concretely, it becomes clear that it is not only as a logical necessity that we say that all actions not initiated by the will must be attributed to them, but that in fact Dante has used the properties of the two remaining appetites to aggregate and character-ize the sins of the remainder of Hell in just the same way he had used the will to determine and characterize the sins of fraud.

Objects of the concupiscible appetite, first of all, are objects per-ceivable by the senses (this is a sensitive appetite), and second, are per-ceived as goods desirable in themselves. (The concupiscible appetite also has for objects things perceived as evils and undesirable or harm-ful in themselves—these are objects of avoidance.) In its radical form, it is the appetite most closely linked to our biological nature, and the most distant from the intellect that must control it.[52] Because of its fundamentally biological character, its proper objects compose what Aristotle calls "necessary" goods—primarily sex and food.[53] In its en-counter with such objects, passions appropriate to things desirable in themselves (and their opposites) are evoked: love, upon perception of them (or hate, if the objects are harmful); desire, which fuels pursuit of the loved object, and from which the appetite takes its name (the equivalent contrary passion is avoidance); joy or delight, upon attain-ment of, or union with, the desired object (or sadness, upon its loss). As befits the most primitive appetite, these are also the most primitive passions. All other passions were said by medieval psychologists to be-gin in these, and to resolve themselves back into them as well.[54]

As Aristotle points out, it is possible, by analogy, to speak of a desire for objects other than the immediately biological as if they were ob-jects of this appetite, as long as these "nonnecessary" goods are desired in the same direct way as the simple goods that are the natural objects of the concupiscible appetite. That is, if other things, for example wealth, are regarded as desirable in themselves, they meet the formal requirements for objects of concupiscence. One can, then, speak of desire or concupiscence for wealth, or honor, or other objects. The us-age is metaphorical, but, insofar as the objects of concupiscence are defined as proposing goods of a certain sort, namely as desirable per se, the usage is unforced.[55] Moreover, those objects are then pursued in the same way as are the proper objects of concupiscence, and are ac-companied by the same passions as the objects of concupiscence.

Aquinas, building his explanation on a citation from 1 John 2: 16, distinguished two concupiscences in just this way. For our purposes, what is important to note is that he believed both were appropriately called concupiscence.

> There are, indeed, two kinds of concupiscence, as was concluded previously [1a2æ 30, 3]. One concupiscence is natural, and is concupiscence for those things by which our bodily nature is maintained, both in regards to the preservation of the individual (food and drink and other things of this sort), and also in regard to the preservation of the species (sexual desires and procreation). An inordinate appetite for these things is called *concupiscence of the flesh.* The other concupiscence is a spiritual concupiscence, a concupiscence for things that have nothing to do with sensible pleasures or the sustenance of the body, but which are pleasurable on account of the apprehension of the imagination or a similar sort of comprehension—things such as money, fine clothes, and things of this sort. And this spiritual concupiscence is named *concupiscence of the eyes.* (*ST,* 1a2æ 77, 5)

An Aristotelian would recognize immediately that the objects of the concupiscible appetite are identical to the objects of the virtue temperance (and its opposed vice, intemperance), and also of continence and incontinence when these are taken in their strict sense. We recall that many of the sinners in upper Hell should more properly be said to have acted through the vice of intemperance (insofar as habitual and deliberate), rather than through incontinence properly so-called. Yet, as we also took note, a proper Aristotelian understanding of intemperance (or vice in general) would be problematic for Dante's notion of sin, both because for Aristotle the vicious are essentially unconscious of the wrongness of their actions, and also because vice implies repeated and habitual wrongdoing, while many in Hell are condemned for acts that could not be said to be habitual. (It is unlikely, for example, that the first sinners we encounter in Hell—Paolo and Francesca—would have been considered vicious in an Aristotelian sense.) However, the effective coincidence of the objects of intemperance and incontinence with the objects of the concupiscible appetite provides Dante a solution.

In his discussion of incontinence in the *Ethics,* Aristotle points out that properly speaking one is not called continent or incontinent with respect to any object, but only with respect to those same objects that we have described as "necessary" goods. Sex, food, certain other physical goods—these are the objects of continence and incontinence, as well as of temperance and intemperance. The very same objects, we have noted, are the objects of the concupiscible appetite.[56] But further, as a primitive appetite, the concupiscible appetite is malleable enough that it can be directed to objects beyond its original or natural objects, and by incorporating these easy extensions, it becomes possible to describe the actions of all of the sinners in upper Hell as dependent upon the operation of the concupiscible appetite. When Virgil characterizes all of the sins of upper Hell as *incontinenza*, the usage may not be properly Aristotelian, but medieval associations of Aristotelian virtues and vices with specific appetites made it possible to recognize in all of those sins, whether properly incontinence or vice, a common set of objects pursued in a common manner. This, we can see, is the same strategy that Dante had used with respect to *malizia*. Some of the fraudulent sinners are properly speaking malicious; others acted without vice's settled habits. Yet all of their actions pursued the same object, and pursued it in the same manner, an object and a manner associated, again, with a specific appetite. In both cases, using the appetite to characterize the actions enables Dante to find a common description of the nature of these actions which avoids having to deal with the distinction between habitual sinful actions and unique sinful actions. For Dante, what the sins of upper Hell have in common, what distinguishes them (whether truly vicious or merely occasional acts) from all other sorts of sins, and what makes it comprehensible to speak of all of them as incontinence, is their common origin in concupiscence, the appetitive impulse that is the natural spur to incontinence proper.

The third of the appetites recognized in the medieval interpretation of Aristotle, the irascible appetite, has as its objects what the Middle Ages called "arduous" goods (and their opposites): objects of sense perception that are not desirable in themselves, but are desirable, though they themselves may be evil or painful, for the sake of other goods desirable in themselves.[57] (The contrary objects of the irascible appetite, that is, its objects of avoidance, are evils perceived as such that are at the same time difficult to avoid. They are therefore "arduous evils," rather than simple ones.) In the case of good or evil objects of this appetite, effort is required, whether to attain a difficult good or avoid a difficult evil. Yet such objects, difficult though they be, are indeed pursued (or sought to be avoided), and thus the irascible is properly said to be an appetite.[58] Since the irascible appetite too is tied to the body, passions are undergone during its operation, just as had been the case with the concupiscible appetite. In the operation of irascibility, any of five passions may be evoked depending on the nature of the object encountered: hope or despair, in the face of goods difficult to attain (or believed to be difficult to attain), the one when one expects to be able to attain the good albeit with effort, the other when one believes attainment is impossible; courage or fear, in the face of evils difficult to avoid; anger, in the face of evils already present. It is from its signal passion, anger, that the irascible appetite takes its name, as the concupiscible appetite took its from its characteristic passion. In the end, the passions of the irascible appetite resolve themselves back into the simpler passions of the concupiscible appetite: to joy if the good is attained (or evil avoided); to sadness if not. Anger begins in sadness that results from the presence of the evil that evokes it, though it expects to resolve itself into the pleasure of revenge or vindication.[59]

Consideration of the role of the irascible appetite will solve our last remaining problem with Virgil's characterization of the nature of sins located in distinct areas of Hell. Since many of the sins Virgil had described as *con frode* were accompanied by violence, we recognized a problem in understanding how the description *con forza* specified sins of a nature distinct from the fraudulent. The malicious sins that Virgil calls *con forza,* and which are punished in the seventh circle of Hell, can, however, be distinguished from the violent actions of the eighth and ninth circles to the extent that they originate in passion rather than calculation.[60] Now, the passions associated with the actions of the seventh circle cannot be attributed to the concupiscible appetite. Rather, the passions that are impulses to violent acts are passions associated with the irascible appetite, anger predominant among them. And, just as Dante was able to determine the sins appropriate to upper Hell by recognizing in them a common character resulting from their common origin in the concupiscible appetite, so he could determine that the injuries of circle seven demanded separate consideration (from the injuries of the eighth and ninth circles) because of a distinctive common character they received from their origin in the irascible appetite, a character significantly different from the character of the sins of circles eight and nine, even when those sins involved violence.

That the sins of the violent against neighbors (of the first *girone* of the seventh circle) take their origin from, or are accompanied by, anger has never been doubted by readers of the *Commedia*. The other sins of violence of the seventh circle can also be related to irascibility if we consider that, just as the concupiscible appetite exhibited a certain malleability with respect to its objects, so a similar malleability can be found in the irascible appetite. Someone can desire wealth (though not a natural object of concupiscence) in a manner structurally identical to the desire for food or sex. It is appropriate to speak of such a person as having a concupiscent desire for wealth, complete with the familiar concupiscent passions. In the *Inferno*, we can note similar analogical extensions in the relationship of sinner to object with respect to the irascible appetite in *gironi* two and three of circle seven. That is, just as the desire for wealth is not merely a metaphor of concupiscence but actually manifests the same relationship to its object as concupiscence does to its more natural objects, so the violent toward self, God, or nature manifest toward these objects the same relationship as would usually be manifested toward a difficult good or evil that is a natural object of the irascible appetite. To the extent that these sinners treated self, God, or nature as difficult goods or evils or present evils, we would expect them to manifest the passions associated with such objects just as if in a natural operation of the irascible appetite: anger, fear, despair. And, indeed, we do see this. The figure of Capaneus in the third *girone* of the seventh circle (*Inf.* xiv, 43–66) provides an immediate example of the way in which the irascible appetite can be carried over in regard to objects not naturally its own, complete with its characteristic passions.[61] Not only is his speech suffused with rage; not only does he describe his struggle with God as a vendetta (*Inf.* xiv, 60) — that is, as an appropriate object for anger — but his astounding refusal to drop this anger even now that he is condemned to Hell testifies to a voracious hunger for this struggle, and stands as a model of that *pursuit* of the arduous that is the essential character of the irascible appetite as appetite.[62] (We should remember, however, that anger is not the only passion associated with the irascible appetite, nor is the pursuit of vengeance with which anger is associated the only action of this appetite. Other passions and actions also conform to the structure of this appetite, and it is on this basis that later we will consider Dante's inclusion of the sixth circle, of the heretics, within the category of sins originating in the irascible appetite.)

Earlier in this chapter we took note of the motives that constrained Dante in attempting to use Aristotle as the source for the structure of

Hell: first, that a distinction crucial to Aristotle, between vice and incontinence, was irrelevant or misleading in a Christian context; second, that Aristotle's conviction that the truly vicious would also be least conscious of their guilt was untenable from a Christian perspective; third, that despite these problems justice demanded that Dante choose a system for Hell whose basis was natural or philosophical, rather than theological or revealed. Pagans too must be able to recognize the justice of their damnation, which means that the principles according to which they are damned must be accessible to the human understanding even without the benefit of revealed truth. Dante's use of the three appetites as the underlying principles of the organization of Hell deals with all three constraints.

First, as we have mentioned in passing, associating sins with appetites makes it possible to describe the common and distinctive character shared by sinful actions that arise from a given appetite without our having to decide whether the action is the result of a firm habit (that is, is a vice), or is a singular occurrence. In either case, the action receives its character, and an estimation of its gravity from the nature of the appetite. Second, once the issue of vice/incontinence is put aside, the issue of accountability is easily solved, even for the worst sins, since the natural relation of the appetites and the reason in action confirms the responsibility of all individuals for their actions.[63] Each of the appetites is, to a greater or lesser extent, obedient to reason and controllable by it. This is what distinguishes them from the merely biological aspects of our nature and our soul, such as functions of nutrition and growth, which are not controllable by reason.[64] Thus, even when actions are proposed by the appetites, it always remains within an individual's choice whether to perform them or not, so that from the standpoint of the appetites people remain accountable for their actions, and are open to praise or blame based on them. Finally, medieval doctrines of action based on the appetites are wholly naturalistic explanations of action, and therefore of sin. These are explanations, that is, that could be discoverable by, and comprehensible to, any person at any moment in time, merely by consideration of human nature. They therefore neither require knowledge of revealed truth to recognize that a given action is a sin or not, nor allow any plea of ignorance of revealed truth to exculpate anyone from the charge of sin.

Using the appetites as the principles of the genera of sin identified by Virgil not only accounts for the groupings into which specific sins fall, it also accounts for the order in which they appear and, therefore, for the structure of Hell. For, embodied within psychological explorations of the appetites was also a natural order among the appetites that could serve as the criterion by which to determine the relative gravity of sins to each other.[65] Since all actions begin in appetite, the natural relation in the soul of the three appetites to one another creates an ordered relation of the seriousness of wrong actions committed through them. An axiom of ancient and medieval ethics was that the reason must direct action if action is to be moral. When an impulse to action arises in a faculty distant from the reason, the reason experiences greater difficulty in directing the action than when the motive is nearer to the reason. How difficult the reason's task is in controlling action provides a measure of how harshly to judge the reason's incapacity to do so when sins are committed. The farther an appetite is from the reason, the harder it is for the reason to master the appetite, and therefore the lesser the blame attaching to a disordered act of that appetite. According to this principle, then, the worst acts would originate in the will, since—inasmuch as the intellectual appetite is itself a part of the reason—it ought to be easiest for the reason to control. On the other hand, since the body is distinct from the mind, actions undertaken at the urging of the two sensitive appetites (which are attached to the body and operate with passion) are less rational, and therefore less serious than those committed through the will.[66] Passion mitigates culpability (*ST,* 1a2æ 77, 6). The sensitive appetites are able to overpower the intellect because of the passions with which their operations are inextricably accompanied, given their intimate connection to the body. Passions aroused by the appetites in the presence of their appropriate objects physically alter the body of the individual experiencing them. (People with appetites brought into proper order by good habits experience less dramatic passions, undergo less significant physical modification, and confront their intellects with less serious challenges to control.)[67] Since our intellect is housed in a body, the body's changes affect the operation of the reason, in precisely the same way that sickness alters both the capacity to sense things and the capacity to think about them.[68] Just as no one would find someone culpable in an unqualified sense for actions or judgments undertaken during the course of a disease, so the operation of strong passions requires a partial suspension of the blame that would usually attach to actions that result from them. Of course, since the virulence with which we experience passions is itself within our own control, it is not that passion wholly excuses sin.[69] Yet, because passion removes some responsibility for one's actions, it is only passionless actions that can occur without excuse.

The first distinction between appetites concerns their relation to passions and the body. But among sins dependent on sensitive appetites, those originating in the concupiscible appetite are the least grave. As the appetite farthest removed from the reason, closest (in its primary operations) to the body, and closest to the simplest and most direct forms of pleasure, the concupiscible appetite is inherently the most difficult to control.

> The stronger the impulse to sin, the less a man sins. . . . Carnal sins have the more vehement impulse—namely, the very concupiscence of the flesh that is innate in us. . . . As the Philosopher says, . . . concupiscence . . . participates less in reason. (*ST*, 1a2æ 73, 5 and ad 3)

Since the reason would have the greatest struggle in controlling this appetite, less blame attaches to failure to win the struggle.[70] The lesser gravity of sins arising in the concupiscible appetite explains their location in upper Hell.

Actions committed through the irascible appetite are worse than those committed through the concupiscible. Insofar as there are passions, often powerful, associated with the irascible appetite, the culpability of wrong actions undertaken at its prompting is diminished relative to wrong actions that arise in the will.[71] Aristotle notes that though it cannot be said in an unqualified sense, it is possible to speak of inappropriately angry people as incontinent *with respect to anger*. Those acting through anger, or the irascible appetite, are thus overcome and mastered in a way analogous to those overcome by concupiscence. But "incontinence" with respect to anger differs in two critical respects from incontinence with respect to concupiscible passions. First, the irascible appetite as a whole participates in reason to a greater extent than does the concupiscible. It is not so immediately connected to the biological as the concupiscible is, and requires, in fact, specific judgments of the reason as to the arduousness of the attainment of its object, and, in the case of anger, as to whether an evil has occurred that requires an angry response. Anger, Aristotle says, "listens to reason."[72] The concupiscible appetite with which temperance and intemperance, and continence and incontinence (properly speaking), are concerned waits on no such judgment before making its demands for satisfaction. But since anger and the irascible appetite are to a certain extent rational in their origin, they should be more naturally controllable by reason than concupiscence. Failure to control irascible appetitiveness, therefore, is more blameworthy than the equivalent failure with concupiscence. Second, with respect to anger, at least, the actions that occur as a result of its operation involve injury to other people. Aristotle and Aquinas concur that actions that injure others are worse than improper actions that are entirely personal (and that constitute, for the most part, the sins of concupiscence).[73] The sins of violence, which we interpret as those originating in irascibility, are one category of Virgil's *malizia* for this reason.

For both reasons, then, sins originating in the irascible appetite are more blameworthy than sins originating in concupiscence. They share with concupiscent sins an origin in passion, however, and an underlying structure of incontinence—that is, of passion overwhelming the judgment of reason. In the *Ethics,* persons who commit unjust acts under the influence of anger are distinguished from those properly called unjust. It is easy, therefore, to see Dante's reasoning in placing sins of irascibility in a middle position in Hell. Insofar as the sins arise in passion, as is also true of concupiscence, some of their culpability is removed. These sins cannot be considered the worst of sins, since their source is not the most properly human faculty, the intellect. Reason has been overpowered in these sins. But, on the other hand, the reason has been overpowered by passions that it ought to have been able to control more easily than the passions that confront it under the influence of concupiscence. Thus, the blame attaching to the reason's failure here is greater than in the sins originating in the concupiscible appetite, and so the appropriate location of these sins, while not the lowest part of Hell, neither should be upper Hell.

The lowest part of Hell is reserved by Dante for sins of the intellectual appetite, the will. Where the objects of the concupiscible and irascible appetites are objects perceived by the senses (or proposed by the imagination, recreating sensations), the objects of the will are goods apprehended solely by the reason. Such objects either may be the soul's final good, happiness (in the strictly human context) or blessedness, or they may be general goods, not specified until the moment of action into particular objects perceivable by the senses.[74] We can get a sense of how abstract, and dispassionate, the objects of the will are by considering how different a motive that "gain" is which is the general object of the will (and motive for injustice) from the *passion* for possession that we see in those who are incontinent with respect to wealth. The unjust do not have a *hunger* for wealth. Rather, they have made a calculation that there is profit in a certain course of action, and they pursue it, to the injury of others, for that profit. Because the will is part of the intellect, this calculation can be made without passion. Just as the man who sleeps with a woman for profit is more properly said to be moved by cupidity than by lust, so the pursuit of gain in this sense is also a passionless exercise, quite distinct from the action of the avaricious in circle four of Hell.[75] Because the will's actions are passionless, and because the will as intellectual appetite has the most intimate connection to the intellect itself—the most properly human of the faculties—sins of the will are the worst of human sins.[76]

So, in the end, it is indeed Aristotle who provides the structure of Hell, though Aristotle as he was interpreted by the Middle Ages. The medieval psychological doctrine of three appetites, in which all action arises, provided a way of concretizing Aristotle's moral distinctions, and provided Dante a means of distinguishing and characterizing sins. The natural hierarchy of the appetites placed them in an order Dante could use; as the appetites can be ordered from the most commonly animal to the most properly human, so are sins from the least blameworthy to the most: sins of concupiscence, which Dante calls sins of incontinence; sins of irascibility (for the most part, sins of violence); sins of the will, calculated sins of fraud.[77]

PART II

THE POETIC APPLICATION OF THE
STRUCTURE OF HELL

The Contrapasso *and the Relation between
Poetic Details and Structure*

The medieval Aristotelian psychological theory implicit in Virgil's description of the geography of Hell gave Dante only the skeleton of the *Inferno.* What we experience in the poem itself is that theory made concrete and vivid in the incidents and descriptions of the narrative.

Many of the poetic details of the *Inferno* are intuitively comprehensible, but others are more obscure; and to the extent that we understand Dante's interpretation of Aristotle, we have a powerful clue both for illuminating his more obscure poetic choices and also for more fully understanding even the familiar ones. Nor does this process of illumination occur in one direction only. If our awareness of how Dante may have used Aristotle casts light on the incidents of the poem, it is equally the case that the incidents in their turn often suggest to us nuances of how Dante specifically understood the Aristotelian text he used as his philosophical source.

All of the poetic details are significant—location, geography, climate, physical appearance—all are surely intended to make concrete the abstract theory that determined the placement of a particular sin in a particular place in Hell. But foremost among the details, of course, are the punishments with which the damned are tormented. The punishments are the most compelling of the details. Physical descriptions of place appear from time to time in the *Inferno,* sometimes with more detail, sometimes less. But the punishments are always before our eyes, and it is the vividness with which Dante treats them that gives the *cantica* its force. We must be self-conscious and deliberate, then, in determining how best to interpret these most important narrative events in the context of Hell's structure and the structure of sin it embodies. Moreover, our decision with respect to the punishments will effectively determine what we will look for in the other poetic details as well. So, we must state our position with respect to what Dante once, and commentators many times, called the *contrapasso* that the damned endure.

My conviction is that we must distinguish the figurative principle of the punishments that we see the damned souls undergoing in Hell from that of the corrections we see souls undertaking in Purgatory. What we see in the punishments of the damned are figurative replications of the actions or natures of the sins themselves. When, later, we see purgatorial corrections, what we see are figures that show actions opposite in nature to the vices being purged.[78] For Hell, the principle is enunciated by Bertram de Born, in the eighth circle of Hell:

> Io feci il padre e 'l figlio in sè ribelli:
> Achitofèl non fè più d'Absalone
> e di Davìd coi malvagi punzelli.

> Perch'io parti' così giunte persone,
> partito porto il mio cerebro, lasso!
> dal suo principio ch'è in questo troncone.
> Così s'osserva in me lo contrapasso.
> (*Inf.* xxviii, 136–42)[79]

Considering how important the notion of the *contrapasso*—presumably not any individual punishment itself, but the principle of justice that informs all of the punishments—is to the poem, it is strange to realize that this passage is the only time in the whole of the *Commedia* that Dante uses the term *contrapasso*. That being the case, given also how late in the *Inferno* it is before Dante deals with the principle explicitly, the location he chooses as the one in which to call attention to the principle is probably also significant. Bertram says that having divided others, he is now himself divided. He is punished among the sowers of discord, the *seminator di scandalo e di scisma* (*Inf.* xxviii, 35). Now, *seminator* is also a word that Dante only uses once in the entire *Commedia*, and given the nature of the principle Bertram enunciates, it is a noun pregnant with meaning. If Dante has waited until encountering these sowers of discord before making the notion of a *contrapasso* explicit, it is, I believe, so we can hear the echo of Paul in Galatians: "Quæ enim seminaverit homo, hæc et metet" (Gal. 6:7), Whatever a man sows, so shall he reap. And this is precisely what Bertram is undergoing. Having sown division, he has now reaped it. In his case, he now undergoes what he did; in other cases, we recognize that sinners continue to engage in the activity that was their sin (rather than to suffer its effects); but in whichever of these two patterns Dante chooses, the image we are given in the punishment, as we see in Bertram's case, is an image in which we can recognize the essential action of the sin that is being punished.

The principle of the corrections of Purgatory, as stated by Omberto Aldobrandesco, is exactly the opposite. Omberto recognizes that the correction imposed upon him among the proud consists in doing what he should have done, but did not do, while alive:

> E qui convien ch'io questo peso porti
> per lei, tanto che a Dio si sodisfaccia,
> poi ch'io nol fe' tra' vivi, qui tra' morti.
> (*Purg.* xi, 70–72)[80]

The purpose of Purgatory is the undoing of the vices that had afflicted the now repentant sinners while alive. Vices cannot be removed by a repetition of one's vicious actions: an Aristotelian would understand that such repetition would merely serve to confirm a vicious habit. Hence, it is altogether necessary as well as appropriate that the undoing of their sinful states be accomplished, and represented to us, by actions that are the opposites of the sins they had committed. It cannot at all be said of the sinners undergoing rehabilitation in Purgatory that they have reaped what they sowed.[81] Quite the contrary, whether we look at the corrections they undertake or the ultimate result of those corrections. Having sown a stiff neck, Omberto reaps its opposite, a bent one. Or, one might say, having sown sin, Omberto will eventually reap, because of his repentence, blessedness. Purgatory moves by opposition, and the *contrapasso* in the *Purgatorio* must be recognized as demanding correction through action opposed to the sin that is to be corrected.

In the *Inferno*, the descriptions Dante gives of the punishments are meant to embody, make concrete, external, and visible, the intentions, motives, and choices that inform the various sins.[82] In punishing the damned through the actions of their own sins, these punishments effectively become dramatizations of the underlying nature of each sin, making manifest what may have been obscured or concealed in the original act. In our world, sinful actions inevitably present themselves to us veiled by a cloud of circumstantial detail, detail that makes it difficult to separate what is essentially sinful about the act from the accidents amidst which we perceive it. In his striking descriptions of their punishments, Dante is able to propose the essences of the sins stripped of worldly circumstance, and ultimately, if not immediately, more capable of being understood.[83] The general nature of this poetic principle has long been the common possession of readers of the *Inferno*. The parallelism of many of the punishments to the sins they punish is almost intuitively apparent. We see the lustful now driven by a whirlwind that is the image of the passion that drove them while alive; the violent, moved by anger—a "heating of the blood around the heart," as the Middle Ages would express it[84]—find themselves eternally surrounded by boiling blood; the traitors, so coldly calculating as to betray family, country, sovereign for gain, are set in ice.

While I believe that Dante is unwavering in his application of the principle that the punishment mirrors the sin in the *Inferno*, there has always been controversy regarding either the principle in general or its applicability in particular cases. The likely source of ambiguity on which disagreement could be based is Dante's practice of sometimes showing sinners re-enacting the specific actions of their sins in their punishments, and other times undergoing the effects of those actions. His choice of active or passive representations is presumably dictated by poetic judgment. Sometimes the passive image may be more effective; in other cases, the active. But this practice can lead to a verbal equivocation, since in the case of passive representations, it is possible to say that the sinners are being punished by the "contrary" of their sin (since acting and undergoing are indeed contraries). Hence, some readers have fallen into the trap of saying, rather too casually, that these sinners are punished by the "opposite" of their sins.[85] But while it would be proper to say that the souls in Purgatory are being purged by the opposite of their sins, the sinners in Hell are not tormented by a sin's opposites, but by the sin itself. In the case of the schismatics, already noted, they are punished by undergoing what they once practiced. Their punishment is passive, relative to the action that was their sin, but they are nonetheless punished by the sin itself, and their passion provides an image of the sin, not its opposite.[86]

There is a powerful double sense of justice in punishing the damned by the re-enactment of their sins. First, these sins were actions freely chosen by the souls themselves during their lives. What could be more just than to allow them to continue to practice those illusory goods (now revealed as pains) which they had preferred to the one true good?[87] Second, justice demands that the damned be beyond change. Were they still capable of change, they could be capable of repentance, and then it would be unjust to continue their punishment eternally.[88] Unlike the souls of Purgatory, then, the damned must remain fixed in the damnable choices they made while alive.[89] And indeed, while undergoing their punishments, they undergo without cease the experience of their same damnable activities. In doing so, they thereby become ever more fixed in the characteristic actions that damned them, since it is the repetition of a certain manner of acting that, for an Aristotelian, renders a specific state of character more stable and durable. As they repeat these damnable actions, they repeatedly and justly incur the condemnation for these actions that has doomed them to their places. They become, if one can say it, more perfectly damned with every iteration of the sin that is their punishment.[90]

(In Purgatory, by contrast, whose purpose is precisely change, and where the allegorical goal of the narrative is to illuminate the virtues that are the opposites of the seven capital vices, the corrections we see in the literal narrative must, for a double reason, exhibit activities opposite to the vices.[91] They must do so, first, in order to be able to serve as figures for their coordinate virtues. They do so as well because of the consistent Aristotelian theory of action that underlies both the *Inferno* and the *Purgatorio*. If bad habits are inculcated and made durable by repetition of bad actions, good habits must be made durable by the repetition of proper activities.)

The *contrapasso* is first of all an ethical or theological principle. Justice directs that the damned be punished by the very actions for which they were damned; ethics instructs that the rehabilitation of bad habits be by an opposing regimen. But it is the *poet's* application of this theological principle that directs how we are to interpret the poetic details of the poem in the light of the structure of Hell (and later of Purgatory). The poet maintains faith with the principle of justice and consistency with the structure of Hell by making the individual sin and its genus resemble that structure—whether we mean that the punishment shows us the action of the sin or physical details illuminate particular aspects of the sin. (In Purgatory, though this will be relevant primarily to the next chapter, our strategy would call for the opposite conclusion. Details are consistent with the structure of Purgatory when they reflect virtuous conduct, the opposite of the vices under correction.)

As we read the *Inferno*, we are encouraged to consider the specific actions engaged in by the damned, and the circumstances in which they engage in them, as furnishing clues to the nature of the sin whose punishment they are. These figurative representations of the sins are often simultaneously obscure and transparent: obscure, insofar as they often do not at first resemble their sins or the occasions of the sins; transparent, insofar as they ultimately provide a starker and therefore clearer picture of the real nature of the sin. What to our eyes makes the punishments initially seem dissimilar to their sins is that the sins, as we have noted, occur in this world surrounded by circumstances— including deceptions, self-deceptions, and rationalizations on the part of the sinners—which have all disappeared in Hell.[92] So these do not look like the sins as we know them. Yet, at the moment that we do recognize the sins in these punishments, we have made a breakthrough in recognizing the underlying action that was the real nature of the sin. We are invited by Dante to use the details of punishments to confirm familiar aspects of the sins, and also to suggest hitherto unacknowledged or obscure aspects of them.[93] Indeed, where we see punishments whose relation to their sins is not immediately apparent to us, we ought not imagine that Dante has suddenly employed a different principle, but, rather, that he is demanding that we consider the sin in an unexpected light, leading us thereby to a reinterpretation of its nature. Where we find sins "doubled," as it were—that is, where we find Dante punishing in two locations, as two sins, actions that we conventionally consider only one sin—we must make an effort to recognize what significant difference Dante may be attempting to exhibit by this diversity of embodiment and location.

As the details of punishments of the individual sins make visible and illuminate the natures of the sins, so grouping sins together in geographical regions of Hell objectifies what we would usually encounter as philosophical distinctions. Geographical proximity of punishments (and so of sins) must imply affinities in the natures of these sins. Distances between circles should reflect differences in nature.[94] Descriptions of geographical or geological separations or barriers between regions, then, are the figurative equivalent of philosophical distinctions between sins of substantially different natures. Where no barriers or separations exist—where, that is, Dante and Virgil can simply walk between circles—their continuous movement should be the image of an essential continuity or kinship existing between discrete sins. (And when we look to this figurative strategy, we immediately recognize that Dante uses it to confirm Virgil's articulation of the structure of Hell in canto xi. Between each of the broad categories of sin Virgil describes there are geographical or geological barriers; between the individual sins within those groupings we find, on the other hand, a continuous, and usually unobstructed route for Dante and Virgil to follow.) Finally, to the punishments and their locations we should add for consideration details of climate and geology, the functionaries whom Dante posts to superintend locations, and the behaviors of the sinners Dante encounters.[95] All of these concrete imagistic details contribute content to the structure of sin embodied in the structure of Hell, at the same time that our understanding of their significance is guided by the principles according to which that structure was articulated.

One fundamental aspect of the poetic use of the structure of Hell bears repeating. The underlying philosophical structure of the *Inferno* is the architectonic principle of the narrative, establishing its order and directing the selection of appropriate figurative detail for the poem's incidents. But, as was already mentioned in the introduction, the existence of this architectonic principle does not constrain Dante *poeta;* rather, it provides the opportunity for a real poetic liberation, freeing him from an otherwise impossible poetic task. Consider: if we had no theological or philosophical context in which to understand that, and why, certain sins in their nature were worse than others, Dante's descriptions of their punishment—by themselves—would have had to embody simultaneously both the essence of the sin and the degree of its gravity. Not only would the details of punishments have to be figures of the diverse sins, the punishments would themselves have to be ordered in such a way that each punishment would unequivocally appear worse to every reader, thus indicating the increasing seriousness of the sins encountered. Who could imagine it possible to do this? In the natural scheme of things, is it worse to be burned in a fiery tomb? Or to be hacked in half at every completed circuit of Hell? Is it worse to be up to one's neck in boiling blood or in excrement? In the *natural* scheme of things, it does not, of course, matter at all, and individual readers find different punishments more horrific or disgusting for what will always be purely personal reasons. But the geographical location of the punishments gives an unequivocal measurement of their differing seriousnesses, so that we do not have to do so.

That the circles of Hell (and the sins represented in them) follow an ordered sequence that itself incorporates an explanation of the increasing seriousness of the sins frees Dante from having to undertake this impossible poetic feat. The primary geographic feature of Hell furnishes the initial and most straightforward of the poetic figures: the depth in Hell in which a sin is punished indicates its seriousness; downward is worse. Inasmuch as the regions of Hell are associated with the appetites that are the sources of all action, and inasmuch as the appetites are themselves ordered in terms of rationality or controllability by the reason (and, hence, culpability in the failure to control them), attribution of sins to the appropriate appetite locates the sin with respect to its seriousness, and therefore determines its physical location in the geography of Hell. Since we conclude from geography alone that to be punished lower in Hell is worse (whether or not the punishments for sins lower in Hell are ones we would personally consider more painful than for sins above them), Dante is freed to select punishments on the basis of how effectively they provide an image of the sins of which they are punishments.[96]

Upper Hell: The Region of Concupiscence

Virgil identifies upper Hell as the region of sins of incontinence. As has been argued above, we will have to adapt the Aristotle he cites to understand it properly.[97] Nonetheless, all of the sinners of this region, and this is especially easy to see if we initially consider only the more straightforward examples, would share the one characteristic common to intemperance and to incontinence properly so called within medieval Aristotelian usage: the objects of their sinful actions were objects of the concupiscible appetite.

The earliest circles of sinners show us sins of concupiscence in their most basic form. The sins of lust and gluttony (in circles two and three) are naturally associated with that appetite, for their objects are explicitly those "necessary" goods that are the natural objects of both intemperance and incontinence for Aristotle and medieval Aristotelians. But Dante does not leave their association only at the abstract level of the definitions of these sins. The imagery of the poem too in both instances supports the identification of these sins with the appetite that is the source both of these two sins and of the moral states of intemperance and incontinence. The buffeting of the lustful by winds outside of their control and beyond their strength to resist (*Inf.* v, 31–33) is a straightforward poetic embodiment of the passion that, as one would say figuratively, "drove" them to their sins, and now literally drives them in Hell. The *bufera* that moves them embodies, as well, the quality of "otherness" that passions, with their source in the body, always seem to present to the reasoning soul, for in its confrontation with passion the intellect is conscious of being compelled by forces opposed to its wishes, and therefore apparently exterior to itself. And indeed, throughout the poetic imagery of these earliest circles, we can see consistent emphasis on the corporeality of these sins, either in the energy of the whirlwind of the lustful or the gross materiality of the gluttons.

Initially, the punishment of the gluttons and the circumstantial details surrounding it seem worlds removed from their sin; perhaps it even seems its opposite. What we have in this case, however, is the first instance of how unfamiliar a sin may appear to us when represented in a figurative form that strips away worldly trappings that obscure its real nature. In its naked form the sin seems unfamiliar to us, but Dante is nonetheless not describing the sin's opposite here, but the sin itself.

Our first indication that this is so is the placing of the three-headed dog, Cerberus (Dante calls specific attention to the appetitive side of these three heads, of course, by describing not merely three heads, but three gullets, *gole; Inf.* vi, 13–15), as the superintendent of the circle of the gluttons. To use a dog as functionary is to confront the reader with the common animal (that is to say, biological) nature of this sin, as would be appropriate for an act of concupiscence, and with its distance from the rational soul that should control it. Cerberus is content to eat the rotting mud that Virgil hurls to him (*Inf.* vi, 25–29), and in this image we are directed to consider that, despite the luxury with which gluttons often surround themselves, such display is mere pretense. The essence of gluttony is filling one's belly. It is, in a sense, the sin most purely directed to corporeality. The glutton strives to be ever more corporeal, and this impulse finds its grotesque embodiment in the final description of the souls of the gluttons as nearly indistinguishable from the mud in which they lie. Indeed, they are the substance of the mud in which they lie ("Sì trapassammo per sozza mistura / dell'ombre e della pioggia"; *Inf.* vi, 100–101). Having made their decision to pursue corporeality, they have managed now to become completely corporeal. They are now mere matter.[98]

Only these two sins in upper Hell can claim a natural connection to concupiscence. But in the description of their journey, Virgil and Dante are able to walk from the first circle of Hell through the fourth without encountering any physical barrier or requiring any alternative or exceptional means of transport. If we take the most straightforward figurative interpretation of the physical contiguity of these realms, we would conclude that Dante is using it to indicate that these four specific sins all fall into a single, more general category of sin. As all four circles share a single "continent," so the sins punished in the four share some significant substrate. We know from Virgil's explanation, of course, that all of these sins were to be seen in common as sins of incontinence. We, in turn, recognize that the actions of this region form a single category because all take their origin in the concupiscible appetite. Dante, in fact, has gone further. In asking Virgil about the meaning of the location of the sins of upper Hell, we should note, he had explicitly included the fifth circle too in upper Hell: "quei della palude pingue" (*Inf.* xi, 70: this is the fifth circle; verse 71 describes the second and third, verse 72 the fourth circle). When Virgil does not correct him, we must conclude that it too, though only equivocally part of this "continent," should be included in the same category of sin. Here, in fact, our seeing that the principle of what Dante calls incontinence is actually the common origin of all of these sins in the concupiscible appetite is what makes it possible to bring even the initially less straightforward cases of upper Hell into line.

Every appetite has its natural objects and also a characteristic way of pursuing them. But the appetitive faculties are naturally malleable, and it is possible to direct them toward objects that are not their natural objects, and still have them pursue (or avoid) these new objects in the same way their natural objects would be pursued. Indeed, an entity or experience becomes the object of a given appetite when it is pursued as that appetite would. Any object pursued as a simple good, and for immediate gratification, whether a natural object of the concupiscible appetite or not, is properly speaking an object of concupiscence. This principle explains both the presence of the sins of circles four and five in upper Hell, and also the "doubling" we see of certain sins from upper Hell in lower Hell. In circles four and five we see objects that are not naturally objects of the concupiscible appetite treated as if they were.[99] In lower Hell, what seem to be familiar sins treated a second time will turn out to be instances of a different appetite taking over something that naturally is an object of concupiscence, but treating the object in a different way, that is, in a way appropriate to the new appetite.

The fourth circle furnishes our first example of an analogical sin of concupiscence, an extension of the operation of the appetite to objects that do not naturally belong to it. The ambiguous nature of such a sin is indicated from the start in our encounter with the functionary who superintends the circle, Pluto. In place of the straightforwardly animal Cerberus whom we saw superintending the straightforwardly corporeal and concupiscent sin of gluttony, Pluto is himself ambiguous. Is Dante showing us an animal or the mythological god? The mythological figure, of course, should appear human, and even this Pluto is human insofar as he is able to utter words. But the words are inarticulate, and all remaining description of him stresses the animal: Virgil, probably figuratively, calls him a wolf ("lupo"; *Inf.* vii, 8); Dante describes him, probably not so figuratively, as a savage beast ("la fiera crudele"; *Inf.* vii, 15).[100] The ambiguity is appropriate, for what we find punished here are actions that have as objects purely human and abstract goods, yet which pursue these objects in a manner closer to the animal, or biological, manner of the concupiscible appetite when in pursuit of "necessary" or animal goods.

Dante does not name the kind of sinner we discover in this circle. Editors often call them the avaricious and prodigal, though some English translations label them hoarders and spendthrifts. *Hoarders* ought to be preferred to *avaricious* for that party in this paired set of sinners, I believe, because *avarice* is itself an ambiguous term in the context of the *Commedia*, potentially applicable to sins of very different qualities. The "avarice" we see here in the fourth circle, if avarice it must be called, is an appetite altogether different from the pursuit of gain that is the motive of injustice (which, though it can also be called avarice, might perhaps better be called "covetousness" or "cupidity": see *ST*, 2a2æ 118, 3, cited above).[101] The hoarders of the fourth circle are not interested in "profit"—the advantage to be gained by wealth—but rather in the mere possession of wealth. As Virgil describes the two kinds of sinner punished here:

> Mal dare e mal tener lo mondo pulcro
> ha tolto loro, e posti a questa zuffa.
> (*Inf.* vii, 58–59)

Wealth (whether to possess or squander) is desired as an end in itself, and is itself the source of pleasure. In this respect, though the object of appetite to these sinners is not one that can properly be said to be an object of concupiscence, their appetitive tendency toward it is identical to the tendency of concupiscence toward its proper objects. The hoarder is to wealth as the glutton is to food. And in this case too the pursuit of the desired good is accompanied by a passion that is wholly lacking in that avarice or cupidity associated with injustice. The frenzy with which the hoarders and spendthrifts push their weights and the violence with which they collide poetically embody the drive of the appetite; the material but indistinct "weights" (*pesi*) they move and the slogans they hurl at one another suggest the abstractness of the object of the appetite (*Inf.* vii, 25–35). We see in the fourth circle an example of the malleability of appetite. The concupiscible appetite, by nature the most immediate and concrete of appetites, is here directed to an abstract object, though retaining through this choice of object the identical structure of pleasure and pursuit that it manifests in its natural operation. By participating in the structure of concupiscence, the hoarders and spendthrifts participate also in the moral qualities of concupiscent sin. Many sins involving wealth are assigned by Dante to much lower locations in Hell. But the sinners of circle four share the same diminished culpability that characterizes the other sinners in upper Hell. They are slaves to passion in a way that matches the lustful and the gluttonous. That they are punished below these two representatives of the real force of concupiscence probably reflects a greater culpability that should be assigned to those enslaved to objects that are only abstractions. Money cannot exercise the same truly animal attraction for the concupiscible appetite that sex and food can. To let it do so, as the hoarders and spendthrifts do, is perverse, and more blameworthy than natural concupiscence.[102] Yet insofar as they act in the grip of the same pattern of passion as the naturally concupiscent, they act in a way most distant from reason, and their incontinence is of lesser gravity.

The most perverse of the mutations of the concupiscible appetite is found, as is appropriate, in the lowest circle of upper Hell: circle five, the circle of the wrathful and sullen. Dante explicitly included this circle in upper Hell, and therefore among the sins that Virgil characterized as "of incontinence," despite what would otherwise appear to be similarities to the sins of violence in lower Hell. Moreover, to the extent that concrete details of geography and of Virgil's and Dante's passage through geographical regions stand as figures for abstract philosophical distinctions, we should recognize that no more emphatic distinction is signaled poetically by Dante than that between upper and lower Hell. No passage between circles is as difficult for Virgil and Dante to accomplish. It requires, first of all, another method of transportation than walking. This is Dante's most familiar means of indicating a separation between regions and, therefore, a distinction between sins of different natures. But not only does Dante make a simple distinction by these means, he reinforces the distinction by further poetic detail, as if to indicate that the distance between the natures of the sins of upper and lower Hell is even greater than in other cases. Not only must Virgil and Dante cross a body of water, they must pass through a gate, a gate that is defended and that they themselves do not have the power to force. It takes nothing less than the intervention of a celestial messenger to make it possible for the two travelers to reach lower Hell. No passage is more fraught with violent emotion in its accomplishment.

That so great a distinction is called for is probably to be explained by a crucial difference between sins of concupiscence and all others. It is possible to regard sins of concupiscence as sins in which the reason, which should control appetite, is at war with its natural enemy, the body. What Dante calls incontinence is a sin because the reason should win even against this opponent. But in the natural conflict that exists between mind and body, we find a degree of exculpation for the sin. In all of the sins of lower Hell, however, the reason is participant, either as originator or as collaborator, and in this regard the sins of lower Hell are categorically worse than those of upper Hell. Taking into account this fundamental distinction between upper and lower Hell, Dante unequivocally places the wrathful and sullen in upper Hell.

At the same time, though, Dante provides telling poetic details in circle five that seem to imply an intention to regard the sins of this circle as somehow transitional or mixed between those of upper and lower Hell. The fifth circle, the Styx, is the only example in the poem of a geographical feature that separates regions (as the Acheron did, but not the Phlegeton of circle seven) which is also itself the circle in which a sin is punished. We can reasonably surmise that this image was Dante's way of alerting us figuratively that the sin punished here might appropriately be considered in the light of the characteristics of both "banks" of this river. Moreover, though Dante will have picked up the description of the river Styx as a marsh (rather than a true river) from the *Æneid* (*Æneid* vi, 323: "Stygiamque paludem"), what was only a vague description in Virgil's poem is made vividly concrete in the *Commedia* as Dante describes the mud with which sinners are coated or in which they swim or bubble (*Inf.* vii, 109–11, 117–20, 127–29). Dante calls such vivid attention to the mud of the Styx to remind us that the marsh is simultaneously earth and water, and in its mixed material nature we presumably find another figure of the mixed nature of the sins punished there. The geographical and geological clues are such as to imply most forcibly that the sins of circle five have a combined or transitional character: while sins of upper Hell, they nonetheless reflect properties of lower Hell at the same time.[103]

> ... Figlio, or vedi
> l'anime di color cui vinse l'ira.
>
> (*Inf.* vii, 115–16)

Virgil describes the wrathful as overcome by anger ("color cui vinse l'ira"), and taken together with the general characterization of the sins of upper Hell as sins of incontinence, this has led commentators to define the sinners of this circle as the "incontinent with respect to anger,"[104] finding in this way an explanation of the combination we see here of the sins of incontinence of upper Hell and the sins of violence in circle seven. But such an explanation encounters many of the same problems regarding "incontinence" that we have earlier explored, and can only be properly understood by taking account of what we have discovered would have been Dante's interpretation of the term.

Aristotle had spoken of persons incontinent with respect to anger in book seven of the *Ethics*, but his usage there, as throughout his discussion of incontinence, is intended to distinguish the incontinently angry from the *viciously* angry. But that distinction is not a Dantean distinction. On the one hand, there is every reason to believe that many of wrathful in circle five are not merely incontinent with respect to anger but are vicious with respect to it. Nor, on the other, would we want to say that the wrathful could be distinguished from the violent of circle seven as incontinent from vicious, for we are likely to find the same phenomenon with respect to the sinners of circle seven, as with the wrathful. Many of the violent were surely viciously violent; others may have been merely incontinently violent, in Aristotelian terms.

Moreover, as we have discussed much earlier in this chapter, the violent of the seventh circle are themselves portrayed by Dante as having been in some way driven to violence by passion. They are not deliberately violent, though some of the fraudulent are. Consequently, it would be possible to say that the violent of the seventh circle too were conquered by some passion, of which anger is surely the most likely. Indeed, with respect to the wrathful particularly, it is not immediately apparent how they are to be distinguished from the violent. Both the violent and the wrathful are seemingly moved by anger. Both have done injury. We know that the violent have committed injury, since that is how Virgil has defined them. No such direct statement is made concerning the wrathful, but how could the wrathful—especially the consistently wrathful, as, for example, Filippo Argenti—*not* have done injury to others?[105] Neither can we say that the violent of circle seven act more deliberately than the wrathful of circle five, since even Aristotle denies that those acting from anger act deliberately, an interpretation with which I believe Dante more or less agrees (though always maintaining the individual's responsibility for such action).[106] Nor can we say that the violent are violent for the sake of profit since, although there are certainly instances where profit accrued to the violent for their actions, there are others where there is none.[107] The best examples of deliberate and profitable violence, as we have already seen, are found in the ninth circle, where we see sinners who committed murder for gain, but those acts were not based on anger or any other passion.

The acts of the wrathful of circle five and of the violent in circle seven, then, seem identical, and both sets of sinners act from the impulse of some passion, and yet Dante manifestly distinguishes the two groups of sinners. We can only make proper sense of their locations by understanding the incontinence of the wrathful in the Dantean, not Aristotelian, sense, a sense that makes it possible to recognize that while both wrathful and violent are overcome by a passion, they are overcome in different ways, appropriate to different appetites. In the most extreme, and perverse, of the transformations of the concupiscible appetite, what the sinners of the fifth circle have done is to take objects and passions that are natural to the irascible appetite and use and experience them as if they were objects and passions of the concupiscible appetite. The wrathful share violence and injury with the sinners of circle seven. But what is theirs alone is that they take the same kind of pleasure in anger and objects of anger that more conventionally concupiscent sinners take in more properly concupiscible objects. Though the wrathful commit injury, it is not the end, *'l fine,* of their action (though such is the end for the violent of circle seven). For the wrathful, the end is anger in itself, anger as if it were actually pleasant. Anger is not naturally a pleasant emotion, and it is not pleasant to the straightforwardly violent of circle seven; it is revenge that is pleasant to a person angry in a natural way. But the wrathful find anger pleasant in itself. Anger is properly a response to a perceived prior injury. The wrathful apparently can be angry almost spontaneously. Not only do the wrathful find pleasure in something naturally painful, but this pleasure makes it possible for them to evoke the emotion without its natural stimuli. Enjoying anger as they do, they transform any object into an object that evokes anger.[108] This is the mixed nature of their sin: the material is normally the material of the irascible appetite, but it is here experienced in a structure normally proper to the concupiscible.[109]

The sullen commit a similarly perverse act, though the outcome is opposite: they take pleasant objects and make them occasions for sadness.[110] Here too the disorder is of the concupiscible appetite. The pleasant things in which they take no pleasure are pleasant things of this sensible world. (Despite Dante's calling these sinners *accidiosi*, they do not commit the theological sin of acedia: that is, a sadness in regard to spiritual goods, goods of the next world, not this.)[111] The sensibly pleasant is the natural object of the concupiscible appetite, and that is where these souls' sin resides.

The wrathful find the unpleasant pleasant; the sullen find the pleasant unpleasant. Both have inverted the normal pattern of concupiscence, and in doing so have invented its most perverse manifestation. For their perversity the sinners of circle five are punished in the lowest location of upper Hell. By comparison, the extension of concupiscence to wealth, the sins of the fourth circle, seems almost natural. And yet, however perverse their choice of object, the appetite actually initiating the action is concupiscence. Joy and sadness are passions of the concupiscible appetite, even when it is joy in painful things, such as anger, and sadness in pleasant things. The sins of the fifth circle in their own way confirm that the common foundation of all of the sins of upper Hell is their origin in the disordered operation of the concupiscible appetite, whether it is operating on its proper objects, or analogically extended objects, or even perversely inverted objects.[112]

(We should say a brief word about the damned in the first circle. These souls, of course, have *committed* no sin. Nonetheless, Dante is explicit that this circle too is connected to the circles of the incontinent. The transition from the first circle to the second, where we first encounter souls condemned for active sin, is easier than the equivalent transition from the second to the third, and in the ease of movement between them an unbroken and untroubled physical connection is implied and in that a firm philosophical connection figuratively expressed. Though the souls of the first circle committed no sin, they suffered from and died in sin, since they lacked baptism [*Inf.* iv, 33–36]. That the souls in Limbo are condemned for their inescapable participation in original sin is the key to their location in the region identified with concupiscence. Original sin is innate to us. It is part of our biological nature, and in that respect directly linked to the concupiscible appetite, which, in its radical form, has also a purely biological origin. Moreover, original sin is transmitted from generation to generation through concupiscence. For both these reasons, we find that in medieval treatises original sin is described as having an essentially concupiscent nature. To Aquinas, original sin, as committed by Adam and Eve, while formally a sin of the will turning away from God, was materially a turning to mutable goods, which he identifies with concupiscence.[113] To Peter Lombard, original sin was both transmitted concupiscently, and was, because of its identification with the *lex membrorum* [or the *lex carnis*], by its nature concupiscent.)[114]

Lower Hell 1: The Region of Irascibility

Every detail of Dante's poetry points to or reinforces the connection between the irascible appetite and the sins of circles six and seven. This is the realm of fire and of heat, with all of their associations with emotions generally, and with anger specifically.[115] From the first sight of the city of Dis, the fires within it are prominent:

> E io: «Maestro, già le sue meschite
> là entro certe nella valle cerno,
> vermiglie come se di foco uscite
> fossero.» Ed ei mi disse: «Il foco etterno
> ch'entro l'affoca le dimostra rosse,
> come tu vedi in questo basso inferno.»
> (*Inf.* viii, 70–75)

The image of irascibility provided by these fires (and other fires in the realm) is immediately taken up by both the belligerent opposition of the city's guardians to the entry of Virgil and Dante, and also by the irascible passions that Virgil must arouse in himself to make good their entry:

> . . . la città dolente,
> u' non potemo intrare omai sanz'ira.
> (*Inf.* ix, 32–33)[116]

The guardians Dante encounters in this realm also reinforce characteristics of irascibility through the images their persons present. We first meet the Erinyes, described as ferocious (*feroci*), and reflecting a particular special quality of the irascible appetite in their very shapes. According to medieval Aristotelians, irascibility participates more extensively in rationality than the concupiscible appetite does.[117] Each of its passions depends in an essential way on some degree of calculation or estimation. Anger arises from the estimation that an injury has occurred; courage or fear, hope or desperation is experienced depending on one's estimation of the possibility or impossibility of achieving an arduous good or avoiding an arduous evil. Nonetheless, irascibility is a sensitive appetite. Its objects are objects of sense, and its operation is accompanied by passion, as was the operation of the more purely biological concupiscible appetite. Insofar as animal figures and descriptions were used in upper Hell as images of the biological underpinnings of the concupiscible appetite, the half-human, half-animal appearance of the Erinyes provides an appropriate image of the partly biological, partly rational character of the irascible appetite. Indeed, throughout this section of Hell the superintendents appear in mixed natures: on the one hand, the Erinyes, Minotaur, and Centaurs, who are associated with violence and with the specific irascible passion, anger;[118] and on the other, Medusa and the other Gorgons whose power of turning people to stone may be Dante's gesture at the paralyzing properties of fear and despair, which are also irascible passions. (Though at the wall of Dis Dante sees fallen angels, who will reappear in the eighth circle as demons, these angels never appear as guardians encountered in the sixth and seventh circles, while the functionaries he does encounter exhibit these mixed forms.)

As Dante comes within sight of the sinners of the first *girone* of the seventh circle, he explicitly articulates the connection between the sins of violence punished there and anger:

> Oh cieca cupidigia e ira folle,
> che sì ci sproni nella vita corta,
> e nell'etterna poi sì mal c'immolle!
> (*Inf.* xii, 49–51)

The connection is continued in the poetic images of their sins that their punishments give us, for the sinners of this circle are, for the most part, punished in fire or heat that reflects the passion and violence of their sins.[119] There is a direct and intuitive appropriateness to the connection of the simply violent (those of the first *girone*) to the irascible passions, especially anger, and the other significant detail of their punishment reinforces the linkage to anger. They are surrounded by boiling blood, which while it may at first remind us of the blood these sinners have shed, would also remind us of a special, technical significance. In medieval physiological explanations of the passions, anger was described as a heating of the blood around the heart: "ira est 'accensio sanguinis circa cor,' "[120] and for these sinners too, then, we see a punishment that continues them in the activity and state that was their sin.

There is every reason to be skeptical that all the murderers, tyrants, and robbers punished in this circle really believed injuries had been done them such that they would have experienced anger. But we should not be misled into taking too narrow an interpretation of the operation of the irascible appetite. It is named for anger, true, but this appetite operates whenever difficult objects are pursued with passion, whether the passion is anger or another of the irascible passions. None of the actions punished in the seventh circle was characterized by the simple pursuit of pleasure that is the essence of the concupiscible appetite. All, whether motivated by anger or some other passion, involve difficulty, even danger. Thus, even without anger specifically, we could still attribute the actions of murderers, tyrants, and robbers to irascibility. What is important in such an attribution, though, and in these sins' appearance here in the seventh circle is that both are clearly intended to distinguish them from similar actions punished in the eighth or ninth. In the lower circles, we have concluded, these actions were pursued without passion; here, we must conclude, that violence is punished which had passion somehow attached to it. Some of the violent of the first *girone* may indeed have believed themselves injured and acted in anger; others may have acted without anger, but all acted under the influence of those irascible passions that are associated with the pursuit of difficult goods.

In the other two *gironi* of this circle too the irascible nature of the sinful actions is stressed either in explicit descriptions of the sin or in the poetic imagery with which it is presented. These later *gironi*, however, display to us examples of transformations of the fundamental operation of the appetite (as also had the later circles of upper Hell), involving either redirecting the normal action of irascibility to an abnormal object (oneself or one's own possessions) or transforming the action of irascibility analogically so that it might be applied to objects toward which simple irascibility could not be directed (blasphemy, sodomy, usury).

Though the suicides and the squanderers *(gli scialacquatori)* are not overtly punished by flame or heat, the poetic imagery of this *girone* continues to stress the passionateness of their actions, and even to reconnect their actions to anger. The agents who torment them repeat the half-human, half-animal motif of the seventh circle, stressing the mixed corporeal and rational nature of the irascible appetite. The suicides are harassed by the Harpies; the squanderers are pursued by dogs ("nere cagne, bramose e correnti / come veltri ch'uscisser di catena";

Inf. xiii, 125–26), whose animal savagery suggests an equally passionate motivation for these sinners' actions. When Virgil breaks off a twig of the tree that imprisons Pier della Vigna, the weirdness of the punishment may obscure a telling characteristic of the state of these damned souls. Pier's voice hisses from the branch like sap bubbling out when a twig is held to a fire:

> Come d'un stizzo verde ch'arso sia
>   dall'un de' capi, che dall'altro geme
>   e cigola per vento che va via,
> sì della scheggia rotta usciva inseme
>   parole e sangue; ond'io lasciai la cima
>   cadere, e stetti come l'uom che teme.
>   (*Inf.* xiii, 40–45)

We see no overt flame in this *girone,* but heat there surely is. Pier's words bubble out with his blood, and we realize that the blood of these souls too is boiling, though the boiling is internal, just as their violence had been directed inward toward themselves.

Indeed, to judge from the conversation Dante has with Pier, the suicides of the seventh circle are not suicides as we today are most likely to interpret them. They are not suicides of desperation; they did not kill themselves because they had given up hope, or simply lost the will to live. Behind their violent ends are motives much more violent than we commonly find, much closer to the anger with which violence is usually directed at others. Pier describes his state of mind in terms that very much recall the normal operation of irascibility:

> L'animo mio, per disdegnoso gusto,
>   credendo col morir fuggir disdegno,
>   ingiusto fece me contra me giusto.
>   (*Inf.* xiii, 70–72)[121]

Pier had encountered envy and anger from his enemies, and responded with two irascible responses: on the one hand, the attempt to flee their actions; on the other, with anger of his own. (*Disdegno* and *sdegno* in the *Commedia* are often, as I believe here, better translated by *anger* than *disdain*. We should recall that Virgil praises Dante as *alma sdegnosa* when he responds to Filippo Argenti with anger [*Inf.* viii, 44].)[122] Pier's action stems from irascibility, even irascibility in its fundamental form insofar as it can also be seen as an attempt to exact a certain revenge (anger's natural goal) on his enemies.[123] What is unnatural in his response, of course, is his choice of object on which to vent his anger (himself, rather than his enemies) and his means of flight (death). But the fundamental irascibility of Pier's suicide can be more pointedly recognized when we remember that the suicides of the seventh circle are not the first we have encountered. Two notable suicides, Cleopatra and Dido, are punished among the lustful (*Inf.* v, 61–63), rather than among those violent to themselves. As is consistently the case in the *Inferno*, any act (here self-murder) may be ambiguous in its origin, and the origin cannot be understood from the physical event of the act in itself. When Dante shows Cleopatra and Dido being punished with the lustful, he is first of all indicating that even within what would have seemed to be a single sin, suicide, distinctions must be drawn as the act takes on a different character depending on the appetite that prompts it. Cleopatra's and Dido's suicides had their source in their concupiscence, and Dante explicitly states with regard to Dido that she committed suicide for love, that is, under the influence of concupiscible passions ("colei [Dido] che s'ancise amorosa"; *Inf.* v, 61). These suicides lack the irascible passion or intent of Pier's.

An equivalent distinction regarding similar actions driven by different appetites should be made between the squanderers punished in the seventh circle and the spendthrifts of circle four. The squanderers are not more violent than the spendthrifts simply because they do a more thorough job of overspending. We have no evidence in the poem that this is so. But excessive spending can be pursued in two quite different spirits. There can be a pleasure in spending, even in overspending, and the spendthrifts presumably pursue this pleasure. Insofar as it is a simple pleasure they seek, their action is essentially concupiscent. The squanderers, on the other hand, from what we know about the one who is named, may not take any pleasure from their actions, but are driven to destroy their fortunes, rather, as if possessed. Benvenuto's description of the life of Jacopo da Santo Andrea (*Inf.* xiii, 119–35) portrays an individual acting as if in some mad fury.

> Once, when he was at his country house, he heard that a certain lord was coming with a great entourage to dine with him. And because he was not provisioned (nor could he be in so brief a period of time) to the degree that would seem fit for his prodigality, without delay he made use of an extraordinary strategem: for he immediately set fire to all the cottages on his estate, all of which were ready enough for burning, since they were

built from straw, reeds, and cane, as the homes of peasants in the terri-
tory of Padua commonly are. Then, going to meet them, he said he had
done this as a celebration of his joy at their coming, and so that he might
honor them most magnificently. In this he was surely more violent and
more foolish than Nero, for Nero had the houses of the city burned, but
Jacopo his own.[124]

According to Benvenuto, Jacopo's act was even closer to madness
than Nero's, and our sense of acting under a form of compulsion—
under some violent passion, that is—is more strongly reinforced. What
is also apparent to us is that Jacopo's act was as much motivated by
hostility toward his visitors as by any desire to use up his own re-
sources. In this regard, the act is one of anger like normal acts of irascibility; all that is different is that Jacopo himself pays the price for it.

The suicides and squanderers display sins of irascibility in which
the appetite operates normally, except for being directed toward oneself as victim, rather than toward one's enemies. The sinners of the
final *girone* of the seventh circle, by contrast, display an irascibility that
is transformed with respect to its objects and operation, in ways similar to the transformations of the concupiscible appetite in the fourth
and fifth circles. While the suicides and squanderers choose unexpected objects for their irascibility, the sinners of the third *girone* of
circle seven choose impossible objects. It is not only unjust to be angry
with God, it is impossible to seek revenge there. The blasphemous display a quite gratuitous and literally aimless irascibility. What they pre-
tend to do, to be revenged on God, is not only arduous, it is futile.
Precisely because of its futility, it is clear that their anger cannot arise
in calculation; it must have its source in passion. Their punishment in
fire provides an image of the passion, and it is revealed as well in their
actions and Virgil's explanation of their actions. Of Capaneus, the only
blasphemer we meet individually, Virgil makes an explicit point not
only that his punishment in heat and flame is an exact replica of his sin
itself, but also that that sin is one of anger.

> . . . nullo martiro, fuor che la tua rabbia,
> sarebbe al tuo furor dolor compito.
> (*Inf.* xiv, 65–66)

That the sodomites and usurers are also punished in fire is Dante's
indication in their case too of an underlying irascibility in their actions.
Sodomites are not punished for the wrong choice of sexual partners.

That aspect of their sin turns out to be relatively insignificant, as we discover in the *Purgatorio*, where the sin is dealt with no differently (neither in terms of correction nor gravity) from heterosexual lust. The location of the sodomites here in the seventh circle suggests that it is not the sexual dimension of the sin that is being punished. Rather, since the sodomites' choice of sexual partners is, from the standpoint of the conventional understanding of the operation of concupiscence, unnatural, and since to act against nature is by definition arduous, the sodomites' pursuit of sexual pleasure, therefore, cannot fit the pattern of simple lust. Simple concupiscence would not pursue so difficult an object. To do so demanded the perseverance and energy that are characteristic of the irascible appetite, and it is for the disordered operation of that appetite that the sodomites are distinguished from the lustful in the *Inferno* and punished more severely.

All of the sins in circle seven that we have considered so far are clearly passionate, as would be appropriate to the operation of the irascible appetite. But where is the passion in the last of the sins of circle seven, usury? Aquinas defines usury as a sin of injustice, which is much as we would normally expect, insofar as it reflects what we would consider its deliberate nature. But were that the definition Dante had accepted, within the structure of the *Inferno* usurers ought to have been punished in the eighth circle.[125] That Dante located the usurers exactly at the outer edge of the violent, and even somewhat separated from their nearest neighbors, the sodomites, probably signals his awareness that the sin might be considered as calculated in the way the injustices of circles eight and nine are. The usurers are placed right on the border, as it were, with the fraudulent, that is, with those who are dispassionately sinful for profit. But while we might think usury a calculated act, Dante continues the consistently passionate imagery of the rest of the seventh circle, even for the ususers, who are punished by flakes of flaming snow (*Inf.* xvii, 46–54). To the end, Dante also stresses the animalistic nature of these figures (*Inf.* xvii, 49–51 and 74–75), and such references serve to reinforce the notion that these actions are not merely calculated. As with the sodomites, the explanation probably lies with the perversity of the action of usury. To invent and pursue a means of business so contrary to the natural sources of wealth demands a strange kind of nerve and perseverance, and these are traits of irascibility. Since its only end is wealth, however, it is in the closest position to the sins of gain. (And, if the use of animal imagery links these sinners back to the sensitive appetites, their anger at being found in this position—not shame at having committed their sins, but shame at having been discovered [*Inf.* xvii, 66–67]—is a trait they share with the fraudulent.) As was characteristic also of upper Hell, the sins dependent on transformed versions of the appetites, being farthest from the natural operation of the appetite, are located in the lowest circles of the region.

In order more easily to confirm the underlying dependence on the irascible appetite of the sins of the middle region of Hell, we have first dealt with the violent of circle seven, where the appearance of irascible passions—overtly in the actions of the souls or embodied in the imagery with which they are treated—makes the origin of their sins manifest. But the realm of the irascible also unequivocally includes the sixth circle of Hell, the circle of the heretics, since it too is found within the city of Dis, and since from it Virgil and Dante are able to descend to the seventh circle without encountering any geographical or geological separation, or any impediment that necessitates an alternate means of transportation. Such physical contiguity between two circles has been the poetic means of declaring that the sins of the two circles share a common nature, and so it is here too. Moreover, this first poetic indication is supported by another, perhaps even more compelling: the sins of circles six and seven share fire as the means of their torment, and insofar as punishments provide images of their sins, the common form of punishment in these circles must reflect their sins' common passionate nature.

The location and poetic treatment of the heretics lead us to Dante's wholly idiosyncratic definition of this sin as a disordered operation of the irascible appetite. But we should also take note that other structural and narrative details show Dante's systematic exclusion of more conventional definitions of the nature of heresy. We should note, first of all, the error of those far too numerous commentators who have flatly stated that heresy is the one purely Christian sin in Hell.[126] Readers who take this view sometimes use it to explain Virgil's silence with regard to heresy in his description of the structure of Hell, seeing the silence as the prudent reticence of a pagan unwilling to expound on matters of which he cannot have knowledge. But heresy is manifestly *not* a purely Christian sin, if Virgil is correct in saying that the tombs of the sixth circle contain "li eresïarche / co' lor seguaci, d'ogni setta" (*Inf.* ix, 127–28). For the first identified tomb Virgil and Dante encounter—

indeed, a whole section of the cemetery—contains "con Epicuro tutt'i suoi seguaci" (*Inf.* x, 14).[127] In most circles of Hell, Dante encounters or describes at least one pagan and one Christian sinner, and the practice is followed here too. Epicurus is the example from the ancient world (represented, it is true, by two contemporary followers, but that cannot be avoided, given that the heresiarchs are forced farther and farther below ground by their followers); Pope Anastasius II is the representative of the Christian world (*Inf.* xi, 8–9).

But there is an even more significant reason that Dante had no need to consider heresy a wholly Christian sin: although the most common way to define heresy was as a sin of wrong belief,[128] for Dante doctrinal error has nothing to do with the sin. The presence of Saladin, Averroës, and Avicenna in the first circle of Hell proves this to us, for Limbo is not the circle of the "virtuous pagans," as it is sometimes described; it is the circle of the unbaptized who have committed *no* sin. Though from a doctrinal point of view the three great Muslims whom Dante places there surely had wrong beliefs, their location in that circle demonstrates his conviction that they had committed no positive sin.[129] Indeed, Dante's treatment of what we commonly think of as heresy demonstrates his concern to distinguish different aspects of what most would consider a single act. Dante treats activities associated with heresy twice in the *Inferno.* On the one hand, Dante deals with the heretics named as such who are exhibited here in circle six; on the other, he deals separately with the schismatics in the eighth circle, among whom we find the founders of Islam, Mohammed and Ali. But as the presence of Saladin, Averroës, and Avicenna in circle one shows us that one can hold Muslim beliefs without committing sin, so we must conclude that Mohammed and Ali are not punished in the eighth circle for their beliefs, but for having pursued sectarianism to the extent of destroying the community of believers. They are punished among the "seminator di scandalo e di scisma" (*Inf.* xxviii, 35), sinners against charity, according to Aquinas, not against faith.[130] It was not their heterodox doctrine, but their divisive action that condemned them.

Mere intellectual error is no sin to Dante. Sin is an action of a certain sort, though in recognizing this we should also be careful to note that it is not only the leaders of sects who act. So do followers. When Dante distinguishes between schismatism and heresy, it is not as though he were drawing a distinction between founding a sect and following one, such that establishing a sect would condemn one as a schismatic, while simply believing its doctrines one might escape condemnation or receive only that for heresy.[131] Among the heretics of circle six are both the founders of sects and their followers. Thus, for the sin Dante specifically identifies as heresy, there is something sinful even in the simple belief in its doctrines. And if we examine the doctrines of those Dante names as heretics, we discover simultaneously first, that of all of the heresies that might have been included in the *Inferno,* Dante makes an extraordinarily narrow selection, choosing to mention only two, Epicureanism and Photinism; and second, that these two heresies possess a significant doctrinal kinship. It is striking that in his treatment of heresy Dante omits Islam, never mentions any of the early Christian heresies (besides Photinism), nor does he mention any of the significant contemporary heretical movements, such as Catharism.[132] Conversely, the two Dante does choose to mention are scarcely the most natural choices for representatives of heresy as it would most commonly be understood. Though Florentines were accused of Epicureanism, it was not conventionally dealt with in theology as a Christian heresy. It does not appear, for example, in Augustine's treatise on heresy, nor in Thomas's refutation of heretical doctrines in the *Summa Contra Gentiles.*[133] Photinism, for its part, is so obscure a heresy as to be easily confused, by both medieval and modern commentators, with several other sects similar to it in certain respects. Photinus, like Arius, was a monophysite, but had it been monophysism generically that Dante intended to condemn, he would surely have chosen the figure of Arius for the second tomb.[134] When we inquire why, of all heresies, Dante chose these two, we discover they share an important common doctrine.

What is presumably the relevant characteristic of Epicureanism is given to us explicitly by Virgil:

> Suo cimitero da questa parte hanno
> con Epicuro tutt'i suoi seguaci,
> che l'anima col corpo morta fanno.
> (*Inf.* x, 13–15)

The Epicureans are punished in graves for believing that the soul was mortal and had no life beyond the grave. Photinism, with which Pope Anastasius II is identified, albeit mistakenly,[135] though a Christian heresy, held to beliefs that led to conclusions about the future life of the soul which were effectively equivalent to the Epicurean. According to Aquinas, the Photinans, like the Arians, believed that Christ was not God but merely a creature. If anything, the Photinans were even more extreme in this belief than the Arians.

> Others, indeed, who are heretics, relate this generation [of the Son receiving the divine nature from the Father] to an extraneous nature: Photinus and Sabellius to human nature; Arius, not to human nature, but to a certain created nature higher in dignity than that of other creatures. . . . Sabellius, however, differs from Photinus in that Sabellius confesses that Christ truly is God, an eternal equal to the Father, but Photinus does not, nor does Arius. But Photinus holds that he is pure man; Arius that he is as it were a mixture, from a sort of most excellent creature both human and divine. (*SCG*, iv, 7)[136]

Photinans, therefore, more so even than Arians and Sabellians, made a complete denial of the divinity of Christ's nature, and it is for taking this extreme position, presumably, that Dante chose Anastasius to represent heresy rather than the otherwise better-known Arius (of whom after all, with Sabellius, he was aware: see *Par.* xiii, 127). From an orthodox point of view, the consequences of a belief such as Photinus' are very similar to the consequences of believing that the soul is mortal. For Augustine, belief that Christ's incarnation was the incarnation of God is the only basis for the conviction that Christ's sacrifice is sufficient to cancel the debt of original sin:

> For what was so necessary for raising our hopes, and for liberating our mortal minds—dejected by the condition of their very mortality—from despairing of immortality, but to demonstrate to us how much God valued us, how much He loved us? And of this thing, what indeed could be clearer or more shining than this so great proof: that the Son of God, unchangeably good, in himself remaining what he was, and from us and for us taking on what he was not . . . should bear our evils. (*de Trin.*, xiii, 10 [13])

With the necessity for a divine sacrifice commensurate to the magnitude of original sin, Dante explicitly agreed, though casting it as a matter of justice. Given the nature of original sin, only God was capable of the gesture that would cancel it.

> Non potea l'uomo ne' termini suoi
>   mai sodisfar, per non potere ir giuso
>   con umiltate obediendo poi,
> quanto disobediendo intese ir suso;
>   e questa è la cagion per che l'uom fue
>   da poter sodisfar per sè dischiuso.

> Dunque a Dio convenìa con le vie sue
> riparar l'omo a sua intera vita,
> dico con l'una, o ver con amendue....
> ....
> chè più largo fu Dio a dar sè stesso
> per far l'uom sufficiente a rilevarsi,
> che s'elli avesse sol da sè dimesso;
> e tutti li altri modi erano scarsi
> alla giustizia, se 'l Figliuol di Dio
> non fosse umilïato ad incarnarsi.
> (*Par.* vii, 97–105; 115–20)[137]

The Photinans, by denying Christ's divinity, deny the possibility of canceling the debt, and thus, for them, just as for the Epicureans, though for a different reason, the possibility of salvation disappears. This is most obviously so for the Epicureans, of course, since if the soul is mortal there can be no eternal life.[138] But while Photinans may believe the soul itself is immortal, that turns out to be of no use in human salvation, since they deny the only foundation of redemption for this soul. Thus, the two (and only two) heresies that Dante identifies in the sixth circle share a very similar content: that human beings are incapable of an eternal life,[139] a doctrinal content, moreover, that distinguishes them from all other heresies that we might have expected to find represented in this circle. Neither Islam nor any contemporary Christian heresy so emphatically denied the possibility of salvation.

It is by that content, and that content only, that Dante identifies heresy. Other erroneous beliefs can become sinful if they lead to schism but are not sinful in themselves. But this belief in itself is sinful, for Dante, and had been so even for Epicurus' pagan followers. The particular theological error of the belief then accounts for the most notable of the poetic details regarding its punishment. The heretics, whether Epicureans or Photinans, are punished in tombs, for all essentially believed in the death of the soul, or believed in doctrines that were its equivalent in denying the possibility of redemption after death. But it is the other of the poetic details of their punishment—that the tombs are fiery tombs—that directs us to the explanation of why this belief is a sin, and why it is punished where it is.

The fire of the tombs is something the punishment of heresy has in common with the punishment of the violent of the seventh circle, and in both cases it is a figurative indication of passion in the origin of the sin.[140] Passion there must be, indeed, for according to Dante the specific content of heretical belief could never be the conclusion of an intellect functioning normally, since this particular belief was, to him, of all beliefs the most unreasonable. In the *Convivio* he calls a belief in the soul's mortality the stupidest of all bestiality, "intra tutte le bestialitadi quella è stoltissima," because, as he goes on to say, all sources, even most pagan philosophical sources, agree that the soul is immortal:

> Since, if we turn to any writings whatever, whether of the philosophers or of other wise men, all agree in this: that there is in us an immortal part. (*Conv.*, ii, viii, 8)

With such virtually unanimous testimony to the soul's immortality, only an intellect overcome by passion could be persuaded to the opposite opinion. But which passion? For Dante, the passion that is the source of the belief of both the Epicureans and the Photinans, and that is therefore the source of their sin, is despair.[141] Despair is one of the five passions associated with the irascible appetite. It is the passion experienced in the face of a desired good that one judges too difficult ever to accomplish, and which one therefore gives up any hope of possessing. In the face of unanimous philosophical agreement that the soul is immortal, and in the face of the inherent desirability of believing that one will have a life after the body's death, how could one become an Epicurean? In the face of the New Testament, how could one become a Photinan? Only by the conviction, Dante insists, that however desirable a future life would be, it is impossible to achieve. Convinced that such a good was too difficult to possess, those whom Dante calls heretics despaired, and retreated to philosophical sects that provided justifications for their conviction of the impossibility of salvation.

The origin of the sin of heresy as Dante understands it, then, is in the disordered operation of the irascible appetite. Irascibility is named for anger but is the source of other passions too, and it is allowing one of those passions, despair, to overcome reason that leads to heresy. Like the sins of violence, heresy too is more closely tied to the intellect than the sins of concupiscence were, for it depends on a judgment (though mistaken) that the arduous good sought, eternal life, cannot be possessed. Its origin in irascibility explains its connections to the seventh circle, and the common use of fire in its punishment, to stand as the symbol of irascibility.

When Virgil explains to Dante the organization of Hell in canto xi, they had come to a stop at the brink of circle seven, having already traversed the circle of the heretics. As Virgil begins his explanation, their backs are to the sixth circle; the *tre cerchietti* below them comprise only circles seven, eight, and nine. It is those circles that Virgil characterizes as punishing sins of *malizia*. Both the direction in which the two travelers are looking and Virgil's silence indicate that heresy is not to be included among the malicious sins. Had Dante meant us to understand that heresy should be included among the sins of malice, nothing would have been easier, or more natural, than to have had the two travelers stop immediately after their entry into the city of Dis for the explanation of the structure of Hell. Having them traverse the sixth circle before beginning the explanation is a way of dramatically excluding the circle of the heretics from the category of sins that have injury as their end.

At the same time, however, circle six is emphatically within the city of Dis (and thus just as emphatically separated from the sins of concupiscence in upper Hell) and physically connected to circle seven. Circles six and seven share contiguous space, and common images in their punishments, as we have mentioned, and are also physically separated from circles eight and nine. Thus the two categories of sin of these circles are clearly distinguished as a single genus of sin, different from both those above and those below them. It is this category of sin that Dante attributes to the action of the irascible appetite, symbolized by their common punishment in fire which reflects the emotional and spirited nature of that irascible appetite.[142]

The two souls in the sixth circle with whom Dante converses also exemplify their irascible passion as surely as Capaneus' anger embodied his. If despair was the source of their heretical belief, it is also a consequence of such belief. But how people act in the grip of despair is diverse. For some, it leads to paralysis, as Aquinas describes the consequences of Photinism insofar as it denied the possibility of redemption:

> To some, it might seem that man could never attain to this state—that is, that the human intellect be immediately united to the divine essence, as an intellect to its intelligible—because of the immeasurable distance between the two natures. And in this way a man might lose his ardor for searching for beatitude, held back by this very desperation. (*SCG*, iv, 54)[143]

In others it leads to a kind of desperate heroism. Augustine points out that those who have fortitude and a desire for some kind of happy life, but having given up hope of the truly happy life of blessedness, pursue the best life they can, searching for whatever lesser image of immortality they can find:

> So then, he [who has given up any hope of immortality] will do what he can, since he cannot do what he would. This is the whole of the blessedness of these proud mortals—should we laugh at it? or, rather, pity it?—who glory that they live as they will, because willingly they patiently bear what they do not will to happen to them. (*de Trin.*, xiii, 7 [10])[144]

Such a person, Augustine says, "is not truly blessed, but is bravely miserable" (*de Trin.*, xiii, 7 [10]). These people, having renounced a second life, are active in this life, making of it what they can. In Dante's encounter with Farinata and Cavalcante we are given examples of both the sorts of behavior that follow from these beliefs. The nobility of a figure like Farinata has this source, but as heroic as his actions in this life appear, they are based on a sort of desperation, since the actor believes that this is all of immortality he can have. This desperation is at the heart of Benvenuto's description of Farinata:

> He was a follower of Epicurus, and did not believe there was any other world but this one. For which reason, he made the effort to excel in every way in this short life, since he did not hope for a better one.[145]

Farinata's heroism endures as a brave factionalism in the face of an enemy visitor; Cavalcante's more passive despair reappears in his dejected silence when he misunderstands Dante's remark about his son. Cavalcante's response (*Inf.* x, 67–69) shows his reason still overcome by his despair. Were Guido dead and damned, Cavalcante would already know it, for the damned know the fates of those associated with them. That he does not know Guido's fate can only mean, if reasoned through, that Guido is either still alive, or is indeed dead but in, or on his way to, Heaven. But Cavalcante does not stop to reason, nor did he apparently, while alive, and his inability to control his despair is what has led him to this circle.[146] Few figures seem less akin than these two, yet Dante's ostentatiously tangled narrative—Cavalcante dramatically interrupting Dante's discussion with Farinata, which resumes after the equally dramatic exit made by Cavalcante—itself represents the way in which the destiny of these unlike characters is knit together by the sin that is all that is left to them in Hell. These two pursued other, mundane forms of immortality during their lives: politics and family for Farinata, family for Cavalcante. But these substitutes turn out to be no more durable or immortal than their corporeal lives had been. Dante can destroy Farinata's hopes in the immortality of his civic feats and reduce him first to anger and then to sullenness by informing him of his family's defeat; he will destroy Cavalcante's hope and pride in his family and plunge him into despair by an inadvertent remark.

One final point. With Christ's descent into Hell, circles six and seven became even more closely connected than they had been before. That there had always been some physical connection is proved by Virgil's earlier voyage past this point and his action now on this journey with Dante. As he approaches the edge of this circle Virgil does not look for any alternate means of transport to the seventh. That nonaction indicates that on his earlier voyage he had passed this point also on foot, as it were. Now, Virgil comments with surprise when he sees the fallen rock down which he and Dante will clamber to the seventh circle. It had not been there at the time of his first voyage through Hell; and he deduces that the rock slide occurred at the moment Christ descended to Hell (*Inf.* xii, 31–45). At that moment, that is to say, heresy and violence became even more directly connected than they had already been through sharing a common appetite. In this poetic detail Dante links his idiosyncratic conception of heresy to one aspect of more conventional definitions of the sin. Heresy is sometimes defined as wrong belief *pertinaciously* or obstinately adhered to.[147] The persistence in the belief, in the face of the truth, is for most sources a critical component of the sin. That pertinacity, of course, has much in common with violence generally, or with the resistance to perceived evils that is the underlying purpose of the irascible appetite, and is most clearly manifest in anger. Until the descent of Christ to Hell and the Resurrection, which, as Augustine said, "persuaded [people] of what appeared incredible,"[148] adherence to a belief that destroyed hope of salvation could be a sin, inasmuch as it was a disordered operation of an appetite, but could not be described as "pertinacious," because irrefutable evidence of error would be lacking. After the Resurrection, the evidence is there, and any further persistence in such error could fairly be described as pertinacity, and thereby as a form of violence.

Lower Hell 2: The Region of the Will

Dante and Virgil are unable to progress from circle seven to eight by their own powers, and in that obstacle Dante *poeta* indicates a major distinction between sins of circles six and seven (irascible sins) and those of eight and, eventually, nine. Their passage from circle seven to circle eight is accomplished by the monster, Geryon, with the face of a human and the body of a dragon. We should *not* see Geryon as another example of the half-human, half-animal functionaries who were figures of the partly passionate nature of the irascible sins. Geryon is a figure of fraud: he is no mixture of human and animal, but wholly serpent, though with a deceptive human appearance—but not nature. Geryon's body is most likely an image of Satan in the guise of the serpent, the first purveyor of fraud among humans. For in this realm too the functionaries provide images of the sins they superintend.

The superintendents of the eighth circle (where they appear) are demons who were once angels, and their angelic natures, though corrupted, are especially appropriate for indicating the underlying nature of the sins of this circle. In earlier circles, creatures of an animal or mixed nature provided figures for sins that took their origin in appetites we share with animals, or, in the case of irascible sins, that stand midway between the animal and human. But angels are wholly intellectual or spiritual creatures—that is, they are without body. They therefore have no sensitive appetites and thus nothing of the animal about them. Their only appetite, and the source of their movement, is the will.[149] This is also to say, of course, that the only origin of the fallen angels' sin is the will, and that is the explanation of their special appropriateness to sins of this circle, and also the explanation of Dante's restricting his usage of the demons only to this circle. Other accounts of Hell, literary and artistic, represent demons throughout the whole of Hell, but Dante does not, and his restraint is the result of the consistency of his using all poetic details in the *Inferno* to reflect the natures of the sins of their locations. Animal figures would be inappropriate to this circle, as indeed the demons would have been inappropriate figures in earlier circles. The angels, having only a will, act without passion, which is what makes them inappropriate figures for the passionate sins of the two sensitive appetites. But this same property makes them altogether appropriate figures for the circles of fraud, precisely because Dante saw fraudulent sins as also essentially sins of the will.[150]

The sins of circles eight and nine are those sins of malice that are properly identified with injustice in a strict sense, on the basis of injustice's medieval definition as the vice of the intellectual appetite, the will. For Aquinas, frauds were precisely acts of deliberate injustice, and acts solely of the will, and he is explicit that such acts have covetousness only (in the general sense of "gain," rather than the appetitive sense of the fourth circle) as their object. For this reason, they do not arise in the passions of the two sensitive appetites.

> On account of the vehemence of pleasure and concupiscence, lust suppresses the reason totally, so that it cannot proceed into act. In the aforesaid vices [craftiness, guile, and fraud], however, there is a certain use of the reason, though you may say an inordinate one. For this reason, the aforesaid vices do not arise directly from lust. (*ST*, 2a2æ 55, 8, ad 1)

> Anger has a sudden movement, whence it acts precipitously and without counsel (which the aforesaid vices do use, though inordinately). When some men use ambushes in the killing of others this does not proceed from anger, but, rather, from hatred. (*ST*, 2a2æ 55, 8, ad 3)

> Therefore, the aforesaid vices [i.e., craftiness, guile, fraud] arise most of all from covetousness.[151] (*ST*, 2a2æ 55, 8)

But if frauds are perpetrated without either concupiscible or irascible passions, it is clear from Aquinas' need to draw these distinctions that many actions that appear similar to them could be pursued for other, more passionate motives. The narrative and structure of the *Inferno* incorporate Dante's awareness of this distinction, for we see that the circles of fraud (especially circle eight) are the location of several instances of "doubled" sins: that is, of sins that appear to be punished more than once in Hell—once here in the circles of fraud, once in some higher circle. On such occasions we see Dante taking what would conventionally be thought of as a single sinful act, and distinguishing what he believed were sins different in nature though sharing the same appearance. The reappearance, as it were, of an earlier sin in circles eight or nine is Dante's narrative exhortation to us to take note of his distinguishing a purely calculated action from the earlier passionate one.

Panderers and seducers, for example, deal in lust but do not themselves act out of lust. They act for money or advancement, and have their place far distant from the lustful. They act for the gain they calculate will accrue from the sin, and this pursuit of gain is an act of the will, not of the concupiscible appetite. Thieves too are distant from the rapacious of circle seven, schismatics from the heretical of circle six. The deliberate nature of fraudulent sins makes them morally worse, for they lack the passionate impulse that both mitigated the culpability of sensitive sins, and also invested those sins with a certain honesty or authenticity. To take an action that might be pursued spontaneously from passion and instead to pursue it calculatedly and dispassionately is to make a grotesque parody of the original action. And as a part of Dante's adaptation of his punishments to furnish images of their sins, some of the punishments of the fraudulent construct their image of the fraudulence of the sin by being structured as parodies of the punishments for the passionate sins with which they could be confused. The panderers and seducers, for example, wheel by each other in self-propelled mimicry of the gale that drives the lustful (*Inf.* xviii, 25–33).[152] The *bufera* of circle two was an external force to the lustful, providing a figure of a force outside reason that overcomes the reason. But to walk in circles under one's own power, as the panderers and seducers do, indicates the intimacy of the motive that the will furnishes. These sinners cannot say they were driven by something outside their control. The will's desires are reasoned and deliberate. Likewise, the thieves of the eighth circle melt into one another like wax, and are concealed in smoke during the transformation, but without the fire of the seventh circle where the rapacious are punished (*Inf.* xxv, 46–138). This is flame without heat, an image of transmutation, as they make theirs what belonged to others, not an image of passion.[153] The schismatics are not punished together with the rest of their communities of co-believers as were the heretics in the sixth circle; rather, the schismatics find themselves split apart even from themselves (*Inf.* xxviii, 30–36).

If one set of parodic similarities in punishments compels us to distinguish sins of earlier circles from their fraudulent counterparts, other parodies suggest similarities we might otherwise overlook between sins propelled by the will and those impelled by passion. Actions of quite different natures result when the actions spring from different motive appetites. The flatterers, covered in excrement, seem to have serviced a more depraved yearning than did the gluttons, covered in mud. The simoniacs, stuffed into baptismal fonts rather than tombs, and played over by a flame without heat, remind us that their action is as damaging as that of the heretics, but without the mitigating quality of sincere belief that the heat of the heretics figured. The barrators, in a canal of pitch rather than a river of blood, remind us that the sale of justice is injury without violence: just as destructive of society, but for murkier, less passionate motives, and therefore more sordid. And Ulysses, speaking out of a flame that does not burn him, reminds us that the power of his fraudulent, coolly calculated eloquence made others burn to accomplish difficult things—true irascibility—while he remained unmoved by those passions.[154]

All of the sins of circle eight, as sins of the will, were passionless in their origin. We see displays of emotions in this circle, but they are emotions experienced after the fact, not in the commission of the sin. If the tears of the sorcerers fall on their buttocks, it is in part because they are weeping too late.[155] Vanni Fucci was not angry in the commission of his theft, but experiences anger at Dante's discovery of him in Hell—the anger, or frustration, of the fraud found out.[156] We can discover the passions of concupiscence and irascibility in the eighth circle, but they too are parodic—they were not the origins of the sin, they are the responses to the sins' punishments.[157] And if much of the parody of the circles of the fraudulent involves emotions that are not real, fire that does not burn, then the perfection of the adaptation of punishment to sin is also the most perfect parody of the appetitive impulse.

The worst of the sins of the will are the frauds against family, country, guest, and lord of the ninth circle. These are not simple injustices, they are sins against that charity that demands love of neighbor. Those who can feel so little charity, so little love as to commit the compounded frauds of these betrayals exhibit an appetite so devoid of love as to be perversely moved without any passion, any semblance of the normal desire that accompanies action.[158] The horror of such utterly dispassionate sins calls forth from Dante his most horrific image of punishment and, thereby, sin: a frozen lake, which not only represents the coldness of their actions, unmoved by passion, but also displays the fundamental consequences of sins of this sort, an increasing incapacity for any kind of movement or action. Movement depends on appetite, and appetite must exhibit love in some form. But these worst of sinners have reduced all their action to a single appetite, and to that in its most extreme, and therefore its most limited, form. As they strip themselves of love, they lose the capacity even for appetition and movement, those punished in each later section of this circle becoming further encased in ice, and less and less capable of motion or expression. In the end they are represented not only as cold but as frozen. Having chosen to be unmoved by love, they now remain literally fixed in that choice. Unmoved by the warmth of love in life, they are now punished by perfect immobility.

The Poetic Value of Dante's Innovations

The organization of Hell that we have been considering—a division of the geography of Hell into three regions, corresponding to three classes of sin according to the three appetites that constitute the source of every human action—is Dante's response to a specific set of poetic and theological needs: that the principle of organization order sins according to their seriousness, that it be able to take account of individual sinful actions as well as habitual states, and that it be one knowable even by pagans, so that there can be one single rule of justice for Christians and non-Christians alike. We need scarcely add that the organization should be as poetically lucid as possible. Dante's solution, we noted, was not orthodoxly Aristotelian or Thomistic. We could multiply examples of Dante's divergence from Aristotle and Aquinas, but that would not be the point. It is likely, rather, that Dante believed himself working in the spirit of Aristotle and Aquinas, and indeed, the way in which he diverges from them exhibits a characteristically medieval respect for their authority.

In Aquinas' and in most other medieval discussions of sin, the nature of a given sin and its seriousness are determined by the object of the sin, for the object is first in intention in the mind, and therefore constitutes the formal and final causes of action.[159] It is this principle that Dante rejects, and replaces with one of his own—or, rather, does not reject outright, but reinterprets to his needs, making use of the same authorities to justify his reinterpretation. Aquinas had stated that "movement takes its species from the term *whereto* and not from the term *wherefrom*" (*ST,* 2a2æ 118, 7, ad 2), that is, from the object, which is the end of the action, rather than from the appetite, which is its origin. Dante's innovation is to collapse the distinction, making the appetite "wherefrom" the principal determinant of the object "whereto." He does so starting from the reflection that it is appropriate to say that an object receives its character as an object not from itself, necessarily, but from the appetite that pursues it as an object. What Dante recognized was the natural malleability of the appetites as initiators of action. There are, indeed, objects that are natural objects for individual appetites, but appetites and their associated passions have the plasticity to attach themselves to and pursue other objects and actions than the simply natural. In doing so, they alter the character of these new objects, transforming them from whatever they were before into objects of the appetite pursuing them.

For Aquinas the appetite is only the subject of the sin, not its object; its efficient cause, not its formal cause.

> The subject of a sin is principally that part of the soul to which the moving cause of the sin primarily pertains. So that, if the cause moving someone to sin is that sensual pleasure which pertains to the concupiscible power as its proper object, it follows that the concupiscible power is the proper subject of the sin. (*ST,* 1a2æ 83, 2)

For Dante, there were two substantial benefits to using the efficient cause to distinguish sins from one another. First, using the efficient cause was the most direct way of reducing the ambiguity that can result wherever the same physical object can be pursued for two quite distinct motives. Throughout Aristotelian discussions of moral action, this ambiguity is explored. (Aristotle's own double treatment, in the *Ethics,* of the same actions as sometimes instances of injustice and sometimes of other vices is an example of this.) In Dante, these ambiguities are resolved by referring consideration of any object to the appetite that pursues it and thereby gives it its univocal character. That is, any object pursued as an object of concupiscence (i.e., as a simply desirable good) can be properly recognized as a concupiscible object whatever its original nature might have been. We have seen the operation of this principle in the pursuit of abstract goods as if naturally concupiscible in the fourth circle and in the transformation of naturally irascible objects into concupiscible objects on the part of the wrathful in the fifth circle.

The second benefit that accrued to Dante in using the appetites to distinguish sins is that the human appetites embody in themselves a natural order of eminence, and therefore generate a natural order for the gravity of sins. Dante's order of sin may not correspond to common notions of the seriousness of sins, nor even to the orders that appear in Aristotle, Aquinas, or other medieval theologians. It corresponds, rather, to the state of the individual committing the sin. That theft—or flattery!—should be considered a worse sin than murder can only be justified by a judgment regarding the state of the agent, not the nature of the effect on the victim, which is the object intended. That some suicides, such as Dido and Cleopatra, are punished in ways different from others demands a distinction not of the object as physical act (which is identical), but of the intention itself. In Dante's system, sins are grouped together when they share a common appetite, and the three great regions are ordered overall by the greater seriousness—

which here means the greater humanity—of the appetite.[160] Within each of the regions, the ordering of sins as increasingly blameworthy corresponds to increasingly depraved uses of the human faculty represented by the appetite. Thus, within each region we see sins ordered from simpler and more natural operations of the appetite to more perverse and unnatural operations. In upper Hell we move from the best operation of unregenerated human nature (that is to say, human virtue, in the first circle) through the natural concupiscible passions (lust, gluttony), to abstract concupiscible passions (concerning money), to the perversion of transforming irascible objects into concupiscible objects. In the second region we move from the natural operation of unregenerate irascibility (despair at the possibility of happiness based only on human ability), to natural operations of irascibility, to increasingly unnatural forms of violence.[161] In the region of the sins of the will, the order of sins moves from merely fictitious frauds, to frauds that require actual fabrication, to frauds that deny the fundamental— and natural—bonds of human association and love, and that are, therefore, the most unnatural of all uses of the will or of any appetite.

Because this order follows the *natural* order of the appetites, it requires no knowledge of revealed truth to be understood. Anyone who understands the nature of the human soul, in Dante's interpretation, simultaneously understands the nature of sin, and also the order of the seriousness of sins. Justice was the motive for creating Hell (*Inf.* iii, 4), and justice requires that the reasons for being sent to Hell have been known to sinners long before they ever get there, and long before these truths would be revealed in the New Testament. The psychological structure we see providing the structure of the *Inferno* demonstrates how justice is served. And it also provides a critical link to the structures and meanings of the remainder of the *Commedia*.

The appetitive powers through which sins are articulated in the *Inferno* are powers that are the sources of every action, not only of sin.[162] Rectified, these same powers could also be the sources of beatitude. The powers that, through disorder, eventuate in sin are the powers that we find under correction in Purgatory. Once purified and transformed, they will be discovered to be the powers that operate to our beatitude in Heaven. The powers that we first encounter in the organization of Hell provide a framework also for our understanding of the other two realms of the next world. That this is so, and why it is so, are the subjects of the remainder of this inquiry.

2

Purgatorio

Purgatory is different from either Hell or Heaven by being a place of change. No soul in Hell will ever change in any substantial way. The actions that have condemned the damned to Hell have already reached their completion, indeed their perfection, though it is a perfection in evil. In the same way, the souls in Heaven have accomplished the perfection of their natures, and those natures will remain fixed forever. At the Last Judgment, these souls will participate in two final events: the blessed will be reunited to their perfected bodies; the damned will find the punishments they suffer made more perfect. In neither case will these events alter the nature of the souls to whom they occur; rather, these events are themselves the final perfecting complement to natures that have already reached their final states. The blessed in Heaven have the opportunity to enact their perfected natures for eternity. For the damned, their most perfect punishment is the eternal re-enactment of the sins they have committed. Hell, as we would poetically expect, parodies Heaven's eternal perfection in the endless iteration of the same evil action.

But Purgatory is different. The souls in Purgatory will alter their characters in the most significant way in the course of their purgation; that is the purpose of their being there. Purgatory is not merely a place in which, incarcerated for a certain time, souls repay a debt of justice for evil actions they have performed. Such, indeed, was Aquinas' position.[1] But for Dante, there is positive work to be done. The diseased souls of the sinful but redeemed must be made healthy; they must be released from sin, not by pardon, merely, but by therapy. What is ugly must be made beautiful. Purgatory, therefore, has a double aspect: one facing our world, one facing Heaven.

Our discussion must reflect the double nature of this realm and of the matching doctrines Dante proposes about it. There is change from one state to another, but from what? to what? and in what? What is there in the soul that can be changed by the corrections we examine in Purgatory? And what is the final state to which the souls must be transformed? In the first part of this chapter we will consider Purgatory in its aspect that still reflects our life in this world: What about the human soul undergoes correction? In the second part we will consider Purgatory in the aspect that faces toward Heaven: For what purposes are these corrections intended? And what new light does our answer to that question throw on the corrections themselves? Indeed, I think we should be conscious from the outset that when we redirect our attention to the final purpose of the purgatorial corrections, all of our initial conclusions made in the first part of the chapter will themselves have to undergo a kind of transformation. We will not abandon them; but we will discover that all along they too have had a double significance embodied in them, one worldly, one celestial. The narrative structure and the psychological effects of the *Commedia* are designed to exploit this moment of reversal to encourage us to pursue the surprising doctrinal principle on which they are based.

PART I
PURGATORY IN THE LIGHT OF SIN

The Apparently Defective Symmetry of Hell and Purgatory

The difficulties we experience in understanding the structure of Purgatory are oddly similar to the problems we encountered with respect to the organization of Hell. For this realm too there is no lack of explicit statement by Dante (through Virgil) about its organization. What is problematic is that the explanation, as was the case in the *Inferno,* seems to provide less illumination than it promises or owes. In canto xvii of the *Purgatorio,* Virgil explains to Dante that the seven *gironi* through which they are to travel in Purgatory can be grouped according to the nature of the love that was manifested in the actions of the sinners undergoing purgation in each. Three *gironi* are assigned to those who loved the wrong things, namely the harm of their neighbors; one *girone* is allotted to those who did not love the good sufficiently; three are allocated for the correction of too avid a love of good things that should not have been loved so much, that is, worldly things.

> Ma quando al mal si torce [l'amore], o con più cura
> o con men che non dee corre nel bene,
> contra 'l fattore adovra sua fattura.
> (*Purg.* xvii, 100–102)[2]

While these categories can certainly be used to describe the actions being purged in their respective *gironi,* the identification of three categories of sin is not pursued in the narrative with the same consistency and detail as had been Virgil's equivalent explanation of the structure of Hell. The distribution into three categories finds no echo in geographic separations or other poetic details, as had been the case in the *Inferno.* Each *girone* of Purgatory is simply separate from the others; no rivers, chasms, or walls suggest generic groupings of *gironi* into regions; and Dante and Virgil travel through all seven *gironi* by their own powers, without need for assistance or alternate means of transport. To this extent, we find little reinforcement of the structure Virgil proposes.

If we turn to the relation of this realm to the one we have just exited for an explanation of its structure, we encounter new problems. The actions being purged in the *gironi* of Purgatory are most frequently called sins by Dante, and that name is reinforced by the seven letters *P* (for *peccato*) first incised on the forehead of Dante *personaggio,* and one by one erased as he journeys through Purgatory. But the seven named sins of Purgatory are not the eight species of sins (nine, counting original sin) of Hell. There seem to be obscure symmetries between the two realms—as, indeed, we would expect there should be, since both are concerned, if in different ways, with the same subject, sin—but these half-symmetries tease our understanding with their simultaneous parallelism (perhaps *reciprocity* would be a better term) and incompleteness.[3]

In the narrative, we are told that the reciprocity of the two realms has existed from the moment of their simultaneous creation, which we discover when Virgil is compelled to explain to Dante the apparent reversal of the direction of their journey as they leave Hell. The existence of Hell and Purgatory in opposite hemispheres, the source of Dante's confusion, is explained by the single event that created them both: Satan's fall from Heaven.

> Da questa parte cadde giù dal cielo;
> e la terra, che pria di qua si sporse,
> per paura di lui fè del mar velo,

> e venne all'emisperio nostro; e forse
> per fuggir lui lasciò qui luogo voto
> quella ch'appar di qua, e su ricorse.
> (*Inf.* xxxiv, 121–26)

As the earth fled in terror from Satan, it created both the land mass of the Northern Hemisphere and the ocean of the Southern. In the interior of the earth, the same terror drove earth out of the cavity that would become Hell, upward to form the mountain of Purgatory, the only continent in the southern ocean. Hell and Purgatory were therefore created together precisely at the moment that sin first entered the world. The material reciprocity of action and reaction in this one event is what suggests to us that, in addition to their twinned birth, the two realms ought to share some symmetrical relationship. What was done in one hemisphere could be undone in the other. We tend to think of the two realms existing, in fact, as mirror images of one another, even though if we imagine how the realms are spatially oriented to one another, we are forced to recognize that visually they would not actually appear as reflections at all, but as cones both tapering to points oriented in the same direction.

Their physical relation notwithstanding, our experience of the realms is very close to one of mirror images (as had been the experience of Dante *personaggio*), since the fundamental physical descriptions of Hell and Purgatory, and the significance implied by these descriptions, support our conviction of their reciprocal relationship. In both realms the same, most intuitive, organization of space denotes the seriousness of the sins encountered. The lower one is in Hell, the more serious the sin; the same is true of Purgatory. Since for Dante and Virgil the direction of travel in Hell is downward, the worst sins are encountered last. But with the direction of travel in Purgatory upward, the order of experience is reversed: the worst sins are encountered first, and it is this inversion that initially creates our sense of the realms as mirror images.[4]

The simple spatial figure is reinforced in both *cantiche* by a second poetic figure based on weight. Any movement downward in Hell is accompanied by an increase in weight, so that Virgil can say that the center of the earth, where Satan is fixed, is "'l punto / al qual si traggon d'ogni parte i pesi" (*Inf.* xxxiv, 110–11). (It is for this reason that it is no foolish play on words to speak of the gravity of sins.) In Purgatory, by contrast, movement upward is accompanied at every stage by a decrease in weight, so that as Dante passes from one *girone* to another, he finds it increasingly easy to rise. Other critical aspects of the order of narrative in both *cantiche,* moreover, also reinforce our conviction of the symmetrical, and reciprocal, relation of the two realms. The upper three *gironi* of Purgatory correspond, apparently exactly, with the upper three circles of those *punished* in Hell; that is, with circles two through five.[5] Traveling in Hell, Dante first encounters lust, gluttony, avarice; in Purgatory the order is identical but reversed: avarice, gluttony, lust. And at the end of the *Purgatorio* we further discover that the entire passage of the two realms has been circumscribed by rivers and woods. Passage into Hell requires crossing the Acheron, passage out of Purgatory crossing Lethe. And if Dante's falling into sin has placed him in a dark wood at the beginning of the *Commedia,* his exit from sin finds him in another wood the opposite of that one.[6]

But if we are convinced of a certain general symmetry and reciprocity between Hell and Purgatory, when we move to the level of particular detail that relationship seems seriously challenged. At the simplest, most material level, we cannot escape recognizing from the outset that Hell and Purgatory are not divided into the same number of regions. Hell has eight circles of punishment (nine, if Limbo is included), Purgatory only seven. While three of the *gironi* of Purgatory seem to match three circles in Hell, the remaining four *gironi* have no immediately apparent relation to the five other circles of sin in Hell. One aspect of Purgatory's organization makes this incompatibility inevitable, though to point it out is not in itself to offer a solution, since pointing it out merely calls for further explanation. Purgatory is organized by what are popularly called the seven deadly sins, which constitute a relatively late, and entirely Christian distribution of sin.[7] Using a Christian taxonomy is perhaps both appropriate and also just for the realm of Purgatory, since none enters or passes through Purgatory who has not been baptized and has died in the Christian faith. We recall, however, that justice also demanded the opposite for Hell: that it be organized by principles that have their origin in nature, rather than Christian faith, so that they could be articulated by philosophy and understood by anyone. Only thus would it be just to condemn even pagans for their actions. Since two quite different taxonomic principles are used for the two realms, it is not surprising that sins appear in one realm that do not appear in the other. None of the sins of fraud that appear in circles eight and nine of Hell, for example, appears in Purgatory. Hell generally, in fact, is far more detailed than Purgatory. Looked at from the other side, while lust, gluttony, and avarice in Purgatory seem matched in Hell, and perhaps Purgatory's anger could be more or less directly related to the sins of violence in Hell, none of the remaining three of the four most serious deadly sins (pride, envy, sloth) appears in Hell.

The divergences between the two realms become even more serious with only a little probing, since even where sins of the same name, or activities of apparently similar natures, appear in both realms they are sometimes treated so differently in the two realms as to compel us to conclude that the names are used, or the actions understood, in quite different senses. Often they, or their figurative representatives, appear in locations so different, relative to the respective order of each realm, as to challenge the symmetry of the realms rather than support it. Homosexuality, for example, is purged in Purgatory as a species of lust, the "lightest" of the deadly sins. In Hell, however, nothing was said of its relation to lust; rather, it was punished in lower Hell (a location of considerably greater seriousness than the *girone* in which it appears in Purgatory) as a sin of violence. Similarly, the Centaurs, who in Hell were so closely associated with the most direct form of violence as to be the functionaries of the first section of the seventh circle, appear in Purgatory among the examples of the vice of gluttony, in the second "lightest" *girone* (*Purg.* xxiv, 121–23). Cain, who gave his name to one of the regions of the lowest circle of Hell, is used in Purgatory as an example—not of the worst deadly sin (that is, the one punished in the lowest *girone*), but of only the second deadliest sin, that is, in the second *girone* (*Purg.* xiv, 130–35).[8]

The complexity of the relationship between the two realms can be exemplified by the description Hugh Capet gives to Dante of the crimes of his descendants:

> Lì cominciò con forza e con menzogna
> la sua rapina; e poscia, per ammenda,
> Pontì e Normandia prese e Guascogna.
> Carlo venne in Italia e, per vicenda,
> vittima fè di Curradino; e poi
> ripinse al ciel Tommaso, per ammenda.
> (*Purg.* xx, 64–69)

His descendants have committed rapine and murder, yet, as his subsequent apostrophe indicates, Hugh is merely using them as examples that show the destructive force of *avarice,* which he is himself purging in the fifth *girone* of Purgatory:

> O avarizia, che puoi tu più farne,
>> poscia c' ha' il mio sangue a te sì tratto.
>> (*Purg.* xx, 82–83)

Similarly, when Hugh later describes to Dante the *exempla* of avarice that are shouted by the penitent of this *girone* to remind them of the nature of the sin they now wish to avoid, the figures he mentions, while intended, we must remember, only as examples of avarice, are individuals whose crimes in pursuit of avarice compass the commission of an even more extensive range of horrifying actions than had his relatives, and include theft, betrayal, murder, and parricide.

> Noi repetiam Pigmalïon allotta,
>> cui traditore e ladro e parricida
>> fece la voglia sua dell'oro ghiotta;
> . . . .
> ed in infamia tutto il monte gira
>> Polinestòr ch'ancise Polidoro.
>> (*Purg.* xx, 103–5; 114–15)[9]

From its location in Purgatory (it is the third highest, or "lightest," *girone*) we are surely directed to conclude that avarice can be considered one of the "lighter" deadly sins. But we know very well where the actions that Hugh says were committed for it would be punished in Hell, had they gone unrepented: not in the third circle of sins, but in the seventh, eighth, and ninth circles, for these are a catalogue of the worst of malicious sins, and they would find their punishment in the lowest circles of Hell.

Hugh's statements initially seem to make the relationship between Hell and Purgatory more problematic, for his statements undermine those few parts of Purgatory that seemed reassuringly parallel to parts of Hell. Hell had circles for the lustful, gluttonous, and avaricious; Purgatory has *gironi* for the same sinners. But Hugh's statements demonstrate to us that though both realms have such locations, they are not populated by the same sorts of sinners. While it is probable that sinners in the fourth circle of Hell would have spent time in the fifth *girone* of Purgatory had they repented, it is certain that many sinners whom Hugh describes as suffering from the same avarice he did were, or would have been, consigned to circles of Hell far lower than the fourth. We noted a similar dislocation in the disparate treatment of homosexuality in the two realms. Some of the lustful of Purgatory would have been treated to far worse fates had they not repented than the fate of those called lustful in Hell. If these apparently identical terms, *avarice* and *lust,* are manifestly not used with the same significance in the two realms, we have no choice but to conclude that even those sections of the realms that at first seemed symmetrical to us may not be so in fact.

Sin and Vice

The teasingly near, but imperfect, alignment of the organizational members of the two realms frustrates our understanding of their relationship, and has led, of course, to attempts to reconcile the two orders.[10] In almost all cases, the attempts have centered on trying to find all of each realm's sins in the other realm, though under different names, or concealed within different groupings. That readers have attempted to find direct correspondences between the two realms testifies to the tenacity of our conviction that the two realms have some symmetrical relationship. But trying to discover one uniform set of sins for both realms is doomed to failure, for the two realms in fact deal with fundamentally different activities and states, which reflect the essentially different purposes the two realms serve. It is this difference in the nature of their subjects that frustrates us in aligning the two realms. At the same time, once we identify their different subjects and inquire into the relation between them, it becomes possible to discover the true relationship of the structures of the realms.

Hugh's statements, however problematic they first appear in regard to finding a direct parallelism between Hell and Purgatory, in fact embody the significant relationship that exists between the deadly sins purged in Purgatory and the sins punished in Hell. When Hugh uses the term *avarice* to explain the criminal actions committed by his descendants and by the figures who are the *exempla* of this *girone,* his usage is immediately familiar to us. Hugh is explaining what we would most often call the "motive" for their crimes.[11] As Hugh describes it, his descendants acted violently or fraudulently to steal Pontì and Normandy and Gascony because they were motivated by avarice.

Charles of Anjou murdered Conradin and Pygmalion of Tyre his uncle Sicheus for the same motive.

Thus, the avarice of Purgatory does not merely describe actions that involve the obsessive acquisition of material wealth, as the sin of avarice did in Hell. Rather, it describes an attitude or state of character that may lead individuals to commit actions far worse than the hoarding of possessions we encountered in Hell. The avarice of Hell, on the other hand, does not denote a state of character that functions as a motive that might eventuate in any of several actions. Rather, it describes a unique kind of action: not a motive for action, that is to say, but an action in itself. Any given action may be the expression of quite different motives or states of character. Similarly, any given state of character may seek expression in actions of very different natures. There is a relation between motives and subsequent actions, but it is a fluid and contingent relation. Many who share the same motive act very differently. It is the fluidity of the relationship between motive and action that explains the frequent lack of parallelism between Hell and Purgatory with respect to the locations in which we find individual sinners.

The primary distinction that must be made in order to understand the relationship between Hell and Purgatory is between sin, as an action of a certain sort, and vice, as a state of character.[12] Sins (*peccata* in Latin; *peccati* in Italian) such as we find in Hell are dealt with by Dante (and would be so understood in medieval ethical discussions) as concrete and individual actions. The location in which one finds a figure in Hell reflects that specific action, not the character of the individual. Vanni Fucci, as we have previously noted, is punished among the thieves for a singular—and not especially characteristic—action (*Inf.* xxiv, 97–151). By character and temperament, Vanni was a violent man, but he is not punished with the violent but with the thieves.[13] On the other hand, what are commonly called in English the seven deadly sins, which we find as the divisions of Purgatory, are not, strictly speaking, sins in this earlier sense at all; they are vices. Even medieval discussions occasionally use the terms *peccatum* and *vitium* interchangeably,[14] but in both the first explicit and codified appearances of these seven and in later discussions,[15] these seven sins are always initially described as vices. They are not, properly speaking, the "seven deadly sins," rather, they are the Seven Capital Vices, and it is in their nature as vices that they are capital, that is, the head or origin of other vices and sins.

Virtues and vices, according to Aristotle and Aquinas (and this view would have been widely accepted in medieval psychology), are not actions, but habits: dispositions of the powers of the soul which condition the manner in which these powers operate. The "subject" of a virtue is some power or capacity that can function well or badly. Most generally, "the term virtue signifies a certain disposition by which something is suitably disposed in accordance with the mode of its nature" (*ST,* 1a2æ 71, 1).[16] (Vices, by contrast, are habits that dispose powers to faulty operation.) Virtues "determine" their powers to perform their natural functions:

> Virtue denotes a certain perfection of a power. The perfection of any-
> thing is principally considered in its ordering to its end. But the end of a
> power is its act. Hence, a power is said to be perfect insofar as it is deter-
> mined to its act. (*ST,* 1a2æ 55, 1)

In the realm of ethics, the powers that are the subjects of virtues and vices—that is, the powers that can acquire habits that make them tend toward good operation or bad—are those powers, appetitive or rational, that operate in the process of making deliberate choices of action. Since powers do have natural ends and operations, the goodness or badness of their operation is primarily judged in reference to these natural ends. Vices are habits that dispose these powers to bad operation in the sense of operation that deviates from the natural purpose of the powers. Vices can therefore be spoken of as against nature. Similarly, since morally good actions exhibit a certain orderliness that is the result of the orderliness of the reasonable deliberation that precedes them, vices, which lead to bad actions that lack this orderliness, can also be described as disorderly habits. Like all habits, moral virtues and vices are acquired by repeated action, and, like all habits, they are settled and firm dispositions. They are not easily lost or altered once acquired.[17]

Since habits dispose powers to operation, virtues and vices become the formative causes of the individual actions that may be carried out by these powers, though they are potentially the causes of a wide array of actions. That a given power is badly disposed to its operation because of some vicious habit does not determine precisely which defective action will be undertaken when that power is put into operation. But having a bad habit will certainly make it more likely that whatever action is eventually undertaken will be effected in a disorderly manner, and probably to improper ends. Medieval discussions of the seven capital vices found them to be both capital and deadly not only as predispositions to individual evil actions, but as predispositions to further vices as well.

> The term capital is used in respect of the head . . . as metaphorically any initiating and directing principle is called the head. . . . Thus a vice is said to be capital if it is one from which other vices arise, especially insofar as it is their origin as a final cause, which is a formal origin, as was stated above [1a2æ 18, 6 and 72, 6]. For this reason, a capital vice is not only the originating principle of other vices, it is also in a certain sense their leading principle. For an art or habit to which the end belongs always rules and controls those things which are ordered to the end. Whence Gregory [*Moralia*, xxxi, 17] likens the capital vices to the leaders of armies. (*ST*, 1a2æ 84, 3)

It is these seven most serious of all bad habits that we find being purged in the seven *gironi* of Purgatory, not individual actions, as had been punished in Hell. These are the two different subjects with which the two realms deal, and if Hell and Purgatory seem to stand in a complicated and sometimes obscure relationship to one another, it is because actions and habits stand in much the same relation to each other. Even when we know that a person possesses a given habit, we cannot predict with certainty what singular action the person will take.[18] Yet at the same time, our inability to make such a prediction does not belie the existence of an intimate relation between habit and act.

Habit and the Purpose of Purgatory

That Purgatory is organized by habits while Hell is organized by actions reflects the fundamentally different purposes of the two realms. Hell is organized by actions because it is the place of punishment, and it is action—that is, sin—that is blameworthy and that demands punishment:

> Evil is more general than sin, just as good is more general than right. For every privation of good in anything whatever constitutes a principle of evil; but a sin, properly speaking, consists in an act which is done for some end, and that lacks the due order to that end. (*ST*, 1a2æ 21, 1)

> Properly speaking, sin denotes an inordinate act. (*ST*, 1a2æ 71, 1)

Merit or blame is not assigned to habits in themselves—that is, to virtues or vices—nor do habits per se call for reward or punishment.

Habit holds a middle state between power and act. For it is manifest that, in good and evil, act is placed above power, for, as it is said [*Metaphys.*, ix, 19], it is better to act well than to be able to act well. Similarly, doing evil is more blameworthy than the capacity to do evil. Whence it follows that in both goodness and badness a habit holds a middle status between power and act. So, while a good or bad habit surpasses a power in goodness or badness, it is at the same time surpassed by a [good or evil] act. This is also apparent because no habit is said to be good or evil except as it inclines us to good or evil action. (*ST,* 1a2æ 71, 3)[19]

No merit attaches to good actions that were never performed. Similarly, no blame, properly speaking, can be attached to bad actions that were suppressed. The case of continent persons illuminates the question of justice embodied in this distinction. The continent possess bad habits, but by force of will or intellect manage to avoid acting on them. We recognize that continence is a defective moral state, relative to virtue; and we know, moreover, that a life of continence is more painful than a life of virtue. Nonetheless, the *actions* of the continent are no less upright than those of the virtuous, even if accomplished differently from the way the virtuous would. To punish the continent for habits they have never indulged would be unjust; they have done nothing wrong.

It is sin that is due punishment (*ST,* 1a2æ 87, 6 and 87, 7). As the place of punishment, therefore, Hell can justly punish only sins—that is, acts, not vices. Hence, the discrete circles of Hell correspond to actions of different natures, and the order of the gravity of the sins corresponds to the nature of the actions themselves. Purgatory, on the other hand, is not a place of punishment, but rather of correction. (There is no correction in Hell, inasmuch as justice only allows eternal punishment of those eternally fixed in their sins.) And what is corrected in Purgatory are vices, not actions. There is no way to correct an action once it has occurred. What is done cannot be taken back. The only appropriate subjects of correction are states, that is, habits, that lead, or can lead, to sinful actions, for these states may yet be altered, even if already completed action cannot. This is why the two realms are divided differently. The individual *gironi* of Purgatory correspond to vices that preceded the sinful acts of the sinners being purged; the circles of Hell, for their part, correspond to specific sins (that is, actions) that have been performed.[20]

There is a further consequence to organizing Purgatory by vices, that is to say, by habits. If the purpose of the suffering undergone in

Purgatory is to remove the seven capital vices, there must be a transformed and purified state of character that is the goal of this correction—that is, the soul with its bad habits reformed into good habits. And there must be, moreover, some reason that it is desirable to achieve this state. From the very start of the *Purgatorio,* Dante does indeed inform us that the purpose of this realm is the transformation of the souls who are sent there. Throughout the *Purgatorio,* Dante stresses the goal of rectification, explicitly often, and implicitly constantly in the altered nature of the *contrapasso* that we see exhibited in the scenes of this *cantica.*

> E canterò di quel secondo regno
> dove l'umano spirito si purga
> e di salire al ciel diventa degno.
> 　　　　　　　　　　(*Purg.* i, 4–6)

The goal of the process is the capacity to rise to a life in Heaven. Dante describes the vices that are being purged as weights that impede souls from rising to Heaven (cf. *Purg.* xi, 34–36), or as wounds that must be healed (*piaghe; Purg.* ix, 114)—and he has Cato state directly that until these defects are removed, the soul is not capable of a life in Heaven:

> Correte al monte a spogliarvi lo scoglio
> ch'esser non lascia a voi Dio manifesto.
> 　　　　　　　　　　(*Purg.* ii, 122–23)

As Dante *personaggio* replicates the action of purgation, he experiences a growing ability to move toward Heaven. At the moment that he completes the symbolic purgation of the first of his vices, he is immediately aware of an unexpected lightness:

> Ond'io: «Maestro, dì, qual cosa greve
> levata s'è da me, che nulla quasi
> per me fatica, andando, si riceve?»
> 　　　　　　　　　　(*Purg.* xii, 118–20)

To which Virgil replies by explaining:

> Rispuose: «Quando i P che son rimasi
> ancor nel volto tuo presso che stinti,
> saranno come l'un del tutto rasi,
> fier li tuoi piè dal buon voler sì vinti,
> che non pur non fatica sentiranno,
> ma fia diletto loro esser sospinti».
> 　　　　　　　　　　(*Purg.* xii, 121–26)

The sinful *actions* committed by the souls in Purgatory have already been forgiven. Were that not so, the souls would be in Hell rather than Purgatory. But though the actions are now behind them, the dispositions, that is, vices, that led to those actions are not themselves necessarily removed by that forgiveness.[21]

> The stain of sin remains in the soul even after the act of sin is past. . . .
> Even given that this act of sin—by which a man withdrew from the light
> of reason or divine law—has ceased, it is not the case that the man at
> once returns to what he was. (*ST,* 1a2æ 86, 2)[22]

A soul still suffering from one of the capital vices retains the "stain of sin" as a defective condition. Purgatory is the means by which this defect is removed, by which the original beauty of the soul is restored. The souls in Purgatory have the obligation and desire to follow this route: "ire a farsi belle" (*Purg.* ii, 75). The removal of their defects, and the restoration of their original beauty are the goal of the souls there, to one of whom Dante can say: "O creatura che ti mondi / per tornar bella a colui che ti fece" (*Purg.* xvi, 31–32). It is only by this restoration that the souls are fit to enter Heaven. But since this restoration means the removal of a condition that disposes the soul to improper action, the particular sense of beauty that is meant here must have to do with the restoration of an original capacity for proper action. The vicious soul is effectively a diseased soul. Its operations do not incline to their natural and intended ends. Omberto Aldobrandesco speaks of himself and his whole family as *sick* with pride:

> Io sono Omberto; e non pur a me danno
> superbia fè, chè tutt'i miei consorti
> ha ella tratti seco nel malanno.
> (*Purg.* xi, 67–69)

Understanding the vicious soul as diseased is also implicit in Virgil's description of Dante's state at the end of his own purification, for Virgil says that Dante is not only free, and upright, but healthy too.

> Libero, dritto e sano è tuo arbitrio,
> e fallo fora non fare a suo senno:
> per ch'io te sovra te corono e mitrio.
> (*Purg.* xxvii, 140–42)

What makes a soul healthy in this context is that it is free of dispositions to wrong action and therefore perfect with respect to proper operation. That, indeed, is what health in general is. In such a state the soul can also be spoken of as free, for it is no longer enslaved by tendencies that compel it to improper, because unnatural, action. Perfection understood in this operational sense is the result of the acquisition of the virtues that belong to the soul and its faculties, for, as was cited above, it is virtue that is the perfection of a power insofar as it disposes it to right operation.[23] Restoring a soul to full health, then, means acquiring the suite of virtues that perfect all of the soul's powers. Thus, the souls in Purgatory become healthy by substituting the virtues of their soul for the sicknesses—the vices—they previously possessed. Acquiring these virtues is what souls undertake in Purgatory to become worthy of rising to Heaven.

Therapy and the Contrapasso in Purgatory

The nature of the corrections imposed upon the souls in Purgatory confirms this understanding of the soul's sickness and health, for the corrections appear in forms that are characteristic of how vices are transformed into virtues. Vices, for Aristotle, are corrected by remedies that drive the soul toward pleasures that are opposed to the pleasures that led to vice, until the soul becomes habituated to desiring these new pleasures, and so is straightened.

> [Our natural aptitude to a given action] is made apparent by the delight or sadness evoked in us. Then we must force ourselves to its contrary, for by steering ourselves as far as possible away from sin, we will arrive at the mean. And this is what those straightening bent timbers do. (*EN*, ii, 9; 1109b5–8)[24]

Dante has Virgil echo this Aristotelian passage in his conversation with Forese Donati, when he speaks of Purgatory as "la montagna / che drizza voi che 'l mondo fece torti" (*Purg.* xxiii, 125–26). Purgatory straightens what the world made bent. The *contrapasso*, considered as the principle that determines what is appropriate for a soul to suffer after death, takes on an appropriately different form in Purgatory from what it had in Hell, reflecting Purgatory's different purpose and the means of accomplishing the purpose. As we noted in the first chapter, the damned souls were compelled to endless iteration of the sin for which they were damned. That was the *contrapasso* in Hell. But we also noted that in Purgatory we see souls compelled to enact essentially the *opposite* of the actions to which they had tended while alive, and of which they now repent.[25] We can now understand why this is the *contrapasso* in Purgatory, since we can now recognize its appropriateness for the correction of dispositions, rather than the punishment of actions. Omberto Aldobrandesco states the new principle that applies in Purgatory, in a passage that has already been cited. The correction of his vice of pride consists in the self-abasement he should have undertaken while alive.

> E qui convien ch'io questo peso porti
> per lei, tanto che a Dio si sodisfaccia,
> poi ch'io nol fe' tra' vivi, qui tra' morti.
> (*Purg.* xi, 70–72)

Had Omberto bent his proud neck while alive (it is now his stone that does so: "[il] sasso / che la cervice mia superba doma"; *Purg.* xi, 52–53), he would not have formed in himself the habit, the capital vice, known as pride. But since he did acquire that habit, he can lose it only by a purgatorial action that drags him in the opposite direction from his vice in order to inculcate its contrary disposition.

Neither virtues nor vices are acquired by a single act. Reiteration of a virtuous action is what removes the habit of vice that had been acquired by the reiteration of vicious actions. As Aquinas says: "We may then universally sum up in one sentence: like actions produce like habits."[26] Since the souls of sinners in Purgatory had been habituated to feel the wrong pleasures, they need encouragement to pursue their opposites. In the narrative of the *Purgatorio,* the penitent souls in each *girone* are encouraged to right action by examples of the virtue they should be acquiring in the *girone,* and discouraged from continuing in their old habits by examples of the vice. As Virgil says of the correction of the envious (the statement is clearly meant to apply to all *gironi*), "Lo fren vuol esser del contrario [to the virtue] sono" (*Purg.* xiii, 40). At the end of their purification by opposed action, the souls can indeed be said to have been straightened (in Aristotle's sense), and this meaning too is incorporated in Virgil's description of Dante's state at the completion of this part of his journey: healthy *(sano),* free *(libero),* and *dritto*—"upright," yes, but in the metaphor of the *Ethics,* "straight" too (*Purg.* xxvii, 140).

The rehabituation of their vices into virtues which the penitent accomplish by action the contrary of the vice is also the necessary procedure for removing the "stain" of sin—the enduring disposition to sin even after individual acts of sin are past—which had rendered their souls unworthy of Heaven:

> A man does not at once return to what he was [before sinning], but a certain motion of the will contrary to the first [sinful] motion is required. (*ST,* 1a2æ 86, 2)[27]

With this restoration of the souls' unstained state, they are free to rise to Heaven, and Virgil's declaration to Dante that his soul is *libero* acquires a further meaning. To Aristotle, the virtuous soul is free because it is not enslaved to passions. Being virtuous is being free *from* these encumberances. At the end of the *Purgatorio,* the souls also have the freedom *to* do something, to rise to Heaven. From the start, Dante's voyage through Purgatory had been described as a search for freedom ("Or ti piaccia gradir la sua venuta: / libertà va cercando"; *Purg.* i, 70–71), and at its end he is proclaimed upright, healthy, and free because these three states are the same.

Finally, two other important aspects of the narrative of the *Purgatorio* confirm that the subject of the *cantica* is the reformation of habits, or vices. First, unlike the souls in Hell, who undergo a single eternal punishment, the souls in Purgatory may be required to undergo multiple corrections, and for differing lengths of time. Insofar as the powers of the soul are multiple, any one or several of the powers might be afflicted by one vice or several. And insofar as some habits may be more deeply ingrained than others, the courses of treatment by opposed movement may take longer in some cases than others. Statius declares to Dante and Virgil that he spent five hundred years in the fifth *girone* purging his prodigality, after spending four hundred years in the fourth purging his lack of religious zeal (and, since some three hundred years are yet unaccounted for, they must have been spent either in the antepurgatory or in some other *girone* or *gironi* on the mountain). Unlike Hell, where the soul is fixed in the image of the worst evil it had committed, the restoration of health to a soul requires the removal of *all* vices that may encumber it. That the souls in Purgatory expect to have to visit several of the *gironi* confirms that it is the alteration of dispositions that is the purpose of this realm. Only after the acquisition of the appropriate virtues for every one of the soul's powers can the soul be said to be wholly healthy, and wholly free. Every vice is a weight binding the soul to its earlier sinful patterns of action, and only when all of these weights have been removed does the soul feel light enough to be able to rise toward Heaven:

> Della mondizia sol voler fa prova,
> che, tutto libero a mutar convento,
> l'alma sorprende, e di voler le giova.
> Prima vuol ben, ma non lascia il talento
> che divina giustizia, contra voglia,
> come fu al peccar, pone al tormento.
>
> (*Purg.* xxi, 61–66)

Similarly, the way in which Dante describes the state of the soul after it has completed its time in any individual *girone* is a second confirmation that the purgation accomplished in each *girone* is the acquisition of a new habit. At the exit of each *girone,* the angel of that exit sings a Beatitude to signify that the purified soul, at the completion of its stay in the *girone,* now possesses that Beatitude. One enters the *girone* with one quality, a vicious habit, and one exits with another, cured, lightened, and blessed. The Beatitude replaces the vice, and this is also apparently true for Dante *personaggio,* since at each such moment when he exits a *girone* another *P* is erased from his forehead, and the angel sings the Beatitude for him.

Now, Dante's use of the Beatitudes as signs of virtuous habits opposed to the capital vices is not a technically authorized usage, since in scholastic discussions the Beatitudes were not virtues. Beatitudes differ from virtues, Aquinas says, "not as habit from habit, but as act from habit" (*ST,* 1a2æ 69, 1). (*Act* is used here in the technical Aristotelian sense of an actual perfected operation of a power.) Properly speaking, a Beatitude, insofar as it means the state or experience of being blessed, could not be merely a habit that readies us for right action; properly speaking, it should only be used of the real possession of the happiness that comes from the actual performance of right action. In this technical sense, the Beatitudes were seen as beyond virtues—as the actualizations, or completions, of virtue.

But Dante cannot be using the Beatitudes in this strict technical sense, since in that sense the souls who exit individual *gironi* in Purgatory could not properly be said to possess, or to exhibit or experience, the Beatitudes. (Nor, indeed, could it properly be said of souls still in this world, of whom the Beatitudes were first pronounced.) For a medieval Aristotelian, true blessedness cannot be a merely partial blessedness. One could not be blessed in one respect but not in others. In a proper sense, no single Beatitude can really be experienced until all of the Beatitudes have been acquired; and true and complete blessedness can be enjoyed only in the soul's perfect actions in Heaven, not at the end of any individual *girone* in Purgatory. (The case of Statius is again instructive: while he would have had the Beatitude of the fourth *girone* pronounced for him as he exited that *girone,* there were still some five hundred years of suffering to be undergone as correction before he could rise to Heaven. It is impossible to say that for those five hundred years he was *blessed* in the proper sense of the term.) Recognizing these limitations, we must conclude that Dante's use of the Beatitudes as discrete qualities attributed to souls at the moment of the acquisition of individual good habits—but long before the souls are actually blessed—signals his loose and untechnical use of the term.

In such a freer sense, Dante could indeed use the Beatitudes as if they were virtues. And it is worth pointing out that such a usage does have a medieval sanction. Aquinas notes that it is possible to speak of individuals as blessed in, as it were, anticipation of later final blessedness, simply because their character and actions convince one that they have the qualities, the dispositions, necessary to achieve final blessedness:

> Someone is said already to possess an end on account of the hope of obtaining the end. Whence the Philosopher said [*EN*, i, 9] that "children are called happy in hope"; and the Apostle says [Rom. 8:24] *We have been saved by hope.* Indeed, hope of following through to the end arises from something moving suitably toward an end, and approaching it. . . . And a person moves toward the end of blessedness, and approaches it, through the operation of the virtues. (*ST,* 1a2æ 69, 1)[28]

> So, therefore, those things which are touched on in the Beatitudes as merits [that is, those clauses "Blessed are the . . ."] are certain preparations or dispositions to blessedness (whether perfect or inchoate); and those things which are set as rewards ["for they shall . . ."] can be either perfect blessedness itself (and in this sense they pertain to our future life), or they can be a certain inchoate blessedness, as there is in perfect men (and in this sense the rewards pertain to our present life). But when someone begins to perfect himself in the acts of the virtues and the gifts, it can be hoped that he will arrive at perfection both in this life and in the next. (*ST,* 1a2æ 69, 2)

For those still completing their purgation, any Beatitude attributed to them must be attributed in this anticipatory way, and to refer not to their actual possession of blessedness, but to their *disposition* for it, and insofar as a disposition to action, only a habit or virtue for acting in this blessed way. Until the completion of Purgatory, that applies to all souls therein, and to each of the Beatitudes until, with the acquisition of the last, all are possessed. But this anticipatory usage is exactly what Dante is doing: using the Beatitudes to stand for the dispositions, habits, or virtues that now move the purged souls in the direction of their happiness, as their vices had disposed them to move in the opposite direction.[29] Thus, Dante's use of the Beatitudes as if habits is a further confirmation that the purpose of Purgatory is to inculcate virtues. If Dante uses the Beatitudes instead of more familiar names of virtues to indicate the healthy state of a soul after removing its vices, the reason is because the Beatitudes embody in themselves a description of the blessed actions that are to come with the restoration of the soul's healthy disposition. As we shall consider in the second part of this chapter, that is essential to the dynamic of the narrative of this *cantica*.

Habits and Powers

Habits, and therefore virtues and vices, are dispositions of powers, and stand midway between the power, as pure potentiality, and the completed act. Habits condition powers to eventuate consistently, that is, to be actualized, in one kind of action rather than another. Virtues dispose the powers to their proper completed act. Vices dispose powers to acts just as surely as virtues do but to disordered or improper acts.[30] But of which powers are we speaking? Recognizing, as we have done, that Hell punishes acts while Purgatory corrects habits (and recognizing that the relation between a habit and its eventual act is often tangled or obscure) may be sufficient to explain the dissimilarities that exist between the structures of Hell and Purgatory, but is not sufficient to explain their similarities. It is only by considering which are the powers whose habits are corrected in Purgatory that the deeper connection between the two realms emerges, and with it the explanation of what similarity does exist in their structures.

In ancient and medieval discussions of biology and psychology, the excellent disposition of any power can be said to be a virtue, if the term is used in its broadest sense.[31] But in discussions of ethics, as we have already touched on briefly, virtue is understood in a more limited, technical sense, as applying to certain specific powers. Some powers, which perform only one fixed function, can be said to be naturally determined to the actions that constitute their ends. Powers related to nutrition and growth, for example, are of this sort. In normal conditions of health, these powers perform their functions properly. Only disease or some similar natural disorder causes them to operate badly. In their cases, the term *virtue* actually signifies nothing more than their satisfactory natural operation. Their virtue is not an additional state that "disposes" them as powers. They have been "disposed" by nature.

But where a power is capable of aiming at, and accomplishing, diverse ends (where it is not, as it would be said, "determined" to any single act), its operation requires something to direct, or dispose, it to one end rather than another. This disposition is habit, and habits that determine a power of this sort to good operation are virtues in a sense different from the natural virtues of healthily operating physiological powers.

> Every power which can be ordered to action in diverse ways requires a habit by which it is disposed well to its act. . . . Since it is necessary for the end of human life that the appetitive power be inclined to a determinate object—to which it is not inclined by its nature as a power, which is capable of many and diverse things—it is therefore necessary that in the will and the other appetitive powers there be certain inclining qualities, which are called habits. (*ST*, 1a2æ 50, 5 and ad 1)[32]

While any power can be said to have a virtue, our most common usage of the term, as well as the starting point of discussions of ethics, takes "virtue" in this latter sense of habit, as does Dante's usage in his discussions of sin, both in Hell and Purgatory.[33]

Within ethical discussions, a further distinction is also crucial. Since the acts about which moral virtue is concerned are voluntary and deliberate acts, the powers that one would properly consider to be those disposed by *moral* virtues to right operation—in the technical vocabulary, the "subjects" of the habits or virtues—must be those specific powers by which our voluntary and deliberate actions are performed, whether well or badly. Voluntary and deliberate actions are rational in some sense (this distinguishes them from the actions of animals), but not all rational activities are germane to questions of morality. Purely speculative activities of the intellect, for example, are not. So, while the powers of the speculative intellect are capable of being actualized in many different ways, and therefore also stand in need of, and indeed do possess, habits by which their operation is disposed to proper operation, these habits of the intellect, while intellectual virtues, are not moral virtues. They perfect our speculation but do not affect those actions that are the province of morality.[34] The moral virtues (and vices) are habits of those rational powers involved in action properly so called, not of those whose end is merely thought. And in medieval psychology, such a description pointed immediately to a particular set of powers.

> Indeed, moral virtue is so called from *mos,* insofar as *mos* signifies a certain natural (or as if natural) inclination to a certain kind of action. . . . It is evident that inclination to act properly regards the appetitive faculty, to which it belongs to move all the powers to action, as was made clear previously [1a2æ 9, 1]. And therefore not every virtue is called a moral virtue, but only that virtue which is of the appetitive faculty. . . . Only that virtue which is of the appetitive part of the soul effects right choice. For it has been stated above [1a2æ 13, 1] that choice is an act of the appetitive part. Hence, a habit of choice—which is to say a principle of choice— can only be that habit which perfects the appetitive faculty. (*ST,* 1a2æ 58, 1 and ad 2)

The powers that are the subjects of moral virtues, then, are the three appetitive powers, the will, the irascible appetite, and the concupiscible appetite:

> The subject of that habit which is called virtue simply can only be the will, or some other power insofar as it is moved by the will. The reason for this is that the will moves all the other powers which are in some way rational to their acts. . . . The irascible and concupiscible appetites . . . can be considered to participate in reason because it is innate in them to obey the reason. And thus the irascible and concupiscible appetites can be subjects of human virtue. Indeed, they are principles of human action insofar as they participate in reason, and for such powers we must posit virtues. (*ST,* 1a2æ 56, 3 and 4)[35]

This sudden reappearance of the appetites should not really surprise us, since the explanation Dante has Virgil give of the arrangement of the seven capital vices in Purgatory is not only consonant with but essentially confirms the linkage of vices to appetites. The starting point and fundamental principle of Virgil's explanation is that every action, virtue, and vice can be understood as the operation of love:

> «Nè creator nè creatura mai»
> cominciò el, «figliuol, fu sanza amore,
> o naturale o d'animo; e tu 'l sai.
> . . . .
> Quinci comprender puoi ch'esser convene
> amor sementa in voi d'ogni virtute
> e d'ogne operazion che merta pene.»
> (*Purg.* xvii, 91–93, 103–5)

By making this declaration, however, Dante again indicates his agreement with the Aristotelian principle that effectively traces back all movement, and therefore all action, virtue, and vice, to the operation of appetite. The only powers, then, to whose virtues, vices, and operations praise and blame, reward and punishment can attach have to be the appetitive powers, for it is only to these powers that love properly belongs, and it is from these powers that all action begins.[36]

> Love *[amor]* is the first movement of the will and of every appetitive faculty. (*ST,* 1a 20, 1)[37]

> It is manifest, therefore, that the power of the soul which is called the appetite is the moving cause. . . . If moving causes are considered formally and according to their species, there will be a single moving cause—that is, either the object of appetite or the appetitive power.[38]

Nor is it only in this general discussion of structure in canto xvii that Dante expresses this connection. He repeatedly stresses the appetitiveness of the seven capital vices in descriptions of the vices given by Virgil, or in descriptions of the sinners purging these vices. The vices of lust and gluttony are naturally associated with the appetites, and we can easily understand avarice in that sense too. But Dante goes further, having Virgil associate anger, metaphorically, with gluttony: "della vendetta ghiotto" (*Purg.* xvii, 122), and describe pride as a kind of hunger:

> È chi per esser suo vicin soppresso
> spera eccellenza, e sol per questo brama
> ch'el sia di sua grandezza in basso messo.
> (*Purg.* xvii, 115–17)

At this point, of course, we recognize that the capital vices that are the subject of the *Purgatorio* are dispositions of the same appetitive powers whose completed sinful operations provided the organization of the *Inferno*. It could not really have been otherwise. Appetites, as the ultimate basis of all movement, are on the one hand the active origin of actions, good and bad, and on the other, are the powers that are the subjects of habits to dispose them to good or bad action.[39] Thus, the *gironi* of Purgatory share a common substrate with the circles of Hell: dispositions in one, actions in the other are distinguished and organized by their relation to the same three appetites.[40] It is this common appetitive substructure that explains both the manifest similarities between the organizations of Hell and Purgatory and also the equally manifest dissimilarities. The teasing parallelism of the two realms arises from the fact that both structures are derived not only from the same three appetites, but also from the same natural order that exists among the appetitive powers. At the same time, however, the unavoidably contingent relationship between habits and actions (even of the same power) accounts for the divergences between the structures of the two realms.

The divergences are all at the level of individual sins and specific vices, and they arise because, while virtues and vices dispose powers to actions of a given sort, they do not inevitably and completely determine the character of every individual action. Virtues and vices are dispositions of appetitive powers only with regard to those powers' ends.

> In order that a choice be good, two things are required: first, that the intention (of the end) be fit—and this comes to be through moral virtue, which inclines the appetitive faculty to a good suitable to the reason, which is a fit end. (*ST,* 1a2æ 58, 4)[41]

Appetites initiate movement by the pursuit or avoidance of their ends (seen as various goods or evils), and capital vices, as vices, furnish the *ends* of actions.[42] But while virtues and vices dispose us habitually to select good or bad ends, they do not determine the means we use to accomplish those ends. Knowing that someone was well or badly disposed toward certain objects considered as goods, or toward certain passions associated with those objects, would not tell us what that person would actually do in pursuing those objects or reacting to those passions.

Knowing which appetite is affected by a given vice does not in itself predict how satisfaction of the vice will be sought, because as individual beings, we act as integral agents. We do not necessarily use only one power at a time; rather, we bring all of our powers to bear in the attempt to accomplish our ends. If avarice or gluttony, as a habit of the concupiscible appetite, proposes an end to us, we will first try to pursue the end as would be normal for an object of concupiscence. But if the accomplishment of that end seems difficult or is impeded by others, our attempt to accomplish it is likely to bring our irascible power into operation. The resulting action may be violent, then, or involve anger, and thus the action itself—though not the end for which it was intended—will exhibit the characteristics not of the concupiscible appetite that initiated it, but of the irascible appetite that executed it. If the best way to fulfill a gluttonous or avaricious design is through fraud, our intelligence and will are likely to swing into action to accomplish it, and the resulting action will appear not simply as the outcome of a concupiscible appetite, but rather as the product of the intellectual appetite, with the calculation and injustice associated with that appetite. Consider, for example, someone with vices with respect to the acquisition of wealth. That end, the possession of wealth, might be accomplished by means ranging from the legal but obsessive pursuit of commercial activities, through murder, theft, fraud. One vice alone, then, could be the cause of a wide variety of actions of significantly different character, each one reflecting in its ultimate playing out a different one of the appetitive faculties.[43] The examples we considered above (of Hugh's descendants, *inter alia*) reveal precisely this open-endedness with regard to the initiating vice and the eventual concrete action.[44] Much of what seems initially misaligned between Purgatory and Hell has its origin in this variability of the means to an end. Because Hell punishes action, the sins are punished in connection with the appetites that executed the final act, and gave it its ultimate character. Purgatory, however, rehabilitates the vices in which actions originated, not the acts in which they ended.[45]

There is nothing novel in linking the seven capital vices to the appetitive powers. Philosophical consistency essentially demands that if the capital vices truly are vices, they must be dispositions of some powers. Consequently, other medieval discussions of the seven capital vices, and other discussions of their appearance in the *Commedia,* also link the vices to the three appetites—though in some cases linking them only to the two sensitive appetites.[46] But as Dante's association in the *Inferno* of particular sins with the three appetites was idiosyncratic, so is his association of particular capital vices with the appetites in the *Purgatorio.* Dante's most significant innovation is linking two of the vices, pride and envy, to the intellectual appetite, the will. And even in his association of certain capital vices with the concupiscible and irascible appetites, Dante often makes decisions quite different from those of other authors.[47] But what drives Dante's departures from other medieval treatments and his idiosyncratic alignment of vices with specific appetitive powers is his double sense of the fundamental symmetry of Hell and Purgatory: first, that there exists a consistent explanation of the motives of action in both realms, and second, that one consistent principle of the seriousness of actions applies in both realms. Because Dante saw the initiation of mortal sins in all three of the appetites, and because he believed that the capital vices are the sources of all other vices and sins, he believed that the capital vices, in turn, had to be vices of all three appetites. And since it was the natural order that existed between the appetites that determined the seriousness of individual sins and the order of their appearance in the *Inferno*, so that same principle of order had to determine the appearance of the capital vices in the *Purgatorio*. The worst of sins were committed through the operation of the will; his sense of just symmetry, therefore, would insist to Dante that the will would also be the subject of the worst vices. That earlier readers of the poem have not been able to recognize the common structure possessed by Purgatory and Hell is a result of their not recognizing first of all the underlying role played by appetite in the organization of the *Inferno*, so that they could subsequently recognize the same appetites in a similar role in the *Purgatorio*.

Hell and Purgatory in this poem are indeed symmetrical, but not at the "surface" level, not at the level of individual sins and vices. Where they are symmetrical is at the level of the appetites, which in the one instance execute the sins and in the other are the subjects of the capital vices. As one descends in Hell, one descends through the circles of the sins of concupiscence to circles of sins of irascibility, and from there to circles whose sins have their source in the will itself. As one ascends in Purgatory, one ascends from *gironi* in which the vices purged are vices of the will, to *gironi* whose vices are defects of the irascible appetite, to *gironi*, finally, whose vices are vices of the concupiscible appetite. For Dante, as we will explore below, the vices of pride and envy are vices of the will; anger and sloth are vices of the appetite that deals with arduous goods, the irascible appetite; avarice, gluttony, and lust are vices of the concupiscible appetite.

In both Hell and Purgatory, the order of the circles or *gironi*, of punishments or purgations, reflects the same principle: that sins or vices are more serious the more properly human they are; the more they involve the rational faculties that are the property of human beings, and that ought to direct human action. Hence, both sins and vices of the will are more serious than sins and vices of the sensitive appetites because the will is itself rational. Sins and vices of the irascible appetite are more serious than those of the concupiscible because the irascible appetite, while a sensitive appetitive power, has a closer connection to the reason than the concupiscible appetite does. As has already been mentioned, the upward movement in Purgatory is the symmetrically opposite poetic figure of this principle to the downward movement in Hell.

In both realms the least serious sins and vices—those highest in either realm—are associated with the concupiscible appetite. (We must remember that, though the names are identical, in one realm lust, gluttony, and avarice refer to acts of concupiscence and in the other to concupiscent dispositions.) To say these sins and vices are least blameworthy because farthest from being properly human is simultaneously to say that they are closest to biological or natural functions, and closest therefore to being naturally good. In speaking of the vices of the concupiscible appetite in the *Purgatorio*, Virgil specifically points out that the three lightest vices, which are vices of this appetite, pursue real, though secondary, goods. This is one indication of this appetite's closeness to strictly biological faculties. Natural powers are naturally adapted to their purposes, and go wrong only if their pursuit of the end is impeded.[48] The concupiscible appetite too is adapted to real goods, though its defect is that it pursues them too avidly.

> Altro ben è che non fa l'uom felice;
> non è felicità, non è la bona
> essenza, d'ogni ben frutto e radice.
> L'amor ch'ad esso troppo s'abbandona,
> di sovr'a noi si piange per tre cerchi.
> (*Purg.* xvii, 133–37)

The origin of these vices in the pursuit of genuine goods is also reflected in the nature of their purgation. The sinners purging these vices do not undergo treatment by action literally opposed to their past action (as do the penitent in the four other *gironi*) but seem, rather, to undergo radical diets. They pursue the same ends as they had but with extreme restrictions on their ability to pursue them. The reason for this difference in treatment is that the concupiscible appetite is close to naturally good. Its defect is in excess, not in the direction of its operation. With respect to the concupiscible appetite, it is this excess, not its aim, that must be reformed by contrary action. Thus, the corrections of these souls take the form of bringing the impulse of pursuit back into measure, as diet is intended to do. By contrast, the purgations of vices lower on the mountain of Purgatory very much take the form of compelling the sinner to actions whose aims are the opposite of the original vice.

As we begin to consider the individual vices, however, we should keep in mind that the surface similarity between certain vices and sins is deceptive, as are, in a way, the names given both sins and vices. Habits of lust, gluttony, and avarice, we know, may result in actions with natures very different from what these habits would imply. Certain acts of lust may require a kind of violence, and the operation of the irascible appetite; certain acts of avarice may require not merely violence but even fraud. Whatever similarities exist must not cause us to forget that entities of very different natures go under the same name in the two realms. Anger in Hell is a *passion* of the irascible appetite; it is a reaction to a perceived wrong, an emotional spur to violence. In Purgatory, anger does not name the passion of the irascible appetite, but a vice: a *habit* of anger, a disposition (not simply a passion) of the same appetite. In Purgatory, likewise, lust, gluttony, and avarice do not name acts of this nature, but states of character: weaknesses or defects of the concupiscible appetite in respect of these three objects.

The Seven Capital Vices and the Three Appetites: The Underlying Symmetry of Hell and Purgatory

Deciding that the seven capital vices are vices of the appetitive powers, and concluding that the process of purgation consists in the healing of the appetites are only the first steps toward explaining the organization of Purgatory, since determinations would still need to be made as to which vices are properly attached to which appetites, and as to the order in which we find individual vices. Indeed, Dante's overall distribution of the vices to the appetites—his association of pride and envy to the will, of anger and sloth to the irascible appetite, and of avarice, gluttony, and lust to the concupiscible appetite—are essentially unique to him. There already existed other associations of the seven capital vices to appetites, based frequently on literal interpretations of either the vice's name, or key words in its definition, and quite different from the alignment Dante proposes.[49] In Aquinas, for example, envy and sloth are both associated with the concupiscible appetite because of the appearance of the word *sadness* in their definitions.[50] Envy was defined as sadness at others' good fortune, sloth as sadness in regard to spiritual matters (indeed, sloth, *acedia,* often appears explicitly as sadness, *tristitia,* in medieval lists of the capital vices). Aquinas reasons that since sadness is a passion of the concupiscible appetite, these vices should be associated with that appetite. Avarice as a vice was associated by Aquinas with the will, the intellectual appetite, by etymology of its Greek equivalent, πλεονεξία. Since πλεονεξία means, literally, having (or the desire to have) more, Aquinas argues that "more" must imply "more than is just," and inasmuch as justice is a virtue of the will, avarice must be a defect in regard to liberality, a virtue "annexed" to justice, and therefore a vice of the will.[51]

Dante ignored these competing systems and invented his own structure of associations of vices with appetites for two reasons: first, in order to maintain the consistent principle that the worst vices (as also had been true for the worst sins) should be associated with the will; second, in order to be more concrete about the nature of the appetites and more sensitive to the character of the appetitive impulses that lie behind the vices than had been the discussions of other theologians. To associate envy and sloth with the concupiscible appetite on the basis of their "sadness," for example, as was done by Aquinas and others, is less profound and more ambiguous than it might at first appear. Sadness, or pain, is the ultimate passion of every unsuccessful appetitive movement (as joy or pleasure is of any successful one), whether it be the failure to attain something desired, or the failure to avoid something hated. Every unsuccessful instance of appetition resolves itself into sadness, as Aquinas himself argued, whichever of the three appetites was the subject of the original appetitive movement.[52] (Dante makes an explicit reference, for example, to the pain, *dolor,* in which anger begins [*Purg.* xv, 95], and Aquinas himself would certainly agree with such an identification.)[53] But on such a basis, one could theoretically associate any of the first four capital vices with the concupiscible appetite (along with the final three, which seem naturally to belong to it), though to do so would obscure the essential differences that exist between the vices.

The specific sadness, or pain, that accompanies envy has a source different from that of the sadness associated with anger, for example, or with sloth. We understand this intuitively. The envious make an estimation (however erroneous) of their own worth, and are saddened by the good fortune of others insofar as they feel these others are less worthy of good fortune than they. Their sadness depends on what is an extremely abstract, though incorrect, calculation. The sadness of anger, by contrast, comes from suffering, or believing one has suffered, an actual injury. The sadness of sloth is despair at the hopelessness of accomplishing something desired but believed to be out of reach. Of the three sadnesses, this is the most passive, and it leads to further passivity. The sadness of anger is passionate and leads to vigorous, often violent, action. The sadness of envy is cerebral, in a certain sense. In each case the process that terminates in sadness is different, in ways that reflect the fundamentally different structures of the habits of action that define the vices. To conclude that these vices were all vices of the same appetitive faculty, the concupiscible, on the basis of sharing this one emotion would be to confuse vices whose appetitive impulses and structures were fundamentally and significantly different.[54] For this reason, I believe, Dante sought a different principle for associating vices with appetites, one that took more accurate account of the characteristically different objects the appetites have, and reflected more sensitively the characteristically different ways in which they operate on those objects.

For both pride and envy, Dante stresses three aspects of the vices that associate them both intuitively and technically with the will: the interpersonal nature of these vices, the mental calculation that is an essential component of each, and the immaterial nature of the goods that are erroneously pursued by possessors of the vices. The interpersonal dimension is immediately apparent in Virgil's explanations of the natures of the proud and the envious.

> È chi per esser suo vicin soppresso
> spera eccellenza, e sol per questo brama
> ch'el sia di sua grandezza in basso messo:
> è chi podere, grazia, onore e fama
> teme di perder perch'altri sormonti,
> onde s'attrista sì che 'l contrario ama.
> (*Purg.* xvii, 115–20)

Now, Aquinas' definition of pride (common also to other medieval writers) made the vice essentially personal rather than interpersonal, emphasizing the improper *estimation* of one's own worth rather than, as Dante did, the desire to diminish the stature of another: "Pride [*superbia*] is so called because someone willfully strives toward what is above [*supra*] him. . . . But right reason holds that anyone's will should be drawn toward what is proportionate to him" (*ST,* 2a2æ 162, 1).[55] Further: "Humility observes the rule of right reason, according to which a person makes a true estimate of himself [i.e., of his worth]. It is precisely this rule of right reason that pride does not observe, but pride makes people estimate themselves as more than they are" (*ST*, 2a2æ 162, 3, ad 2). Aquinas' definitions do not involve others at all. With respect to envy, Aquinas specifically rejects Virgil's formulation involving imagined threats from others (*ST*, 2a2æ 36, 1), seeing it merely as an inverted concupiscence: "[The envious man] grieves over what he should rejoice at, that is, his neighbor's good" (*ST*, 2a2æ 36, 2).

But Dante's formulation is not unconsidered. Virgil specifically refers to the will to *injure* another as the heart of pride: "È chi per esser suo vicin soppresso / spera eccellenza." The proud wish to injure others pre-emptively, as we would say, to preserve their own position. Dante's purpose in making this claim is to bring the definition of this vice into the realm of injustice. It is distinctly unconventional to conceive of pride as related to injustice, but by making this relation, Dante can link pride to the will. Linking envy to one's fear of another's success is Dante's way of associating that vice too with the realm of injustice and, thereby, with the will. Readers of Dante's text have noticed that the definitions Virgil gives of these two vices tend to muddy the distinctions between them, at least as the vices are conventionally distinguished in other sources.[56] Indeed, this is so. But Dante's purpose in bringing the two definitions so inconveniently close to one another is to stress precisely that the two share characteristics that associate both of them with injustice and the will.[57]

From his very first comment on these vices, Dante stresses two other shared characteristics that link them to the will. On the one hand, he stresses their rational component, for the will is, after all, the intellectual appetite: "O superbi cristian, miseri lassi, / che, della vista della mente infermi, / fidanza avete ne' retrosi passi" (*Purg.* x, 121–23). The envious too are described as having their intelligence clouded: "se tosto grazia resolva le schiume / di vostra cosci̇enza sì che chiaro / per essa scenda della mente il fiume" (*Purg.* xiii, 88–90). (The penance too of the envious suggests an intellectual fault, for it is their sight that undergoes correction, of all senses the least corporeal, and the one most closely tied to the intellect.) On the other, Dante stresses that the goods at which both pride and envy aim are those abstract objects that are in their abstractness essentially associated with the will. While Guido del Duca condemns human striving after goods that cannot be shared—"o gente umana, perchè poni 'l core / là 'v'è mestier di consorte divieto?" (*Purg.* xiv, 86–87)—the goods that Virgil specifically cites as the objects of pride and envy—excellence, privilege, honor, fame, and power (*Purg.* xvii, 116, 118)—are objects rather of the intellectual appetite than of any sensitive appetite, as has been discussed in the previous chapter.[58]

Moreover, an indirect, but significant, confirmation of the intellectuality of pride and envy, and therefore of their association with the will, can be found in the attribution of these vices to the fallen angels and to Satan.[59] Angels have no sensitive appetite, only an intellectual appetite, the will. The fact that they can be vulnerable to these vices at all (and pride is a vice we know to be unequivocally associated with the fallen angels) must imply that the proper subject of these vices is the will. Even Aquinas admits (despite his association elsewhere of envy with the concupiscible appetite) that angels can be afflicted with these vices, and only these vices, as the result of their wholly intellectual nature.

> Only those sins can be in the evil angels by which a spiritual nature can be afflicted. Now, it does not happen that a spiritual nature is affected by goods which are proper to bodies, but only by those which can be found in spiritual things. . . . Whence an angel's first sin cannot be anything other than pride. But, as a consequence of this, it was possible for envy to be in them too. (*ST,* 1a 63, 2)

So too do the individual examples of these vices (or their opposed virtues) confirm for us their association with injustice and with the will. Omberto Aldobrandesco, among the penitent, states that because of his hereditary pride, "non pensando alla comune madre, / ogn'uomo ebbi in despetto" (*Purg.* xi, 63–64). Pride in his family led him so to overestimate his worth as to ignore the common nature that demands that all humans be loved as we love ourselves. Virgil's definition of the proud echoes this injunction by specifically emphasizing the relation to one's neighbor (*vicin; Purg.* xvii, 115–16), rather than the personal estimation involved. Trajan, among the *exempla* of the virtue opposed to the vice of pride (*Purg.* x, 73–93), provides a different sort of confirmation of Dante's linkage of this vice to injustice. While the first two *exempla*, Mary and David, straightforwardly exemplify the virtue or Beatitude opposed to pride, that is, humility, we would be hard pressed to discover any hint of humility in the story of Trajan's conversation with the widow. Rather, the factors—and they must be the operative virtues in this instance—that convince Trajan to assist the widow are justice and pity (*Purg.* x, 93).[60] Virgil appeals to these same qualities—*giustizia e pietà*—at *Purgatorio* xi, 37, in asking the proud for directions to the way to the next *girone*. It will be these qualities, he says, that will allow the proud, once purified, to rise higher on the mountain. It is in associating pride and envy with injustice that Dante effectively assigns them as the capital vices to the will, since, as we have discussed in the first chapter of this essay, justice and injustice are the habits that regulate, well or badly, our relations to others, and therefore if pride and envy are in some way equivalent to injustice as defects in our relations to our neighbors, then they too must be vices of the will.

Just as Dante attributes two vices to the will, he attributes two, anger and sloth, to the irascible appetite. Because the two vices seem so completely different from each other, Dante's rationale for attributing them to the same appetite is not immediately transparent. But the pairing of two such diverse vices in the irascible appetite is reminiscent of the unexpected common substrate of heresy and violence (circles six and seven in Hell). That the vice of anger is a defect of the irascible appetite hardly needs argument. The passion anger is a passion of that appetite, and indeed gives its name to the appetite. A vice of the same name would presumably signify an inappropriate and habitual predilection to that passion, and in most cases, one supposes, acting in response to it. Dante makes a notable effort to indicate that the passion itself is neutral with respect to sin. He alters the text of the Beatitude sung at the exit of this *girone* in order to make clear this very point. "Blessed are the peacemakers," the angel sings, "who are without *sinful* anger" ("che son sanz'ira mala"; *Purg.* xvii, 68–69). The revised Beatitude implies that the *pacifici* are possessed of a good anger, and therefore that the vice must be a disposition to excessive or wrongly directed passion. The goodness of the peacemakers' anger must be that their anger, as a passion, is felt at appropriate moments and to the proper degree. The *pacifici* must be those whose irascible faculty has been virtuously habituated to experience the passion rightly. It is not the passion that defines a vice or virtue, but the standing well or badly with respect to the passion.[61]

> A passion of the sensitive appetite is good to the extent that it is ruled by reason; if it sets aside the order of reason, it is evil. But the order of reason in regard to anger can be considered in two respects. First, with respect to the appetible object toward which it tends, and this is revenge.

Hence, if someone desires to take revenge in accordance with the order of reason, this is a laudable appetite for anger, and is called "zealous anger." If, however, someone desires to take revenge in some way that is opposed to the order of reason (for example, if he desires to punish someone who does not deserve it, or to a greater extent than he deserves, or not following the lawful order, or not for the proper end, which is the preservation of justice and the correction of faults), then this will be a vicious appetite for anger, and is called vicious anger. The second way in which the order of reason in regard to anger can be considered is in respect of the manner of being angry: namely that the movement of anger not burn immoderately, neither internally nor externally; since if this rule be passed over, there can be no anger without sin, even if the person desires a just revenge. (*ST,* 2a2æ 158, 2)[62]

Just as had been the case with the damned in Hell, the location of the penitent in Purgatory reflects Dante's judgment of the culpability of vices from the standpoint of the nature of the appetitive faculty involved, rather than of the consequences for others of the sins or vices. Had we not recognized this previously, the location of the angry in the third *girone* now makes this clear. The viciously angry love the misfortune of others ("'l mal che s'ama è del prossimo"; *Purg.* xvii, 113) just as the proud and envious do. (In some cases, it is probable that the actions undertaken by the proud and envious were as violent as those undertaken by the angry. Indeed, it is possible that someone with the habit of anger might choose expressions of the anger that were not overtly violent, yet would still have to purge this habit in the third *girone.*) But the angry are treated as if they possessed a "lighter" vice than pride or envy, purging it, we see, in a higher *girone,* because in Purgatory defective habits of character that arise under the influence of passions are less culpable (as in Hell had been actions initiated with passion) than those that are defective without such prompting. That is, bad habits of the sensitive appetites, conditioned as they are by the passionate impulses of these appetites, are less culpable than bad habits of the will, whose corruption cannot be attributed to, nor therefore mitigated by, any passion.

In their turn, sins and defective habits of the irascible appetite are more culpable than those of the concupiscible because they depend in part on a kind of judgment or estimation—that an injury, in the case of anger, has been done. Nonetheless, since the passion of anger is so powerful a passion, its capacity to overpower the reason reduces the culpability of sins committed while in its grip. That the *exempla* of the vice of anger and its associated virtue are presented to Dante as ecstatic visions (*Purg.* xv, 85–86) is also probably a narrative reflection of the passionate nature of this appetite. The *exempla* of the first two *gironi* had been mediated by apprehensive faculties, sight or hearing. But the *exempla* of this *girone* appear immediately in the heart and mind, and therefore dramatically testify to the immediacy of the emotions associated with this appetite.

The correction applied to the souls of the angry requires special comment. Those readers who have directly addressed this matter have seen the correction of the angry in smoke as a figurative representation of the vice of the *girone,* just as in an equivalent place in the *Inferno* the violent were punished in flame.[63] Were this the case, it would be the only time in the *Purgatorio* that Dante followed such a procedure (with the possible other exception of the lustful, whom we will consider separately later). In all other *gironi* inside Purgatory, we see those undergoing purgation engaging in virtuous activity to inculcate virtue by repetition. The proud, who would not bow their heads while alive, now are compelled to stoop; the envious, who looked askance at others' good fortune, now cannot look; the slothful, who were slow in their spiritual duties, now hurry to complete them; the gluttonous are placed on a diet. If it is possible to find an interpretation of the smoke by which the angry are purified which proposes the *opposite* of the vice of anger, we know that that would better preserve the consistency of Dante's poetic principles.

It is significant, I believe, that the angry undergo correction in smoke but not in fire. Flame and heat are appropriate metaphors for the *passion* of anger, indeed, and so Dante used them in the *Inferno* for those sins that took their origin in that passion. But here, in the third *girone,* it is noteworthy that Dante mentions neither flame nor heat. It is, rather, another property of smoke to which Dante gives prominence. While smoke is often an accompaniment to fire, it is also a sign of the extinguishing of fire, and this can especially be true of smoke of the sort that Dante here describes: thick, choking, acrid, "a sentir di così aspro pelo; / che l'occhio stare aperto non sofferse" (*Purg.* xvi, 6–7). The figure Dante proposes is one appropriate to the putting out of the flame of anger.[64] This figure of extinguishing is probably further extended by Virgil when he tells Dante that the ecstatic visions that provide the *exempla* of this *girone* are immediate to his mind and heart

so that his heart may be opened to the *water* of peace. It is the quench-
ing of flames of anger that occurs in this *girone:*

> Ciò che vedesti fu perchè non scuse
> d'aprir lo core all'acque della pace
> che dall'etterno fonte son diffuse.
> (*Purg.* xv, 130–32)

Unlike the vices of the will, which are transformed by total eradica-
tion, the vice of anger must be restrained and controlled, though not
eradicated. The vice of anger is the vice of an appetite (and passion)
that can be susceptible to virtuous application, once the operation of
the appetite has been brought under the control of the reason. The
vices of the sensitive appetites are essentially habits of disobedience to
reason. With vices of the will, that is not so. Since the reason itself is
corrupt in their cases, the bad habits that corrupted the will must be
replaced by their opposites. In distinguishing virtuous from vicious
anger, Aquinas states that envy admits of no such distinction:

> Envy specifically implies a certain evil, for it is sadness with respect to
> others' goods, which in and of itself is opposed to reason. . . . But this is
> not the case with anger, which is an appetite for revenge, for it is possible
> to desire revenge both well and badly. (*ST,* 2a2æ 158, 1)

While the vice of anger must be removed, the passion of anger will
not be. Rather, it will be tamed and controlled. For the souls in this
girone, the fires of anger are being taught to go out, and that is why
there are no flames and Dante *personaggio* feels no heat. While there is
no heat in this *girone,* its smoke testifies to the extinguishing of these
fires, and it is the putting out of the flames of anger which makes possible the appearance of a virtuous anger, properly directed, and mod-
erated, or perhaps even without passion. An anger or something like it,
that is, such as God and the angels experience, as Aquinas states,[65] and
at the end of their purgation, according to the angel at the exit of this
girone, also the *pacifici.*

Dante's attribution of the vice of sloth also to the irascible appetite is straightforward as long as we recall that, although the irascible appetite is named for one of its passions, anger, the appetite has
a far more extensive scope. It is the appetite that pursues "arduous"
goods of every sort. The defective habit the slothful are correcting is
their lack of zeal in pursuit of an arduous but most important end. In
medieval psychology, not to pursue a difficult good with sufficient

energy would also have been seen as a defect of irascibility (with associated passions of fear or despair). The difficult end in this case is salvation, and the slothful were negligent in the spiritual duties necessary for its pursuit. Dante's treatment of the slothful is relatively brief, but both his description of them, and the *exempla* of the vice cast the vice (which is often viewed as a purely spiritual failing) in terms that relate it directly to the functions of the irascible appetite. In performing the opposite of their vice which is their purgatorial *contrapasso*, the slothful seem to be gripped by a fervor that recalls the heatedness of much activity occasioned by the irascible appetite: "O gente in cui fervore aguto adesso / ricompie forse negligenza e indugio" (*Purg.* xviii, 106–7). And, in a strategy very like the use of Trajan as an example of the link between humility and justice, Dante's second *exemplum* of the vice is a purely secular example of deficient ardor in the face of difficult goods. The Trojans who would not follow Aeneas lacked in the simplest terms that perseverance that it is one of the functions of the irascible appetite to provide: "quella [gente] che l'affanno non sofferse / fino alla fine" (*Purg.* xviii, 136–37).[66] Through this example, as with Trajan's, Dante links a vice that in the *Purgatorio* has a theological application to the normal functions of a natural appetite.

Although Aquinas made a different association than did Dante, attributing sloth to the concupiscible appetite on the grounds that it is a vice with respect to a passion of the concupiscible appetite, sadness,[67] much in Aquinas can actually be used to support Dante's association with the irascible. Aquinas on other occasions describes the arduousness of the pursuit of spiritual goods, in terms of the sacrifices required,[68] and the fundamental arduousness of these goods as ends, given the impossibility of attaining them without Grace.[69] Perhaps even more clearly, for our purposes, Aquinas admits that the habit of sloth begins in passions of the irascible appetite—faintheartedness and despair—which, given Dante's principle of associating sins and vices with the appetites in which they arise, would firmly associate sloth with the irascible appetite.[70]

> The spiritual goods about which sloth is saddened are both the end and the means to the end. Flight from the end occurs from despair. Flight from those goods which are means to the end (which are matters about which we take counsel), precisely because it is a difficult end, occurs from faintheartedness. (*ST*, 2a2æ 35, 4 ad 2)

Insofar as the slothful may have been motived by despair (up to a point only, of course, else they would have been damned), their defect in regard to irascibility has a marked affinity to the unrepented defect of the heretics in Hell. Indeed, we can now see that the location of the vices anger and sloth essentially mirrors the location of the sins heresy and violence, in Hell, and that this symmetry of location reflects the underlying association of the two vices and two sins with the same appetite.[71]

Attribution of the final three capital vices to the concupiscible appetite surely poses no conceptual problem. This appetite pursues sensible objects that are good simply and are not arduous. These three vices constitute the most commonly recognized defective habitual dispositions of the appetite with respect to these objects, as did the three parallel sins in Hell comprise actions that originated in this appetite as it pursued such objects. Sex and food are the natural objects of the concupiscible appetite. Riches, though conventional rather than natural, provide an intuitive extension to these objects since it is easy to see the avaricious pursuing riches with the same simplicity as the lustful and gluttonous pursue sex and food. An interesting structural detail also reinforces the association of avarice with the concupiscible appetite. For each of the two appetites we have already considered, Dante associated two capital vices with them. For the concupiscible, there are three. But, as we had also noticed, Dante uses the singing of a Beatitude at the exit from a *girone* as an indication of the replacement of the vicious habit by a virtue. For the two *gironi,* five and six, Dante uses but one Beatitude. That is, he takes the Beatitude that begins "Blessed are they who hunger and thirst," and divides it between the two *gironi.* The angel at the exit of the fifth *girone* (of avarice) sings, "Blessed are they who thirst . . ." (*Purg.* xxii, 1–6); the second half of this Beatitude is saved for the gluttonous and is sung by the angel at the exit of the sixth *girone:* "Blessed are they who hunger . . ." (*Purg.* xxiv, 151–54). Literal and transformed gluttony are thereby linked through sharing a Beatitude, and by doing this, Dante also signals that avarice shares with gluttony an underlying, authentically concupiscent nature.[72] Both can be seen as vices of material acquisition, one physical, one conventional.

As noted earlier, the objects of the concupiscible appetite are simple goods and undeniably goods. Its vices, then, do not come from pursuing evils but from the disordered, usually excessive, pursuit of goods, often at the expense of better, spiritual goods.

> Altro ben è che non fa l'uom felice;
> non è felicità, non è la bona
> essenza, d'ogni ben frutto e radice.
> L'amor ch'ad esso troppo s'abbandona,
> di sovr'a noi si piange per tre cerchi.
> (*Purg.* xvii, 133–37)

Since the goods pursued truly are goods, Dante must make an adaptation in the application of Purgatory's *contrapasso*. It would be inappropriate to correct the vice of this appetite by demanding the pursuit of objects that were the opposites of the objects of the vices, for those would be evils, not goods. Nor would it be appropriate to remove the appetite altogether. For the vices of the concupiscible appetite, rather, replacement of vices by virtues requires bringing the operation of the appetite back into its proper measure. The *contrapasso* for two of these *gironi* (of the avaricious and the gluttonous) thus shows us the transformation of vice into virtue being effected by the equivalent of a radical diet regimen. The angel at the exit of the sixth *girone* sings an extended and, as it were, glossed version of the appropriate Beatitude which stresses what it means to reform these habits:

> . . . Beati cui alluma
> tanto di grazia, che l'amor del gusto
> nel petto lor troppo disir non fuma,
> esurïendo sempre quanto è giusto!
> (*Purg.* xxiv, 151–54)

Here, as elsewhere in Purgatory, especially in the *gironi* that are associated with sensitive appetites, the angel indicates that there is a virtuous operation of the appetite, as long as the appetite follows a just measure. Inasmuch as avarice could be considered the most abstract and extensive pursuit of worldly goods, it demands a most complete controlling of its appetite. The ordeal of the avaricious involves the most rigorous diet: having spent all their energy in the pursuit of wealth, they are now physically restrained from pursuit of anything:

> Come avarizia spense a ciascun bene
> lo nostro amore, onde operar perdèsi,
> così giustizia qui stretti ne tene,
> ne' piedi e nelle man legati e presi;
> e quanto fia piacer del giusto sire,
> tanto staremo immobili e distesi.
> (*Purg.* xix, 121–26)

Having valued dust too much, they recognize now that it is only dust. The penitent souls cleave to dust gladly, since they know that by cleaving to dust they are reorienting their appetite by turning away from what they had done in the past, that is, cleaving to other more esteemed (but no less ephemeral) objects. In the words of the Psalm to which Dante alludes in this episode ("Adhæsit pavimento anima mea"; *Purg.* xix, 73, which is equivalent to Ps. 119 [118]:25), these souls pray that their hearts be turned from avarice and vanity to the way to God: "Inclina cor meum in testimonia tua et non in avaritiam. Averte oculos meos ne videant vanitatem, in via tua vivifica me" (Ps. 119 [118]:36–37).[73] The hearts of the avaricious will still yearn after objects—the appetite is not being eliminated but reordered—but they will be spiritual, not worldly objects. In a similar way, the gluttonous retrain their appetite by allowing it to operate, yet frustrating its end (*Purg.* xxiii, 61–72; xxiv, 103–14). They hunger for food but are kept from it, so that over time their souls, like those of the avaricious, will come no longer to desire it but will desire spiritual sustenance instead. At that point, their appetite will have been rehabituated, and a new virtue will have replaced the vice of gluttony.

The *contrapasso* of the lustful also stresses reformation, though this is initially obscured or treated ambiguously because of the special problems of finding appropriate poetic figures for the vice in connection with its opposed virtue. After all, one cannot say that love, even improper love, should be reformed by the opposite of love. That would clearly be wrong. Love could only be reformed by love. In poetic terms, virtue and vice are here hard to distinguish. And so Dante exploits the multivalence of the metaphor of fire to indicate this near paradox. Fire is used frequently enough, even by Dante in certain instances, as a metaphor of passion. Thus, in some contexts there would be nothing unexpected in using the image of fire to represent the passions associated with lust. But fire has so many associations attached to it that it can be used as a metaphor for other qualities as well. The fire of the seventh *girone* does not represent passion and therefore vice. This fire is a figure for the correcting and refining fire of charity, which removes the impurity of lust from these souls, and leaves in its place not lust but love. Since charity is also love, fire is as metaphorically appropriate to it as it also is to carnal love. At the same time, however, we call easily to mind the refiner's fire (echoed in the accompanying Beatitude, "Blessed are the pure of heart" [*Purg.* xxvii, 8]), and therefore the replacement of this vice by a purified virtue.[74] For the lustful too, then, there is a *contrapasso* that does not entail either the opposite of the appetite, or its suppression, but its transformation through an appropriate regimen. Dante describes the effect of these flames as a cure *(tal cura)* and a diet *(tai pasti)* by which the final wound on their souls is healed (*Purg.* xxv, 138–39).

One of the continually impressive qualities of Dante's creative gift is the way in which the selection of the most effective poetic solutions likewise corresponds to the theological orderliness that Dante also sought. From the standpoint of poetry, Dante's selection of the appetites, their habits and actions, for the organizations of Hell and Purgatory provided a system more intuitive, more concrete, and more consistent than alternative philosophical structures. But choosing this poetically straightforward order had a secondary, and surely not insignificant, result on the purely doctrinal, and not poetic, level. Dante presents the capital vices to us in an order that completely follows that of Gregory (in whose writings they were first codified) and of most medieval authorities.[75] But while this was the received order of the vices, and while there was also a received general sense that the list generally progressed from the worst vice to those of lesser gravity, no medieval authority in fact proposed what might be the principled basis for the specific order in which the vices appeared in the list. (Gregory had described how each subsequent vice was derived for the one preceding, but hardly in a principled way.) In addition to its poetic utility, then, Dante's association of the vices with the appetites supplied an explanation for the otherwise unexplained order of the capital vices: as Dante understood the subjects of these vices (that is, the appetites of which they are vices), the seven capital vices fall naturally into this order because this order—though only for Dante; not for those who associate the vices with appetites different from those he does—follows the natural order of the appetites and therefore of the proper humanity and seriousness of the actions and dispositions that belong to them.[76]

Virgil's words to Dante at the end of canto xxvii—his last words to him, as we later discover—summarize the rehabilitative aspects of Purgatory. Dante *personaggio*, standing for the souls of the dead who have also ascended this mountain, has not merely paid some price for his sins and vices, he has, more importantly, transformed himself and his soul's powers:

Non aspettar mio dir più nè mio cenno:
libero, dritto e sano è tuo arbitrio,
e fallo fora non fare a suo senno:
per ch' io te sovra te corono e mitrio.
(*Purg.* xxvii, 139–42)

Healthy, for vices are diseases or wounds of the soul (*Purg.* ii, 122; *Purg.* ix, 113–14; *Purg.* xv, 80; *Purg.* xxv, 139); upright or straight, for what was bent has been straightened by the application of contrary cures; and free, for the virtuous state of a soul is also its liberation from impulses that enslave it by compelling it to act in ways fundamentally opposed to its nature. When Virgil crowns Dante as sovereign of himself, this autonomy is precisely the condition of the virtuous man, and that has been the goal and purpose of the journey through Purgatory (*Purg.* i, 71).

The geographies of Hell and Purgatory indicate the condition of the soul as represented by a specific location. As we approach the end of the narrative of the *Purgatorio*, Dante's spatial location again corresponds to his emphasis on rehabilitation, by stressing the symmetry of the first two *cantiche* of the *Commedia*. Having awakened, at the beginning of the poem, lost to sin in a dark wood, and having had to cross a river into Hell to make his way back, at the end of the *Purgatorio* the poet describes himself as freeing himself from the vices that enslaved him by way of another dark wood, and across another river, in order to reach a new location, the terrestrial paradise, representing the state of the sinlessness of mankind. This paradise is not merely the place that Adam and Eve inhabited before having committed their sin. More importantly, while they inhabited it, they were still perfect for the function for which they had been created. Vices and other spiritual defects entered human life only after that sin.[77] When Dante *personaggio* enters this paradise he has not merely been forgiven his sins (it is likely that that took place, allegorically, when he emerged into Purgatory at the beginning of the *Purgatorio*, and was indicated to us poetically both by his rebaptism by Virgil [*Purg.* i, 121–29] and by his admission to Purgatory proper in canto ix); his soul has in fact been cleansed of the vices that lead to sin. Thus, Dante (or any other purified soul) emerges into the terrestrial paradise in the same perfect state that Adam and Eve had originally possessed there. For Dante *personaggio*, therefore, having descended into a state of sin, he has now climbed back out of it, and, from a *human* perspective, his journey is in fact complete at this moment. The purely human dimension of the poem is exhausted in the symmetry that exists between Hell and Purgatory. Purgatory undoes the damage that was done the soul by the vices that led to the sins we see punished and explained in Hell. But that the poem is meant to have a dimension beyond the human is what accounts for the fact that the *Commedia* does not end with the *Purgatorio,* even though it could be said that at this moment the salvation of Dante's soul—Beatrice's motive in sending Virgil to aid Dante—has been accomplished. And that the poem has a dimension beyond the human also compels us to make a critical reconsideration of the significance of the purgatorial journey we have witnessed.

PART II

PURGATORY IN THE LIGHT OF HEAVEN

Virtues and the Afterlife

The very solutions we have reached in the first part of this chapter create, or uncover, a new problem for us. At the beginning of the chapter I had said a moment would come at which we would have to reinterpret all of the conclusions we had reached to that point. This is the moment. Indeed, the need for reinterpretation at this moment is very much part of Dante's overall poetic strategy in the *Commedia.* For the souls Dante encounters, Purgatory is a place of transition and transformation; for us his readers, the *Purgatorio* fulfills much the same function within our understanding of the poem.[78]

The symmetry we have discovered in the structures of the *Inferno* and the *Purgatorio* is fundamental to Dante's exposition, and to our initial understanding, of the nature of sin and of how to avoid sin. Since sinful actions have their origin in appetites, and vicious habits their residence in them, philosophical consistency requires that the two realms be symmetrical. But poetic effectiveness militates for this symmetry too. The initial suggestion of symmetry in the narrative details of Hell and Purgatory is what urged, and encouraged, us to look for a principle that could explain the symmetry. It is thus that we discovered the appetitive conception of the nature of action which underlies both regions and informs the symmetry. At the same time, the apparent inconsistencies between the two realms spurred us to other considerations, compelling us to recognize the real but complicated relationship that obtains between habits and actions. The existence and embodiment of the underlying structure common to both *cantiche* makes the reader's discovery of Dante's principles of action possible. Yet, however far we have come, we cannot stop at this point, nor does Dante wish us to, for of course the *Commedia* does not stop here either.

It might appear, at first, that we could stop here, for as we noted at the end of the previous section, the purpose of Dante's journey is apparently accomplished at the end of the *Purgatorio*. For his part, Dante *personaggio* has been cleansed of the sins that would have otherwise doomed him; for our parts, we have seen the undoing in Purgatory of the evil acts of Hell and through this symmetry have come to understand the basis both of sin and of pious action. Yet the specific content of this solution, in the context of the poetic details of the poem and the explanations Dante gives of them, creates a new problem of primary and overriding significance.

That Dante designates disorders of the appetitive faculties as the source of vices and sins is manifestly relevant to pious action in this world, and to salvation. Medieval interpretations of Aristotelian ethics stressed the goal of bringing the appetitive powers into properly orderly operation. But the relevance of this structure to the penitent souls Dante encounters in Purgatory (and even, in a sense, to the damned souls in Hell) is not at all manifest. The recovery of the health of his own faculties is indubitably valuable to Dante *personaggio*, who can now return to the world able to act without sin; understood allegorically, this same account would be equally valuable to Dante's readers, who also must live and act in the world. For both Dante and his readers, knowing the appetitive nature of action is an aid to good action, insofar as it maps out for us what vices must be avoided or cured to avoid the sinful acts that might be obstacles to salvation. But the same most definitively cannot be said of the souls of Purgatory. They are not returning to the world of action. The narrative insists that their rehabilitation is for the sake of their entry into Heaven. But to say this is to pose two momentous questions.

On the one hand, in what way would these souls need rectification of their appetitive faculties for their lives in Heaven? Rectification of the appetites by which action is initiated in this world scarcely seems relevant to that new life. These appetitive faculties would seem to have to disappear, and even their virtues with them, for want of any function to perform in Heaven.

> And so we must say that moral virtues of this sort will not endure in the future life as far as concerns what is material in them, for there will be no place in the future life for concupiscences, or the delights of food or sex; nor will there be fear or daring regarding the danger of death; nor distributions of nor commerce in things which are employed in this life. (*ST*, 1a2æ 67, 1)

Just as importantly, and far more troubling, it is not even clear that these souls continue to possess appetitive faculties that might require purification. Indeed, the medieval Aristotelian tradition that Dante uses so extensively denied that the sensitive appetites endured beyond the grave. All that could be eternal in a human soul, according to this tradition, were its intellectual faculties, reason and will foremost among them. The sensitive faculties (whether of apprehension, as the five senses, or of appetition, the concupiscible and irascible appetites) would, because of their dependence on the body, have to disappear almost entirely with the body's death. And, as they perished, so did their virtues.

> All the powers of the soul are related to the soul itself as to their principle. But for some powers, their relation is to the soul alone as their subject. Such is the case for the intellect and will, and powers of this sort necessarily remain in the soul even after the body is destroyed. Other powers, however, have their subject in the conjoined soul and body, as is the case for all of the powers of the sensitive and nutritive parts. When the subject is destroyed, accidents cannot continue to exist. Therefore, once the conjoined [soul and body] is destroyed, powers of this sort do not remain actually, but remain only virtually in the soul, as in their principle or root. So it is false to say that powers of this sort remain in the soul even after the destruction of the body; and it is even more false to say that the actualities of these powers remain in the separated soul, because such powers have no actuality except through bodily organs. (*ST*, 1a 77, 8)[79]

As we read the *Purgatorio,* our first impression is that Dante seems to accept this view of the endurance of human faculties. When Statius explains to Dante about the quieting of the sensitive faculties at death, he uses terms that are very close to Aquinas' concerning what endures, and in what state.

> Quando Lachèsis non ha più del lino,
>   solvesi [l'anima] dalla carne, ed in virtute
>   ne porta seco e l'umano e 'l divino:

l'altre potenze tutte quante mute;
memoria, intelligenza e volontade
in atto molto più che prima agute.
(*Purg.* xxv, 79–84)

Memory, intelligence, and will—all of them intellectual faculties—
become more acute at death, with the muting of the "other" powers, by
which are meant, presumably, the sensitive powers of apprehension
and appetition. The *in virtute* that expresses how the faculties endure
in the soul separated from its body seems to echo Aquinas' declaration
that the sensitive powers exist after death only "virtually" (*virtute tan-
tum*), as a root. At first glance, this appears a properly Aristotelian or
Thomistic interpretation.[80] But his statement that both the human *and*
the divine parts of the soul survive *in virtute* suggests that Dante's interpretation of his Aristotelian authorities cannot be exactly orthodox.
If we assume, as most readers do, that by the "human" part Dante
means the sensitive faculties of the soul, and by the "divine" the intellectual, then it is not clear why the divine part is said to be there only
virtually.[81] Nor, for that matter, is it exactly orthodox to call the sensitive appetites "human." They are in fact, as Statius also acknowledges
in a passage we will consider in the next section of this chapter (*Par.*
xxv, 52–60), faculties we share with all other animals.

These are merely semantic indications that Dante's understanding
of how faculties endure in the separated soul diverges from standard
medieval interpretations. Far more serious evidence is found in the
content of the narrative of the *Purgatorio,* for Dante consistently presents us with incidents not only in which do souls undergoing purgation seem to be acting in ways firmly associated with the sensitive
appetites, but in which the reformation of these appetites is the explicit purpose of the ordeals the souls undergo. Even Statius' declaration about the muting of faculties, which seems so consistent with
standard interpretations, is made in response to a question by Dante
(*Purg.* xxv, 20–21) concerning how it could be possible for the souls of
the gluttonous—being incorporeal, after all—to show the effects of the
starvation diet that is reforming them. Dante himself, that is, calls
attention to the supposed axiom of the falling away of the sensitive
faculties at death, and elicits an answer from Statius that makes an explicit declaration that no sooner has the soul been liberated from both
body and the sensitive faculties than it recreates both a surrogate body
and what appear to be those same faculties!

> Tosto che loco lì la circunscrive,
> > la virtù informativa raggia intorno
> > così e quanto nelle membra vive:
> e come l'aere, quand'è ben pïorno,
> > per l'altrui raggio che 'n sè si reflette,
> > di diversi color diventa adorno;
> così l'aere vicin quivi si mette
> > in quella forma che in lui suggella
> > virtüalmente l'alma che ristette;
> e simigliante poi alla fiammella
> > che segue il foco là 'vunque si muta,
> > segue lo spirto sua forma novella.
> > > (*Purg.* xxv, 88–99)[82]

The identical formative power of the soul which first articulated a body and its powers in flesh, after death does so in the air; and as the desires and passions of the soul were executed and exhibited in this life through and in the body, so are they after death in this aerial body.[83]

> Però che quindi ha poscia sua paruta,
> > è chiamata ombra; e quindi organa poi
> > ciascun sentire infino alla veduta.
> Quindi parliamo e quindi ridiam noi;
> > quindi facciam le lacrime e' sospiri
> > che per lo monte aver sentiti puoi.
> Secondo che ci affiggono i disiri
> > e li altri affetti, l'ombra si figura;
> > e quest'è la cagion di che tu miri.
> > > (*Purg.* xxv, 100–08)

The aerial body is created by a soul in Purgatory precisely to allow for the reformation of the soul's faculties; and Statius is explicit that it is specifically the appetitive faculties that are the subjects of this reformation. He speaks of the aerial body reflecting desires (*disiri*) and passions (*affetti*), which we know can be experienced only through the appetites. There is nothing here about the rehabilitation of any of the apprehensive or purely reasoning faculties. Statius never speaks of a rectification of the memory or the intellect, nor would an aerial *body* be needed for those faculties.

Equally unconventional with his apparent insistence on the endurance of the sensitive appetites after death is Dante's description of the state of the soul once it has purged its vices. The narrative of the *Purgatorio* makes clear that as each vice is removed from a soul, the soul comes into the possession of a Beatitude that is the opposite of the vice. (More properly, as noted above, we should say that the soul is in a condition that would allow it to actualize that Beatitude, once arrived in Heaven.) But within classical and medieval discussions of morality, the three appetitive faculties had vices and virtues that were natural to them, but these standard virtues are emphatically *not* the six Beatitudes that Dante stretches to serve as the opposites of the seven capital vices. (For that matter, of course, neither were the seven capital vices the natural vices of the three appetites.) The primary natural virtue and vice of the will, according to conventional systems of ethics, were justice and injustice; of the irascible appetite, courage and cowardice; of the concupiscible, temperance and intemperance. But these three cardinal virtues (justice, courage, temperance) are nowhere to be seen in the *Purgatorio.* Or, rather, they are only to be seen in a number of *exempla,* as a way of suggesting to us that a link exists between the conventional virtues of the appetitive faculties and the Beatitudes with which Dante replaces them. As we look at the whole of the *Purgatorio,* we recognize that while Dante sees the purgatorial process as one of replacing vices with virtues, he is at the same time deliberately substituting a new set of virtues for an older one. That substitution is at the heart of the transformation of our interpretation of the meaning of the symmetry that exists between the first two *cantiche* of the poem. It begins to suggest how the reformation of the appetitive faculties might be important to the life of the soul in Heaven, and it begins to suggest that the faculties that are undergoing reformation may be different from what we first believed them to be.

Though Hell and Purgatory are both organized by the appetitive faculties, their orientations, we might say, are different. Hell punishes actions of this world, and the appetites as we understand them in the *Inferno* are our natural appetites. In Purgatory it is the vices of these same appetitive faculties which must be transformed into virtues, but Purgatory is oriented to the life of Heaven, not the earth. The virtues of a life in this world are not appropriate for the life of Heaven.[84] As we have already mentioned, there is no need for courage or temperance in Heaven, at least not in their usual or proper forms. And so, those cardinal virtues that prepare the human soul for perfect operation in regard to its actions in this world are likely to be irrelevant or insufficient to perfect the soul for the new operations it will be called upon to perform in Heaven. If Purgatory is to transform souls appropriately for

their future (and not merely demand some accounting for sins committed in the past)—and Dante repeatedly stresses that this is the purpose of the rehabilitation undergone in Purgatory—it must somehow
transform mundane vices not merely into their conventional counterparts, the mundane virtues, but into ultramundane virtues.

When Dante links the Beatitudes to the three appetitive faculties,
and indicates at the exit of each *girone* that the soul has acquired a
Beatitude rather than one of the cardinal virtues, it is clear that he intends the Beatitudes to fulfill this role of ultramundane virtues.[85] They
will replace the cardinal virtues, whose only proper field of activity was
this world, with new habits that dispose the soul to action that is not of
this world. An equivalent conceptual role had been played, though
negatively, by the seven capital vices. The seven vices are themselves
different from the conventional vices of the three appetites. They are
not the dispositions of natural powers which incline the powers to defective operations in this world. Rather, they are specifically the faulty
habits that would keep the soul from successfully rising to, and performing in, the next world. They are vices of the soul not from the perspective of morals, but from the perspective of salvation.[86]

The matching pairs of the seven capital vices and Beatitudes are the
poetic means Dante uses in the *Purgatorio* to direct us to transform
our understanding of the soul in a way equivalent to the transformation Purgatory itself is intended to accomplish on the souls who pass
through it. Neither the capital vices nor the Beatitudes are the "proper"
or natural vices or virtues of their appetitive powers. But powers may
be perfected by multiple virtues, if they have multiple purposes to fulfill. The cardinal virtues perfect the soul for actions of this world, the
Beatitudes for actions of the next. If courage, temperance, and justice
do not prepare us for life in Heaven, it is also the case that humility,
piety, gentleness, and zeal do little to prepare us for a natural life in
this world. Yet these qualities, celebrated by the Beatitudes, and used
by Dante as a new set of virtues, are explicitly the qualities that are
required for the ability to reach Heaven and to live our lives there.[87]
Thus, in using the Beatitudes as virtues, Dante compels us to begin to
consider what will be the action of the soul in Heaven, and what powers and dispositions it must possess to act successfully, and therefore
blessedly, there. We know that the qualities celebrated in the Beatitudes
are aimed at activity in Heaven, rather than in this world, because
those who possess them are not only said to be happy (the goal of the

cardinal virtues of philosophers and of our natural lives) but are said to be blessed. But Dante goes further than this. Up to this moment, we have believed the Beatitudes were habits perfecting our three appetites. But if the Beatitudes are to be habits to perfect powers for their heavenly operation, they must be habits of powers that endure and operate in Heaven. That they must be compels us to consider the powers of which they are the habits in a strikingly new light.

The Origin of the Soul and the Endurance of the Soul's Powers after Death

The purpose of a virtue is to dispose its power to proper operation, and the Beatitudes are acquired, as ultramundane virtues, for operations not of this life but of the next. Since the Beatitudes are virtues for the operations of separated souls in Heaven, they must therefore be virtues of faculties that themselves endure in Heaven, after the soul has been separated from its body. But five of the seven capital vices the Beatitudes replace were vices of two faculties—that is, of the two sensitive appetites—that would not conventionally have been believed to endure in the separated soul. How can the Beatitudes perfect the soul for action in Heaven if they perfect powers that the soul does not possess or use in Heaven? That is the central problem of the *Purgatorio*, and its solution alters utterly our understanding of the human soul and its faculties.

When, in Purgatory and with a view to action in Heaven, a Beatitude replaces a vice of any of the appetitive faculties, Dante is asserting that the faculty that receives the Beatitude continues in operation in the life of the soul in Heaven.[88] The crux of the problem is that every authority whom Dante is likely to have consulted would have argued that the life of Heaven is an intellectual life, not a sensitive one. As we have already considered, the same authorities would further argue that the sensitive appetites, being powers that depend on sensitive apprehension, and that accomplish their ends in the management of corporeal organs, themselves die with the body, and neither they nor their virtues survive in the separated soul. Thus, they ought not to be capable of being the faculties that are the subjects of virtues of operation for the separated soul.

Yet Dante not only insists that the Beatitudes replace the capital vices (and must they not, then, have a common substrate?), but, as we not only see in incidents in the *Purgatorio* but have specifically explained to us, he also insists that the souls of the dead recreate aerial versions of their corporeal organs, through which what appear to us to be sensitive powers continue to operate, act, and suffer in Purgatory. It is these powers, apparently, that acquire the Beatitudes when their vicious habits are corrected. That Dante was acutely aware of how paradoxical and problematic these descriptions are is proved to us by the length and care he gives to their explanation. Indeed, the paradox of immaterial souls suffering corporeal pain is one that Dante himself draws attention to, and makes into an explicit subject within the literal narrative of the poem. On reflection, that was an extraordinary thing to do. Had he not called attention to it, we readers would surely have forgiven it, dismissing it as a simple poetic necessity: "What else could he do, after all, but make immaterial sufferings visible by materializing them?" But Dante rubs our noses in the paradox and finally, within the narrative, demands his own explanation of it. The calling attention, of course, is for the sake of this explanation, for it is the explanation— the very fact that Dante takes the paradox seriously, as a truth of the afterlife—that points to its more extensive significance.

The moment that Dante chooses to address the paradox is, from a poetic point of view, surprisingly late in the *Commedia,* and that late location is itself significant. The occasion is Dante's surprise at the apparent emaciation of the souls of the gluttons whom he, Virgil, and Statius have just left in the sixth *girone* (*Purg.* xxv, 19–108). So starved have the gluttons been by their diet that their bodies have wasted almost entirely away. Suddenly, the absurdity of the situation seems finally to strike Dante: they have no bodies that could be wasting away! ("Come si può far magro / là dove l'uopo di nodrir non tocca?" [*Purg.* xxv, 20–21].) As soon as the question is raised, it calls into doubt the narrative reality of all the sufferings we have encountered, whether the eternal torments of the damned or the corrections of the saved. None of the dead sinners possesses a body, yet all undergo what appear to be corporeal sufferings. Poetically, Dante might simply never have raised the question. To ask the question, though, and thereby to make necessary an answer, is to take the question seriously, not as a matter of metaphor but as a natural phenomenon of the supernatural world. It will receive from Dante not merely a poetic apology or pretense but a theological explanation.

The moment at which Dante raises the question is no accident, but is itself a clue to the application and significance of the answer. After all, this question might well have been raised at any moment from the time that Virgil and Dante crossed through the gates of Hell and encountered the first souls in its vestibule.[89] And since most readers, in fact, ask themselves the question from early on in the poem, had Dante's motive been simply to quiet our aesthetic doubts, he would have done better to have raised this question and given us its answer as early as possible in the *Inferno*. While the gluttonous provide a striking example of the underlying paradox, many other incidents do too, especially incidents in the *Inferno*. But the moment at which Dante does raise and deal with the issue is cannily chosen. It comes just at the moment at which we must transform our understanding of action and suffering from models appropriate to this world to models appropriate to the next.

Once Dante moves the poem from Purgatory to Heaven any questions regarding what of human nature persists into Heaven, and how that nature operates in its blessed life should already have been settled. The paradoxes and problems regarding the Beatitudes as virtues, with which we began this section, constitute part of these questions to be resolved. Dante chooses the gluttonous as the opportunity for his explanation because they provide the last unambiguous example of an apparently corporeal ordeal before he leaves Purgatory and enters Heaven, and the explanation we receive here from Statius serves to reorient our thinking with regard to action in this life and the next, and the faculties by which we engage in action. (I stress that this is the last *unambiguous* opportunity. We might think it would have been better to have given the explanation in the very last *girone* of Purgatory rather than in the next to last. But I believe Dante may well have been afraid that we would doubt the actual physicality of the fire in which the lustful are purged. Were we to think that fire was a spiritual fire, we would not interpret their ordeal as exhibiting this central paradox. By contrast, the loss of "weight" by those who have none to start with is unequivocally paradoxical.)

Thus, it is clearly deliberate that we get Dante's solution to this paradox not at the first moment when we might have wanted it to understand what is going on in Hell and Purgatory; we get the explanation at the last possible moment in which we might think the souls still possessed bodies, in order to explain something about what we will see in Heaven where souls most definitively do not have bodies.

The particular solution Dante proposes in the voice of Statius is in fact meant to complete our reorientation from faculties and virtues of this world to faculties and virtues of the next, and to resolve the problem of which faculties it is that have the Beatitudes as their virtues by explaining to us what it is about the human soul that endures after death. In formulating his solution Dante relies on familiar philosophical and theological authorities, but interprets them in a unique way, consistent with the letter of what they have said but manifesting a whole new spirit than would have conventionally been discovered in these texts.

Statius' explanation of the phenomena Dante has seen, not only in the sixth *girone* but throughout Hell and Purgatory, has two quite distinct parts. One part, which we have already cited in the preceding section of this chapter, describes the recreation of aerial bodies by the souls after death (*Purg.* xxv, 79–108). This is the only part of his explanation that is actually a direct answer to the question that Dante *personaggio* had asked. But before Statius gives Dante this answer, he precedes it with an even longer description of the origin of the human soul (*Purg.* xxv, 34–78), presumably because Dante *poeta* believed that the explanation of the aerial bodies could be properly understood only by first understanding the origin and nature of the soul. Much has been written concerning Statius' account of the origin of the soul, and all commentators have recognized that the very length of the account, as well as its clear references back to philosophical and theological sources on the question, indicates the importance Dante felt should be given to it.[90] Yet none of the many studies has explained what makes this account relevant to the question Dante had originally asked or the direction he intended to go with its answer.

Statius' account of the natural history of the human soul is even more controversial than his explanation of the creation of those aerial bodies that had confused Dante and led to this discussion.[91] Since I believe that Dante knew he was constructing a novel interpretation of his sources and a novel explanation of the nature of the human soul, I also believe he was perfectly aware how controversial his account was. But the account he constructed was adapted precisely to the paradoxical phenomenon he was attempting to explain. Since the souls of the gluttonous that are the occasion of Dante's question are immortal souls separated from their original, material bodies, the powers that we see operating in them in Purgatory (as well, of course, as in the souls in Hell and Heaven) must perforce be powers that, by their spiritual and incorporeal nature, are immortal and capable of enduring in the separated soul. But throughout the first two *cantiche* (including here with the gluttons), Dante has shown us image after image in which souls after death seem still capable of suffering passions that we recognize as appetitive passions. Moreover, in the *Purgatorio* it appears that the apparently appetitive faculties to which these passions belong must undergo rectification to prepare the soul for action in Heaven. What we have consistently been shown, and what Statius' explanation of the aerial bodies seems to confirm, is that even the separated soul was capable of functions that at least resemble appetitive operations. Statius' explanation of the origin of the soul demonstrates that these incidents were not merely poetic figures. It is not for poetic convenience only that Dante shows souls acting in apparently appetitive ways; he believed that they did. The account of the origin of the soul was constructed in the way it was precisely to explain how and why even the separated soul could exhibit such operations.

Within Statius' account, the history of any human soul has two distinct stages, and the fact that it does is both the source of the theological paradox Dante is exploring and also the source of its solution. The first stage is wholly natural, in which the soul develops in exactly the same way that the soul of any other animal develops. When that first stage is complete, and the embryo has accomplished this purely animal development, a second, decisive moment occurs, unique to human beings and precisely what distinguishes them from animals. At this second stage, and by direct divine intervention, what had previously been essentially an animal soul is now made essentially human. The controversial aspects of Dante's explanation, and its novelty, focus on the related issues of the status of the soon-to-be human soul prior to the second stage, and of the manner of change wrought on the embryonic soul by the moment of divine intervention.

The beginning of Statius' account, of the first stage of the development of the soul, describes activities of the human soul that are common in every respect to the development of the souls of all other animals. The origin of the soul follows that of the conception and growth of any animal soul, an origin and growth that is wholly corporeal. The human soul itself, therefore, is in its earliest stages wholly corporeal. As formal and efficient cause of the life of the animal that, in this case, will eventually be a child, the soul begins as a material biological entity formed in the blood of its father. As was conventional in ancient and medieval physiology, the mother provides the matter this soul will animate and organize.

> Sangue perfetto, che mai non si beve
>   dall'assetate vene, e si rimane
>   quasi alimento che di mensa leve,
> prende nel core a tutte membra umane
>   virtute informativa, come quello
>   ch'a farsi quelle per le vene vane.
> Ancor digesto, scende ov'è più bello
>   tacer che dire; e quindi poscia geme
>   sovr'altrui sangue in natural vasello.
>   (*Purg.* xxv, 37–45)

Once joined in the womb to its matter, the soul impresses on the matter the physical form of the body for which it is the soul, as well as the functional forms of, and organs for, the faculties it must possess to live. This, indeed, is the nature and purpose of the soul of a living organism, and it is by its organization of the creature's powers that the soul makes it possible for the creature to live. It is the capacity of the soul to perform this formative function—or, more precisely, as we shall see, a transformed version of the capacity—that Statius will later say the soul exercises after death in the creation of an aerial body.

> Anima fatta la virtute attiva
>   qual d'una pianta, in tanto differente,
>   che questa è in via e quella è già a riva,
> tanto ovra poi, che già si move e sente,
>   come fungo marino; e indi imprende
>   ad organar le posse ond'è semente.
> Or si spiega, figliuolo, or si distende
>   la virtù ch'è dal cor del generante,
>   dove natura a tutte membra intende.
>   (*Purg.* xxv, 52–60)[92]

This soul is a complete soul, and the embryo it has informed is a complete and perfect embryo, except that neither is yet human. Statius makes that explicit in the verse that immediately follows the verses cited above, when he says that he knows that at this point Dante will want to know what it is that can make what is merely animal human: "come d'animal divenga fante" (*Purg.* xxv, 61). The stages that Statius has described, from conception through to the articulation of all members and organs, are those of the development of a perfect *animal*.[93]

The embryonic soul has followed the stages of animal growth and has brought them to completion. But all of these stages have been wholly corporeal, as is the soul that has performed them also therefore corporeal. This indeed is one of the reasons that this soul is not yet human. Nothing in this soul is yet intellectual, and therefore nothing in it is immortal. If this were a human soul, the human soul would be mortal.

But while Statius stresses that the soul of this embryo is still short of being human, he also stresses that this soul is not a vegetable soul but an animal soul. The meaning of the distinction would be clear in the context of medieval science, though at this moment in the *Commedia* it also takes on a significance beyond the merely scientific. The first of the soul's functions can be seen as purely vegetative; that is, nutrition and growth, functions that not only do humans share with animals, but animals share with plants. But, as Statius puts it, this embryo's soul does not exercise these functions the way a plant does but the way an animal (that is, a creature "che già si move e sente") does. For a plant, these functions are the fulfillment of the sum total of its soul's capacities and the completion of its purpose; the plant is *già a riva*. An animal's soul carries out these functions merely instrumentally in support of its proper functions of movement and sensation. For an animal, these functions are only *in via*.

The significance of the distinction is tied to a second Aristotelian and neo-Aristotelian scientific principle: that any living creature possesses one, and only one, soul. Any living thing can have only one substantial form, and since the soul of a living creature is its substantial form, any creature can have only a single soul.

> First, an animal would not be one absolutely in which there were several souls. For nothing is one absolutely except because of its single form, through which the thing has its being. (*ST,* 1a 76, 3)[94]

This is also the position that Statius enunciates, stressing that even at its final stage of development the human soul is a single soul ("un'alma sola"; *Purg.* xxv, 74). Indeed, the unity of the soul was a question Dante felt it important enough not only to raise explicitly here, but to have mentioned twice before in Purgatory (perhaps as a sort of empirical preparation for this discussion: *Purg.* iv, 1–6; *Purg.* xvii, 19–24).[95] The question arises in the first place, as Statius alludes to here, from recognizing that even the simplest of animals exercises functions that are different from, and supplemental to, the functions of a plant, which is an even simpler living thing. The functions of growth and reproduction are the total life of a plant, Statius reminds us; its soul is the formal cause of those functions and that life. Animals perform these functions, but also functions of apprehension and movement (*Purg.* xxv, 52–57). Ought one therefore to say that animals have two souls, since, on the one hand, they have the capacity to perform the vegetative functions (and to articulate faculties to perform them), but, on the other, they also perform functions of sensation and movement, which necessarily require an informing cause different from the simply vegetative? For medieval Aristotelians, the answer to this question was No, and it is this answer that Statius gives.

It is impossible that an animal have two souls—an animal soul superadded to a vegetable soul. No creature can have more than a single soul. An animal, therefore, must have an animal soul capable of also performing the functions of the vegetable soul.[96] This is what Statius says by implication when he says that, though the embryonic soul in its very first operations *(anima fatta)* performs only vegetative functions, it does so not as a plant does but as an animal. It has not added an animal soul to a prior vegetative soul. This embryo has always had an animal soul, as a direct result of its genetic history. Since the soul takes its nature from what has generated it, this soul, having been formed from the blood of its father, inherits the material, animal nature of its father. An animal soul is thus always an animal soul; and even when it performs vegetative functions, it does so as an animal function.

> So, therefore, the vegetative [soul] which exists apart from a sensitive soul is a different species of soul [from the sensitive], and has a different productive cause. However, there is the very same productive cause for both the sensitive [soul] and the vegetative [power] that exists in a sensitive soul.[97]

When Statius says that the embryonic soul performs animal functions in the manner of a sponge ("come fungo marino" [*Purg.* xxv, 56]), he no doubt is pointing out that the animal functions of the embryo are decidedly modest at this stage. But his comparison also simultaneously declares that, however modest, this soul is operating in a way distinct from the operation of a plant's soul. Even the humblest animal is capable of performing two sorts of function, vegetative and sensitive. No plant can do more than the vegetative function.

It is not, of course, animals and plants that are at issue in this discussion. While the question whether the soul of complex living creatures is single or consists of multiple souls arises first—and least controversially—in regard to animals, its most complete expression (and the reason for our interest in it) is encountered in the problem of the integrity or multiplicity of the human soul. For humans exercise functions that other animals do not. In addition to growth and sensation, humans think. Are there, then, three souls in a human being to account for these three functions? Here too the Aristotelian answer must be No, and it is an answer with profound theological consequences, especially within the *Commedia*.

> If, therefore, a man were alive because of one form (that is, the vegetative soul), and an animal because of another form (the sensitive soul), and a man because of another form (the rational, or intellectual, soul), it would follow that man was not one absolutely. . . . Therefore, we must say that in man one and the same soul is sensitive, intellectual, and nutritive. (*ST*, 1a 76, 3)

Because a plant arises from different causes than does an animal, its vegetative soul is proper to its life as a plant, and different from the vegetative *function* that is part of an animal soul.[98] Put the other way around, the vegetative function of an animal is different from that of a plant: it is performed by an animal soul (of different nature and origin than the vegetative soul of a plant) which, as a superior soul, has the capacity to perform two sets of functions: the functions of nutrition and growth, and, in addition, those of sensation and movement. Thus, even the vegetative function in an animal is essentially animal, since it is performed by an animal soul. And thus, even the animal's vegetative functions are marked by the character of the animal soul in which they reside, and of the proper animal cause that created that soul and gave it the nature it has.

We can readily see the applicability of this principle to the human soul. If animals exercise both vegetative and sensitive functions but possess only one soul, human beings must possess only a single soul though exercising the three functions of growth, sensation, and thought. As the animal soul is a sensitive soul that incorporates the vegetative functions, the human soul must be an intellectual soul that incorporates the vegetative and sensitive functions. As the powers of the animal soul that perform vegetative functions must be fundamentally and essentially animal since the animal has only a single, unified soul—that is, the vegetative functions are carried out by essentially sensitive powers that have the superior capacity of being able also to perform these vegetative functions—so the vegetative and sensitive functions of the human soul must be performed by essentially human powers—that is, by essentially intellectual powers that have the superior capacity of being able also to perform vegetative and sensitive functions.

> Therefore, the intellectual soul contains in its faculties [or, contains virtually] whatever belongs to the sensitive soul of brute animals, and to the nutritive soul of plants. (*ST,* 1a 76, 3)[99]

But what makes a soul intellectual and essentially human is not biologically inheritable. Since heredity occurs through material transmission, the inheritable soul can only be corporeal, and therefore not intellectual. On this virtually all medieval participants to this dispute agree,[100] and thus the creation of the distinctly human, because intellectual, soul requires some form of external agency. But implied in the creation of this soul, since it too can be no other than a single soul, is that the intellectual soul cannot merely be superadded to supplement a sensitive soul that continues to exist. Rather, the intellectual soul itself must be capable of performing the two lesser functions. Those lesser functions thus do not survive in humans as vestiges of an earlier animal soul—that would give human beings more than one soul. Rather, these lesser functions must be performed in the human soul by functions of the intellectual soul itself.

> If it is stated this way, therefore—that the vegetative and sensitive functions that exist in the intellectual soul are from the same extrinsic cause as is the intellectual soul—nothing unsuitable follows. For it is not unsuitable that the effect of a superior agent have some power which is also possessed by the effect of an inferior agent, and even more. So, too, in the case of the intellectual soul. Although it exists because of an exterior agent, it nevertheless possesses the powers which vegetative and sensitive souls do, which exist because of inferior agents.[101]

With respect to the intellectual soul, the "extrinsic cause" is God. Aquinas' argument makes two assertions. The first is that the vegetative and sensitive functions of an intellectual creature (a human being) are different from the vegetative and sensitive functions of either plants or animals. What were distinct souls to plants and animals are merely internalized powers to the human soul. (As what had been a distinct soul to a plant is merely a nutritive power to an animal.) The human soul is an intellectual soul exercising both the vegetative and sensitive powers, in the same way that the sensitive soul of animals exercises vegetative powers. The second assertion is one that I think is implicit in the conviction that the intellectual soul must have its origin in God, namely, that all three functions have been part of the intellectual soul from the moment of its origin in God. Since the soul, even the intellectual soul, must be a single soul, at the moment God implants this intellectual soul in the human embryo, it is implanted already capable of exercising those functions.

Aquinas accounted for the unity of the human soul by speaking of the "supersession" of one soul by another.[102] I believe that Nardi is correct in saying that Dante does not subscribe to the notion of supersession (indeed, as we will consider, he describes a quite different process),[103] but the two doctrines that Dante has Statius enunciate are consonant with Aquinas in two essential respects: that the human soul operates in a way unique to it, distinct from the animal soul it once was, in the same way an animal soul is distinct from a vegetable soul; and that this character of the human soul is one it receives at the moment that God's intervention makes it human. This is what Dante expresses in Statius' explanation of the final stage of transformation— it is now no longer appropriate to say "development"—of the human soul.[104] The moment at which "animal divenga fante" follows the completed operation of the animal soul with which conception began, and requires the direct intervention of God (as "extrinsic cause," as Aquinas would have expressed it).

> ... Sì tosto come al feto
> l'articular del cerebro è perfetto,
> lo motor primo a lui si volge lieto
> sovra tant'arte di natura, e spira
> spirito novo, di vertù repleto,
> che ciò che trova attivo quivi, tira
> in sua sustanzia, e fassi un'alma sola,
> che vive e sente e sè in sè rigira.
> (*Purg.* xxv, 68–75)

Statius stresses that the human soul, though now capable of three fundamentally different living actions, has only a single substance, and a single soul. In Statius' explanation, the new substance of the human soul is acquired by the transformation of the earlier soul into something different from what it had been. The doctrine is different from both Aquinas' and Albert's, and gives the greatest emphasis to the miracle performed in the creation of the human soul.[105] What Statius most forcibly seems to be saying, somewhat obscurely in his "philosophical" discussion but very clearly in the simile he uses to illuminate it, is that the intellectual soul of human beings is no replacement of one or two earlier souls, but a transformation of an earlier animal soul, by direct divine intervention, into a soul of a wholly intellectual nature that in its new nature has the capacity also of performing the sensitive and vegetative functions.

There would be a possible ambiguity if we took Statius' use of the word *spirito* (*Purg.* xxv, 72) specifically to refer to a new complete soul being breathed into the human embryo. (Taken this way, his statement of the origin of the human soul would replicate Aquinas' theory of supersession.) But the simile that follows seems to give a different meaning to *spirito*, emphasizing transformation rather than replacement.

> E perchè meno ammiri la parola,
> guarda il calor del sol che si fa vino,
> giunto all'omor che della vite cola.
> (*Purg.* xxv, 76–78)

The sun does not replace grape juice with wine, it turns grape juice into wine, at least in the terms of the simile. In doing so, it alters the nature of the grape juice. The sun's heat is not wine; neither is grape juice wine. Wine is a unique substance different from grape juice, and as a different substance, it possesses a different formal cause than does grape juice. The alteration cannot be accomplished, in the philosophical terms of this discussion, by the addition of a secondary formal cause to grape juice's original form. Any nature can possess only a single form. A vinous form must therefore replace the original form of the grape juice. The nature of the grape juice must be altered; it must become, here in an engagingly concrete way, "spiritualized." Through the action of an external agency, the nature of heat and the nature of grape juice are simultaneously transformed into something with a new, integral nature of its own.

Dante is arguing that in a proper and profound sense, that is also precisely what happens in the creation of the human soul. Up to the moment of God's intervention, the growth of the embryo and its development of vegetative and sensitive functions and organs have been strictly natural, animal, corporeal. But at a crucial moment a

137

supernatural event takes place. By the breathing in of a new spirit, the formerly merely natural soul is literally spiritualized. This divine spirit has the power *(vertù)* to bring the other, lower power into its own nature, creating a single substance that can perform vegetative functions *(vive)*, apprehensive functions *(sente)*, and intellectual functions *(sè in sè rigira)*. Strikingly, in the simile that Statius uses, it is not the grape juice but the heat of the sun that becomes wine. The sun's heat "assumes" the grape juice to become wine; the new spirit infused into the human embryo similarly assumes the body and corporeal functions in becoming human.[106] The key here is that it is the higher power that gives its character to the new creature. Wine is not grape juice with alcohol added; it is a new substance of its own. The human soul is not an animal soul with an added intellectual power; it is an intellectual substance of its own.[107]

Since the human soul is, by this transformation, entirely intellectual, having received its nature and character from its external cause, what we see in the human soul as sensitive and nutritive faculties are no longer the sensitive or vegetative faculties or functions as they had previously existed in plants and animals. Rather, just as the vegetative functions of an animal are essentially animal, not vegetative, so both the vegetative and sensitive functions of a human soul are essentially intellectual. There is a proof of this in Statius' explanation of the action of the separated soul in creating an aerial body. The ability of the soul to recreate sensitive faculties and organs in air, rather than flesh, is possible only because this formative power is itself fundamentally an intellectual power. The original, proper sensitive faculties of the original animal soul were articulated and operated through organs of flesh. That is all the corporeal soul knew how to do. In Purgatory, the soul finds itself capable of abstracting these powers from their original corporeal attachment, and of using them to refashion organs in a new medium. That it can do so is a function of the human soul's being (after its transformation by God) essentially intellectual.

(An equivalent adaptation can be seen in the vegetative operations of an animal soul. For plants, which have only vegetative functions, those functions operate through an appropriate set of organs and processes: roots, leaves, photosynthesis. In animals, the sensitive soul performing these functions must adapt these functions to animal life by abstracting them from their original connection to certain botanical organs and recasting them in organs suitable for an animal that moves and feels. That the animal soul can escape the genetic attachment of vegetative processes to vegetable organs is a result of the animal soul's being wholly animal, or sensitive, and merely performing its version of this vegetative function. In an equivalent way, the sensitive functions in humans are performed by wholly human—that is to say, intellectual—faculties operating through appropriate media: in flesh, while alive in this world; on other, unnatural, media, such as air, after death. That the human soul can escape its genetic attachment to corporeal organs and processes is proof of its essentially intellectual nature.)

Since it is an intellectual substance, the human soul is capable of being separated from the matter that forms no part of its intellectual nature:

> Therefore, when a form has some operation in accordance with one of its powers or virtues apart from any connection to its matter, that form itself it is which has being, nor does it exist only through the being of the composite, as other forms do, but, rather, the composite exists through its being. Therefore, that form which exists through the being of the composite is destroyed when the composite is destroyed; but that form through whose being the composite exists (and which does not itself exist through the composite's being) is not destroyed when the composite is destroyed.[108]

But what we now recognize is that, for Dante, the intellectual soul that can be separated from its body, and that therefore can survive after the death of the body, consists not merely of the faculty of reason, but also of capacities that in other creatures would not be considered intellectual at all. For human beings, however, who are essentially and integrally intellectual, these same capacities have to exist as operations of the intellectual soul. The intellectual soul that exists independently after the death of the body, therefore, is that same complete and integral human soul that possessed all of the faculties—intellectual, sensitive, nutritive—from its creation, or in Dante's case transformation, by God. In the souls in Purgatory, we see a new composite of soul and aerial body existing and operating through the unique power of the intellectual soul.

But what we must now also recognize is that when these same souls were alive in this world, their terrestrially living composite of soul and corporeal body was actually existing and operating from the same unique intellectual cause. That is, if it is the purely intellectual soul that operates the aerial organs and experiences the aerial equivalents of sensitive appetites and passions in Purgatory, it was also the purely intellectual soul that had operated the corporeal organs and experienced the corporeal equivalents of sensitive appetites and passions in this world.

We see the same complement of powers in action in Purgatory as we had in this life because, within Dante's interpretation of the nature of the human soul, all of these powers in human beings were in fact intellectual from the moment they became human beings, and therefore all of these powers can survive the corporeal body's death—even the powers we seem to recognize as appetitive powers. What is crucial here, as Statius effectively points out, is that there has been no essential change in the soul's nature between life and death. All that has changed is the matter on and through which the soul operates and, more importantly, the end for which the soul operates. The same intellectual soul is performing the same informative and directive functions in both states: on flesh in this world, on the surrounding air, as necessary, in the next.

Revising Our Understanding of Human Action and of the Purpose of Purgatory

At this point we are able to resolve the dilemma that had been created for us, on the one hand, by the symmetry of Hell and Purgatory (which directed us to discover the appetitive foundation of all action) and, on the other, by the necessity that any faculties that exist in the afterlife be spiritual rather than corporeal faculties (which seemed to render impossible an appetitive structure to these two realms of the next world). But resolving the dilemma also compels us to reinterpret the nature of the appetitive faculties that provide the structure of Hell and Purgatory. Dante had asked Statius (*Purg.* xxv, 20–21) how it was possible for disembodied souls to suffer bodily torments. In asking the question, Dante assumes that what he is seeing (and representing to us) actually are corporeal sufferings; that is, that the soul somehow has a body, and also the sensitive faculties that operate through the body. The short answer to Dante's question is that indeed these souls do have bodies, aerial bodies, in which they suffer and through those sufferings straighten and rehabilitate their viciously disposed faculties. But Dante *poeta* precedes this direct answer with an account of the origin of the soul because without that account, Statius' answer regarding aerial bodies would be either incomprehensible or misunderstood.

For although Dante assumes, as we would, that the torments are corporeal and are meant to correct disorders of those faculties linked to the body, Statius' account of the origin of the soul tells us that it is not disorders of the sensitive appetites or the sensory organs that we see figured in the aerial bodies of these souls. We had believed (and Dante *personaggio* acts as if he believes) that as we watch the damned in the *Inferno* or the penitent in the *Purgatorio* we are watching *bodies* suffer. We might have been encouraged in that belief not only by the vividness of Dante's descriptions, but by knowing that medieval authorities had also spoken of corporeal suffering after death. But what Statius makes clear to us is that all the suffering we have seen is wholly intellectual suffering. The aerial bodies appear to be suffering only because they reflect the intellectual suffering of the souls.[109]

To inform a body is what a human soul does. It cannot do otherwise without violating its nature. The soul has its powers and motions, and naturally exercises them on the matter to hand. But among this intellectual soul's powers are also those capacities it has for fulfilling animal and vegetative functions, and so we can see those too reflected in the aerial body. And since the body informed by a soul resembles that soul, the disordered condition of the soul's powers in the state of sin or vice naturally results in impressions in matter of those disorders, at least until the disorders have been removed by appropriate rehabilitation, as Dante has Statius express:

> Secondo che ci affiggono i disiri
> e li altri affetti, l'ombra si figura.
> (*Purg.* xxv, 106–7)[110]

The desires and affections that we have seen in the souls of the next world, then, are affections of the intellectual soul; they merely *appear* to be affections of the sensitive soul. As mentioned earlier, the ability of the souls to create aerial bodies is itself a proof of this, for the original sensitive faculties would have been, if truly corporeal, inextricably tied to human flesh as their medium.[111] Authentically animal sensitive powers would not be capable of using the air for their actions and sufferings. Only a more abstract and intellectual power would be capable of this extension. And even something that initially appears as nothing more than a running joke in the *Purgatorio*—repeated comments made by souls in Purgatory about the solidity of Dante's body—can now be seen to have been a narrative means of pushing us in the direction of confronting the necessarily intellectual nature of the appetitive actions we see. By having the souls in Purgatory express surprise at Dante's corporeality, we are reminded, again and again, of their own *incorporeality*. By reminding us of this, Dante forces us, again and again, to confront the paradox that, although the souls seem to be suffering corporeal pain, in fact they cannot possibly be experiencing this, not having bodies. Their pain, and the faculties by which they experience it, must ultimately be intellectual. On the basis of Statius' account, we must conclude that all of the *human* appetites, even those that appear to be sensitive appetites, are ultimately intellectual in origin and character.

How can Hell and Purgatory share an appetitive structure when there are no bodies in either realm for two of the appetites to operate on? They can share this structure because, for Dante, all of the human appetitive faculties are ultimately intellectual. In saying that, we also discover Dante's explanation of the purpose of Purgatory. There could be no utility to reforming habits of faculties that will have no further reason to operate. If the sensitive appetites no longer exist in the soul after death, they no longer need virtues to perfect them. There is no occasion for moral virtue in Heaven. That being the case, were Purgatory organized according to the three appetites as we have understood them up to this point, such an organization would be philosophically foolish, since the reformation of such appetites would serve no purpose.

One explanation for the need for rehabilitating these faculties would be for their direction of the glorified bodies the saved will possess following the bodily resurrection. That is the only use that Aquinas sees for the sensitive appetites.

> There is a twofold state after this life: one before the resurrection, when souls will be separated from their bodies; another after the resurrection, when the soul will once again be united with its body. In this latter, resurrected, state there will be irrational faculties in the bodily organs just as now; hence, it will also be possible for there to be fortitude in the irascible appetite and temperance in the concupiscible insofar as each faculty shall be perfectly disposed to obeying the reason. But in the state before the resurrection, the irrational parts will not be in the soul actually, but only in their roots in its essence. (*ST*, 1a2æ 67, 1 ad 3)

Without doubt, Dante not only believed in the bodily resurrection but also in this use of the sensitive faculties. He referred explicitly to the final perfection of the glorified human soul in the state that follows the resurrection (cf. *Inf.* vi, 100–111; and especially *Par.* xiv, 37–60). But in the *Purgatorio,* Dante is also explicit that the faculties of the soul must be rehabilitated not only for their later reunion with their bodies, but specifically to be capable of rising into Heaven. The purpose of Purgatory is to become worthy of rising to Heaven:

> . . . quel secondo regno
> dove l'umano spirito si purga
> e di salire al ciel diventa degno.
> (*Purg.* i, 4–6)

The vices the souls possess until their purification keep the souls from being able to enter Heaven: "lo scoglio / ch'esser non lascia a voi Dio manifesto" (*Purg.* ii, 122–23). Whatever later use there may be for the faculties that can be afflicted with these vices, the faculties must be in a perfected state even for their separated life before their reunion with their bodies.

When we recognize that the appetitive functions that we know as the will, irascible, and concupiscible appetites are at base all of them operations of the intellectual soul, the significance of the rehabilitation undergone in Purgatory is suddenly shifted to a higher plane.[112] If what we had originally believed to be operations of sensitive appetites are actually and most importantly diverse operations of the intellectual soul, given that the intellectual soul does survive the death of the body, then the reformation of its operations might well be critical to the proper functioning of the separated soul, that is, to its ultimate blessedness. And while moral virtues are surely inappropriate to Heaven, other perfecting qualities that adapt the intellectual soul to the operations that will make it blessed may well be needed. It is the acquisition of these qualities that we see in the *Purgatorio.* We do not see the rehabilitation of the will and the sensitive appetites by the acquisition of worldly virtues. We see the rehabilitation of those intellectual capacities that were in fact the *origins* of the human sensitive appetites as well as of the will by new virtues adequate to the operations these intellectual faculties will perform in the future life of the soul.[113]

Since the same capacities are involved in both worlds, the new virtues will naturally bear a certain resemblance to the more familiar worldly virtues. But they will take on a new cast appropriate to their purely intellectual natures.

> We must say that moral virtues of this sort will not endure in the future life as far as concerns what is material in them, for there will be no place in the future life for concupiscences, or the delights of food or sex; nor will there be fear or daring regarding the danger of death; nor distributions of, or commerce in, the things which are employed in this present life. But insofar as concerns what is formal, the virtues will remain most perfectly in the blessed after this life, insofar as everyone's reason will be most right concerning those things which pertain to him in that state. And the appetitive faculty too will be moved wholly following the order of the reason in those things which pertain to that state. Whence Augustine says [*de Trin.*, xiv, 9] that "there shall be prudence without risk of error; fortitude without the annoyance of tolerating evils; temperance without the resistance of the desires. So that it will be the work of prudence not to prefer nor to take as equal any other good to God; it will be the work of fortitude to cling with greatest firmness to Him; of temperance to delight in Him, free of any harmful defect." Concerning justice, it is clear what act it will accomplish there: namely, to be subject to God, since even in this life subjection to one's superior pertains to justice. (*ST,* 1a2æ 67, 1)[114]

Aquinas had spoken of the sensitive appetites as existing only in their roots in the separated soul. We can see Dante's position either as rejecting the Thomistic interpretation, or, as I believe more likely, as Dante imagining he was providing a gloss or interpretation of what might be meant by these powers existing as "roots." For Dante, all three appetites exist in the soul after death because all were originally and have always remained operations of the intellectual soul. At the moment that the animal soul of the embryo is spiritualized into an intellectual, human soul, all operations of the soul are spiritualized and intellectualized, and what were operations of the sensitive appetite in animals are in human beings in fact operations of the intellectual appetite, the will, specially adapted to the senses and bodily organs.

Even Aquinas, though he denied that the will has irascible or concupiscible components properly speaking, recognized operations in the will that are similar to these appetites. According to Aquinas, any motion of the irascible or the concupiscible appetite which occurs accompanied by passion in those appetites can also exist in the will free from passion.[115] Indeed, for Aquinas it is as a disposition of the will that actions of one capital vice or another become mortal rather than venial.[116]

> Love, concupiscence, and such can be understood in two ways. On the one hand, as they are understood as specific passions, arising from a certain excitation or disturbance of the soul. This is how they are commonly understood, and in this sense are only in the sensitive appetite. But in another sense they signify a simple affection without passion or excitation of the soul, and in this sense they are acts of the will, and it is in this sense that they are attributed to angels, and to God. But if they are taken in this sense, they do not pertain to different powers, but to one power only, called the will. . . . The will itself can be said to be irascible, inasmuch as it wishes to combat evil, but not from the impulse of passion, but rather from a judgment of the reason. In the same way it can be said to be concupiscible on account of its desire for good. It is in this way that charity and hope can be said to be in the concupiscible and the irascible—that is, in the will insofar as it is ordered to acts of this sort. (*ST,* 1a 82, 5 ad 1 and 2)[117]

It is these operations of the will that Dante intends as the faculties undergoing rehabilitation in Purgatory. In Dante's sense, these operations of the will are well and truly the roots of the appetites. These primal operations of the will are the source from which the sensitive appetites spring, to become adapted to the corporeal requirements of the human soul-body complex.[118] Insofar as these operations exist in the will and its powers, they can be said to endure beyond death, and, indeed, can be said to belong to the other separated intellectual substances, that is, to the angels and to God.

Insofar as there are distinct acts or operations of the will, there must also be perfections, that is, virtues, of these operations, although, as is clear in trying to discuss them with respect to the angels, either new names will have to be found for these virtues, or the old names will have to submit to redefinition.

> Temperance, in respect of its being a human virtue, is concerned with the concupiscence of sensitive pleasures, which pertains to the concupiscible power. Similarly, fortitude is concerned with daring and fear, which belong to the irascible. As a human virtue, then, temperance is in the concupiscible part, fortitude in the irascible. In this sense, they [these virtues] are not found in angels. For they have no passions regarding concupiscibles nor fear or daring, which need to be regulated by temperance and fortitude. But temperance can be said to exist in them in respect of their exhibiting their moderation of will in accord with the

divine will. And fortitude is said to be in them in respect of their firmly carrying out the divine will. All of this is done by the will, not by irascible or concupiscible powers. (*ST,* 1a 59, 4)[119]

Virgil does not say to Dante at the conclusion of his journey through Purgatory that Dante's appetites are healthy, upright, and free. He says that it is Dante's *will* that has reached that happy condition. The sins and vices that bring souls to Purgatory and demand first forgiveness and then correction were the acts of the composite of intellectual and sensitive appetites with which human beings exist and act in this world. But it is not really the three worldly appetites that we see undergoing rehabilitation in Purgatory. Neither do we see souls in Purgatory acquiring the cardinal virtues that were the virtues of those worldly appetites. Rather, as is also most appropriate for their coming life in Heaven, what we see being rehabilitated are operations of the intellectual soul more fundamental than the worldly appetites, and of which those appetites are merely corporeal extensions. If the worldly appetites were defective in their operations, their defects merely mirror more serious defects of those intellectual movements that lie behind them and inform them. And so it is those intellectual movements that must be reformed, and that we see being reformed in Purgatory. It is only when those motions of the will are perfected by the virtues the Beatitudes celebrate that it is proper to say that that separated soul which is the eternal part of a person is "puro e disposto a salire alle stelle" (*Purg.* xxxiii, 145).

Purgatory, we had said, is a realm of transformation. But the transformation Dante exhibits in this *cantica* is more than simply a transformation from the sins of this world to the purity of the next. The very subject of the entire poem is transformed as we watch. The souls who enter Purgatory do so because of sinful actions they have committed based on vices of the appetites that drive all human action. In the course of their purgation, the souls not only lose the vices that once enslaved them, they also acquire virtues whose intended operation is not of this world but of the next. Because of their change from vices of this world to virtues of the next, we might be tempted to say that souls exiting Purgatory are not merely purer than when they entered but are of a new and different nature. But this would not be true. The soul has always been of the same nature, but it took the regimen of Purgatory to reveal that real nature to us, since that nature was concealed or obscured by flesh and worldly pursuits. What looks like a change in nature is merely the stripping away of the limitations that the matter and habits of the corporeal world place on the free activity of the soul and its powers. Entering with worldly weaknesses (and, for that matter, with strengths that were of value only in worldly affairs), the souls leave capable of the activity they will perform in Heaven. And since that activity is the unimpeded operation of intellectual powers that were the soul's first *human* possession, that divinized activity is also the activity for which the souls were originally created. The activity of the soul in Heaven, for which the acquisition of the Beatitudes throughout Purgatory prepares, is thus the most natural of the activities the soul might perform, and it is for this reason that it is the soul's happiness and blessedness.[120]

3

Paradiso

Of the three *cantiche* of the *Commedia*, the *Paradiso* is the most fundamentally—one might say, organically—allegorical. It is the only *cantica* in which the use of the events of the literal narrative for figurative purposes is itself made an explicit part of that literal narrative. In the previous two *cantiche*, Dante *poeta* had, by gestures external to the action of the poem, called the reader's attention to the existence of allegorical meanings for the literal events Dante *personaggio* was experiencing.[1] But in the *Paradiso* the principle that literal appearances and events represent meanings existing at levels beyond the poem becomes itself a part of the experience of Dante *personaggio*. Allegory is no longer a matter of the poet's stepping out of the poem and self-consciously reminding us of the artifice of the poetry; rather, the characters of the poem themselves explicitly declare to Dante that what passes before his eyes as literal action is, in this realm, nothing less than divine artifice.

It is Beatrice who first and most authoritatively tells Dante that what he experiences at the literal level is not the truth of Paradise. What he sees is a poetic fiction. Its purpose, like the purpose of the *Commedia* itself in its allegorical significances, is to make manifest to Dante's limited human intelligence, by making manifest to his senses, meanings that actually exist on another, more abstract, plane. The blessed souls Dante meets in Heaven do not reside in the diverse spheres in which he encounters them. They reside together in one single Heaven. Their appearance in the spheres is merely a corporeal sign, adapted to Dante's intellect, which, in its weakness, can function only by means of such signs.[2]

> De' Serafin colui che più s'india,
>   Moïsè, Samuèl, e quel Giovanni
>   che prender vuoli, io dico, non Maria,

> non hanno in altro cielo i loro scanni
>   che questi spirti che mo t'appariro,
> . . . .
> ma tutti fanno bello il primo giro.
> . . . .
> Qui si mostraron, non perchè sortita
>   sia questa spera lor, ma per far segno
>   della celestïal c'ha men salita.
> Così parlar conviensi al vostro ingegno,
>   però che solo da sensato apprende
>   ciò che fa poscia d'intelletto degno.
> Per questo la Scrittura condescende
>   a vostra facultate, e piedi e mano
>   attribuisce a Dio, ed altro intende.
>   (*Par.* iv, 28–32, 34, 37–45)

Not only have the souls in Heaven arrayed themselves in fictive locations, their very appearance is itself illusory or enigmatic. Dante discovers, in speaking to Justinian in cantos v and vi, that even as Justinian becomes the more willing to answer Dante's questions, the happiness Justinian feels in this action renders the light in which he is enveloped more intense, and this paradoxically conceals him more completely from Dante.[3]

> Sì come il sol che si cela elli stessi
>   per troppa luce, come 'l caldo ha rose
>   le temperanze di vapori spessi;
> per più letizia sì mi si nascose
>   dentro al suo raggio la figura santa;
>   e così chiusa chiusa mi rispose.
>   (*Par.* v, 133–38)

Nor is it only when Dante is still relatively inexperienced with Paradise, that is, in the early cantos of the *Paradiso*, that he is unable to see through to the truth of these figures. He experiences the same difficulty almost to the very end of his journey. When, having already traveled through the greater part of Paradise, Dante specifically asks Saint Benedict to show him his face, rather than merely the flame that envelops him, Benedict refuses, cautioning Dante that such direct sight can only be accomplished in the last and highest location of Heaven, and reminding him, by implication, that until that time all the sights he sees remain only *imagini* "*coverte.*" Only in that sphere that is beyond place and time could Dante hope to see the truth.

«Però ti priego, e tu, padre, m'accerta
  s'io posso prender tanta grazia, ch'io
  ti veggia con imagine scoverta.»
Ond'elli: «Frate, il tuo alto disio
  s'adempierà in su l'ultima spera,
  ove s'adempion tutti li altri e 'l mio.
Ivi è perfetta, matura ed intera
  ciascuna disïanza; in quella sola
  è ogni parte là ove sempr'era,
perchè non è in loco, e non s'impola.
(*Par.* xxii, 58–67)

Until that moment, nothing that Dante sees is truly what it is. And yet, everything that Dante sees has significance. The fictions he perceives were prepared precisely because of their capacity to convey meaning to him. They are not mere fictions, Beatrice says, they are signs. If Dante does not, cannot, see the truth of Paradise directly, what he sees is at least a reflection of that truth. Indeed, reflection is one of the central themes of the *Paradiso*. Throughout this *cantica*, the words *figura* and *segno* and *specchio* recur, resonate, and become simultaneously problematic and heuristic. The very light that conceals the reality of the souls from Dante is in fact itself reflected light. Figures reflect truth, but truth embodied is also truth concealed, to a certain extent, as Beatrice, Justinian, and Benedict all remind us. We should note, and I believe are encouraged to note, that this same ambiguous quality is inherent also to poetry and allegory. The images of the souls Dante sees and the images of the poem which he presents to us share a common nature, and it is that nature that renders them at once revelatory and obscuring. They must be concrete so that he can perceive them, and to be concrete they must be manifested to him (and us) as particulars as if they were physical entities that existed in a discrete place at a determinate time. But the truth they aspire to convey is itself immaterial and eternal, universal and indivisible. In effect, the very process of allegory becomes an issue in the literal story of the third *cantica*,[4] for the literal level of the *Paradiso* again and again draws attention to the need for, and the difficulty of, allegorical interpretation.

At the same time, however, interpretation of these images is rendered difficult for us because the figures we are given seem so much less suggestive than the figures Dante had provided in the first two *cantiche*. Insofar as images depend on concreteness and presence for conveying their truths, whether to Dante or to us, the images of the first two *cantiche* seem more successful and compelling to the extent that the punishments and corrections of Hell and Purgatory are richer in circumstantial detail. Each of those details is a resource and an occasion to the reader to interpret the underlying natures of the sins and virtues to which respective ordeals are related. But the Heaven of the *Paradiso* seems frustratingly devoid of such detail. One could argue that a picture of souls in Heaven ought to lack such concrete details since Heaven is beyond circumstance, but however theologically appropriate such an argument might be, it does not speak to the explicit poetic requirements of the *cantica*. Inasmuch as the souls have explicitly descended to merely fictive locations for Dante's and our edification, why must these fictions be such pallid fictions?

Yet, for all that the incidents of the *Paradiso* fall short of the vividness of the incidents of the *Inferno* and the *Purgatorio,* they nonetheless constitute figures clear enough in the aspects that matter for us to construct our interpretation of the *cantica*. The first and fundamental figure of the *Paradiso* is the structure of Heaven itself: the locations in which souls appear to Dante—those locations, coupled with the identities and characters of the individuals he meets in them. Compared with the events of the first two *cantiche,* this figure no doubt appears abstract, but we and Dante have been told by Beatrice that their appearance in those locations is Heaven's fiction created expressly for him. And as a figure it has been rather cannily adapted to an even more abstract truth it is intended to illuminate. There is a paradox in what Beatrice has told Dante: on the one hand, she seems to claim that blessedness is identical for all in Heaven; and yet the means by which Dante has Heaven explained to him, and the content of that explanation, assert and re-emphasize differences in the reasons for which people have been blessed and in the nature of their blessedness. The problematic truth of the *Paradiso* is a truth about ordering, and is reflected in a figure that first and foremost embodies order. In the four sections of this chapter we will consider the character of the order of Heaven, the source of that order, and its significance.

The Order of Blessedness

There is, after all, an order to Heaven just as there had been to Hell and Purgatory, and while Beatrice does not give Dante an explicit explanation of the principle that articulates that order (as Virgil had of Hell and Purgatory), her statement that the souls have dispersed themselves to the locations that compose this order for didactic purposes—to render comprehensible by his limited human intellect some truth regarding Heaven—provides a guarantee that this order is in itself significant, and that it exists to be interpreted so that its significance be understood. The structure of Paradise, the number and order of the celestial spheres through which Beatrice and Dante travel, thus plays the identical functional role as had the circles of Hell and the *gironi* of Purgatory. Discovering the principle that underlies its order, and discovering the principle by which souls are assigned to one or another sphere becomes the means of determining both the common nature and also the individual specification of blessedness, in the same way that discovering the principle that directed the orders of Hell and Purgatory revealed to us the general nature and specific qualities of sin and redemption.

As an allegorical image, the order of the celestial spheres also explicitly shares the primary and fundamental figurative strategy that is embodied in the orders of the two other realms. As descent in Hell reflected the increasing seriousness of the sins there punished; as ascent in Purgatory reflected the diminishing seriousness of the vices to be purged; so ascent through the spheres of Paradise reflects an increasing blessedness of the souls Dante encounters and the activities they represent. But even to make so intuitive an assertion confronts us with a paradox. The passage we have already cited from Beatrice implies that there is no difference in the blessedness of souls and angels in Heaven, and yet the existence of difference is unequivocally supported not only by the order of the spheres, but also by the statements of the souls with whom Dante converses. Insofar as all souls, whatever their natures and characters, inhabit the same Heaven, as Beatrice declares (*Par.* iv, 28–33; and, indeed, she does not restrict this statement only to human souls: the highest order of angels shares this habitation with all human souls), all are equally blessed. And yet the comments of souls he questions frequently distinguish souls from each other in terms of their blessedness.[5]

Piccarda Donati, in the first sphere, is sensitive to the fact that her location appears lowly to Dante (it is she who so characterizes it), and admits that its lowliness is a result of her own failings:

> E questa sorte che par giù cotanto,
>   però n'è data, perchè fuor negletti
>   li nostri vóti, e vòti in alcun canto.
>   (*Par.* iii, 55–57)

When Dante asks her whether she would not prefer to be closer so that she might see God better, he, on his side, makes a natural assumption that distance from God must diminish, or at least set a limit to, the joy she can experience in Heaven.

> Ma dimmi: voi che siete qui felici,
>   disiderate voi più alto loco
>   per più vedere e per più farvi amici?
>   (*Par.* iii, 64–66)

Piccarda does not deny that this is so. Her charity, and the pleasure she takes in conforming to God's will, which has assigned this location to her, restrains her desire (*Par.* iii, 70–75). But in the very act of condemning any desire to be higher in Heaven as discordant to God's will, she perforce recognizes that a "higher" does exist in Heaven, to which other souls, if not she, might appropriately aspire. And when she says that charity makes her wish only for what she has ("che fa volerne / sol quel ch'avemo, e d'altro non ci asseta" [*Par.* iii, 71–72]), she implies that other souls do indeed have more of blessedness than she. Justinian, in the next sphere, understands that his appearance in a relatively lowly sphere mirrors his merit, and his human shortcomings, and that this location provides a figure of the measure of reward he has earned. At the same time, of course, the location also implies other higher rewards he has not merited or received. Since divine justice would inevitably match reward to merit, and since recognizing the operation of divine justice would give a blessed soul pleasure, that recognition makes even the awareness of possessing a lesser reward sweet.

> Questa picciola stella si correda
>   di buoni spirti che son stati attivi
>   perchè onore e fama li succeda:

e quando li disiri poggian quivi,
   sì disvïando, pur convien che i raggi
   del vero amore in su poggin men vivi.
Ma nel commensurar di nostri gaggi
   col merto è parte di nostra letizia,
   perchè non li vedem minor nè maggi.
Quindi addolcisce la viva giustizia
   in noi l'affetto sì, che non si puote
   torcer già mai ad alcuna nequizia.

(*Par.* vi, 112–23)

But that in his case, as in Piccarda's, it is justice that restrains desire, and tempers it so that it does not turn to envy, demonstrates Justinian's awareness too that there are in fact greater rewards than those he has received, reserved for others of greater merit or grace who, we recognize as we read this passage, will manifest themselves to Dante in higher spheres. Indeed, at the same moment that Beatrice informs Dante that all souls, whatever their grandeur or modesty, live in the one empyrean sphere, she does also admit that souls experience joy diversely, and that their appearance in the various celestial spheres provides a sign of their achievement in what she calls "rising" among the heavenly ranks:

Ma tutti fanno bello il primo giro,
   e differentemente han dolce vita
   per sentir più e men l'etterno spiro.
Qui si mostraron, non perchè sortita
   sia questa spera lor, ma per far segno
   della celestïal c'ha men salita.

(*Par.* iv, 34–39)

Even in the *candida rosa,* that one true habitation of all blessed souls, location reflects merit. Bernard of Clairvaux points Beatrice out to Dante "nel trono che suoi merti le sortiro" (*Par.* xxxi, 68–69); Adam and Peter sit closest to Mary, highest up on the rose, while other souls are arranged downward from them (*Par.* xxxii, 115–26); and those souls who are in Heaven for merits not their own (infants and children) sit below those who are there in reward of their own actions (*Par.* xxxii, 40–45).[6] Even among the angels, as Beatrice explains, greater closeness to God brings increased delight, and this greater reward reflects merit, or it might be more proper to say vision, which in their case is the same.

E dei saper che tutti hanno diletto
    quanto la sua veduta si profonda
    nel vero in che si queta ogni intelletto.
Quinci si può veder come si fonda
    l'esser beato nell'atto che vede,
    non in quel ch'ama, che poscia seconda;
e del vedere è misura mercede,
    che grazia partorisce e buona voglia:
    così di grado in grado si procede.

(Par. xxviii, 106–14)

But if we admit that there exist grades of blessedness among the souls and angels in Heaven, in what sense or senses can it be appropriate to say that souls are more or less blessed? The outline of an answer to this question had been given through the figure of Solomon in the fourteenth canto, and it is in the context of his earlier statement that we can understand the full significance of Beatrice's application of his principle to angels. Solomon, indeed, had already provided the principle that explains the assertion that Beatrice makes regarding the diverse blessedness of angels, and the principle he had enunciated makes her assertion effectively true of blessed human souls as well: that is, joy and delight are proportional to the vision the souls have of God.

Solomon had called attention to what is probably the most frequently repeated poetic figure of the *Paradiso:* that in looking at God souls become filled by, and in turn reflect, the light of God; and that, within the spatial metaphor of the spheres, as the spheres that souls occupy are closer to God, the brightness of the souls increases. Dante had already noticed this, and will continue to throughout the *Paradiso,* both in the souls he encounters and in the increasing brightness of Beatrice's eyes, as they approach God during the journey. According to Solomon, the diverse brilliance with which souls manifest themselves to Dante depends on the ardor of their love; that, in turn, depends on the acuity of their vision; and that acuity on the measure of grace each soul has received.

. . . Quanto fia lunga la festa
    di paradiso, tanto il nostro amore
    si raggerà dintorno cotal vesta.
La sua chiarezza seguita l'ardore;
    l'ardor la visïone, e quella è tanta,
    quant'ha di grazia sovra suo valore.

(Par. xiv, 37–42)

Solomon takes the dependence of acuity of vision on grace in a most concrete sense: in his explanation, the grace bestowed on the souls is divine light itself, light that serves as a necessary condition to sight, presumably, as in most discussions of the process of seeing, as the medium of vision.[7]

> ...ciò che ne dona
>   di gratuito lume il sommo bene,
>   lume ch'a lui veder ne condiziona.
>   (*Par.* xiv, 46–48)

This explanation of the principle of the souls' brilliance in turn explains and fills out an observation that Dante *personaggio* had made earlier in the *Paradiso,* in his first address to Justinian. There, he had noticed that the light within which Justinian was concealed seemed to have its source in Justinian's eyes:

> Io veggio ben sì come tu t'annidi
>   nel proprio lume, e che delli occhi il traggi,
>   perch'e' corusca sì come tu ridi.
>   (*Par.* v, 124–26)

But Dante's original conclusion, we now see, was incomplete. While the souls' eyes do indeed provide the light that clothes them, they are not the source of that light. They diffuse light only because they reflect light they themselves have first received from God. Souls appear brighter or dimmer to Dante to the extent that they have received more or less of this light, and in the spatial metaphor of the *Paradiso,* they do so as they are closer to God or farther away. In the context of Solomon's explanation, however, we come to realize that what Dante initially experienced as a merely phenomenal change in the appearance of the souls embodies, and is a figure for, a far more significant spiritual difference. Inasmuch as the same light that alters the appearance of the souls is also the necessary condition of their vision, those souls that appear brighter to Dante because they have received more light are also more capable of apprehending God by means of that light.

Beatrice has told Dante that what he sees is only a corporeal representation, adapted to his intellect, of the truth of Heaven, and in the explanation of these phenomena we see two interlocking figures. Location and brilliance become two metaphors of the same quality. "Closeness," in the sense of occupying a sphere closer to God, is merely the physical or spatial manifestation of "having received greater grace." Greater brightness in the appearance of the souls signifies the same thing. Since we know, in the physical world, that brightness is proportionate to the distance from the source of light, the two images of brilliance and location mutually confirm each other. But the physical properties of distance and illumination also embody an even more important doctrine.

According to Solomon, in seeing God more clearly the souls experience more love. But more important still is the consequence drawn by Beatrice in a passage we have already cited. Since delight is proportionate to apprehension—"tutti hanno diletto / quanto la sua veduta si profonda / nel vero" (*Par.* xxviii, 106–8)—a soul's greater ability to see God will also bring it more joy. It is in this specific respect that it turns out to be possible to distinguish degrees of blessedness among the souls in Heaven.[8] The amount of delight, or blessedness, a soul experiences depends on the soul's capacity for the activity in which delight resides. Some souls, being more capable, will inevitably experience more delight. It is that difference in capacity that is given its figurative expression in the respective locations of the souls in Heaven as Dante encounters them.

The principle not only provides a concrete basis for recognizing differences in the blessedness of souls, it also explains why souls feel no envy in regard of these differences. For if the greater or lesser degrees of blessedness are the consequence of greater or lesser capacities for apprehension, and only of that, then it can be said of every soul that the blessedness it receives is not only as much as it is entitled to, but as much as it is capable of. It is not, therefore, only out of a sense of duty and obedience that souls do not envy those who experience more blessedness than they. Souls recognize that they experience all the blessedness that they can. It is not possible for them to experience more joy than they do (they do not have the acuity to do so), and so, they have no reason to feel deprived or envious.

That this is so also provides a solution to the paradox with which we began this consideration. Why are we shown souls in discrete spheres if all inhabit the same Heaven? Or, perhaps at this stage the question is more pressing looked at from the other perspective: If souls are distinguishable by the amounts of grace they have received, how is it proper to say they all inhabit the same Heaven? Both aspects are now reconcilable. All souls inhabit the same Heaven insofar as all souls are completely blessed. (In an Aristotelian sense we might even say, more properly, that they are perfectly blessed.) As some souls have greater capacities for blessedness, however, their complete blessedness could be said, in a relative sense only, to be greater than that of others. But no soul is, or feels that it is, in any way deficient in its blessedness. The perfection of all souls' blessedness is expressed in their true location in a single Heaven. Their differing capacities for blessed activity are expressed in the discrete spheres in which Dante encounters them.

We should note, finally, that the principle of rewarding pious souls with all the joy they are capable of experiencing is effectively identical to the principle of punishing the damned by making them pursue eternally the same delights that condemned them to Hell. It is not proper, one supposes, to speak of a *"contrapasso"* in Heaven, but the principle of punishing and rewarding souls with what delighted them (and to the extent it delighted them) runs uniformly from Heaven to Hell, and testifies to the simplicity, in a theological sense, of divine justice.[9]

Merit and Character

But if the explanations given by Beatrice and Solomon show us how it is possible that souls experience different degrees of blessedness, they do not yet explain why different souls would have these different capacities. For in the process as Solomon describes it, the differing capacities of souls to apprehend God and experience blessedness is attributed to their greater or lesser possession of the gratuitous light that provides a medium for vision. What is missing, to this point, is an explanation as to why the individual souls (and presumably, the more general human activities and qualities they represent) should receive the differing amounts of grace that they do, and which then condition their degress of blessedness. Solomon states that the grace souls receive is beyond their merits (*sovra suo valore*), but that declaration does not imply that the amount they receive is arbitrary.[10] Even the minimum of grace, after all, could be said to be beyond human merit. For Dante, no human being could merit salvation by his or her own actions alone. The magnitude of the debt incurred by original sin, and human incapacity to repay it, is the fundamental human condition that demands the incarnation of Christ for its solution. This theological commonplace is given explicit statement by Beatrice at *Paradiso* vii, 19–51, and vii, 85–120.[11] But knowing that all grace is beyond human power will still not explain why some souls receive more grace than others.

As souls do manifest themselves to Dante, they do so as if the principle that allotted them different amounts of grace and indicated where they should locate themselves to make this manifest did somehow operate as if in reward of their lives and according to the actions that characterized their lives. Dante does not meet random individual souls in his journey; he meets souls gathered in groups who all pursued common ends, sometimes, we might even say, common professions. All the souls of the fourth sphere were philosophers or theologians; all of the sixth, rulers. The souls of each of the first three spheres exhibit distinguishing defects in their lives. Insofar as groups of souls are presented to Dante in a hierarchical order in his upward journey through the spheres, we as readers are presented with an exposition that seems inescapably to declare that the measures of grace allotted these souls were based on the nature of the actions that characterized their lives. Human action may not be sufficient to merit the grace that makes possible the vision of God, yet the character of that action seems to bear a direct relation to the measure of grace and blessedness any soul does receive.

If I keep using circumlocutions regarding what receives a given measure of grace, such as "the character of the actions to which certain souls were most akin," or "the actions that characterized an individual's life," rather than simply saying "they deeds they did" or "the actions they undertook," it is because I believe that one of Dante's motives in speaking about the allotting of grace as being "beyond merit" was to bypass any merely conventional estimation of merit as the basis of the order we discover in Heaven. For if we consider the souls we encounter, and the places in which we encounter them, it becomes clear that, while souls are arranged in Heaven according to some common active characteristics, we cannot say in any simple way that souls find themselves placed in Heaven according to the actions they took while alive.

It is only as we read the *Paradiso* that we see how critical it is to understand the principle of order and reward in Heaven, though we could have come to grips with this problem at any moment in the *Purgatorio*, had we stopped to ask the question, Where will any of these many souls whom we are watching suffer for their vices be located in Heaven once they have completed their corrections in Purgatory?

Where, for example, will someone like Buonconte da Montefeltro, a sinner to the last instant of his life, be placed? This is not a question with which Dante deals in the *Purgatorio,* nor, for that matter, in the *Paradiso,* except implicitly by his placement of souls in Heaven, about certain of whom we know just enough to see how problematic any answer to the question must be. For from the very first cantos of the *Paradiso* we encounter souls who make the simplest answer to the question untenable.

Our initial impulse would be to assume that justice demands that a person such as Buonconte, and any other whose life had been predominantly sinful, must find his ultimate place in the lowest spheres of Heaven. We would be assuming a material connection between the piety of one's earthly life and the measure of one's reward. The more pious the life, the higher one's place in Heaven; the more sinful, the lower. Yet several of the blessed souls we encounter in the lowest spheres show that Dante's understanding of the allocation of heavenly rewards does not follow any such material conception of justice. In the *Purgatorio,* we have been given a simple test for measuring the relative piety or sinfulness of someone's life. The amount of time spent in Purgatory, we are told, corresponds to the number and recalcitrance of the vices possessed by a sinner. Since the recalcitrance of vice depends directly on the degree to which the bad habit that is the vice has been practiced, the number of years spent in Purgatory provides a rough but fair measure of the ingrained sinfulness of a person's soul, irrespective of his or her ultimate salvation. Those who spend the least time in Purgatory, then, do so because their lives were freest of vice and sin. The simplest and most conventional sense of justice would expect that such souls should wind up placed highest in Heaven; those who have spent longer in Purgatory should be lower. But virtually from the start of the *Paradiso* we find Dante contradicting such a conclusion.

Charles Martel, for example, had been dead only five years when Dante encounters him in Heaven. Even if he is only just arrived in Heaven (which he neither says nor implies) and therefore had spent five years in Purgatory, if we compare that with Statius' twelve hundred years of purgation, we would have to conclude that his sins were insignificant. We would have to reach a similar conclusion concerning Piccarda Donati. Although the date of her death is not known precisely, given her brother Forese's recent death (such that hers would probably not have preceded it much in time), she too must have arrived in

Heaven with no, or scarcely any, stop in Purgatory. Indeed, Piccarda's life was exemplary in its holy beauty to her family and friends, and Forese was convinced that her prompt entry into Heaven was just recompense for that:

> La mia sorella, che tra bella e bona
> non so qual fosse più, triunfa lieta
> nell'alto Olimpo già di sua corona.
> (*Purg.* xxiv, 13–15)

But Dante *poeta* places her in the lowest sphere of Heaven, and Piccarda herself, as was cited above, calls attention to the lowliness of her station, and its justice. Charles Martel manifests himself to Dante only in the third sphere. In both cases, we find figures treated in a way that minimizes their blessedness and holiness despite their having led lives so pure as to require almost no purgation of vice. Yet if souls with so little sin in them are assigned so small a measure of grace, where is there room for justice in the handling of souls whose sins were far greater? Buonconte da Montefeltro, we have been told, had already spent eleven years in the antepurgatory before Dante met him there, and was to spend many more in that spot (a period at least equal to the length of his life) before he could even begin the process of purgation. But despite his sinful life, Buonconte will inevitably be rewarded at least as generously as Piccarda, for there is in fact no way to allot him less grace than she: there is no sphere lower than hers with which he could be associated. Were Dante to imagine him associated with any other sphere, his reward would in fact be beyond hers. Since we are sure that the order of Heaven must embody a principle of just reward, it cannot be the simple piety or sinfulness of these individuals' lives that is being rewarded.

The question is not merely hypothetical, since it seems clear that Dante could indeed imagine a person like Buonconte rewarded more generously than Piccarda, to judge from his placement of certain highly equivocal figures, if not outright sinners, in far more elevated positions than those occupied by the relatively pure Piccarda and Charles. Siger de Brabant and Joachim da Fiore, both condemned by their contemporaries for heretical writings, appear in the *Commedia* among the theologians.[12] Even more perplexing, when we consider their lives overall, are some of the kings to whom Dante calls special attention in the sixth sphere by placing them so as to form the eye of the eagle, which is the central poetic image of their sphere:

> Perchè de' fuochi ond'io figura fommi,
> quelli onde l'occhio in testa mi scintilla,
> e' di tutti lor gradi son li sommi.
> (*Par.* xx, 34–36)

But though all kings are given grace far greater than Piccarda's or Charles's (they are rewarded in the sixth sphere), and though those who form the eye are singled out even among kings, it cannot be for the sinlessness or general holiness of their lives. These specially distinguished kings are led by David, an adulterer and murderer, followed by two kings, Constantine and Hezekiah, whose actions led ultimately to disaster, though they are exonerated because of the rectitude of their intentions.[13] These three are then followed by two pagans, Trajan and Ripheus,[14] and finally William the Good of Sicily, about whom all that the commentators declare is that he was generous and more just than his predecessor or his successors.[15] What leads to their appearance in this sixth sphere cannot be the conventional moral quality of their earthly lives. That, apparently, must be seen as no more than secondary; possibly it is even irrelevant.[16] And that Dante takes such a casual attitude toward the actual events of the lives of the souls he meets when it comes to determining their placement in Heaven is what has led me to be so periphrastic in describing what it is about their actions or lives that actually does determine their location.

Yet if the actual earthly piety or sinfulness does not play a determining role in the grace awarded souls, as revealed in the order in which they manifest themselves to Dante, their distribution among the spheres is nonetheless meant to reveal significant distinctions in the origin (as well as measure) of the blessedness of these souls and others like them. But, then, what principles are being used? If we look at the question of finding a principle to determine the order from Dante's standpoint as he composed the poem, we can recognize that the very question of how to distinguish souls presents both poetic and theological problems. Certain criteria, it turns out, cannot be used. The current state of the souls, for example, cannot be used to make the distinction. Upon emerging from Purgatory, all souls should, in a sense, have become equally pure, and therefore their current (now eternal) purity is something they have in common and will not distinguish them from one another. We might look to the pasts of these souls for *differentiæ*, but, as we have already noticed, we cannot use the degree of purity of those pasts as the criterion and yet place them in the order of Heaven that we find in the *Paradiso*.

Indeed, as we consider the nature of the poetic problem, it becomes clear that any criterion to be used for distinguishing the source of the blessedness of the souls must meet some difficult and demanding conditions. On the one hand, even if we reject the purity of the souls' pasts as the standard against which to judge their rewards, the criteria we choose should still reflect some quality or qualities of the souls' earthly lives. This is so for a double reason: First, because justice, in a sense, demands it. We need to see that reward follows human action in some sense at least. Second, the criteria must reflect earthly lives because it is in fact only in their earthly lives that we see distinctions (rather than commonalities) between these souls. But if the needs of human understanding require that the criteria reflect something of earthly action, other—we may say, eternal—needs place further demands on the poet in making his distinctions. For at the same time that the criteria must reflect this world, they must also reflect qualities that are not of this world, and this demand too is for a double reason. First, it would seem that criteria for distinguishing souls in Heaven should reflect qualities that endure in some fashion into their immortal lives, and hence that could serve as eternal and unchanging grounds for the souls' distinction. Second, if the order of Heaven that we are to be presented is to reflect earthly estimations of the value of human activities as little as it does, the standards by which the estimations of the *Paradiso* are made must have their origin elsewhere than in human judgment.

The fourth canto of the *Paradiso* begins with Dante *personaggio* torn between two different questions: how to estimate Piccarda's "merit," and how to account for her location in a particular celestial sphere (*Par.* iv, 19–24). The way in which Beatrice addresses the problem points us toward those qualities that Dante believed provided the basis according to which grace is allotted to individual souls. Beatrice takes and restates Dante's question as to why souls appear in a given sphere as if he were wondering whether Plato was correct in believing souls originated each in its own planet, to which it returned at its death. She then answers his question by first rejecting the Platonic notion that individual souls return to the different stars by which they were created (*Par.* iv, 49–54).

Quel che Timeo dell'anime argomenta
non è simile a ciò che qui si vede,
però che, come dice, par che senta.
Dice che l'alma alla sua stella riede,
credendo quella quindi esser decisa
quando natura per forma la diede.

(*Par.* iv, 49–54)

Her rejection is for two reasons. On the one hand, she explains, the souls Dante encounters do not actually reside in the spheres in which he sees them. They merely manifest themselves to him there. (We have already cited this passage above.) Thus, properly speaking, no souls return to any planet. On the other hand, though, Beatrice also condemns any belief that human souls were created by the lesser intelligences who move the planets and stars. The consensus among commentators is that she does so on the grounds that such belief is inconsistent with the freedom of the will.[17] It is equally likely, and for the argument of the passage more appropriate, that she condemns it because, as Statius had previously stated (*Purg.* xxv, 70–72) and as Charles Martel repeats (*Par.* vii, 142–43), the creation of each human soul is an individual creative act of God, not of any lesser minister. But, at the same time that she rejects the doctrine that souls return to these stars that move in the spheres as if to their homes, Beatrice does state explicitly that the souls manifest themselves to Dante in these spheres to indicate the stars to which the praise and blame for their actions—though not the origin of their existence—must be attributed.

S'elli [Timæus] intende tornare a queste ruote
l'onor della influenza e 'l biasmo, forse
in alcun vero suo arco percuote.

(*Par.* iv, 58–60)

Thus, while Beatrice says it is wrong to believe that the stars create souls, she agrees that it is correct to assign to their influence over human action the formative power to which praise or blame is due. Asking, Why praise *and* blame? convinces us that it is influence over character of which we are speaking, rather than over individual actions. It is not that some stars produce wholly praiseworthy results and others wholly blameworthy. Certainly, the meaning intended is that the stars give their shape to the character of a person born under their influence.[18] Whether persons use that character for good or ill is a matter of their free choice. But good *or* ill, their actions will reflect the influence of that star, with its characteristic and characterizing qualities.

That the stars were responsible for personal character was an ancient and medieval commonplace, and Dante gives ample evidence of his agreement in it.[19] The extent of the stars' influence, and the manner of exerting that influence was, however, open to considerable and significant dispute. Aquinas, for example, repeatedly and consistently argued that the stars could influence human character only through their influence over the human body, and over character, therefore, only indirectly, through the body's influence over those parts of the soul (for example, the sensitive appetites) with unbreakable connections to the body.[20]

Dante, for his part, does not restrict the stars' influence only to transient (or even enduring but merely mortal) inclinations based on the operation of bodily passions. According to Beatrice, praise and blame can be attributed to the stars, even when we consider praise and blame in the context of eternal reward. Thus, in the *Paradiso*, the stars seem to have influence even over the immortal and immaterial aspects of human character. Already in the *Purgatorio*, Marco Lombardo's discussion of free will (*Purg.* xvi, 65–93), while assigning final responsibility for good or evil actions to free choice, admitted that the roots of human action were to be found in the spheres ("Lo cielo i vostri movimenti inizia"; *Purg.* xvi, 73). Charles Martel's lengthy explanation of how it is that worse children may be born to better fathers not only testifies to Dante's belief in the principle of the stars' influencing human character, but articulates the specific role played by the stars in doing so.[21]

Charles calls attention, first of all, to how significantly different the characters are between individuals. They are different enough to make civil government the greatest terrestrial good. Were characters not so different, that would not be true. When Charles makes this argument, Dante *personaggio* agrees completely (*Par.* viii, 115–20). Such different effects, Charles argues (*Par.* viii, 122–35), must have their own diverse causes, but the corporeal nature of humans will not account for these differences. Matter in itself is unchanging, and so cannot account for the differences in character. By inheritance, were that the only cause, people would never differ. They differ by what informs that matter: the spheres, which imprint their formative influence on the soul, as agents of divine providence.

La circular natura, ch'è suggello
   alla cera mortal, fa ben sua arte,
   ma non distingue l'un dall'altro ostello.
Quinci addivien ch'Esaù si diparte
   per seme da Iacòb; e vien Quirino
   da sì vil padre, che si rende a Marte.
Natura generata il suo cammino
   simil farebbe sempre a' generanti,
   se non vincesse il proveder divino.
           (*Par.* viii, 127–35)[22]

And so powerful is this formative influence on the characters of individuals, so innately ingrained, that is to say, are the characters of individual humans, that to try to train someone to a life contrary to this character is both futile and counterproductive.

Sempre natura, se fortuna trova
   discorde a sè, com'ogni altra semente
   fuor di sua regïon, fa mala prova.
E se 'l mondo là giù ponesse mente
   al fondamento che natura pone,
   seguendo lui, avrìa buona la gente.
Ma voi torcete alla religïone
   tal che fia nato a cignersi la spada,
   e fate re di tal ch'è da sermone:
onde la traccia vostra è fuor di strada.
           (*Par.* viii, 139–48)

As Statius had before him, Charles argues for the uniqueness of the creation of the human soul. One cannot say that the human soul "grows," like the souls of animals or plants. Plant and animal souls do grow from the material of the parents, whose formative power is itself material (*Purg.* xxv, 37–60). But the human soul is divine in its origin, both directly and indirectly. It has its existence directly from God ("ma vostra vita sanza mezzo spira / la somma beninanza"; *Par.* vii, 142–43; cf. *Purg.* xxv, 70–75); it receives its character indirectly from the spheres, which carry out the will of God.

Lo ben che tutto il regno che tu scandi
   volge e contenta, fa esser virtute
   sua provedenza in questi corpi grandi.
E non pur le nature provedute
   sono in la mente ch'è da sè perfetta,
   ma esse insieme con la lor salute:

per che quantunque quest'arco saetta
disposto cade a proveduto fine,
sì come cosa in suo segno diretta.
(*Par.* viii, 97–105)[23]

With its character determined from the beginning of its life as a human, a human soul can be said to grow only in the sense that actualizing the potential given it by its creator and its creator's instruments is also a sort of coming into being. The soul does not grow by adding new properties or capacities. It has been given its own. It does, however, progressively actualize the capacities it was given, and in that sense grows into the character that at first was only potential. How the imprint of the planets is actualized in the concrete actions of an individual—both in terms of which particular actions actualize that potency and in terms of whether they are good or evil actions—is the result of that person's free will. In this network of causes, no conflict exists between the operations of predestination and free will. God and his agents predetermine the general character of the actions an individual will undertake; the individual undertakes the particular actions by free choice.[24]

When souls manifest themselves to Dante in the spheres, they do so in order to exhibit to him to which stars' influence their actions (with resulting praise and blame), and their degree of blessedness, should be attributed. Souls appear in the poem in those spheres whose influence informed the characters that they spent their lives actualizing, whether the actions of their lives were good or evil.[25] That is the poetic principle affirmed in declarations by Cunizza and Folquet of Marseilles, speaking in the sphere of Venus:

Cunizza fui chiamata, e qui refulgo
perchè mi vinse il lume d'esta stella;
. . . .
. . . e questo cielo
di me [Folquet] s'imprenta, com'io fe' di lui.
(*Par.* ix, 32–33, 95–96)

Cunizza confirms that souls are distributed among spheres in Heaven according to the celestial influences that defined the character of their souls and impressed this character on their actions.[26] But pointedly she does not say that souls are distributed in Heaven according to the good or bad results of their actions, and in that omission expresses a principle of merit and grace very different from the conventional. The principle does respect the different characters of an individual's life on earth, which we said our sense of justice and poetry demanded. Giving a specific definition to a human character, after all, would surely find its reflections in the signal actions persons perform while alive (albeit, in some cases, obscurely), insofar as a character shaped in a certain way would regularly produce actions that were, as we would say, characteristic. Thus, the placement of souls in Heaven, insofar as it corresponds to the definition of their characters, reflects their individuality. Moreover, the definition given a soul's character is precisely a property that would endure in the soul even after its separation from the body, and thus this principle furnishes a standard for the eternal distinction of the souls in Heaven.[27]

But, at the same time, the shaping or defining influence of the stars would be reflected in all of a person's actions, irrespective of whether those actions were good or ill. Even sinners, then, can be used to embody and call attention to these defining influences, since their bad actions will share a recognizably characteristic shape with the good actions of those virtuous souls who were moved by the same celestial influence. Here, the principle departs from our conventional assessments of merit, though in a way that is also poetically liberating to Dante. Forgiven sinners will be rewarded in the same way as saints, if both have been defined by the influence of the same star. Perhaps this is even appropriate, since, as we have already considered, all souls in Heaven ultimately are equally sinless, either because of the original purity of their lives, or through the purgation of their vices. In any case, in determining the location in Heaven of the souls he encounters, Dante needed no longer to worry about assessing the moral value of their human actions. Rather, he could order the souls by reflection on the underlying nature or character of their actions and their capacities for action.

This, presumably, is what would explain the appearance in relatively exalted spheres of souls whose human life exhibited vice as well as virtue; it would also direct our forecasts as to the ultimate location of souls we have encountered in Purgatory. Once sinfulness/sinlessness is removed as the primary criterion for the location of souls, a soul such as Buonconte da Montefeltro's would most naturally manifest itself in that sphere whose power informed his capacities, even though those capacities found expression in his life most frequently in sinful actions. In many cases, this will result in placing notable sinners above the souls of individuals whose lives were much purer. But we have already been told that grace is awarded *sovra valore*, and the location of the souls exhibits to Dante a hierarchy not of good works but of capacity. The blessed souls, clearly, see no injustice in this allocation: they recognize that some souls, in their formation, were graced with a greater *capacity* for apprehending God. Some people with such souls may not have used this capacity well while alive, but the capacity must be as enduring as the soul itself that was shaped to that capacity; that is to say, immortal. And so, having overcome the evil actions and habits of their lives through forgiveness and purgation, these souls in Heaven necessarily acquire greater blessedness, since they will now exercise their capacity in its perfected state.[28] We have here the perfect inversion of the punishments of Hell. As the damned are condemned to practice eternally a clarified version of their defining sinful acts, the blessed are rewarded by the opportunity to practice eternally a clarified version of their defining spiritual qualities. There is only one justice, and since it is one that gives to our natures what is most natural, and therefore most desirable, to them, nothing could be more just.

The Quality, Not Quantity, of Holiness

But which capacities? And why are they in this order? For to conclude that souls are rewarded according to their capacities for action rather than their actual living actions provides only a riddling explanation of their location in Heaven if it cannot answer these two fundamental questions. That the souls' distance from God indicates different degrees of their blessedness—this we understand instinctively. That the souls Dante encounters in different spheres are grouped together because they share common qualities or capacities—this we also accept as poetically straightforward. The order of the celestial spheres in which the groups of souls are found therefore also embodies a hierarchy among these specific diverse capacities. We could expect to conclude, further, that the structure of this order establishes the primary distinctions and outline of the allegorical meaning of this *cantica* by articulating in the groups manifesting themselves in each sphere an enumeration of those human capacities of eternal theological significance. But we will not know the content of that allegory until we can

identify which capacities the spheres articulate, and until we can account for the order in which we find them. Now, we can find our evidence for the identification of the capacities themselves in what we know of the individuals whom Dante encounters, and, to a lesser extent, in what we may know was believed in conventional astrology of the planets and stars as agents and influences over human life. The principle of their order, as we shall see, resides in a special Dantean interpretation of the nature of the spheres.

I believe that we recognize intuitively that the capacities by which Dante distinguishes the grace allotted souls are qualitatively different from one another.[29] The different degrees of blessedness are not to be accounted for simply by the possession of greater or lesser quantities of one single quality of holiness. Our sense of the qualitative differences between spheres is grounded, on the one hand, in declarations by individuals with whom Dante speaks of common traits among all who manifest themselves in a given sphere and, on the other, in the significant differences between the characters of the lives of those who appear in one sphere or another. Some of the spheres are locations for different professions that call for and exhibit different skills or capacities: emperors, theologians, warriors. In other spheres the community is based on a more general common pattern of action or way of life: Justinian says that all who appear to Dante in the sphere of Mercury led active lives for the sake of honor and fame (*Par.* vi, 112–14); Charles Martel and Cunizza explain that in the sphere of Venus appear those who were vanquished by human love (*Par.* viii, 34–39, ix, 32–33).

The homogeneity of souls in each sphere (and their distinction from the souls of other spheres) is of fundamental importance, for in the structure of the *Paradiso* Dante is not arguing that souls receive more grace because they are more holy, but that they receive more grace, and indeed are thereby more holy, because they are of different natures. At an allegorical level, he is also arguing by this structure that the nature of our blessedness is constituted and understood by a number of essentially distinct capacities or activities, embodied piecemeal in the diverse capacities of the souls in their spheres. Given how important it is to Dante, it should not come as a surprise that he does not rely solely on poetic embodiment—which, by its nature, must always be ambiguous and open to misinterpretation—to express the principle. Beatrice supplies an explicit and "scientific" declaration of this principle almost immediately upon her and Dante's arrival in Heaven.

On two occasions in the *Paradiso,* Dante spends the effort—and calls attention to it—to correct earlier statements he had made regarding celestial matters. One regards the proper arrangement of the angelic orders in the celestial hierarchy (*Par.* xxviii, 97–139); the other the origin of the "spots" *(le macchie)* that can be seen on the surface of the moon (*Par.* ii, 46–143). In both instances Dante is correcting statements made in the *Convivio.* Neither seems on its face especially important, and yet both turn out to be of the greatest significance in understanding the underlying structure of the *cantica.* In the latter instance, that of the lunar spots, it is Dante *personaggio* who himself raises the issue to Beatrice, leading her to an explicit refutation of his earlier position. The question of the lunar spots seems throughout of such little importance for its own sake as emphatically to suggest an ulterior motive in Dante's lengthy and otherwise gratuitous treatment of the subject.[30] The content of the explanation with which Dante replaces his earlier position reveals the significance of the passage.

In the *Convivio* (ii, iii, 9), Dante had asserted that the dark and light patches on the surface of the moon were the result of differing densities of lunar material. At Beatrice's prompting, he repeats the hypothesis here (*Par.* ii, 59–60), only to have her refute it and replace it with a quite different explanation. What was wrong with Dante's original proposition, she says, is that it would reduce all questions concerning the differing appearances of celestial bodies to greater or lesser quantities of one single substance or power.

> La spera ottava [of the fixed stars] vi dimostra molti
>   lumi, li quali e nel quale e nel quanto
>   notar si posson di diversi volti.
> Se raro e denso ciò facesser tanto,
>   una sola virtù sarebbe in tutti,
>   più e men distributa e altrettanto.
> (Par. ii, 64–69)

But, Beatrice points out, the stars possess different powers *(virtù)* from one another, and these different powers have to be the result of different formal causes. Since Dante's position would have reduced all formal causes to one only, it is impossible for his original position to explain the distinctive powers the stars exercise.

> Virtù diverse esser convegnon frutti
>   di principii formali, e quei, for ch'uno,
>   seguiterìeno a tua ragion distrutti.
> (Par. ii, 70–72)

The true principle, she explains, is that both the existence of the
stars and their powers are distributed in such a way that each star—
perhaps Dante means each individual star, at the least, certainly each
celestial sphere and its informing star—possesses its proper, individu-
ated, and characterizing powers.[31] Being, once received from the prime
mover, is distributed downward to stars of lower spheres in differing
formal distinctions—distinctions of essence.[32]

> Lo ciel seguente, c'ha tante vedute,
> quell'esser parte per diverse essenze,
> da lui distinte e da lui contenute.
> Li altri giron per varie differenze
> le distinzion che dentro da sè hanno
> dispongono a lor fini e lor semenze.
> (*Par.* ii, 115–20)

When a soul animates a body, it does so by distributing its operation
among the different organs and members of the body. In doing so, the
distinct powers the soul possesses for operation become manifest.
When they do, by virtue of appearing in different organs, their differences from one another also become apparent. The same process,
Beatrice asserts, occurs in the formation of the stars. As the human
soul distributes the exercise of its multiple powers among its diverse
organs, so the many powers possessed unitarily by God are distributed
among the stars. The stars become, as it were, the organs in which the
divine intelligence is displayed, but since it is diverse individual divine
powers that are distributed to them, it is inevitable and natural that as
they manifest the properties of the divine intelligence, they display
readily distinguishable, and essentially different, properties.

> E come l'alma dentro a vostra polve
> per differenti membra e conformate
> a diverse potenze si risolve,
> così l'intelligenza sua bontate
> multiplicata per le stelle spiega,
> girando sè sovra sua unitate.
> (*Par.* ii, 133–38)

It is these differences of qualitative properties that make the stars appear different, not different amounts of one single property.

> Virtù diversa fa diversa lega
> col prezïoso corpo ch'ella avviva,
> nel qual, sì come vita in voi, si lega.

Per la natura lieta onde deriva,
  la virtù mista per lo corpo luce
  come letizia per pupilla viva.
Da essa vien ciò che da luce a luce
  par differente, non da denso e raro;
  essa è il formal principio che produce,
conforme a sua bontà, lo turbo e 'l chiaro.
                              (*Par.* ii, 139–48)

Now, this discussion of the origin of lunar spots can scarcely be thought to be of any importance in itself. It takes its importance—being given where it is, before Dante has encountered even a single soul in Heaven—by being offered to us as the key to interpreting the array of souls we are soon to see. Beatrice corrects Dante regarding lunar spots in order to make explicit the principle that any differences that exist between spheres are differences of essence, differences in the natures of the planets. In their capacity to shape the characters of people, then, the character of the actions they will influence will also exhibit these differences in nature or essence. When Dante learns subsequently from Beatrice that the souls appear to him as they do for a didactic purpose, we can conclude that that purpose is both to make it easier for him to understand to which celestial influences the character of these souls' actions should be attributed, and also to array for him the complete set of distinguishably characteristic human capacities for action. And, finally, when Dante later hears from Solomon that the locations of the souls in Heaven reflect the greater or lesser degrees of grace they have been allotted, we can conclude that the hierarchy of grace that is exhibited across the corporeal Heaven of the poem has been determined according to the essentially different characters of human action as defined by the influence of each of the spheres.[33]

This conclusion enables us to make a new sort of sense out of the declaration that grace is awarded beyond merit *(sovra suo valore)*. For it is not only that God's grace surpasses any human merit, but it is also the case that the grace awarded, as we can now conclude, is a function of divine, rather than human, properties distributed through the stars to human characters. Reward does not follow terrestrial human action; it follows some divine order. Because of this, some sinners, we expect, have received and will receive grace far beyond what they would have deserved on the basis of their prior actions—their merit, in any conventional sense. But at the same time, the grace received is not wholly apart from their qualities as human beings. They receive grace for having a soul of a certain nature. The proximate source of their character is the star that informed their lives (the ultimate source, of course, is God), but precisely by being informed by that star their actions took on its distinct character. Grace does not follow the purity or sinlessness of their actions, but it reflects their actions since those actions were informed by the character of soul each individual had been given and then freely actualized by choice.[34]

PART II

THE SOURCE OF THE ORDER

OF THE *PARADISO*

The Spheres and the Angelic Hierarchy

As we have already mentioned, unlike his practice in the *Inferno* and the *Purgatorio,* Dante gives no explicit description of the order in which human activities are arrayed in the *Paradiso.* Nonetheless, there is an order that lies behind the order of the spheres and of the human souls who manifest themselves to Dante in them, an order that, like the orders of the two earlier *cantiche,* explains the essential significance of the activities in the order. Behind the order of the spheres, and, indeed, informing that order, is the hierarchy of angels, and understanding Dante's interpretation of that hierarchy and its significance is the key to understanding the decisions he has made in his placement of human activities in Heaven, as well as the significance of that placement.

Treatment of the angelic or celestial hierarchy—the hierarchical arrangement of different classes, called orders, of angels—was a specialized theological topic. Dante has Beatrice make an appropriately circumscribed reference to the topic as a specialized subject in her brief discussion of the sphere in which the angels manifest themselves to Dante, the ninth and highest moving sphere (*Par.* xxviii, 97–139). But for Dante, the hierarchy of angels took on an importance far more extensive than its special discipline.

By the sixth century if not earlier, Christian angelology had identified nine different classes of angels (the nine are conventionally called orders), and arranged them in higher or lower ranks, corresponding to their closeness to God. At the same time, medieval astronomy, as we know, had identified nine moving celestial spheres that, in their greater distance from the earth as the center of the material universe, could also be said to be arranged based on their closeness to God. (In addition to the nine moving spheres, a tenth immobile sphere—for Dante, the empyrean—was also recognized.)[35] For each of these moving spheres, its proper motion was initiated and superintended by a spiritual entity—an intelligent, noncorporeal being—which was called the sphere's "intelligence."[36] Surprisingly enough, no author prior to Dante seems to have made what would otherwise appear an irresistible symbolic and theological concordance: the assignment of each order of the angelic hierarchy to one of the celestial spheres, matching them by their relative position within the order of spheres or the angelic hierarchy.[37]

At least as early as the *Convivio*, however, Dante had associated the nine planetary spheres with the nine orders of angels: "The first point to be made is that the movers of the heavens are substances independent of matter, that is, they are Intelligences, popularly known as angels" (*Conv.*, ii, iv, 2). Each sphere was superintended by a different order of angels (often, as here, called "hierarchies" in themselves): "The moving heavens, which are nine, tell their numbers, orders, and hierarchies" ("Li numeri, li ordini, le gerarchie narrano li cieli mobili, che sono nove"; *Conv.*, ii, v, 12).[38] Within the *Commedia*, this association can be seen to acquire a most profound significance: every human being's character, we have been told, is shaped by one star or planet that influences that character at birth; but in the light of this conviction expressed in the *Convivio*, it is clear that the stars and planets themselves, being only corporeal entities, however august, have received their characters and their characterizing powers from the intelligences (that is, the angels) who are their movers.[39] Thus, it is the diverse natures of the different angelic orders—about which theological texts had much to say—which were the actual causes of the diversity of human characters.[40]

In the passage of canto ii (already cited), in which Beatrice explained that differences in the appearance of the heavenly bodies correspond to essential qualitative differences between those bodies, she also related those differences specifically to the motors that move the heavenly bodies, that is, their intelligences:[41]

> Lo moto e la virtù de' santi giri,
> come dal fabbro l'arte del martello,
> da' beati motor convien che spiri;

> e 'l ciel cui tanti lumi fanno bello,
> della mente profonda che lui volve
> prende l'image e fassene suggello.
> (*Par.* ii, 127–32)

In context, her simile is especially appropriate: the hammer's "art"—its ability to produce a specific result—bears the imprint of its user, the smith; the powers *(virtù)* of the spheres bear the imprint of their angelic movers *(da' beati motor)*.[42] But, as we learn from her in canto iv, the *virtù* of these spheres are their capacities to give form to the human characters over whom they had influence. Human character, therefore, must be said ultimately to have been "artfully" shaped by the angelic orders who use stars and planets as instruments for their work.[43]

To the extent that anything was known about the properties of angels—and much had been written, both directly and indirectly about them—those properties could be used to identify which human activities were appropriately associated with given angelic orders and the planetary spheres they superintended. The hierarchy in which human activities were arrayed would then simply, and from Dante's perspective, naturally, follow the angelic hierarchy. Our task is to discover the significance of the hierarchy Dante follows in the *Paradiso*, in order to recognize how that hierarchy determines why grace is allotted to human activities in the order with which we are presented.

The order that Dante uses in the *Paradiso* is different from the one he used in the *Convivio*, as is confirmed for us by Beatrice in canto xxviii (*Par.* xxviii, 97–139). It is the order articulated by one of the most important sources in angelology, the sixth-century neo-Platonic author known as pseudo-Dionysius the Areopagite. In his *Celestial Hierarchy*, Dionysius had divided the corps of angels into nine orders called, to use the English translations of the names by which they were known in Latin: seraphim, cherubim, thrones, dominations, virtues, powers, principalities, archangels, and angels.[44] In the *Convivio*, Dante had followed a competing arrangement of the angelic orders, that of Gregory the Great.[45] The difference between the two arrangements seems to be—not only to modern eyes, but even to medieval commentators[46]—relatively minor, but the change from Gregory's system to Dionysius' was apparently significant enough to Dante to warrant his making no fewer than three explicit references to the fact that he had changed his opinion.[47] If it was important enough for Dante to make a point of his shift to Dionysius' arrangement, we ought to conclude that the specific properties attributed to the angels in Dionysius' arrangement, and in discussions of Dionysius' text, were of serious significance to Dante in determining the nature of the human activities that he, in turn, associated with the angelic orders.[48]

Human Properties, Angelic Properties, Divine Properties

Two kinds of statement on which Dante could draw had been made regarding the angelic hierarchy and the properties of angels. There were, of course, direct statements about the orders of angels made in primary texts such as Dionysius' and Gregory's and in commentaries on their texts by both major and minor medieval authors. But probably even more significant, and perhaps the explanation for Dante's minute concern to be as correct as he possibly could regarding the arrangement of the angelic hierarchy, was the fundamental and momentous declaration about the angelic hierarchy implicit in the assumption (common to all authors by the twelfth century) that the order of the hierarchy reflected the nature of God and, even more specifically, the Trinity. For Dante (and he was not alone in this), the order of the spheres, the order of the angelic intelligences who move them, and indeed, the entire created universe reflect and manifest the image of their Creator. With respect to the angelic orders, the ultimate source of this interpretation is pseudo-Dionysius the Areopagite.

For Dionysius, the hierarchy not only reflects the image of God, it is also the means of making its members (and members of other hierarchies) as much like God as possible.

> Hierarchy, according to me, is a sacred order, a science, an activity that assimilates itself, as much as possible, to deiformity, and, proportionally to the illuminations which God has given it, raises itself—to the extent of its capacity—to the imitation of God. . . . The goal of hierarchy, therefore, is assimiliation to and union with God, to the extent possible. . . . Hierarchy receives the imprint of God's most divine beauty to the extent it can, and it also makes its celebrants perfect sacred images of God, the clearest and purest of mirrors, receptive to the primordial light, the divine ray. . . . And so, when one speaks of hierarchy one signifies in general a certain sacred disposition, an image of the divine splendor, which accomplishes in its orders and sciences the sanctifying mysteries of its own illumination, and which assimilates itself, as much as is right, to its own principle. (*CH*, iii, 1–2; 1044c–1045b)[49]

The Dionysian interpretation that the angelic hierarchy was ordered to the image of God came to be incorporated into all medieval
tracts on angelology, whether they followed Dionysius' arrangement of
the hierarchy or some other.[50] None of Dante's likely sources would
have questioned the principle, and Dante himself is consistent in ad-
hering to it, whether in the *Convivio*, where he followed Gregory's
arrangement of the angelic orders, or in the *Commedia*, after he had
adopted Dionysius' arrangement. For Dante (as, indeed, was true
also for Dionysius and, in qualified senses, for many authorities), all of
creation reflected this image.

> ... Le cose tutte quante
> hanno ordine tra loro, e questo è forma
> che l'universo a Dio fa simigliante.
> (*Par.* i, 103–5)

But while the rest of creation necessarily resembled God in some
way, it could do so only in the way, as Aquinas says, any finished work
is informed by and bears the image of the artist who made it (a description that finds an echo in Beatrice's statement that the physical
heavens embody, display, and articulate the divine nature "come dal
fabbro l'arte del martello" [*Par.* ii, 128]—as the hammer's work reflects
the carpenter).[51] To exhibit the *image* of God was a special property
shared only by angels and humans, and of the two, the angels exhibit
the image most completely.[52]

This specific theological interpretation of the implicit content of
the angelic hierarchy is what guaranteed to Dante the appropriateness
of using that hierarchy not only as the template for the organization of
Heaven, but precisely as the means of determining the degrees of human blessedness that would be made manifest in the *Paradiso* through
that organization. The actions of the different angelic orders determine the character of human individuals and human action through
the intermediary of the planets under whose influence the individuals
are born. Inasmuch as the angelic hierarchy matches the order of the
planetary spheres, the hierarchy of human actions determined by the
operation of those spheres will in turn exactly match—in fact, it has its
origin in—the angelic hierarchy. But if the explanation of the order of
the angelic hierarchy is to be found in the resemblance of this order
to the divine nature, then the order of human activities exhibited to
Dante in the *Paradiso* will find its explanation in the resemblance it too

has to the divine nature, a resemblance given to it by the angelic orders. For Dante, then, the angelic hierarchy is not merely a convenient
pre-existing structure to use to explain the order of the souls encountered in Heaven, it is precisely the best, most natural, even most necessary structure.[53]

The real, and significant, relationship of human characters, angelic
orders, and divine nature is repeatedly emphasized throughout the
Paradiso. The interlocking metaphors of mirrors, reflections, and images are the most vivid repeated poetic figures in the *cantica.* Starting
from Dionysius' declaration that the individual angels and their hierarchy as a whole constitute a mirror that reflects the divine image—
"hierarchy . . . makes its celebrants perfect sacred images of God, the
clearest and purest of mirrors, receptive to the primordial light, the divine ray" (*CH,* iii, 2; 1044d–1045a)—Dante again and again refers to
souls as mirrors that reflect the light of God; to angels reflecting specific characteristics of God's nature; to the whole of creation bearing
the imprint of that nature. And yet, if we wish to understand the profound combination of poetic and theological power in Dante's use of
the angelic hierarchy, a more revealing metaphor would be to describe
the celestial hierarchy as a *prism* that disperses the incomprehensible
unity of the divine nature into discrete and separately comprehensible
properties and powers in the same way that the unity of white light is
dispersed into a spectrum of discrete colors. A similar metaphor is at
work in Beatrice's final statement to Dante regarding the orders of angels in the ninth sphere: a multiplicity of mirrors is necessary to be
able to reflect piecemeal the greatness that God possesses in unity:

> Vedi l'eccelso omai e la larghezza
>   dell'etterno valor, poscia che tanti
>   speculi fatti s'ha in che si spezza,
> uno manendo in sè come davanti.
>   (*Par.* xxix, 142–45)[54]

The angels distribute, through their own differentiated natures and
their further distinct and differentiated stellar and planetary instruments, discrete and, as it were, fragmentary, aspects of the indivisible
divine nature into individual human characters.[55] In doing so, the angels introduce dissimilarity where there was originally only unity. For
Dionysius, the distinction between the simplicity of God and the multiplicity of everything created is perhaps the first of distinctions to be

made if we are to understand our incapacity to comprehend the divine nature.[56] Any image of God—that is to say, any reflection of God in any medium—even the best image, such as the angelic hierarchy provides, introduces diversity into what was unitary, dissimilarity into something that exists only as purely itself.[57] Yet, while the angels are thus the first source of our dissimilarity to God, that very dissimilarity provides our only opportunity to understand the divine nature in any form and at all.

According to Dionysius—and Dante agrees completely with this—having become dissimilar to God in our multiplicity, our understanding inevitably must begin in multiplicity.[58] However distant the angels' own multiplicity may be from God's simplicity, the angels and their hierarchy are actually, and for this very reason, the best evidence—best in the sense of best adapted to our faulty comprehension—that we have of the divine nature. The multiplicity of the angels' natures, a multiplicity that is nonetheless a refracted image of the divine nature, provides material on which our understandings can operate. This is the poetic justification for Dante's use of the hierarchy to organize Heaven. Ultimately (though this will be the subject of the next chapter of this book), the organization will make it possible not only to understand the nature of blessedness (by embodying and making possible the discovery of the principle according to which grace is allotted), but also to come to a more profound understanding of God's nature (insofar as we come to see the activities arrayed in this hierarchy as reflections—or, should we say, "refractions"—of aspects of that nature).

The Angelic Hierarchy and the Persons of the Trinity

For Dante, the refraction of God's simple nature into the diversity of creation means a distribution of God's single substance into nine new substances, each reflecting a different aspect of God's nature. This is the declaration made in the *Commedia* about the nine angelic orders by Aquinas *personaggio*:

> Ciò che non more e ciò che può morire
>   non è se non splendor di quella idea
>   che partorisce, amando, il nostro sire:
> chè quella viva luce che sì mea
>   dal suo lucente, che non si disuna
>   da lui nè dall'amor ch'a lor s'intrea,

per sua bontate il suo raggiare aduna,
quasi specchiato, in nove sussistenze,
etternalmente rimanendosi una.
Quindi discende all'ultime potenze
giù d'atto in atto, tanto divenendo,
che più non fa che brevi contingenze;
e queste contingenze essere intendo
le cose generate, che produce
con seme e sanza seme il ciel movendo.

(*Par.* xiii, 52–66)

But an understanding of the way in which the nine orders of angels articulate nine divisions of the divine nature begins with an initial division of the nine orders into three triads (each of three orders), reflecting in these three triads the persons of the Trinity. This had been Dante's conviction also in the *Convivio:*

> Both the number of the hierarchies and the number of the orders enable us with great confidence to give an account of their contemplation. For since the divine Majesty exists in three persons who constitute a single substantial being, the contemplation of these persons can take three forms. The supreme power of the Father can be contemplated; on this the first hierarchy gazes, that is, the hierarchy that is first in nobility and last reckoning from our position. The supreme wisdom of the Son can be contemplated; on this the second hierarchy gazes. The supreme and burning love of the Holy Spirit can be contemplated; on this the lowest hierarchy gazes, the hierarchy which, being closest to us, offers us a share of the gifts it receives. (*Conv.,* ii, v, 7–8)

That the nine orders of angels were distributed into three triads (and sometimes these triads too were called "hierarchies," as in this passage) and that this distribution three times reflected the three persons were already common conclusions by the thirteenth century.[59] The basis, again, is implicit in Dionysius, who had distributed his nine orders into the three lesser hierarchies, and though he made no explicit link between the triads and the Trinity, it was an easy step to see the parallelism to the Trinity as simply a further particularization of how the hierarchy as a whole imitated God. (Moreover, there is in Dionysius a direct statement that each of the orders of angels reflects God in a different way, and therein the implication that each order reflects a different aspect of the divine nature: "Each name of these beings superior to us [i.e., angels] signifies their deiform properties by which they imitate God" [*CH*, viii, 1; 1053d]).[60]

While medieval sources might disagree concerning the arrangement of the particular orders of angels, or their assignment to one or another of the triads, by the time Dante was writing, there was no disagreement that the triads did reflect the Trinity.[61] The triad of angels closest to humans was associated with the Holy Spirit, reflecting the special affinity of the Spirit to human beings.[62] The triad of angels farthest from humans, and therein most divine, was associated with the Father. The middle triad was associated with the Son. Dante uses this assignment in the *Convivio*, and while he makes no explicit mention of the association of these triads with the Trinity in the *Paradiso*, there is no reason not to believe that he continued to be convinced of the appropriateness of the interpretation.[63] Beatrice's enumeration in canto xxviii of the nine orders of angels divides them into three triads (now following Dionysius' sequence of orders, as well as his triadic principle), and nothing contradicts the association of those triads with the persons of the Trinity as was conventional, and as had appeared in the *Convivio*.

For some commentators on the angelic hierarchy, Dante among them, the full nine orders of angels could be said to furnish an even more detailed image of God by taking the trinitarian principle of the triads and applying it to the three orders that composed each of the triads. The source of this exegetical strategy is again Dionysius, and in this regard too Dante was always more essentially Dionysian in his interpretations of the angelic orders than he was Gregorian. At the heart of Dionysius' doctrine was the conviction that the orderliness of hierarchies in general implied that the principle that ordered them would be identically applied to each of their parts, as well as to the hierarchy as a whole.[64]

> The superessential Harmony of all things has so provided for the holy and beautiful ordering of each of its reasoning and intellectual beings, that it has made itself one single sacred and beautiful order of hierarchies, and so we see every hierarchy divided into first, middle, and final powers. Indeed, each one of these dispositions itself, properly speaking, has been divided according to these same divine harmonies. . . . One could reasonably add here that each soul—both celestial and human—possesses first, middle, and final orders and powers, which the souls manifest proportionately to the proper upliftings which they have been given. (*CH*, x, 2–3; 1058d–1059b)[65]

> One thing should be known first of all: that the holy resolutions of the formed images signify the same sanctifying dispositions of the celestial essences, and sometimes having been sanctified, and other times

sanctifying in turn, and both those sanctified earlier, and themselves, all having first, middle, and final powers. (*CH*, xv, 1; 1065a/b)

The result of a consistent application of this strategy to all levels of the angelic hierarchy (indeed, Dionysius extended these same principles to human levels of hierarchy)[66] was an intricate formal structure within which the otherwise obscure nature of individual orders of angels could be illuminated by considering their natures as the result of a complex combination of attributes that could be predicted based on the location of their order in the hierarchy. The three triads of the hierarchy as a whole had been associated, as we have seen, with distinct persons of the Trinity. But each of the three orders within each triad could also be associated in a secondary way with a person of the Trinity. This secondary association would supplement the triad's primary association, and between them a more detailed sense of the nature of a given angelic order could be concluded.[67]

It should be said that not all writers on angelology were interested in so intricate an application of this principle, or in applying it rigorously to all nine of the orders. But in the *Convivio* Dante not only showed himself aware of the strategy, he showed he believed it ought to be applied across all nine orders:

Since, further, each person of the divine Trinity can be considered in three ways, each hierarchy [i.e., each triad] contains three orders which contemplate in different ways. The Father can be considered simply with respect to himself. . . . The Father can be considered in terms of his relationship to the Son. . . . Again, the Father can be considered in terms of the procession of the Holy Spirit from him. . . . Both the Son and the Holy Spirit can be contemplated in a similar way. There must, therefore, be nine kinds of contemplative spirits who gaze into that light which alone sees itself completely. (*Conv.*, ii, v, 8–11)

In the *Convivio*, Dante worked out the articulation of the orders of angels according to these permutations of different persons of the Trinity only for the highest triad of angels. But given that in context his purpose was to explain the special nature of an order that appeared in the lowest triad, it is clear that, though he did not enumerate the combination of persons associated with each angelic order, he believed such a combination does exist for each order. And, as he expresses it, the completed pattern of these combinations provided the most perfect image of God:

The moving heavens, which are nine, tell their numbers, orders, and hierarchies; the tenth proclaims the very unity and stability of God. As the Psalmist says: "The heavens speak of the glory of God, and the firmament proclaims the work of His hands." (*Conv.*, ii, v, 12)

At a wholly abstract level, we can see how temptingly attractive this compounded trinitarian image within a trinitarian image would have been to mystical or figurative exegetes. In a certain sense, it might even be seen as not especially mystical. It could be seen simply as an attempt to make use of the known orderliness of creation to deduce characteristics of spiritual creatures about whom human reason could have no direct knowledge. Since the angelic nature of each triad reflected, as image, attributes of the person of the Trinity associated with its location in the hierarchy, the same could be said, though presumably in an attenuated sense, of each of the individual orders within a triad. That is, in some lesser degree, attributes that would be characteristic of an entire triad occupying a given location in the celestial hierarchy as a whole could also be said to characterize in a secondary way those individual angelic orders that stood in equivalent or parallel positions within their triads. One could then reason about the nature of an individual angelic order by considering its character as defined, first of all, by the primary attributes of its triad, and then by qualifying or reinforcing these primary attributes with secondary attributes determined by discovering and applying to it the attributes appropriate to its location within its triad. In a theological sense, the source of all these attributes would be the persons of the Trinity with whom given locations were associated, though certain attributes might also be discovered in specific descriptions of the natures of given orders of angels either from the Bible or from other writings on angels.

At the concrete level, however, of matching persons of the Trinity to individual orders within the three triads, the abstractly attractive project became unexpectedly difficult. Few commentators tried to explain the working out of the schematism for all nine orders; those who did, Dante included, I believe, were faced with conflicting principles they could not have resolved, and were therefore forced to find accommodations to minimize these conflicts.[68] There was general agreement, as has been mentioned previously, that the highest triad should be associated with the Father, the middle with the Son, the lowest (the triad nearest to human beings) with the Holy Spirit, but after that agreement broke down. The most straightforward application of the symmetry Dionysius asserted existed throughout the hierarchy would have directed using the same associations of person and location within each triad. Unfortunately, to do so involved conflict with other, equally authoritative principles. (Rather than burden the argument at this point with a discussion of the problems inherent in any of the solutions, I have relegated that discussion to Appendix 3.) The arrangement that I believe Dante followed in the assignment of persons to orders inside each triad was therefore a sort of compromise between the conflicting principles. It was, at least, a compromise that relied on a consensus of the commentaries on Dionysius' and Gregory's texts.

Most writers on angelology went through the process of associating persons of the Trinity with individual orders of angels only for the three orders in the highest triad (if they bothered to make these associations at all). In almost all cases, the pattern they used assigned seraphim secondarily to the Holy Spirit (the triad as a whole, we remember, was associated primarily with the Father); cherubim to the Son; and thrones to the Father. My conviction is that Dante used this same pattern throughout the angelic hierarchy when it came to associating persons with the orders of angels within each triad. Thus, in the intricate fabric he established of combinatory relations of the persons of the Trinity to the angelic orders, I believe we would be correct in concluding that Dante wove the fabric in the following way: for primary attributes, the highest triad of angels would be associated with the Father, the middle with the Son, the lowest with the Holy Spirit; for secondary attributes, however, within any given triad, the highest order would be associated with the Holy Spirit, the middle again with the Son, the lowest with the Father.[69] All members of the highest triad, then, would be associated primarily with the Father. Seraphim would be, as mentioned above, secondarily associated with the Holy Spirit; cherubim with the Son; thrones with the Father. All members of the middle triad would be associated primarily with the Son; with dominations secondarily associated with the Holy Spirit; virtues with the Son; powers with the Father. All members of the lowest triad would be associated primarily with the Holy Spirit; with principalities secondarily associated with the Holy Spirit, archangels with the Son, and angels with the Father.

PART III

THE MEANING OF THE ORDER
OF THE *PARADISO*

Angelic Qualities and Human Character

The only point of our consideration of angelology is for the light it sheds on the principles by which Dante assigned *human* souls to one or another location in Heaven, and the help it gives us in understanding the meaning of this assignment. Dionysius had explicitly extended the identical hierarchical principles throughout all of intelligent creation: to the angelic hierarchy, first of all, then to the ecclesiastical hierarchy, and ultimately to every individual intellectual creature, within whom too, again explicitly, one could find the same distinctions and structures as underlay the angelic hierarchy. In just the same way that the angelic hierarchy was an image of God, the human soul is also an image of God, and it and its activities must also embody in their own way the structure of divine attributes we find first of all among the angelic orders.

> One could reasonably add here that each soul—both celestial and human—possesses first, middle, and final orders and powers, which the souls manifest proportionately to the proper upliftings which they have been given. (*CH*, x, 2–3; 1059a/b)

As Dante would have understood it, *angelic orders* are arranged as they are because of the relations of the individual orders to individual persons of the Trinity. *Planets and their spheres* in which souls manifest themselves to Dante necessarily embody the same relations, for the planets acquire the characteristics they possess from the angelic intelligences who move them, and these characteristics, therefore, will exhibit the attributes of those angels as well as the complex of relations to the Trinity which characterizes the different orders of angels.[70] Insofar as the planets can be held praise- or blameworthy for their influence on human action or character, as Beatrice declares to Dante that they can be, they are so because they transmit their qualities to humans, which is to say that they transmit the same angelic characteristics, the same angelic relations to human beings. *Human action or character* is thus itself informed by the same principle as the angelic hierarchy is, though at two removes: that is, human character is informed by the complex interrelation of divine attributes that we can see reflected in angels and spheres, after these attributes have been transmitted by them to people.[71]

When Dante *poeta* has souls manifest themselves to Dante *personaggio* in particular spheres, therefore, it reflects his conviction that there exists an affinity between their actions or characters and the combined divine or angelic attributes that characterize the angels and planets associated with those spheres.[72] Dante could then use everything he knew about the angels and about how they manifested the divine attributes appropriate to their locations in the angelic hierarchy, and everything he might additionally conclude about the attributes of the divine natures associated with those same locations, as a means for providing the structure by which he could discriminate that certain human natures or activities were more or less blessed, and the criteria by which he could recognize what was significant in the differences among them.

Filling the map of the nine heavens with the symbolic content of the divine attributes provides the allegorical content of the third *cantica:* a new estimation of the value of various human activities, not in worldly terms, but in terms of the rewards these activities receive in Heaven. When it came time to find material with which to fill the map, Dante had a wide array of sources on which he could draw. Since the outline of the map came from the hierarchy of the orders of angels, he could use, first of all, attributes of those angelic orders, as discussed in the Bible, or in treatises on angelology, and especially in Dionysius' *Celestial Hierarchy* and the commentaries on it. Since, further, all agreed that the angelic orders and their hierarchy represented the image of God, two further sources for the content of the map opened up: direct statements in treatises on angelology that associated divine attributes with specific angelic orders, and discussions of the attributes of hierarchy in general, to the extent that these discussions might sometimes reveal attributes of the Trinity that could be used to explain the natures of certain angelic orders or provide clues to the meaning of the placement of a given angelic order in a given location. In medieval treatises, the three persons of the Trinity might be described by any of several different sets of three qualities; the triple divisions of the angelic hierarchy, and of the three orders of angels within each division, could be similarly described by theologians by diverse, but parallel, sets of properties. Any of these sets, singly or in combination, could be

drawn upon, should Dante wish, to furnish clues to the proper location of given human activities, or to provide new descriptions of the
real nature of those activities.

Dionysius, for example, had declared that every hierarchy embodied and instilled order, knowledge, and activity (*CH*, iii, 1; 1044c).
With three terms, three triads, and three orders within each triad, there
was an understandable inclination to associate these three qualities
singly with individual locations in the hierarchy, and thence with specific persons of the Trinity who might also be recognized in one or another of these terms. Dante, in turn, could search for these qualities in
the human activities that fell under the direction of angels in those locations, or, to speak more properly in the order of his own invention,
he could use his discovery of these qualities in certain human activities
to direct him to associate those activities with the location in the
spheres that would be determined to possess the same qualities. In
doing so, he would also be associating activities that exhibited these
qualities with the appropriate member of the Trinity. Nor was Dante
limited to terms that appeared in the *Celestial Hierarchy*. Aquinas, in
exploring the Dionysian order, had explained the existence of the three
triads of the overall hierarchy by distinguishing three relations of the
angels to their ends: contemplation or union, government or disposition, and execution.[73] These terms too could be individually related to
persons of the Trinity, and angelic orders or human activities that subsequently exhibited these characters could be associated in primary or
secondary ways with specific persons and the locations in the angelic
hierarchy—and therefore with a specific sphere—also associated with
that person. Dante himself had used certain sets of terms, both in the
Paradiso and earlier in the *Commedia,* to refer to the Trinity—in the
Inferno: Potestate, Sapïenza, and *Amore* (Power, Wisdom, Love; *Inf.* iii,
5–6); in the *Paradiso: Valore, Ardore,* and *Amore* (Strength, Ardor, Love;
Par. xiv, 37–42, and x, 1–3)—and these terms too could be used to
characterize angels or human activities associated with these persons.

Similarly, insofar as other theological discussions may have associated human powers or activities with persons of the Trinity, these
further associations could be used by Dante to fill out his explanation of the relationship between certain human souls and the spheres
and angelic influences to which they were attached in the poem. In
Augustine's *de Trinitate,* the persons were associated with three human
intellectual faculties: the Father with the memory, the Son with the

reason, the Holy Spirit with the will. Aquinas associated three orders of angels with these same faculties, and I believe Dante extended this association to cover all nine orders of angels.[74] Given the concrete connection between angelic and human character in the *Paradiso,* to the extent that angels are associated with a specific faculty (we will deal later with the problem created by Beatrice's explicit statement [*Par.* xxix, 76–81] that angels do not possess a faculty of memory), so they would pass along to the human souls under their influence their special association with the action of a given faculty. Thus, in writing the *Paradiso,* Dante could take the notable manifestation of the operation of a particular faculty in one kind of activity as an indication of where to locate the soul among the spheres.

Finally, if there were conventionally accepted attributes of the planets in whose spheres Dante encounters souls, Dante could use those attributes too to determine in which spheres to place souls whose worldly activities manifested these attributes, to the extent, at least, that even the planets' actions could be seen as reflections of properties whose primary source was the persons of the Trinity. From all of these different sources, then, Dante could amass a great reservoir of terms and descriptions, all of theological significance, all seemingly parallel to the hierarchy through which he intended to explain the ordering of human action and reward. In the intricate interweavings and combining of all of these terms, in the paralleling of the angelic hierarchy as a whole to the persons of the Trinity, in the interior parallelism of individual angelic orders within a triad to the hierarchy as a whole, in the relation of the nine spheres with their planets to the angelic hierarchy and all of these associated angelic and divine properties, Dante could give the human activities manifested in each sphere new definitions, by using their locations in this order to specify unique combinations of divine attributes, and by discovering in these combinations the eternal significances of those activities.

In the previous two *cantiche* of the *Commedia* the underlying allegorical structure was always also indicated in the narrative details of the literal journey. In the *Paradiso* too, despite the almost painfully abstract character of the "geography" of Heaven, Dante again provides just enough narrative detail to confirm the discrimination of three regions in Heaven, corresponding to the three triads of the angelic hierarchy, and constituting our first entrance into the structure of this realm. Although every sphere has its own individual size and speed of rotation, certain spheres are grouped together and their groups distinguished from other groups. Dante signals these groupings to indicate the kinship of spheres in sets of three (reflecting the angelic triads), first by pointing out that the three spheres nearest to the earth can all be said to be within its shadow (*Par.* ix, 118–19). These first three spheres are thus associated with one another, and also are distinguished from the six spheres beyond them which do not lie within earth's shadow. Next, of the remaining six, the three highest spheres are distinguished in their turn from the three middle spheres by being traversed by the golden ladder Jacob had seen (*Par.* xxi, 28–30), which therefore provides a material connection and spiritual bond between them. Indeed, the ladder testifies to the affinity of these three spheres to each other by suggesting easy movement among them, while at the same time distinguishing these spheres from the three below them which are not connected in this way.

Even in such terse descriptions, Dante gives effective poetic expression to the fundamental distinctions between the lives of these three regions. We realize that we are supposed to agree that literally and figuratively the lives of the souls in the lowest three spheres, however virtuous they may have been, were all led in the shadow of this world. The souls of the six (for humans, actually five) spheres above these escaped this terrestrial limit, though that does not mean their lives were equal in all respects. Only the souls of the seventh and eighth spheres spent their lives in that direct contemplation of God that rendered them like the angels of the ninth sphere in the immediacy of their association with God, and their special access to God, and closeness thereby to the angels, is symbolized by their spheres' possession of Jacob's ladder. The souls of the middle three spheres engaged in lives of a middle quality. Not bound by the world's concerns they escape earth's shadow, but insofar as all chose to pursue the active life, however saintly their activity, it kept them from the special access to God that comes from the contemplative life.

The qualities that are distinguished in these three categories, and that Dante saw as constitutive and exhaustive of the human lives and characters recognized in Heaven, are selected and compiled precisely because they are qualities associated with the persons of the Trinity, or with the angelic orders associated with those persons. Having sketched out the general pattern of Dante's strategy, we must now examine in detail how he uses the qualities discovered in his sources to determine and explain the nature of human action and the principle of its reward.

The Middle Triad of Angels and the Middle Three Spheres of Souls

To medieval readers, certain associations of divine characteristics with angelic orders or human activities would be more straightforward and less controversial than others. In all of the commentators who identify angelic orders with persons of the Trinity, the middle position, whether of triads or individual orders within a triad, is assigned to the Son. Hence, the triad composed of the three middle orders, and the three middle spheres that they govern, and the three human activities manifested in those spheres should all reflect characteristics of the Son. In the more complete versions of the combinatorial geometry of these interpretations, the middle order of the middle three ought to exhibit those characteristics in the most intense way, for that order should reflect the Son in both its primary and secondary attributes, while in the two other orders of the middle triad, the primary attributes of the Son would appear in combination with secondary characteristics of other persons.

Two sorts of attributes are characteristically associated with the Son. On the one hand, as the Word, he is associated with wisdom, science, and reason. On the other hand, the central event in the human life of the Son was his passion and the fortitude, even daring or courage, that it implies.[75] Both attributes can be found throughout all three orders of the central triad, both in the descriptions of the angelic orders of that triad, and, most important to us, in the activities of the human souls who manifest themselves to Dante in the spheres of that triad.

Dante would have found his initial associations of these properties with this triad in Dionysius, even though Dionysius, as we have said, never explicitly aligned the persons of the Trinity with specific orders or triads of the celestial hierarchy. For Dante would have noted that within Dionysius' declaration that every hierarchy "is a sacred order, a science, an activity that assimilates itself, as much as possible, to deiformity" (CH, iii, 1; 1044c), the middle term of this declaration (which appears as *scientia* in Latin) very comfortably reflects the Word, and he would have seen that Dionysius ran the Son's two qualities of wisdom and courage together, as the defining properties of every martyr.

God is praised as Reason by the holy scriptures . . . because he is the giver
of reason, intellect, and wisdom. . . . Faith in God is the single foundation
for believers, binding them to the truth, and the truth to them, with
them possessing as believers that simple knowledge of the truth with an
amazing immutability. . . . Thus, as we believe, the principal leaders of
our divine wisdom die for the truth every day, bearing witness in what
they do, in word and deed, to the one true wisdom for Christians; that is,
that of all things this is most simple and most divine, itself the sole, true,
single, simple, divine knowledge. (*Div. nom.*, vii, 4; 1155d–1156c)[76]

While the souls of all three of the middle spheres of the *Paradiso*
exhibit these attributes in one or another way, the souls of the middle
sphere of these three (the souls of the holy warriors and martyrs, in the
sphere of Mars) exhibit them—in what we know of the lives of these
individuals, and in the descriptions and images with which Dante constructs his encounters with them—as we would expect, in the most
direct way. In Dante's linkage of sphere to angelic order, these souls
would have had their characters formed by the order of angels called
virtues, and with regard to this order the quality to which Dionysius
calls special attention, most appropriately, is their fortitude.

The name of the holy virtues signifies a strong and unshakable
courage—their deiformity—in all their operations. There is no weakness
in their undertaking of the divine illuminations. They are powerfully
brought to the imitation of God. Nor do they ever relinquish their
deiform motion to any softness, but firmly bringing themselves to the
transcendent essence and the power that creates all power; and making
themselves into the clearest image of that power (as far as is right), and
turning themselves to it as to the powerful principle of their power, to
the second giver, indeed, of power, and its deiform provider. (*CH*, viii, 1;
1054a–b)[77]

Aquinas in his turn, commenting on this passage in Dionysius, further speaks of the order of virtues as acting as "champion" ("adiuvans
et propugnans"; *In 2 Sent.*, ix, 1, 3), an especially resonant description
in this context, and associates their fortitude with knowledge by arguing that their name "signifies that they undertake fearlessly the Divine
behests appointed to them; and this seems to imply strength of mind"
(*ST*, 1a 108, 5 ad 1).[78] Gregory had attributed the working of miracles
to this order,[79] and Aquinas took that as confirmation of their characteristic vigor and efficacy, since superseding natural law is among the
most arduous of actions.[80]

The planet of this sphere, Mars, by which the virtues would act on human souls had itself long been associated with courage and daring, and thus straightforward, even pagan, poetic practice reinforces the description of the character of souls born under the influence of this sphere. In the context of our present discussion, it is clear that Dante would attribute the characteristics of the planet Mars not to the planet itself but to the angelic virtues that use the planet as their instrument. That is, all known poetic associations with planets or stars would, in the context of the *Paradiso,* undergo a redefinition: what had once been believed to be the influence of the planet would now be understood as the reflected influence of an angelic power with certain attributes, and, ultimately, as the reflected influence of the divine attributes possessed by the angelic order that informed the planet or star.

The souls whom Dante encounters, his ancestor Cacciaguida among them, were either warriors on behalf of the Church, or martyrs, or both. All, therefore, exhibit the Son's attribute of fortitude, and, in the collocation of qualities that Dionysius makes (cited above), also exhibit the attribute of firm knowledge on which such unshakable fortitude must be based. Nor is it incidental or casual that the central poetic figure of this sphere is a cross, formed by these souls as they manifest themselves to Dante. Indeed, the use of the cross in this sphere as its signal distinguishing visual feature—and its use in this sphere only—seems to me a definitive poetic sign of Dante's special association of this fifth sphere with the Son.[81] And Dante *poeta* calls explicit attention to the special affinity the lives and characters of these souls demonstrate to those attributes exhibited by Christ in his passion:

> Qui vince la memoria mia lo 'ngegno;
> chè 'n quella croce lampeggiava Cristo,
> sì ch'io non so trovare essemplo degno;
> ma chi prende sua croce e segue Cristo,
> ancor mi scuserà di quel ch'io lasso,
> vedendo in quell'albór balenar Cristo.
> (*Par.* xiv, 103–8)

While the souls under the influence of the middle order of angels of the middle triad ought most to manifest attributes of the Son, the souls of the other two spheres of the middle triad should also exhibit those attributes forcibly (more so than souls of either the highest or lowest triad, since those triads would primarily be associated with other persons of the Trinity), if not exclusively. And, indeed, the souls manifested in both of the other spheres of this middle region share with the martyrs and warriors the active and arduous attributes of Christ's passion, insofar as we discover that their lives were spent in active and difficult pursuits for others' sakes, thus reflecting Christ's courage and sacrifice in the realm of human activity.[82]

Given that their positions among the spheres would associate other persons of the Trinity with them secondarily, however, we would expect them to reflect qualities additional to and different from those exhibited by the souls of the fifth sphere, to the extent that the angelic orders that informed their characters exhibited properties that combined Christ's attributes with those of the other persons of the Trinity. Thus, according to what we believe was Dante's principle of ordering these combinations, we would expect the souls of the sixth sphere to exhibit a combination of Christ's attributes with significant, if secondary, attributes of the Holy Spirit; and souls of the fourth sphere to exhibit a combination of the Son's attributes with those of the Father. In every case, it would have been on the basis of their exhibiting certain sets of qualities from among the matrix of combinations of divine attributes that Dante would have determined in which spheres souls should be placed in order to make manifest this principle of celestial judgment and order.

That Dante places the just rulers in the sphere of Jupiter would again (as in the case of Mars with the warriors) have an immediate and simple poetic appropriateness, but here too Dante would see another, theologically deeper explanation. If the planet Jupiter is especially associated with rule, it is because, Dante would now say, its sphere is superintended by the angelic order of dominations. Medieval interpretation of the nature of angelic orders always began with analysis of the angels' names, which therefore straightforwardly associates this order with rule. But later discussions could add further content. Aquinas, for whom the whole of the middle triad of the angelic hierarchy is concerned with government and the establishment of peace, sees the upright administration of such government as dependent on the dominations' special character as directors and emperors ("aliquo dirigente et imperante"; *In 2 Sent.*, ix, 1, 3). If this is the nature of the angelic intelligences who direct this sphere, and if the planet of this sphere is also associated with empire, small wonder that those souls who lived the lives of just rulers—or had a character that was capable of such rule—would appear to Dante here.

But within the angelic hierarchy, the character of the dominations (and thereby any souls informed by their influence) would be shaped, given their location in the highest order within their triad, by the addition of attributes of the Holy Spirit to the primary attributes of the Son (associated with the middle triad as a whole). It is exactly that association that gives the dominations their special appropriateness to just rule. The most common of associations regarding the Holy Spirit was with charity, and, on the basis of this association, Augustine could also argue a further association with the faculty of will (the will was, in Augustine, the representation of the Holy Spirit in the image of God in humans).[83]

In the poetry of this sixth sphere Dante exhibits both of these attributes to us, making apparent thereby the influence of the Holy Spirit on the souls of this sphere. When the souls of this sphere first appear to him, before they come to compose the imperial eagle that remains the enduring image of the sphere, they spell out by their lights five words: *Diligite iustitiam qui iudicatis terram*—Love justice, you who rule the earth. The statement as a whole would of course be generically appropriate to just rule, but it has a special appropriateness we can now recognize. Justice, we know, is the cardinal virtue of the will, and if, by being shaped by the attributes of the Holy Spirit the rulers have a significant association with the will, then they would have a special association with this virtue. Moreover, the will is also an appetite, and the rulers, in the message they spell out, exhort others not only to practice justice but to *love* justice: to take it as an object of desire.[84] Both terms in this message—*iustitiam* and *diligite*—have a special relevance to empire because of their combination of divine attributes in which Dante believed the foundation of empire lay.

The dominations who are the intelligences of this sphere are themselves characterized in ways that stress an unceasing striving for true justice, and their pursuit of justice reflects not only the virtues of the will (and Holy Spirit) but also the fortitude and perseverance that are attributes of the Son.[85] The just rulers, in their turn, exhibit both qualities too, and love of justice, in this regard, is the charity that rulers show toward their subjects.[86] It was precisely this combination of qualities, and especially charity, that those princes who are delayed in the antepurgatory lacked.

In the lowest location of the triad, the fourth sphere (the sun) are found the souls most frequently identified as the theologians.[87] Their "planet" too, of course, as a figure for illumination and understanding, had a long poetic association with their occupation, but again their location in the *Paradiso* reflects Dante's conviction that both that figure and their properties are the result of the specific angelic order that governs their sphere. That order was the order of powers, and Dionysius had specifically associated the powers with the intellect: "Their name reveals . . . their beautiful and unconfused ordering to the divine receptions, and the orderliness of their ultramundane and intellectual power" (*CH*, viii, 1; 1054b).[88] Since the fourth sphere is in the middle triad, Dionysius' description ought to reflect attributes of the Son, and indeed is clearly appropriate to one of the Son's primary attributes, wisdom.

However intuitive this association is, it is interesting that Dante does not stop simply with it. Rather, his greatest effort is spent in associating the theologians with the other active and arduous attributes of the Son, in addition to his wisdom. Some of these additional associations come from other statements regarding the nature of the order of powers, some from the implications of the location of this order within the matrix of divine attributes. Gregory, for example, had asserted that one of the special functions of this angelic order was the suppression of enemy powers, and the preservation of the righteous from temptation:

> Those angels are called powers who are more powerful than others in understanding, such that enemy forces are subject to their strength, and such that those enemy forces are restrained by their authority, lest otherwise they succeed in tempting the hearts of men as they wish.[89]

Almost all of the theologians whom Dante *personaggio* is shown could be said to have spent their lives in the defense of the faith and faithful from error.[90] This, indeed, is what is stressed in the longest discussions of this sphere, the encomia of Saint Dominic and Saint Francis. Neither Dominic nor Francis is represented to Dante as associated with this sphere. Their qualities most likely locate them in other, higher spheres. (In the case of Dominic this is merely implicit in his nonappearance here; in Francis's case, we can judge from his lofty position in the *candida rosa* that he occupies a higher place in Heaven.) But their philosophical followers are in this sphere, and what the two greatest of them stress is the almost literally military nature of their war on error. The accounts of Francis and Dominic by Aquinas and Bonaventure *personaggi* (in cantos xi and xii) describe the two saints as warriors. Bonaventure calls Dominic a *paladino* (*Par.* xii, 142), and both Dominic and Francis *campioni* (*Par.* xii, 44). They are both generals of *l'essercito di Cristo* (*Par.* xii, 37). In describing their work as if a martial enterprise, Dante makes clear to us the active nature of theology as he conceives it here in the *Paradiso*.[91] The theologians of the fourth sphere are not idle dreamers. As far as Dante is concerned, they, like the other members of the middle triad, have chosen the active life; true contemplatives are rewarded elsewhere, in a higher sphere. Philosophy and theology, for Dante, are active pursuits, and in this regard reflect the general activity of the middle triad, which in turn reflects the fortitude and action of the Son. Their field of battle may be doctrine, but they are regarded as warriors in ways strikingly and surprisingly similar to their companions in this middle region, the warriors, martyrs, and emperors, individuals who are more conventionally associated with battle.

Aquinas provides a further linkage between the theologians and the other souls of the middle spheres. In his discussion of the powers (the angelic order), he describes the role of these angels as specifically related to understanding what must be done for the sake of justice. The execution of what they determine was the office of the two higher orders of their triad.

> This order [i.e., triad] is disposed to peace in three ways: by a certain order judging what is needful for everyone; and this is the function of the order of powers. . . . But judgments *[sententiæ]* must be efficacious and right, and for them to be efficacious, they require a certain helper and champion, so that nothing that was determined by judgment be impossible to execute; and this is the function of the order of virtues. . . . And that judgments be right requires some ruler or emperor; and this is the function of the order of dominations. (*In 2 Sent.*, ix, 1, 3)

Insofar as the powers stand in this relation to the orders of virtues and dominations, much the same could be said of the theologians, who could be said to provide the *sententiæ* that strengthen the resolve of the militant and that the rulers execute in laws and government.

Within the matrix of the combinations of divine attributes, we would expect that the angelic order, powers, and the theologians who manifest themselves to Dante in the sphere associated with the powers, would exhibit, in addition to their primary attributes received from the Son, secondary attributes from the Father. In the triads of terms Dante uses to refer paraphrastically to the Trinity, the Father is always associated with terms for power (*Potestate, Inf.* iii, 5; *Valore, Par.* x, 3, and *Par.* xiii, 45). Dionysius' description of the powers as assimilating themselves to "that authority which is the source of all power" (*CH,* viii, 1; 1054b) would confirm for Dante their secondary association with the Father. To understand the nature of the order of powers, then, as Dante would have expressed it in the *Convivio,* the Son should be considered in his relation to the Father (cf. *Conv.,* ii, v, 8–11). In relation to the Father, the Son is the Word by which the truth of the Father is expressed, and if it is predictably obscure to us how that might apply to a given angelic order, it has a distinctly intuitive appropriateness, once the connection is articulated, to the activity of the theologians. They, of all of the human figures in the middle spheres, spend their lives in an understanding of the Word. Dante, in fact, seems to refer to this special relation to the Father in the activities of theologians, by reducing their philosophical interests to the fundamental investigation of the process of filiation and procession by which the Trinity is constituted.

> Tal era quivi la quarta famiglia
> dell'alto Padre, che sempre la sazia,
> mostrando come spira e come figlia.
> (*Par.* x, 49–51)

To the extent that in Augustinian discussions the person of the Father would be associated with the faculty of memory (as the Holy Spirit had been with the will), a further aspect of the character of the theologians could be understood as the result of the combination of attributes of both the Son and the Father. Aquinas had linked the third order of the first triad to the memory, and the same association is appropriate to the powers in their triad, not only through the formal symmetry of their location in their triad, but also because of a symmetry in their relationship to the other members of their triad.[92] Their primary association with the Son is played out in their pursuit of wisdom, but as all human intellective activity begins with the memory, the nature of their activity links them to the Father as well. Indeed, the specific functions Aquinas identifies as the activities of the memory while speaking of the thrones—comprehending and retaining—could comfortably be said to be characteristics possessed by the theologians. They too can be said to comprehend and retain truths.[93]

The Lowest Triad of Angels and the Lowest Three Spheres of Souls

As we touched on earlier in this chapter, the location of souls in the lowest three spheres of Heaven surely indicates a certain deficiency in their lives, a state that receives only the most humble reward. But at the same time, we recall, the location cannot simply imply that the souls appearing there were sinful in their lives. Some surely were; others not. By considering, however, the angelic orders associated with these spheres, and the matrix of attributes their locations would assign to these spheres, we can discover a meaning regarding that deficiency which in a sense is distinct from sin, and a significance that indicates how the array of human activities associated with these spheres fits into the organization of Heaven.

That there is deficiency in these spheres is evident, from what we know of the particular souls we encounter there and their histories, and even more importantly from the explicit comments Dante has them make regarding their location in these spheres, comments that, in the narrative context of these meetings, are now especially reliable since informed by their newly acquired heavenly insight. Justinian describes the souls of the second sphere as having fallen short in their lives by deviating from the best end they might have sought:

> Questa picciola stella si correda
> di buoni spirti che son stati attivi
> perchè onore e fama li succeda:
> e quando li disiri poggian quivi,
> sì disvïando, pur convien che i raggi
> del vero amore in su poggin men vivi.
> (*Par.* vi, 112–17)

Piccarda Donati in the first sphere too had recognized that the spatially lower location of herself and other souls in that sphere reflects some deficiency in the actions that had characterized their lives:

> E questa sorte che par giù cotanto,
> però n'è data, perchè fuor negletti
> li nostri vóti, e vòti in alcun canto.
> (*Par.* iii, 55–57)

The comments of Cunizza da Romano in the third sphere, similarly, reflect regret for the past that has assigned her to her sphere, though that regret is overcome by her joy at being in Heaven:

> Cunizza fui chiamata, e qui refulgo
> perchè mi vinse il lume d'esta stella;
> ma lietamente a me medesma indulgo
> la cagion di mia sorte, e non mi noia;
> che parrìa forse forte al vostro vulgo.
>
> (*Par.* ix, 32–36)

A virtually identical sentiment—an acceptance and forgiveness of one's past that perforce reminds one of the weakness of one's past—is echoed by Folquet of Marseilles:

> Non però qui si pente, ma si ride,
> non della colpa, ch'a mente non torna,
> ma del valor ch'ordinò e provide.
>
> (*Par.* ix, 103–5)

But though these souls regret their past, and though it is what they regret that has assigned them to these lower spheres, it would still be a mistake to conclude that these souls are in any way being punished by their relegation to the lower spheres. Cunizza and Folquet testify to their sense of absolution for the sins of their past. Folquet speaks of Rahab's presence in the third sphere as evidence of a double triumph: of Christ's, obviously, to have redeemed her from death, but worthy of notice too was her own triumph in support of Joshua. Her good actions brought her to Heaven, even though her character has in some way assigned her to the third sphere.

> Or sappi che là entro si tranquilla
> Raab; e a nostr'ordine congiunta,
> di lei nel sommo grado si sigilla.
> Da questo cielo, in cui l'ombra s'appunta
> che 'l vostro mondo face, pria ch'altr'alma
> del triunfo di Cristo fu assunta.
> Ben si convenne lei lasciar per palma
> in alcun cielo dell'alta vittoria
> che s'acquistò con l'una e l'altra palma,
> perch'ella favorò la prima gloria
> di Iosuè in su la Terra Santa.
>
> (*Par.* ix, 115–25)

Even in Justinian's explanation of the failings of himself and his companions in the second sphere, he describes them as *buoni spirti:* their motives were honor and fame, terrestrial rather than divine motives, but the actions themselves, and the souls, are nonetheless characterized as good. Finally, as we have mentioned earlier, the rapidity with which Piccarda Donati and Charles Martel have arrived in Heaven testifies in itself to the essential sinlessness of their lives.

Piccarda recognizes that her humble location is the result of her breaking of a vow. But since she was coerced into breaking that vow, Dante asks Beatrice how it is possible to hold someone responsible for an unwilling action. And Beatrice's answer makes clear to us the context in which these judgments are being made:

> Se vïolenza è quando quel che pate
>   nïente conferisce a quel che sforza,
>   non fuor quest'alme per essa scusate;
> chè volontà, se non vuol, non s'ammorza,
>   ma fa come natura face in foco,
>   se mille volte vïolenza il torza.
> Per che, s'ella si piega assai o poco,
>   segue la forza; e così queste fero,
>   possendo rifuggir nel santo loco.
> Se fosse stato lor volere intero,
>   come tenne Lorenzo in su la grada,
>   e fece Muzio alla sua man severo,
> così l'avrìa ripinte per la strada
>   ond'eran tratte, come fuoro sciolte;
>   ma così salda voglia è troppo rada.
>
> *(Par.* iv, 73–87)

"Ma così salda voglia è troppo rada"—a will such as Lawrence's or Mucius' is so rare. So rare? Virtually unheard of, rather! To criticize Piccarda for not being a Lawrence or a Mucius is to criticize her for nothing more than being human rather than superhuman. And therein is the key to the location of these souls and the relation of the first three spheres to the six higher ones. The souls of the first three spheres are not sinners being punished by their lower location. If some were sinners, we know that others were not. But in all of them their powers for good were limited by the common, and real, human limitations under which almost all people act.[94] The human souls of the five succeeding spheres (the ninth sphere contains only angels) exhibit no such limits to their capacities. The qualities of those souls—for whom Lawrence and Mucius, Christian and pagan martyrs, stand as examples—can be said, in the most concrete sense, to be superhuman.

In speaking of Piccarda, Beatrice points out that her defect (and the same is true, we recognize, of the souls of all of the first three spheres) came from considering the human and temporal consequences of her situation and her choices. This is what limited her capacity to act.

> Voglia assoluta non consente al danno;
>   ma consentevi in tanto in quanto teme,
>   se si ritrae, cadere in più affano.
> Però, quando Piccarda quello spreme,
>   della voglia assoluta intende, e io
>   dell'altra; sì che ver diciamo inseme.
>   (*Par.* iv, 109–14)

Piccarda's absolute will was sound. What wavered, however, was what commentators (reflecting scholastic distinctions) have called her "contingent" or "relative" will.[95] Life in this world inescapably poses such choices between greater and lesser dangers. Nothing in Beatrice's comments, and nothing in the evidence we have of the judgment passed on Piccarda and like souls, suggests she made such choices badly or sinfully. But she did make them in a way characteristic of this world, rather than the next. Only a Mucius or a Lawrence can look with such contempt on the values of this world (including, of course, safety and self-preservation) as to hold fast to his "absolute" will without any interference from his "contingent" will.

When Beatrice says that Piccarda falls short of Lawrence she makes a judgment but not a condemnation, and I believe Dante used Piccarda as the object of this judgment precisely to make that distinction clear. Piccarda did not live a sinful life. She could not have arrived in Heaven as swiftly as she had, had that been so. Her defect was that her will was limited in its strength and capacity to the merely human. That is no ground for condemnation. But in the hierarchy of powers and characters that we find in the nine spheres it is a sufficient reason for locating her soul (and those of persons we find in the first three spheres) in spheres lower than those in which we find souls with capacities greater than that. Had Dante begun his discussion of the lower spheres of Heaven with a notoriously sinful soul, we might have misinterpreted the meaning of its location as a condemnation of the sins of its life. By beginning with Piccarda, he forces us to recognize that it was the limits on her capacity for action that made this sphere most appropriate as the location in which to have her manifest herself. And once we recognize that, we will also be in a position to recognize later that souls of greater capacity will appropriately be manifested in the (higher) spheres that reflect those capacities, however sinful their earthly lives may have been.

The earthly limitations of the capacities of the souls of the first three spheres is obviously implicit in the metaphor Dante puts into Folquet of Marseilles's mouth: that these spheres all lie within the earth's shadow ("in cui l'ombra s'appunta / che 'l vostro mondo face"; *Par.* ix, 118–19). But inasmuch as Dante also uses the structure of the angelic hierarchy to order and inform his judgments regarding human activities, the three angelic orders associated with these spheres, which would be the intelligences that informed the human characters of those born under their influence, also reinforce the earthbound nature of these souls.[96]

The characters of these souls again reflect the character of the angelic orders that informed their lives. The lowest triad of angels as a whole—the triad of angels, archangels, and principalities—consistently was assigned a special relation to humanity in medieval angelology. For Dionysius, it is the nature of a hierarchy that entities above have a duty to communicate their superior knowledge to entities below, as a means of illuminating and uplifting their subordinates. Each order in the angelic hierarchy receives illumination from the orders above it and communicates it to the orders below.[97] The orders of angels that are lowest in the hierarchy, having received illumination from angelic orders above them, have a duty to communicate their illuminations to those creatures below them—that is to say, to people.

> As we have already said, the angels complete and fulfill the whole of the dispositions of the heavenly souls as it should be fulfilled, as among the celestial essences they most show the property of being an angel. They are angels [i.e., messengers] far more to us than the earlier [celestial intelligences] were, and so are aptly named "angels" insofar as their hierarchy is more concerned with what is more manifest [to us] and is disposed to the world. . . . The most manifest disposition of principalities, archangels, and angels presides over the human hierarchies. . . . Whence the Bible assigns our hierarchy to the angels. (*CH*, ix, 2; 1056c/d, 1057a)[98]

For Aquinas, indeed, it was in the very nature of the angels of the lowest triad to be adapted to a role of communication to people. These three orders of angels all had understandings that were limited by their relation to this world, in a way that brings their intellects very close to those of human beings. These orders, according to Aquinas, understood the "order of divine providence as it is knowable in particular [i.e., rather than universal] causes" (*SCG*, iii, 80). With understandings most limited in the way that human understandings are limited, these angels are therefore the best interpreters to humans, because most capable of being understood by humans.

> Or things can be known in their proper causes, and this is the mode of the final hierarchy [i.e., triad], for whom the forms are most particular and are proportioned so that they can be understood by our intellects. For this reason this third angelic hierarchy is said to receive the divine light according to its suitability to our hierarchy; whence it is that the orders of the third hierarchy are named as their activities are limited to single men or to a nation. (*In 2 Sent.*, ix, 1, 3)

In the literature on angelology, therefore, these three orders of angels were consistently associated with the Holy Spirit in the Trinity, almost certainly because of a general conviction of the Holy Spirit's special relationship to humanity. With respect to the illumination that raises humanity to beatitude—and this raising is the purpose of all hierarchy—Aquinas declares that the Holy Spirit is the person to whom this agency should be attributed:

> So that a man arrive at the beatitude of divine enjoyment, which is proper to God and in accord with his nature, it is necessary, first, that the man be made like God by spiritual perfections, and then that he act in accordance with these, and in this way he will at last attain to this beatitude. Therefore are the spiritual gifts given us by the Holy Spirit, as was shown, and thus are we configured to God through the Holy Spirit. It is through it that we are rendered fit again for acting well; and it is through this same Spirit that the way to beatitude has been made ready for us. (*SCG*, iv, 21)[99]

Inasmuch as the angels receive their properties from the persons of the Trinity with whom they are associated, the angelic orders of the lowest triad receive their primary characteristics from the Holy Spirit (in the standard angelological interpretation), and if the Spirit has a special role as messenger to humanity and its uplifter to beatitude, then the lowest triad of angels would mirror this role. To medieval angelologists, this would explain the special role of angels as messengers to people, and gloss Dionysius' declaration that these orders had special responsibility for the uplifting of humanity toward God.

But the Holy Spirit, as we know, was also understood by medieval commentators as it was reflected in the faculty of will, principally because of its association with love and charity.[100] The lowest triad of angels should therefore also reflect properties similar to those of the will, and would, in Dante's interpretation, impress these properties on the souls who came under their influence. In this context, there becomes recognizable the general emphasis on deficiencies of the will—the faculty of intellectual appetite—in the characters of the souls who appear in the first three spheres. According to Aquinas, the will was explicitly and necessarily connected to choice. Choice, he said, can be described as "the appetitive faculty [i.e., the will] deliberating."[101]

The defect of the souls in the first sphere, in this regard, was precisely in their wills. They chose, and then unchose, and their lives showed the success of the "contingent" will over the "absolute" will for all those who failed in their vows, and for that reason manifest themselves in the lowest sphere. The importance of vows, Beatrice explains, relates directly to God's greatest gift to his creatures, freedom of the will. That the will can freely bind itself is proof of its freedom, and its primary devotional act.

> Lo maggior don che Dio per sua larghezza
>   fesse creando ed alla sua bontate
>   più conformato e quel ch'e' più apprezza,
> fu della volontà la libertate;
>   di che le creature intelligenti,
>   e tutte e sole, fuoro e son dotate.
> Or ti parrà, se tu quinci argomenti,
>   l'alto valor del voto, s'è si fatto
>   che Dio consenta quando tu consenti;
> chè, nel fermar tra Dio e l'uomo il patto,
>   vittima fassi di questo tesoro,
>   tal quale io dico; e fassi col suo atto.
>   (*Par.* v, 19–30)

Within the matrix of divine attributes built from the symmetries between triads and orders or spheres within triads, the angelic order associated with the sphere of the moon, and therefore the souls under its influence, should reflect attributes of the Holy Spirit in its relation to the Father. In terms we have already been using for attributes of the persons, the order of angels and its sphere, then, should reflect and impress characteristics of the will (from the association of the first triad with the Holy Spirit) in its primary or fundamental or simplest, unqualified activity (from the position of this order as the first in its triad, thus associated with the Father, as primary and fundamental person of the Trinity). The souls whom Dante shows us in the sphere of the moon exhibit a defect of the will in exactly its simplest and unqualified operation. In their cases, they made the right choice but could not keep it. It is *strength* of will (the first characteristic of the faculty) that they lacked. In a world of contingency, their wills succumb to contingency, rather than maintaining the steadiness that would reveal spiritual capacities both above the human and worthy of reward in the higher spheres.

Criticizing the souls of the first sphere, Beatrice laments the rarity of the higher steadiness: "ma così salda voglia è troppo rada" (*Par.* iv, 87). That steadiness is, apparently, a quality associated with the Father as foundation, in each of the angelic triads. In the fourth sphere, also a first sphere of a triad, the theologians provide unshakable conclusions that form the basis of the actions of the souls of the next two spheres. In the seventh sphere, again a first sphere of its triad, Saint Benedict comments on the qualities of his fellow contemplatives in this sphere in terms that refer to precisely the qualities that were deficient in the souls of the sphere of the Moon:

> Qui è Maccario, qui è Romoaldo,
>   qui son li frati miei che dentro ai chiostri
>   fermar li piedi e tennero il cor saldo.
>   (*Par.* xxii, 49–51)

"Fermar li piedi," stood their ground: the phrase repeats Beatrice's metaphor for the act of will implied in making a vow: "il fermar tra Dio e l'uomo il patto." "Il cor saldo": the phrase echoes the "salda voglia" of Beatrice's complaint against those who break their vows. The souls of the contemplatives of the seventh sphere all exhibited a greater capacity for spiritual action. They were unmoved by contingency; they were capable of action beyond that of this world. This firmness, common to all three spheres located first in their triads, is an attribute of the Father. In regard to the will, the souls in the first sphere could show only a human firmness of will. That alone was their defect.

But the souls of the second and third spheres also show deficiencies of the will of much the same sort as those of the first sphere. In their cases, it is not steadiness in their choice that was defective, but the judgments that their wills made. Again, the symmetries of the celestial hierarchy help specify the aspects of the deficiencies. Qualities, attributes, and activities that we see in superhuman forms in the higher spheres in similar locations are manifested in the second and third spheres in their human forms. The middle spheres of triads reflect attributes of the Son, attributes either of wisdom, or, as is especially appropriate to the second sphere, attributes of perseverance, sacrifice, and courage. Though he had stressed their misdirection, Justinian's description of himself and the souls with him in the second sphere also stressed their striving and courage:

> Questa picciola stella si correda
>   di buoni spirti che son stati attivi
>   perchè onore e fama li succeda:
> e quando li disiri poggian quivi,
>   sì disvïando, pur convien che i raggi
>   del vero amore in su poggin men vivi.
>   (*Par.* vi, 112–17)

Honor and fame were not the best motives for their actions, but the actions were good, and the souls were active souls. They displayed the vigor and perseverance on which honor and fame depend, and which link them at the same time to souls in other triads who displayed the same activity, though for better motives. What we see as true fortitude among the militant and martyrs in sphere five and true wisdom among the apostles with Adam in sphere eight appear in their mundane guises as the desire for honor and fame in sphere two. Put another way, the limitless perseverance in pursuit of divine ends that provides the superhuman fortitude that enables one to act as martyr (which qualities of soul are manifested to Dante in the fifth sphere) was, for the souls of the second sphere, reduced to the pursuit of human ends that required, and received, no more than human fortitude. The knowledge of one's human place in a divine creation, which is the only true wisdom, was, for the souls of the second sphere, reduced to a sense of place among humans; and as they replaced the true wisdom of the apostles with a rather foolish wisdom, so they could not pursue, as the apostles had, true glory, but pursued that much lesser glory that exists among mere mortals, fame.

The relation of the third sphere to other spheres in the third location within a triad exhibits the same symmetries. For Dante, the
sphere of Venus had been associated with the influence of love at least
as early as the *Convivio* or the *canzone,* "Voi che 'ntendendo." In the
context of the whole of the celestial hierarchy, its place can be seen as a
reflection of this same common structure. The third angelic order of
each triad would have been, in the interpretation we have been constructing, associated with the Holy Spirit, and, thereby, with love. So
too, in various ways, would have been the planets assigned to these orders. In spheres beyond the merely worldly orbit, the love of the Holy
Spirit would be manifested as charity. Within the shadow of the world,
the love manifested in the sphere of the planet Venus would extend
only to mundane love, though even this would confirm the symmetry
of the influence of divine attributes. The souls who manifest themselves to Dante in this sphere would thus exhibit capacities for love
limited in the same way as souls in the first and second spheres were
limited. In higher spheres the capacity for love is manifested in more
expansive ways: the love of justice on which just rule and community
depend, in the sixth sphere; finally, a love simple enough to be beyond
human capacity, of which only angelic natures are capable, in the ninth.
All three "third" spheres reflect the attributes of the Holy Spirit, each
in appropriately limited or unlimited ways. And inside this common
structure, the position of the third sphere finds its appropriate place
and explanation.

Insofar as the wills of these souls in the first three spheres were
moved by objects somehow other than, or aslant from, what should
have been their only object, their wills were not, as Beatrice says, *salde,*
but were moved by the contingency of this world. (In a similar way,
the knowledge and capacity of the angelic orders of these first three
spheres are also limited by particularity, and to that extent by contingency.) The souls we find in these spheres did not *fermar li piedi,* but
ran after honors, fame, or profane love. They lived within the shadow
of this world, and their capacities had only the strength of this world,
no matter how upright their lives. It is important that we stress *capacity* for action here. The souls of the first sphere, for example, are not
manifested there because of breaking their vows *in se.* Rather, the
breaking of their vows was the result of a deficiency (if we can call it
that) of the power of their wills, and it is that weakness that places
them in the first sphere. Their location reflects the level of spiritual

power they possessed, not the actions that ensued from that power. Unless we are to think that no one who had committed positive sin will appear in any sphere above the first three (which I do not believe is a Dantean interpretation), this is the proper formulation. After all, for those who in their lives were active sinners (not merely mundanely righteous), there were defects not only of the contingent will, but even of the absolute will, insofar as they chose objects in opposition to God, not merely deflections from God. But since I believe that Dante conceived that with the purgation of the souls of sinners their souls were then fit to take their properly spiritualized or glorified position in the order of Heaven, we would expect to find the souls of sinners in appropriate locations throughout the celestial hierarchy. Though the sinners misused their capacities while alive, once purged, the greater capacity of their souls, in comparison with the weaker souls of the first three spheres, would have the opportunity to act rightly, and be recognized, and this would be manifested to Dante in locations in Heaven appropriate to those capacities.[102]

The Highest Triad of Angels and the Highest Two Spheres of Souls

The highest triad of angelic orders superintends three spheres, but in only two of these does Dante encounter human souls. In the *Paradiso*, the ninth sphere is reserved for the manifestation of the angels themselves. Dionysius' statements about this triad explain why human beings appear only up to a certain point in Heaven. The primary properties that he stresses regarding this triad—what distinguishes them from all other angelic orders, and from humans—reflect the immediacy with which its orders contemplate God:[103]

> The first group [of angels] is said to be around God always, and is said to be attentively united with him with no intermediary. . . . Their speculations are contemplative, too, of both sensible and intellectual symbols, but not as if uplifted to God by way of the variety of visions in holy Scripture, but as replete with every immaterial science of the highest light, and as having been brought, as much as is right, to the contemplation of the primordial beauty that informs all beauty, superessential and triply luminous. Their speculations are contemplative also because they have been made worthy to enter into communion with Jesus not by means of holy fictive images (which figure the likeness of God in forms), but by truly approaching him in a primary participation in the knowledge of his divine lights. (*CH*, vi, 2; vii, 1–2; 1049d; 1051c)

This also is what distinguishes the human souls Dante encounters in these spheres from the souls he had previously seen. All the souls in the two final spheres—and only they—can be said to have in one sense or another known God directly, without mediation. The seventh sphere (of Saturn) is the sphere of the contemplatives. What distinguishes them from the theologians, for example, is that their knowledge of God was not discursive (that is to say, mediated), as was the knowledge acquired by theologians, and it is indeed precisely their capacity for ecstatic, nondiscursive (and therefore immediate) knowledge that explains their manifestation in a higher sphere than that of the theologians, and, by implication, their greater grace and in that sense their superiority to them. The souls of the eighth sphere (of the fixed stars) had an even more immediate knowledge of God. To indicate this greater immediacy—whatever its explanation—Dante *poeta* uses the strategy of allowing Dante *personaggio* to meet only four individuals: Saint Peter, Saint James, Saint John, and Adam, all four of whom knew God directly in a way surpassing that of even the contemplatives, since they *literally* knew God directly. Adam spoke to God the Father in the Garden; Peter, James, and John, as apostles, knew Christ both before and after the resurrection, but even more emphatically, as the only witnesses to the transfiguration, they saw Christ in his divine nature and heard the voice of God the Father.[104] (To complete this strategy, though he does not meet her, Dante sees Mary, who also knew God literally, in the distance.)

Such knowledge is undeniably a more authoritatively direct knowledge of God than that possessed by the contemplatives, and thus the apostles and certain other figures appropriately appear in a sphere beyond the contemplatives. Indeed, it would be impossible for any human while alive to surpass such literal knowledge of God, and so this group of souls puts a term to the human souls Dante can find in the spheres. Insofar as we recall that as souls manifest themselves in given spheres they reflect the amount of gratuitous light they had received, and that that light determined their capacity for seeing God, it is clear that no humans have ever received more of that grace than this small group. Only angels might see God more directly and clearly. (Though we should recognize that the common location of both contemplatives and apostles in the highest triad, as well as the poetic figure of Jacob's ladder rising without interruption through Heaven from the seventh sphere, both imply that the contemplatives' knowledge of God is as authentically unmediated, if of a different and lesser nature, as that of the apostles. That the ladder exists only between these spheres also distinguishes these souls from all other human souls below them.) There is a limit to the immediacy of human knowledge of God. Even in Heaven, even face to face, one must believe that the human intelligence, being inferior to the angelic intelligence, will perceive God less perfectly than the angelic intelligence will.

In this triad too Dante's determination of whom to locate here and his strategy for indicating the principles of his decisions to his readers are made by interweaving the full gamut of attributes of different persons of the Trinity, the sets of terms related to the Trinity or to the angelic hierarchy, and also symmetries between related orders of angels. Here too the combinations of the several vocabularies supply the content for his explanation of the nature of the human activities rewarded in these two spheres. With regard to the seventh sphere, its location as the first sphere of the highest triad, and its connection to the angelic order of thrones as its intelligences, suggest certain special aspects in the lives of the contemplatives Dante meets. By their location in the matrix of the celestial hierarchy, thrones are doubly associated with the person of the Father, and would have attributed to them (and thereby, through their agency, to the souls manifesting themselves in this sphere) qualities of order (from Dionysius) and of the foundation upon which other actions are based (Aquinas).[105]

The figures to whom Dante speaks in this sphere, Saint Benedict and Saint Peter Damian, indeed, were not only contemplatives but were directly linked to the *foundation* and spiritual reconstruction of monastic *orders*. (The same is true of Saint Bernard, who replaces Beatrice as Dante's final guide and whom Dante links with the other contemplatives [*Par.* xxxi, 109–11].) In retrospect, we recall that a significant portion of the conversation Dante had in the fourth sphere of the sun—also a first sphere in a triad—concerned Saint Dominic and Saint Francis, also founders of orders. Just as Dante had used Jacob's ladder as a concrete image to indicate the immediate contact of contemplatives with God, Benedict resonantly likens the order he established to that same ladder, as if the Rule of the order provided a means of spiritual ascent; that is, as if his order was the foundation upon which the direct contemplation of God could be based.

Ivi [sc. the tenth sphere] è perfetta, matura ed intera
ciascuna disïanza; in quella sola
è ogni parte là ove sempr'era,
perchè non è in loco, e non s'impola;
e nostra scala infino ad essa varca,
onde così dal viso ti s'invola.
Infin là su la vide il patrïarca
Iacob porgere la superna parte,
quando li apparve d'angeli sì carca.
Ma, per salirla, mo nessun diparte
da terra i piedi, e la regola mia
rimasa è per danno delle carte.

(*Par.* xxii, 64–75)

It is a characteristically Dionysian interpretation to see an order as a means of ascent into deiformity.[106] Dante, picking up this term *(order)* as the first term of a Dionysian triad, points out its appropriateness to the foundation of monastic orders; and in that regard, the location of their founders here in the seventh sphere reflects their affinity to that Dionysian property.

The eighth sphere, of the fixed stars, occupies a middle position in its triad, a position that in the matrix of divine attributes would associate with it, and with its angelic intelligences, the cherubim, attributes of the Son in addition to their primary attributes (from their location in the highest triad) of the Father. For Dionysius and all commentators on angelology, the principal characteristic of the cherubim was wisdom.

The name "cherubim" means "fullness of knowledge" or "outpouring of wisdom." . . . The name cherubim signifies their power to know and to see God, to receive the highest gift of his lights, their power to contemplate the divine beauty in a primordial operative power, their ability to be filled with what is passed to them to bring wisdom, and their capacity generously to communicate the wisdom they have been given with those who come after. (*CH*, vii, 1; 1050a–c)

Wisdom, of course, is one of the principal attributes of the Son, and indeed, the eighth sphere is the one Dante chooses as the place in which to display the triumph of Christ (*Par.* xxiii, 20). It is also the sphere in which, at what might seem a surprisingly late stage in his journey, Dante is examined regarding his understanding of faith, hope, and charity. But this examination, whose stages the poet analogizes to the levels of academic degrees,[107] serves, on the one hand, to remind us of the association of this location with the Son as well as the Father, and, on the other, to give a special significance to the blessedness of the souls in this sphere, by locating the nature of that blessedness in the special knowledge they have of God.

Order and Knowledge

It had been characteristic of the earlier two *cantiche* of the *Commedia* that the activities and characters of souls whom Dante encountered in different locations acquired their complete significance not intrinsically or in the details of their descriptions alone, but by their place in the overall structure of their *cantica*. The same is true of the *Paradiso* and of the souls Dante encounters in Heaven. In the *Paradiso* the narrative details may seem less suggestive to us than those of the earlier *cantiche*, until we recognize that location itself is the primary narrative detail of this *cantica*, and that location in itself is sufficient to direct our allegorical interpretation. Structure is even more significant, perhaps, in the *Paradiso*, since there not only exist juxtapositions and separations, but more complex and subtle parallelisms and symmetries between the spheres of Heaven and their locations absolutely and relative to one another, symmetries sanctioned and even encouraged by the sources Dante used in developing his structure.

Because all locations in Heaven are referred back to specific persons of the Trinity, locations associated with the same person—whether primarily or secondarily—must exhibit common characteristics. The human activities manifested to Dante in those locations must also exhibit at least a human form of those characteristics. In our discussion we have tended to pursue only those relations that explained why a given occupation or activity was located where it was in Heaven. But as parallel locations in the other *cantiche* suggested significant relations between actions that might otherwise not be considered together, the same strategy obtains in the *Paradiso* too. From time to time we have glancingly touched on these relations but without attempting to investigate them more fully. Nor do I intend that here we should spend the time to examine the significance of these relations with the care they might be given. But it is worth mentioning that the structural relations are surely delineated by Dante, and it seems clear that he would want us to pursue the meaning of these relations as a means of understanding the true character of these human activities. For Dante, we must remember, the meaning of these locations is neither arbitrary nor factitious. These locations' associations with persons of the Trinity reveal the most fundamental and significant origins of the characters of angels or souls who appear in those locations. Where we see parallels and affinities, they are parallels grounded in the divine nature that imprints all phenomena.

All middle locations in Heaven—whether we mean the entire middle triad or the middle location within a triad—reflect attributes of the Son. Activities occupying those locations thus have a fundamental affinity, though we might not at first recognize it. (Here, as in the other *cantiche*, especially the *Inferno*, Dante is using structure to draw our attention to affinities we would not otherwise discover.) Theology, martyrdom, empire: these are not activities we would intuitively group together, yet all, Dante insists by locating them together in the middle triad of human activities, share the activity and the qualities of wisdom, fortitude, perseverance, and sacrifice of the Son. The same is true, in however altered a form, of activities that occupy the middle location of other triads. The second sphere contains souls whose good actions were motivated by the worldly goals of honor and fame. If these souls pursued the active life in a predominantly human way, it is nonetheless specifically their activity that Justinian emphasizes: "i buoni spirti attivi" (*Par.* vi, 113). (Were we to ask, What would pursuing the active life in a properly pious way look like? the organization of the *Paradiso* would suggest that the middle spheres outside the shadow of the world would provide an answer: the three perfect activities of the active life would be theology, militancy, and just rule.) Even the souls of the eighth sphere manifest a characteristically active life, though translated to an exalted level that reflects their unmediated connection to God—all of them act as God's agents in creation: Adam of the physical human race; Mary of the physical birth of Christ; the apostles of the community of the Church.[108]

Souls in the lowest locations within their triads exhibit common characteristics of order and communication. Order had been the first of Dionysius' terms for characterizing hierarchies, and the souls of the theologians (in the fourth sphere) and of the contemplatives (in the seventh) both manifest this property. On the one hand, many of those identified as theologians were authors of *summæ*, in which their universal knowledge was marshaled in an orderly form (and even those not properly speaking theologians could comfortably be described as great systematizers of human knowledge); on the other, while the immediacy of the contemplatives' knowledge of God surpassed that of the theologians, the contemplatives Dante meets were themselves founders of monastic *orders,* in which their unmediated approach to God might be pursued.

In another way too Dante indicates the affinity of these locations to order: all three of the lowest spheres (first, fourth, and seventh) are the occasions of the four most significant discussions in the *Paradiso* of the nature of the celestial hierarchy itself, and of the significance of that hierarchy for individual salvation. In the first sphere, Beatrice had furnished Dante his initial explanation of the nature of the hierarchy he was to encounter and its significance (*Par.* iv, 28–63). In canto xiv, in the fourth sphere, Solomon had explained how the brilliance with which he appears to Dante is itself part of the hierarchy of grace:

> . . . Quanto fia lunga la festa
> di paradiso, tanto il nostro amore
> si raggerà dintorno cotal vesta.
> La sua chiarezza seguita l'ardore;
> l'ardor la visïone, e quella è tanta,
> quant'ha di grazia sovra suo valore.
>
> (*Par.* xiv, 37–42)

His explanation can be read as a sort of gloss on Aquinas *personaggio*'s explanation of the origin of the nine spheres (and their hierarchical ordering) in the Trinity, and the way in which their hierarchy reflects that origin (*Par.* xiii, 52–81). In the seventh sphere, Peter Damian's explanation in canto xxi of the nature of both his joy and his appearance to Dante is, as it were, a further gloss on Solomon's explanation:

> Luce divina sopra me s'appunta,
> penetrando per questa in ch'io m'inventro,
> la cui virtù, col mio veder congiunta,
> mi leva sopra me tanto, ch'i' veggio
> la somma essenza della quale è munta.
> Quinci vien l'allegrezza ond'io fiammeggio;
> perch'alla vista mia quant'ella è chiara
> la chiarità della fiamma pareggio.
>
> (*Par.* xxi, 83–90)

The common association to order is tied, as well, to a common association with communication. The lowest triad of the angelic hierarchy as a whole was associated with communication, and the theologians and monastic founders can also be regarded in their roles as the purveyors of spiritual knowledge to their fellow human beings.

The highest locations in triads (as well as the entire highest triad)—the third, sixth, and ninth spheres—all share an association with love, in its many forms, exhibited in turn in the characters of the souls who appear in these locations. Indeed, the hierarchical arrangement of these parallel locations allows us to contemplate the progressive transformation of the spirit as motivated by love. What in the shadow of the earth first appears in the third sphere as terrestrial love, naturally contingent and particular, finds echoes and comparisons in the sixth sphere in the ultramundane love of justice that directs communities, and ultimately, in the ninth sphere, in a simple and immediate love of God that is, in fact, beyond human capacity, and of which only angels are truly capable.

That the activities shown in spheres in symmetrical locations should reflect common qualities in guises of various degrees of purity and simplicity is not merely intricate, exegetical pedantry. It is central both to the fundamental poetic conception of the heavens in the *Paradiso* and to the theological content of this *cantica*. It is also absolutely fundamental (as had been the case too for Dionysius, its ultimate source) to Dante's conviction that the poem was capable of containing and communicating such a theological truth. The order, with its complicated symmetries, was no artifice to Dante; it was a privileged order, whose significances were guaranteed by its origin in the divine nature itself. For Dante, the angels, spheres, and planets are all mirrors that transmit, through their own individuations, evidence of different aspects of that divine nature. So also are the souls he encounters mirrors of these different aspects.

In Dante, as also in Dionysius, the descent from God through the hierarchy or the heavens toward human understandings inescapably implies an increasing dissimilarity between reflection and original, and in that sense an increasing falsification of what is represented. Of all natures, God is most simple but cannot be understood by humans in that nature. God must be distinguished into different aspects if we are to understand the divine nature. The journey downward for both authors replaces an original simplicity with diversity and complexity but does so for the sake of communicability. The highest angels have the most simple natures, humans, of intellectual beings, the most complex. Reflections at a lower level, therefore, always incorporate more diversity, and therefore more dissimilarity from God, than reflections at a higher level. The lower reflections may be more obscure than the higher in an absolute sense, but, however distorted, they remain reflections of divinity. Our recognition of them in their more human forms enables us later to recognize the higher reflections, and to recognize that they are more accurate images of what we had earlier seen only in dimmer forms. Thus, the symmetry of spheres and triads embodies both an interpretive and a representational strategy for Dante. It provides new significance to familiar activities reflected in the three lowest spheres; it enables us to see later activities as ultramundane transformations of the lower.

Predestination, Merit, Reward

The origin of the order of the heavens in the divine nature, and the ordering of human grace according to this divine order, furnish answers to the theologically difficult questions that we encountered early in this chapter. First of all, any apparent contradictions between predestination and freedom of the will find an easy reconciliation. From the stars, especially in the profound sense that Dante constructs, in which human character acquires spiritual qualities through the mediation of angelic intelligences, individual humans receive their innate character. Inherent in that character is a specific capacity to action of a certain sort. Whether that capacity is actualized fully, and whether it is actualized virtuously or viciously, remains squarely in the control of the individual.[109] To that extent—and that extent includes both ordinary decisions that determine the success or failure of everyday actions and also the ultimate decisions on which salvation or damnation depend—the individual is free. Nonetheless, those capacities also constitute a very concrete form of destiny for each individual. As Charles Martel had explained it, the whole enterprise of the celestial spheres driven by their intelligences, *la circular natura*, places its imprint on humans, and its power supersedes even that of heredity *(natura generata)*, which would have held exclusive sway had the stars not intervened, as they do for humans. It is so definitive a force on the soul that action in contradiction to it cannot be truly successful: "fuor di sua regïon, fa mala prova" *(Par. viii, 127–41)*.

Even when one tries to act against this imprinted character, that character informs the action, subverting its intended effect. This, presumably, is the implication of Charles Martel's accompanying declaration (*Par.* viii, 142–48) of the futility of making kings of those shaped by the intelligences to be priests and vice versa. What one gets from these misunderstandings are priests who act like kings and kings unwilling to act other than as preachers. In neither case is the action successful. But even activity in accord with this force does not necessarily result in good action (though it probably results in more successful action). Whether the activity eventuates in good works or in sin depends on the individual's choice of specific ends, and this choice is free and not determined by that imprinted capacity. (For that matter, even action in opposition to this force need not result in sin. It can, by good choice, result in actions that are good in a moral sense, though rarely successful, because against this divinely implanted nature.) Because of this, we can conclude without hesitation that the will is free. It is not within our power to change our natures or character, according to Dante. But it is wholly within our power whether we do good or evil.

At the same time, however, *la circular natura* that forms our character does not act as an independent force; it acts as it does to implement divine providence *(il proveder divino)*, providence so completely determinant as not only to overcome nature, but also to assign the eternal rewards individuals will receive in Heaven ("a queste ruote [tornano] / l'onor della influenza e 'l biasmo" [*Par.* iv, 58–59]), assuming that they have already rightly exercised their free will either by avoiding sin or by freely repenting of it. So to that extent, then—and "that" extent is an eternal extent—we can also conclude without hesitation that the individual destiny of human beings is determined by providence. It is not that free will and predestination need to be reconciled. The key, rather, is understanding their relationship. As Dante establishes it, one's salvation is not a matter of predestination; whether one will or will not be saved depends on one's free choice. But the character of one's actions and the nature of one's blessedness are not a matter of choice. *They* are predestined.

How little anyone's place in Heaven is within human election explains the degrees of blessedness manifested to Dante in the *Paradiso*, and explains why the order in which he encounters souls of greater or lesser blessedness seems humanly inexplicable. For we can now see that Solomon's statement that a soul in Heaven receives grace "beyond its merit" ("sovra suo valore"; *Par.* xiv, 42) means not only that the soul receives more grace than the goodness of its actions warranted, but in fact that, first, the measure of grace it receives has nothing to do with the goodness of its actions at all but with the character of those actions; and, second, and most importantly, that the allocation of grace to actions of diverse characters depends on no human estimation of their value, but wholly on a divine principle in which we participate by God's direction, not our choice.

That is, the degrees of blessedness revealed to Dante during his journey do not correspond to any human estimation of the relative value of actions of the sorts represented by the souls in the different celestial spheres. Emperors are not placed closer to God than theologians because everyone agrees that their activities are more valuable than those of theologians. It is not by any means clear that everyone would agree to that assertion; and even if everyone did agree to it, for Dante that would not be a sufficient reason for their placement. After all, what grounds would there be for certainty that the human reasons for valuing some action correspond to the judgments that God would make of the action? Obviously, none. Yet equally obviously, the order of grace and blessedness, and the organization of the heavens which in the poem has been exhibited to Dante as an embodied image of the order of grace, must be founded on a divine principle.

From the strategic point of view of ordering the souls in the *Paradiso*, Dante really had only one choice. It would be axiomatic that greater godliness should receive greater grace and blessedness, and in the poem would be represented as being located nearer to God. What Dante was fortunate in discovering was a system that, on the one hand, gave a definition to "greater godliness" that was equally axiomatic, and, on the other, provided sufficient clues regarding the nature of godliness so as to make it possible to determine which human activities should be associated with which aspects of godliness.

What is most godly is what is most like God. This is the axiom that expresses the nature of godliness, and determines what among creatures is highest in value and therefore most worthy of grace. Dante could find the axiom in any number of authorities (if authority were needed at all), Dionysius among them. In Dionysius he could also find an explanation of what was most like God: the angelic hierarchy, which is most like God because it constitutes, as a whole, the closest image of God that exists among creatures. Since Dante believed that the different orders of angels moved and informed the stars that shaped human character, the hierarchy of angels and their planets, as we have said, in itself placed human activity and character in the order imposed by God, as long as it could be possible to know which human activities and characters were governed by which angels and stars. Here, the writings on angelology and the Trinity could be employed to determine how the association of human actions with angelic and divine attributes might be made. But, and this is critical to our understanding of Dante's statement about blessedness, the order in which human characters are arranged in the *Paradiso* would, in the end, be seen by Dante as an order imposed on him by the nature of God. One human activity is placed higher in the order than another not by reference to that, or any other, human action. Its place depends only on how by occupying that place *in the hierarchy as a whole* the best image of God might be created.[110]

> ... Le cose tutte quante
>> hanno ordine tra loro, e questo è forma
>> che l'universo a Dio fa simigliante.
> Qui veggion l'alte creature l'orma
>> dell'etterno valore, il qual è fine
>> al quale è fatta la toccata norma.
> Nell'ordine ch'io dico sono accline
>> tutte nature, per diverse sorti,
>> più al principio loro e men vicine;
> onde si muovono a diversi porti
>> per lo gran mar dell'essere, e ciascuna
>> con istinto a lei dato che la porti.
>
> (*Par.* i, 103–14)

Thus, the degree of grace bestowed is *sovra valore* in at least three senses. First, it depends not on the good or ill of individual actions (by the time a soul has reached Heaven not only have any sins been purged, but bad habits reformed), but on the character of those actions, and how that character reflects the angelic nature that formed the character, and, ultimately, the divine nature that disposed even the angelic natures in the identical order. Here we find a solution to the question of where souls whose lives may have been sinful will be rewarded once they reach Heaven: they will be rewarded according to what their character reveals of the divine nature, not according to the actions of their lives. Second, the degree of grace is *sovra valore* because it depends on a divine structure that bears no direct relationship to the value that human beings might put on actions of such characters. Here Dante avoids the risk that his judgments regarding human merit might be influenced by his own partisan prejudices. Souls are rewarded according to criteria that have nothing human about them. And third, no individual human action—of whatever character—has any particular value considered in itself. The value of any and of all actions, whatever their character, comes from their participation in a universe of action that in its totality and form reflects the divine nature. No discrete part of the universe has any value except in relation to the whole. The judgments that Dante makes, then, are radically other than human judgments, and that, of course, would have been their great virtue, for only thus would Dante have had confidence that the organization of Heaven he proposes was both just, in an eternal sense, and heuristic in regard to revealing something of importance of the divine nature.

PART IV
THE ORDER OF THE *PARADISO* IN THE CONTEXT OF THE *COMMEDIA*

The Appetites and the Angels

There is a second structure reflected in the order of the angelic hierarchy. Even as Dante was using that hierarchy, with its associations with attributes of the persons of the Trinity, to organize his presentation of blessed souls and to reveal the principle of blessedness embodied in that organization, that same structure simultaneously embodied for Dante an organization of a very different sort. In the context of the *Commedia* as a whole, that second structure makes possible the construction of one great allegory through all three of the *cantiche* of the poem; and the relation of that second structure to the underlying meaning of the angelic hierarchy directs us to the content of this great allegory.

If we consult the authorities Dante used in characterizing the orders of angels, in arraying the angels to match the attributes of the divine persons, and in arraying human characters to angelic orders, we will find them describing the individual angelic orders and the triads in which they are found in ways that stress properties that are surprisingly and significantly close to the properties of the three human appetites, the will, the irascible, and the concupiscible appetites, whose existence and order provided the structure of the first two *cantiche* of the poem. The same order, as it turns out, informs the *Paradiso* as well.

Once such a statement has been made, it must immediately be qualified. The angels, who are the source of human characters, do not possess sensitive appetites at all; the only appetite that belongs to an intellectual creature is the intellectual appetite, the will.[111] Thus, no order that is based on the nature of angels, as is the order of the *Paradiso*, can be said in the strict sense to follow the order of the three human appetites. What we have in the *Paradiso* is an order that appears to be the same as the order of the human appetites, but that must be understood in a way appropriate to the wholly intellectual nature of both angels and souls whom we encounter in Heaven.[112] Nonetheless, as we will see, the angelic characters are described in a way unequivocally related to human appetitive operations. Moreover, our conclusions from the end of chapter 2 should have prepared us for something like this. At the end of that chapter we had concluded that even what operated in the human body as sensitive appetites had their origin in specialized functions of the will, the intellectual appetite. To the extent that human characters and operations reflect properties of the angelic natures that informed their characters, we should expect to discover similarly specialized intellectual functions in the angels. And, indeed, given our discussions of this chapter, we are prepared to see those angelic functions as the origin of the human. The passages Dante would have found which seemed to describe appetitive operations in the angels would have given him a very concrete sense of how the human intellectual soul could have the capacity to perform the sensitive operations it does.

All of Dante's sources would have agreed that angels possessed a faculty of will, but Dionysius, further, strikingly describes the angels as possessing qualities to whose likeness to the two sensitive appetites, the irascible and the concupiscible, he deliberately draws attention. To point to such a likeness is a deliberate part of his strategy (one, indeed, shared by Dante) for compelling his readers to re-evaluate the nature of those appetites.

> Among irrational beings, anger is a motion born in the passions, and the movement of rage is replete with every irrationality. But among those with intellects [i.e., angels], irascibility must be understood in a different

way, as something, I believe, that demonstrates their courageous rationality and their unmovable coming to rest in the divine and unchanging foundations. Similarly with desire. For irrational beings, we say it is a certain reckless, material, ingrained and incontinent passion (natural or habitual) for the things of this world, an irrational persistence in corporeal pleasure of the sort that compels every animal to pursue the concupiscible objects of sense. But when we apply dissimilar similarities to intellectual beings, and make it appear that they experience desire, this must be understood as a divine love for that immaterial reality above all reason and intellect, an unyielding and capable desire for chaste and impassible contemplation, aiming at the pure and most sublime clarity. (*CH*, ii, 4; 1042b–c)

One could, not improperly, apply physical properties to the celestial powers making use of dissimilar similarities. Thus, anger could be applied to their [the angels'] intellectual fortitude (of which our anger [i.e., human anger] is only the last echo). Even the term desire could be applied to their love of God. (*CH*, xv, 8; 1069b)[113]

Dionysius' language is not only passionate in a literary sense in his description of the angelic attributes; the terms that he uses, and the Latin translations of them, are the standard philosophical terms for appetition and the passions associated with the irascible and concupiscible appetites: θυμός, ἐπιθυμία, and ὁρμή, *furor, amor, irascibile, concupiscentia*.[114] Dionysius, thus, goes beyond merely ascribing to the angels analogical equivalents of the motions of the human will that are vaguely reminiscent of the sensitive appetites; he actually goes as far as describing angelic equivalents of the *passions* that are associated with the sensitive appetites.

In Scotus Eriugena's translation of and commentary on Dionysius' discussion of the angelic forms of desire and love, the technical vocabulary of appetite also appears. Scotus Eriugena writes of the angels' *concupiscentia* and *desiderium*, though the objects of this appetite and passion are of course transferred from the realm of the senses and the material to that of the immaterial beyond intellect and reason.[115]

Then Dionysius says truly that when we use dissimilar similarities drawn from the natural motions of material things lacking reason, and put these powers on intellectual creatures, as if garments of some sort, and then clothe them round with concupiscence, we must understand this concupiscence not as an irrational motion, but as divine love. And this divine love is a laudable concupiscence for immateriality itself, and it

surpasses all reason and intellect.... By all these names it signifies, I believe, a divine virtue which bestows freely on all who desire a sufficient,
robust, and unchangeable power; a power, that is, or purity, which in no
way can be thrown down or conquered by any other power opposed
to it. And all of this is given through the unconfused, serene, and im-
mutable love of the divine beauty, and through the universal uplifting to
that which is truly to be desired: the highest good, that is, which everything that is capable of love desires.[116]

Even Aquinas essentially agrees. He denies, of course, that angels
possess appetites or exhibit passions associated with them. But he does
recognize in the angels qualities of action that are parallel to virtues of
the human sensitive appetites, though attributable in the case of the
angels only to the operation of their will:

> As a human virtue, then, temperance is in the concupiscible part, forti-
> tude in the irascible. In this sense, they [these virtues] are not found in
> angels. For they have no passions regarding concupiscibles nor fear or
> daring, which need to be regulated by temperance and fortitude. But
> temperance can be said to exist in them in respect of their exhibiting
> their moderation of will in accord with the divine will. And fortitude is
> said to be in them in respect of their firmly carrying out the divine will.
> All of this is done by the will, not by irascible or concupiscible powers.
> (*ST,* 1a 59, 4 ad 3)

In regard to demons, these operations appear almost identical to
the operations of the sensitive appetites. Though the demons are themselves purely intellectual creatures, presumably their adherence to sin
has virtually corporealized them, making them more and more like the
human embodiments of these operations.

> They [i.e., the devils] are not evil by nature, but by the lack of angelic
> good.... They are said to be evil because of the weakness of their natural
> operation. Their evil is a false conversion, a stepping outside of their own
> nature, a loss of their essence, an imperfection, an impotence, a weakness
> in the saving virtue that could bring them to perfection, a flight, a fall....
> And so what is this evil in demons? It is irrational anger, mindless desire,
> shameless imagination *(phantasia)*. (*Div. nom.,* iv, 23; 1142c)[117]

But it was not only with regard to individual angels that appetite-
like functions could be discerned. Dante's sources also consistently associated specific appetitive movements with entire orders of angels
in a structure that simultaneously mirrors the known structure of the
human appetites and the structure of relations to the Trinity which

informs the angelic hierarchy. The entire lowest triad of angels and spheres was associated, as we have discussed, with the Holy Spirit, and following Augustine's interpretation of the way in which God's image appears in humans, this association with the Holy Spirit would associate the entire triad with the faculty of the will.[118] This association with the will provided, we saw, the principal ground for Dante's determination of which souls to manifest in the spheres linked to this lowest triad, since the souls who appear in those spheres are those whose lives and characters were determined by the will—or, more correctly, by its human limitations.

Dionysius associated properties that we recognize as irascible with the middle triad of angels, and especially with the middle order within that triad, the order of virtues, by calling attention to their attributes linked to vigorous and arduous effort. In our present context this stress on fortitude is apparent in a passage that was cited earlier:

> The name of the holy virtues signifies a strong and unshakable courage—their deiformity—in all their operations. There is no weakness in their undertaking of the divine illuminations. They are powerfully brought to the imitation of God. Nor do they ever relinquish their deiform motion to any softness, but firmly bringing themselves to the transcendent essence and the power that creates all power; and making themselves into the clearest image of that power (as far as is right), and turning themselves to it as to the powerful principle of their power, to the second giver, indeed, of power, and its deiform provider. (*CH*, viii, 1; 1054a–b)

Scotus Eriugena's Latin translation (in which form, directly or indirectly, Dante is most likely to have encountered Dionysius) stresses their courage, their *incommutabilis virilitas*.[119] And Aquinas' paraphrase of Dionysius in the *Summa theologica* similarly stresses fortitude among the virtues, contrasting it to fear, which of course also would be associated with irascibility in the context of action in this world:

> In another sense, "virtue" can be understood as it implies a certain excess of courage, and it is in this sense that it is the proper name of a particular order. Whence Dionysius says that "the name of the holy virtues signifies a strong and unshakable courage, first in regard to all the divine activities suitable to them, and second in regard to their gazing upward at divine things." And so it signifies that without any fear they undertake those divine tasks which pertain to them, and this seems to pertain to their fortitude of soul. (*ST*, 1a 108, 5 ad 1)

Aquinas also emphasizes that it is on the basis of this fortitude that he assigns the working of miracles to the virtues, for this fortitude is what leads them to undertake and accomplish the most difficult tasks. In doing so, he describes their angelic character in ways that inevitably suggest comparison to the operation of the irascible appetite, since it is precisely the role of the irascible appetite (when functioning properly) to encourage individuals to undertake actions where danger and difficulty oppose obstacles to the successful pursuit of one's desires:

> But judgments *[sententiæ]* must be efficacious and right, and for them to be efficacious, they require a certain helper and champion, so that nothing that was determined by judgment be impossible to execute; and this is the function of the order of virtues, who accomplish the greatest things in every difficult activity pertaining to divine ministries; and for this reason the working of miracles is attributed to them, for acting against the laws of nature is most arduous. (*In 2 Sent.*, ix, 1, 3)[120]

The active power and courage or fortitude of the middle angels—what we might already call their angelic irascibility—is echoed in the descriptions of the dominations. The particular Latin terms Scotus Eriugena chooses stress their severity *(severam Dominationem)*, and their rejection of subjugation and ignominy *(absolutam quamdam et omni ignominia minorationis liberam anagogen)*.[121] Aquinas also cites Dionysius at length to emphasize the quality of firmness in the order of dominations.[122] But the dominations are also said to exercise their dominion humbly, and this qualification of their activity itself is evidence of the seriousness with which the relations of the angelic orders to spiritual versions of the appetites is pursued.[123] The location of the dominations in their triad would give them a secondary association, we recall, with the Holy Spirit, and through the Holy Spirit with the will. Humility, we discovered in the *Purgatorio*, is a virtue of the will, and qualifying the dominations' ardor by humility is parallel to looking at the operation of the irascible appetite tempered with a virtue of the will.

The angelic order of powers was similarly associated with this active ardor, first of all simply by its name,[124] but also by its undertaking of arduous pursuits. Gregory, we recall, had assigned to this order the distinctly irascible functions of suppressing "enemy powers" and preserving the righteous from temptation.[125]

It was with the highest triad of angels that Dante's sources associated those motions that could be described as a form of angelic concupiscence. The seraphim, of course, were said to be named for their burning love for God, but all the orders of the highest triad were said to exist in a uniquely close relation to God (*CH*, vii, 1–2; 1050b–d). The immediacy of their love of God (*CH*, vi, 2; 1049d) is what likens it to concupiscence. For, when we consider the operation of desire from the standpoint of the human appetites, it is in concupiscence that we find that immediacy. Willing an object necessarily involves judgment, since the will is the intellectual appetite. As we have said before, it is the faculty of choice; it is appetite reasoning. But since judgment may be good or bad, willing is susceptible to contingency; moreover, given its appeal to judgment, the will is inevitably in part discursive and mediated.[126] Concupiscence, though, is without judgment, and is in its response essentially immediate. Obviously, angels (and disembodied souls) do not exhibit concupiscence in its strict, corporeal sense, but may be said to exhibit an appetitive response to God as loved object as immediate as the response of concupiscence is to sensible objects.[127] Compared with this immediate love of God, any other response seems mediated, and to that extent diminished. Thus, the highest spheres in the organization of Heaven are reserved for those angelic orders whose love of God has the immediacy and simplicity that the movement of the concupiscible appetite has toward its objects. (There exists a hierarchy also with respect to mediation, for if concupiscence is the least mediated of the appetites, irascibility is nonetheless a more immediate appetitive response than willing or choice. Thus, both triads above the first, insofar as associated with appetites other than the will, exhibit more immediate binding to God than is shown by the will.)

Angelic "Appetites" and Human Character

Descriptions of the angelic orders in such appetitive terms find quite easy reflections in the characters of the souls manifested to Dante in the spheres associated with the orders. The lowest three spheres of souls, we have already mentioned, exhibit the way in which their lives took their character from the operation of their wills. The middle three spheres of souls show us those active souls whose pursuit of ardous goods was superhuman: warriors and martyrs, of course; just rulers; even the theologians, whose lives, we recall, are described not in terms of study but of battle.[128] The souls of the seventh and eighth spheres demonstrate, by their uniquely immediate relations to God, that unmediated love that we have said would be best analogized, in the realm of the sensitive appetites, to the operation of the concupiscible appetite.

To describe the angels in ways that seem to manifest spiritualized versions of human appetition is confirmation that spiritual creatures—and now we are most interested in the separated soul—are capable of acting in ways that we would recognize as spiritual analogues of the movements we know as appetites. While two of those appetites cannot continue to exist in Heaven, certain operations of the will, which does exist in the separated souls, can be likened to those sensitive appetites. Some resemble the concupiscible appetite:

> Love, concupiscence, and such can be understood in two ways. On the one hand, as they are understood as specific passions, arising from a certain excitation or disturbance of the soul. This is how they are commonly understood, and in this sense are only in the sensitive appetite. But in another sense they signify a simple affection without passion or excitation of the soul, and in this sense they are acts of the will, and it is in this sense that they are attributed to angels, and to God. But if they are taken in this sense, they do not pertain to different powers, but to one power only, called the will. . . . The will itself can be said to be irascible, inasmuch as it wishes to combat evil, but not from the impulse of passion, but rather from a judgment of the reason. In the same way it can be said to be concupiscible on account of its desire for good. It is in this way that charity and hope can be said to be in the concupiscible and the irascible—that is, in the will insofar as it is ordered to acts of this sort. (*ST,* 1a 82, 5 ad 1 and 2)[129]

Other operations of the will resemble the operations of the irascible appetite:

> The irascible faculty can be understood in two senses. In the first sense, strictly, and then it is a part of the sensitive appetite; just as anger, properly speaking, is a particular passion of the sensitive appetite. But the irascible faculty can also be understood more broadly, namely as it pertains to the intellectual appetite, to which anger is also sometimes attributed. And it is in this way that we attribute anger to God and the angels: not as a passion, but as the judgment of justice pronouncing judgment. (*ST,* 2a2æ 162, 3)

The rectification of these spiritualized operations would have been the purpose of Purgatory, we concluded, and we can find further confirmation of the existence of such operations in other rectifications of the will with which Dante and his audience would already have been familiar. It would be a maxim of Aristotelian psychology that the existence of distinct virtues indicates either the coordinate existence of distinct faculties, or, at the least, of distinct operations of a single faculty. Dante and his audience would therefore recognize that the existence of three theological virtues effectively confirms the existence of multiple functions of the will—indeed, of multiple functions that themselves were often described in ways echoing descriptions of appetitive faculties, though, again, translated to a spiritual realm. The theological virtues of hope and charity directly perfect the will with respect to the love of God (and so, from a certain point of view, does faith as well), and the existence of multiple habits to perfect this love proves that in loving God multiple actions of appetition occur. Appetitive operations, and their virtues, are specified first by reference to their objects, and we can recognize without hesitation that the way in which the virtues of hope and charity are specified is parallel to the specification of the irascible and concupiscible appetites. Aquinas describes the virtue hope as directed to the appetition of objects identical in one characteristic, arduousness, to those of the irascible appetite, though now transferred to objects that are not sensible but intellectual, as is appropriate to the will, rather than to a sensitive appetite.

> The act of the virtue of hope cannot belong to the sensitive appetite, since the good which is the principal object of this virtue is not any sensible good, but a divine good. Therefore, hope has the higher appetite (the will) as its subject; not the lower appetite to which the irascible appetite belongs. . . . The object of the irascible appetite is an arduous sensible. The object of the virtue hope, on the other hand, is an arduous intelligible (or, rather, something existing above the intellect). (*ST,* 2a2æ 18, 1, and ad 1)

The operation and objects of the virtue charity, likewise, are described in such a way as to remind us of the operation of the concupiscible appetite, insofar as Aquinas distinguishes the directness of charity's operation from that of hope. Charity completes the action of the will simply in loving, without reference to arduousness. In this regard, it resembles, with respect to intellectual goods, the simplicity of operation of the concupiscible appetite, which desired goods simply and directly, apart from arduousness.

Charity perfects the will sufficiently with respect to one act, which is loving. But another virtue is required to perfect it in regard to its other act, which is hoping. (*ST,* 2a2æ 18, 1 ad 2)

The operation of the irascible appetite, we recall, terminates in concupiscence: irascibility is for the sake of concupiscence, and after the arduousness of certain objects of appetition is overcome, the appetitive act is completed in the delight that is a passion properly of the concupiscible appetite.[130] Similarly, the operations of the other theological virtues, faith and hope, find their completion in the operation of charity, which unites the will to God in the same way that the concupiscible appetite united the body to corporeal goods.

But in the order of perfection charity precedes faith and hope inasmuch as both faith and hope are given form by charity and acquire their perfection as virtues from it. Thus charity is the mother of all the virtues and their root, insofar as it is the form of all the virtues as will be stated later [1a2æ 72, 4 and 2a2æ 23, 7 and 8]. (*ST,* 1a2æ 62, 4)

Faith and hope imply a certain imperfection, since faith is of things which are not seen, and hope is of things which are not possessed. (*ST,* 1a2æ 62, 3 ad 2)

The same good is the object of charity and hope. But charity implies union with that good; hope, on the other hand, a certain distance from it. Hence it is that charity does not regard that good as arduous, as hope does, for that to which one is already united is not arduous in character. It is for this reason that charity appears to be more perfect than hope. (*ST,* 2a2æ 23, 6 ad 3)

Even the virtue of faith, though properly a virtue of the intellect, can be said to be a perfecting of the operation of the will as directing the intellect to the apprehension of a certain object as a good.

Faith is that habit of the intellect by which it is disposed to obey the will in its striving for divine truth. For the intellect assents to the truth of faith not as if convinced by reason, but as if commanded to it by the will. (*ST,* 1a 111, 1 ad 1)

Faith pertains to the intellect in regard to the intellect being directed by the will. For this reason, faith must be ordered, as to its end, to the objects of those virtues by which the will is perfected, among which is hope, as will be made manifest below [2a2æ 18, 1]. Therefore the object of hope also is posited in the definition of faith. (*ST,* 2a2æ 4, 1 ad 2)

Since believing pertains to the intellect as it is moved by the will to assent, as has been said [2a2æ 2, 1 ad 3], the object of faith can be understood either from the standpoint of the intellect or from the standpoint of the will which moves the intellect. (*ST,* 2a2æ 2, 2)

These three virtues testify that, although the will is a single appetitive faculty, it possesses three distinct appetitive motions or capacities, which, in regard to intelligible objects, are actualized in appetitive operations equivalent to the operations of the will and the two sensitive appetites in regard to the objects of desire of the soul-body complex in this world. (It should be said, indeed, that it is precisely because the will is capable of these three operations that it was also capable of assuming the control of the sensitive appetites during the time the intellectual soul was united to its body.) It is those operations that we see characterizing the souls who appear to Dante, distributed among appropriate locations in the *Paradiso* to distinguish the operations from one another. It is because the will endures into the next world, and these three operations too, that it was necessary to show the perfecting of these operations in the *Purgatorio.* It is also because of their endurance that it is appropriate to reflect the structure of these appetites in the structure of the *Paradiso.*[131]

Thus, beneath the complexity and intricacy of the theological principles that Dante used to organize the figure of Heaven we are given in the *Paradiso,* we find again a distribution of souls and activities which appears to reflect, albeit in a transformed way, the three appetites, will, irascibility, and concupiscence. The philosophical and poetic motives that led to using such an organizing structure in the first two *cantiche* continue to operate here. Since, as Dante declares in the *Letter to Can Grande,* the field of the *Commedia* is ethics (*Ep. xiii,* 16), it is not surprising that Dante would have pursued the same structure for all three parts of the poem, and it is appropriate that the three *cantiche* all share the same principles. All human action, and perforce all voluntary action, begins and ends in appetition. Insofar as the structure of Heaven too should reflect in some sense the nature of the human actions of the souls who are now blessed in different degrees for those actions, there is a certain inescapability even here that the appetites make their appearance behind the lives and characters of these souls. But two distinct objections should be addressed regarding the appropriateness of using the appetites to organize the narrative of the *Paradiso*.

On the one hand, one might wonder whether it were seemly, for want of a better word, to structure the exposition of the nature of blessedness by appetites. This is really the lesser of the two challenges to such an organization. The angelic motions that resemble appetites have nothing unseemly about them. Indeed, they are not appetites in the sense in which we usually use the term; they appear appetitive only to us. It is clear from the declarations of the souls in the *Paradiso*, as well as from the purpose of the *Purgatorio*, that the appetites of the human souls in Heaven have undergone a transformation that makes them more like the spiritualized motions of the angels than like the corporeal appetites they once were. Everything that we would point to in the operation of the corporeal appetites as making them "unseemly" for use as the structure of Heaven has been stripped from these operations. They have been returned to their original, and intellectual, forms. Souls in Heaven experience desire and love, but without passion; their "appetites" have become as intellectual and spiritualized as those of the angels. This was the work of Purgatory, and it was necessary, so it would seem, precisely so that the once corporeal appetites could be able to operate in their appropriately spiritual way in Heaven. Appetite was not left behind when this world was left behind. But the appetites of this world had to be superseded and refashioned for their operation in the next.

The second ground for objecting to this organization, however, is more serious, and cannot be avoided. It comes from Beatrice's direct statement to Dante that the blessedness of the angels—and the principle must surely apply as well to humans—depends first on the strength of their apprehension of God, not on their love. Love is second.

> E dei saper che tutti [gli angeli] hanno diletto
> quanto la sua veduta si profonda
> nel vero in che si queta ogni intelletto.
> Quinci si può veder come si fonda
> l'esser beato nell'atto che vede,
> non in quel ch'ama, che poscia seconda;
> e del vedere è misura mercede,
> che grazia partorisce e buona voglia:
> così di grado in grado si procede.
>
> (*Par.* xxviii, 106–14)[132]

"*L'atto che vede*"

Though it may initially seem so, there is no contradiction between our discovery of an underlying appetitive structure to the *Paradiso* and Beatrice's declaration that blessedness consists first of all in the act of vision. There is in Beatrice's statement a bold fusion of the technical vocabularies of apprehension and appetition, and this fusion is very much a part of the content of the *Paradiso*. First, delight *(diletto)*, which in classical and medieval psychological discussions was always the final term of the process of appetition, is here attributed to apprehension. Then, in saying that the intellect comes to rest *(si queta)* in the truth, Beatrice is attributing a motion and terminus to apprehension which would also have conventionally been the properties not of apprehension but of appetite.[133] One of the ways of distinguishing apprehension from appetite, indeed, was according to their characteristically different motions. It was appetite that was most properly described as coming to rest *in its object*. Appetites move out toward their objects, and, in possessing them, come to rest in them. That coming to rest is delight. Faculties of apprehension do not properly go out to their objects; rather, they bring their object into themselves.[134] But Beatrice attributes both crucial appetitive properties to apprehension: it is the intellect that comes to rest in its object; it is that rest—of the intellect, not appetite—that is the delight in which beatitude consists.

Beatrice's employing of the terms of appetition to describe the act of apprehension reflects a distinction with regard to apprehension and the intellect which has been implicit throughout the *Paradiso*, and which we must here give its proper emphasis. The profundity of a soul's intellectual vision of God as Beatrice refers to it has no connection to the soul's intelligence, as we would normally use the term, and still less to the soul's erudition. The distant location of the theologians in the *Paradiso* is the clearest proof of that. While the theologians are outside of earth's shadow, by which is indicated their possession of virtues and capacities beyond those of the more worldly blessed, Dante locates them *only just* outside earth's shadow. They are surpassed in location, hence surpassed in spiritual capacity, and, most importantly, in the clarity of their vision of God, by many other souls who could boast neither their learning nor their philosophical or scientific powers. We must conclude, then, that the intellect of which Beatrice is speaking cannot be what we could call the speculative intellect, as Dante also

suggests by using a studiously vague term for the nature of the intellectual apprehension of God. Blessedness is founded in the act of
seeing: "l'atto che vede." Dante avoids terms that would link this apprehension only to abstract or philosophical thought.

To understand the significance of Beatrice's explanation, we must
recognize that while she says that delight depends upon the depth of
vision, she most definitely does not say that that depth of vision depends upon the power of the intellect. Indeed, she says something
quite different from that, and it is that which explains how so many
other souls can surpass even philosophers in their vision of God. There
are three terms in an act of seeing: the object that is to be seen; the organ by which it is seen; and the medium that makes sight actual. Vision
may be clearer, therefore, for any one of three reasons: the object may
be more perfectly visible; the organ may be more acute; or the conditions in which the act of vision takes place may be better. What Beatrice is explaining is that more perfect understanding of God is the
result of more perfect conditions of vision, of a more perfect medium
of vision, of grace, that is—rather than either of the other possible explanations. As far as the other two terms of the act are concerned, they
are easily excluded. It is not possible to distinguish the vision of the
blessed and the angels according to the object of sight, for they all have
their eyes fixed on the same object, and no object can be more perfectly intelligible than God. Neither can degrees in the profundity of
the understanding of God be distinguished on the basis of the second
term of the act, the organ of vision. Some organs of apprehension—
that is, some intellects—are without question more acute than others,
but Dante does not use those distinctions to discriminate among the
diverse depths of the understanding of God. The relatively lowly place
in which he locates the theologians, who, after all, ought to possess the
most acute intellects of all the human souls, demonstrates that.

It remains, then, that diversity in the profundity of the vision of
God depends on diversity of the circumstances in which that act of
vision takes place. That is, in the terms that we would use to describe
such circumstances, and in the terms Dante himself uses, some souls
see God more clearly because they see in stronger light. That is what
is implicit in Beatrice's explanation that grace and a healthy will are
the source of the merit that determines the degree of vision allotted a
soul.

E del vedere è misura mercede,
　　che grazia partorisce e buona voglia:
　　così di grado in grado si procede.
　　　　　　　(*Par.* xxviii, 112–14)

Grace is the light, the medium, that makes the vision of God possible, as Solomon had said earlier in the *Paradiso:*

　. . . ciò che ne dona
　　di gratuito lume il sommo bene,
　　lume ch'a lui veder ne condiziona.
　　　　　　　(*Par.* xiv, 46–48)

And Beatrice, in a further discussion of the angelic vision of God, concurs that the profundity of their vision depends on the clarity of the illumination they receive rather than on the power of their intellects:

　Per che le viste lor furo essaltate
　　con grazia illuminante, e con lor merto.
　　　　　　　(*Par.* xxix, 61–62)[135]

We can at this point tie together two threads as they appear in Beatrice's explanation and in our discussions of the structure of Heaven, and in tying them together we see why in Beatrice's explanation apprehension and appetition become fused. As we have concluded earlier, individuals are distributed to spheres and arrayed in Heaven accordingly as they possessed souls in which were exhibited qualities associated with those spheres and the divine persons whose attributes gave their specific characters to the spheres. Possession of a property determines a soul's location and is the effective content of the soul's merit. It also, however, determines the measure of gratuitous light the soul will receive, and thereby the clarity, or profundity, of its vision of God. In this connection we can comprehend why, as we have seen above, Beatrice consistently links the profundity of vision (and therefore blessedness) to merit as well as to grace: the two are inextricably interwoven because simultaneously determined.[136]

But the faculties and capacities that characterize individual souls and determine their merit are also, as we have discovered, capacities in which we can recognize the spiritual origins of appetite. That this is no accidental or factitious resemblance but a genuine and proper quality of these faculties is embodied in Beatrice's statement that the grace that is the condition of vision can be said to be merited only to the extent that it is *desired:*

E non voglio che dubbi, ma sie certo
che ricever la grazia è meritorio
secondo che l'affetto l'è aperto.
(*Par.* xxix, 64–66)[137]

When Beatrice says, at *Paradiso* xxviii, 111, that love, *[l'atto] ch'ama,*
comes second to apprehension, she is not referring to an operation of
the "appetitive" faculties that provide the structure to the *Paradiso.* She
is merely referring to love as a simple act of appetition. Love of God, in
Heaven, follows apprehension; within an Aristotelian psychology, it
could not be different. How could one desire something that one had
not first apprehended? But while the act of apprehension must precede
this act of love, the capacities that we have been describing as spiritually "appetitive" faculties in fact precede and condition the capacity for
and act of apprehension. Souls are not arrayed among the spheres of
the *Paradiso* according to how much they loved God while alive, even
were it possible to make discriminations along those lines, nor according to the power of their intellect. The distribution that we see is a
distribution according to their *capacities* for loving God, capacities different in quality and in the immediacy of their love. These capacities
are the soul's most primitive functions and, it should be said, its most
divine. The functions precede even apprehension, for—and Dante is
explicit about this—it is as they operate that the soul becomes capable
of greater or lesser depth of apprehension. As the *affetto* is open to
grace, it merits receiving grace; according to the amount of grace it
receives, the apprehensive faculty is able to see God. In this sense, it is
appetite—though we should always qualify such a statement, and our
understanding of it, by remembering that we are actually speaking of
spiritual capacities that only human beings would liken to appetites—
that determines the measure of the profundity of vision, and therefore
of blessedness. And for that reason, it is entirely appropriate, and consistent with Beatrice's statement, that these spiritual faculties provide
the organization of the *Paradiso.*[138]

Because all action begins in appetite, it must also be true that even
contemplation, the action that is the source of blessedness, has, as an
action, its origin too, and its perfection, in desire:

> Although the essence of the contemplative life is in the intellect, it
> nonetheless has its origin in the appetite, insofar as someone is aroused
> to the contemplation of God by charity. And since the end corresponds

to the beginning, it is for this reason that the goal and end of the contemplative life has its being in the appetite, since someone delights in the sight of a loved object, and that very delight excites even greater love of the thing seen. Whence Gregory says that "when someone sees the person he loves, he burns even more in love for him." And this is the ultimate perfection of the contemplative life—namely, not only that the divine truth be seen, but also be loved. (*ST*, 2a2æ 180, 7 ad 1)[139]

Further, while Beatrice declares that being blessed begins in "l'atto che vede," it cannot be said that blessedness ends there. The perfect completion of any act of appetition or desire, as Aquinas says, is delight: the experience of an appetite coming to rest in the possession of the object of desire.[140] The specific delight that is the perfection of that activity in which resides the essence of blessedness is itself an operation of the will—of appetite—rather than of the intellect. According to Aquinas, knowledge precedes love in attaining the object, but love completes that attainment:

> Love is preeminent over knowledge in moving, but knowledge outstrips love in attaining, for "nothing is loved unless it is known," as Augustine says [*de Trin.*, x, 1 and 2]. Therefore, we first attain the intelligible end by action of the intellect, just as we first attain a sensible end through the action of the senses. (*ST*, 1a2æ 3, 4 ad 4)

But:

> The intellect apprehends the end before the will does; nonetheless, motion toward the end begins in the will; and therefore to the will is owed that which is ultimately attained in the attainment of an end, that is, delight or enjoyment. (*ST*, 1a2æ 3, 4 ad 3)

> [Therefore] the essence of blessedness consists in an act of the intellect. But to the will pertains the delight consequent on blessedness, according to what Augustine said [*Confessions*, x, 23] that "blessedness is joy in truth," since that joy itself is the consummation of blessedness. (*ST*, 1a2æ 3, 4)

Desire, therefore, appears at both the beginning and end of contemplation. It initiates contemplation, and it perfects the pleasure that comes from the contemplation of the supreme good.

> First we wish to attain an intelligible end. We attain it by its becoming present to us through an act of the intellect. Then the delighted will comes to rest in this end once attained. (*ST*, 1a2æ 3, 4)

Even of the angels Aquinas speaks of both the coincidence of knowledge and love and the endurance of desire:

The nearer something is to its end, the greater the desire with which it tends to the end, for we see that the natural motion of bodies tends to their ends. The intellects of the separate substances are nearer to divine knowledge than is our intellect. They, therefore, desire knowledge of God more intensely than we do. But we, however much we know God to be and the other things of which we have spoken before [*SCG*, iii, 49], we do not rest from our desire [in this knowledge], but we desire to know God in his essence. The separate substances by their nature desire this even more. Therefore, their desire does not come to rest in the aforesaid knowledge of God. (*SCG*, iii, 50)

When Beatrice describes blessedness as residing in the vision of that truth "in che si queta ogni intelletto," describing the action of the intellect in terms appropriate to the appetite, we hear an echo of Aquinas' description of the appetitive dimension even of contemplation. Souls experience greater delight in Heaven to the extent that they are more capable of apprehending God; but they are capable of that only to the extent that they were capable of desiring the grace that gives them their capacity to apprehend God. In the end, then, the order of the *capacity* of apprehension is identical to the order of the *capacity* of love.[141]

Moreover, the special nature of the object in which the appetite wishes to come to rest gives a pointed appropriateness to the mixed usage we see in Beatrice's description of the blessed operation of the intellect in terms that are most properly used of appetition. In loving God, and seeking to possess God, intellection and appetition become increasingly similar. That Aquinas marks a similar conjunction of the two faculties in regard to the angelic order of seraphim helps to confirm this assimilation. Highest placed among the angels, the seraphim are capable of the most direct and most complete understanding of God, yet they are so because of their capacity for love.

For the highest and first intellects understand the principle of the order of providence in its ultimate end itself, which is the divine goodness (and, indeed, some of them understand this more clearly than others), and these are called seraphim—as it were, the ardent or burning ones— since we are wont to designate as fire intensity of love or desire; and love and desire are in respect to an end. (*SCG*, iii, 80)[142]

God is simultaneously the ultimate object of desire and the ultimate object of intellection. As an object of desire, the will seeks to possess God; but as the most perfectly intelligible object, God can be possessed by the will only through an act of intellection. The more profoundly a soul can understand God, the more profoundly it experiences delight—is more blessed—not because understanding is itself delightful, but because it is through understanding more profoundly that it can possess God more fully, and thus more successfully complete the desire begun in the will. Indeed, the impossibility of separating apprehension and love of God at this level is embodied in another apparent distinction Beatrice makes between apprehension and appetition which functions to suggest as much their identity as their difference. As she and Dante enter the empyrean sphere, she describes the nature of their location in terms that finally completely confound any distinction between the two:

> ... Noi siamo usciti fore
> del maggior corpo al ciel ch'è pura luce:
> luce intellettüal, piena d'amore;
> amor di vero ben, pien di letizia.
>   (*Par.* xxx, 38–41)[143]

Of the three *cantiche* of the *Commedia,* the *Paradiso* far and away depends more on love and desire for action and motivation than the other two. The common words for desire, *disio, disiro,* and *l'affetto,* occur almost twice as frequently in the *Paradiso* as they do in the *Inferno* and *Purgatorio* combined. Virtually no canto of the *Paradiso* passes without some souls (and often Beatrice) explaining to Dante how they are moved by love of God, how they reflect that love, how their desires are attuned to that love. The souls Dante encounters glow in different brilliances also because of the strength with which they love. Nor is this any pallid or abstract love. It is vigorous and represents itself to Dante in the images of passion. The desires of souls are inflamed *(infiammati)* by the Holy Spirit (*Par.* iii, 52–54);[144] they are sped by a thirst *(perpetüa sete)* for God (*Par.* ii, 19–21; cf. *Par.* xv, 64–66). Beatrice herself turns toward God always with desire ("poi si rivolse tutta disïante"; *Par.* v, 86). How could we imagine that Dante would not believe the experience of such a love would inescapably be this vivid? The spheres themselves move at different speeds to mirror their different degrees of love, for love, after all, is the power that moves the stars.[145]

The human activities and characters we see arrayed in the eight spheres in which Dante meets them are arrayed in the order of their knowledge of God only because those activities are first arrayed in the order of the greater capacity for loving God. It is because martyrs and militants exhibit a stronger and more direct love of God, for example, that they surpass theologians in their knowledge of God. We might at first have thought that Beatrice's statement that apprehension comes first in the delight that is the reward of Heaven would dictate that the structure of Heaven should reflect qualities of intellect. But, in fact, it turns out that the best structure in which to reveal what it means to possess a greater understanding of God is a structure based on appetite or love, for greater understanding of God depends not on greater intellect, but on greater love. Moreover, this order of Heaven is also an order of merit, when we remember the very special and restricted sense in which Dante uses the term. For him, merit is determined solely by the receptivity of the soul to the divine grace proferred it. We can see the justice that it be so, for in taking merit in this sense, Dante is able to find a way to have merit yet depend upon our volition. It is by our desiring God that we are rewarded. Were our merit not to depend on our willing, were it to depend only on our intellect, there could be no merit, for merit can depend only on freedom of will.[146]

Love, Blessedness, and the Common Structure of the Three Cantiche

The hierarchy that we encounter in the *Paradiso,* therefore, is at once a hierarchy of appetition and of understanding, and of justice. All souls in Heaven are there because, ultimately, their will desired union with God, but their closeness to or distance from God reflects four different qualities simultaneously. It reflects, first of all, the profundity of their understanding of God. The depth of their knowledge of God must be understood in a double sense, both as it was embodied in their past potentialities and now in their present actuality. Whatever their individual actions had been in their earthly lives, the souls are arrayed as we encounter them in Heaven because of their possession—from birth—of diverse capacities for action (however they chose to realize them while alive), and it is these capacities that Dante *poeta* distinguishes for us by locating the souls with diverse capacities in physically separate spheres. In Heaven, these different capacities (purged of sinful habits, where necessary) are finally perfectly actualized in the contemplation and understanding of God. Beatrice tells us explicitly (*Par.* iv, 28–36), in fact, that the souls of humans, and angels, are not really distinguished from one another by being placed in distinct locations in

Heaven. All souls occupy the same location. The only real distinction among them, angels or humans, is found in their different capacities for understanding God.

But, in the second place, the different locations in which souls manifest themselves to Dante reflect different capacities for the appetitive movement toward God that begins and ends the proper activity of human souls and angels. As souls can be distinguished according to their different capacities of understanding, so they can also be distinguished according to their different capacities for loving. In this final realm, the two kinds of capacity can be distinguished from one another only with difficulty. With regard to the ultimate appetitive object, God, loving and understanding lie very close together. Greater understanding leads to fuller possession of the loved object, and greater delight, which is an appetitive response. Greater love makes possible the more assiduous pursuit of the object, which, given its nature, must be pursued intellectually; thus, greater love receives, because it demands, greater understanding to support it.

This is why all souls in Heaven are happy, and none envious of the souls in locations above them. They understand justice not simply as the differential allocation of grace and blessedness; they understand it as the allocation of as much grace as any given soul is capable of receiving. Every soul has as much grace and as much blessedness as it can have. No soul can ask for more. It is for this reason that Justinian can say that justice "sweetens" their love.

> Ma nel commensurar di nostri gaggi
> col merto è parte di nostra letizia,
> perchè non li vedem minor nè maggi.
> Quindi addolcisce la viva giustizia
> in noi l'affetto sì, che non si puote
> torcer già mai ad alcuna nequizia.
> (*Par.* vi, 118–23)

We do not usually think of justice as sweetening anything, but to these souls justice is no mere intellectual judgment; it is judgment welded to desire and delight. It is because the different orders of angels (and we can safely extend this explanation to the souls of humans) have appetites *(l'affetto)* capable of being open to the degree of grace allotted them that that grace can illuminate their vision to the extent of their capacity and provide them their properly measured reward.

Reward depends on vision, and vision on grace, which illuminates it (*Par.* xxix, 58–66; see also *Par.* xiv, 40–51). As the soul is capable of loving, so is it capable of understanding. This does not say that love precedes apprehension. It says that the capacity for love precedes the capacity for apprehension.[147]

In the *Paradiso* we see the purified and transformed operation of appetite. All souls in Heaven, and the angels, do desire, pursue, and enjoy their appetitive object. We also find the explanation for the need of these appetites, and therefore the reason that the original human appetites needed purification in Purgatory. Insofar as the appetites are capable of being open to grace, so is the soul capable of seeing, and thereby enjoying, God. If souls did not still possess their appetites, they could not also continue to receive grace and continue to enjoy God. This is a much more profound need for appetites than their utility at the moment of the bodily resurrection. Even as separated substances, souls need these spiritualized appetites to be blessed. But these appetites are nothing more than purified forms of appetites and capacities for appetitive action which the souls possessed from the moment they were born, and which they used throughout their lives. When we see that the blessed too carry their desires with them, made newly pristine, to Heaven, we also see the final, heavenly form of the *contrapasso:* for these souls too are rewarded in ways that provide them precisely what they had always loved and pursued, adapted exquisitely to their capacities for love and pursuit. In the *Convivio,* Dante had already expressed a form of such a statement by saying it would describe what has happened "when the soul escapes from sin [and] is made holy and free in its distinctive power" (*Conv.,* ii, i, 7).[148] In the *Commedia,* especially in the relation of the *Paradiso* to the other *cantiche,* Dante was able to make concrete what the capacities were whose exercise in a free and sinless way would constitute blessedness, and to make clear how souls of different characters might be said to possess individually their own distinctive capacities and their own appropriate blessedness.

In speaking of "greater" love or understanding, we must remember that the measure of greater or lesser is not one of the quantity of some single property, but the greater or lesser reward given to qualitatively different properties. It is because of that that the closeness of souls to God reflects a third and a fourth significance. Souls are located more or less closely to God, we have determined, based on the relation of their capacities to attributes of the persons of the Trinity. The double hierarchy of operations of understanding and operations of appetition reflects, therefore, a parallel double distribution of attributes of the Trinity in knowing and willing. Medieval readers would have been familiar with the representation of the Trinity in the three human faculties of memory, intellect, and will. Dante draws our attention to a different representation of the Trinity in the three appetitive faculties. Since all of creation is made to the image of God, and bears God's imprint, there is nothing unnatural in finding that image not only in the intellectual faculties but in the appetitive as well. Since God both knows and wills, the human hierarchy that reflects God must be a hierarchy of both operations. For each of the levels of human understanding and desiring we are encouraged to recognize different aspects of the divine operations.

In all three realms of the *Commedia,* then, we find an underlying narrative structure that follows distinctions that we recognize in the first instance as those between the three appetitive faculties. Punishments, purgations, rewards are all organized by Dante according to distinctions that parallel, if they do not actually depend upon, the distinction between the will and the two sensitive appetitive faculties, the irascible and concupiscible appetites. In Heaven, it is not these three appetites in themselves that are embodied in the order of the angels and their spheres, but, rather, what Aquinas calls the "simple motions of the will" that in angels, and presumably in disembodied souls, operate in ways similar enough to seem to mirror the operations of the corporeal appetites, and that allow us, therefore, to speak analogically of the "anger" of God or angels, or their "love."

That all realms of the *Commedia* are structured by the appetites has moral, poetic, and theological significance. The common structure is what makes possible the construction of a single great allegory that runs through all three *cantiche.* At each new stage, the subject of the preceding *cantica* undergoes a transformation, and, as we will also consider in the final chapter, the order of these transformations itself embodies a significant structure. Since appetite specifically is the origin of all actions, this single, developing structure makes it possible to distinguish all actions from one another, good or evil, temporal or eternal, by the appetites that initiate them. Even more importantly, this particular common structure makes it possible to draw conclusions regarding the proper or improper operation of the faculties on which all of our free actions depend. This, indeed, is one of the intentions of the poem: to demonstrate how, by the exercise of our free will, we justly deserve reward or punishment (*Ep. xiii*, 8).

Moreover, that all realms share the same structure has the most profound theological implications. For in saying that we can find an appetitive structure behind each of the realms of the next world, let no one imagine that we are saying that Dante has organized his poem, and the universe, including the eternal realms of Heaven and Hell, according to these three human faculties. To believe so would be to miss the point entirely. The universe is not made to a human image; it, and every human being, are made to God's. If the three realms beyond the grave exhibit traces that suggest the organization of the three appetitive faculties, it is because they, and the three appetitive faculties themselves, together share the common traces of the properties of God in whose image all were made.[149] For that reason, as Dante had already recognized by the time of the writing of the *Convivio* (*Conv.*, ii, v, 7), understanding the structure of the universe's hierarchy is a means of understanding God, representing that structure in a poem a means of communicating fundamental truths about God's nature.

This, I am convinced, is the essential content of the epiphany Dante has at the conclusion of the *Commedia*. Looking directly at the Trinity, he sees what seems to be a human image, and is absolutely at a loss to explain how such an image can appear there:

> Quella circulazion che sì concetta
> pareva in te come lume reflesso,
> dalli occhi miei alquanto circunspetta,
> dentro da sè, del suo colore stesso,
> me parve pinta della nostra effige;
> per che 'l mio viso in lei tutto era messo.
> Qual è 'l geomètra che tutto s'affige
> per misurar lo cerchio, e non ritrova,
> pensando, quel principio ond'elli indige,
> tal era io a quella vista nova:
> veder volea come si convenne
> l'imago al cerchio e come vi s'indova;
> ma non eran da ciò le proprie penne.
>
> (*Par.* xxxiii, 127–39)

At this moment, Dante has everything exactly backward. The Trinity is not painted in any regard with our image. We are stamped with its.[150] What Dante initially thinks he recognizes as a human image in God is in fact what there is in the nature of God that has made people to God's image. He has, in fact, been encountering that image in every realm through which he has passed, exhibited in the structure of the three *cantiche* just as it is in the structure of the human soul. The diversity, multiplicity, and complexity of the journey and its details were merely the necessary consequences of the distance of these other places and souls from God of whom they were all images. God is most simple and most intelligible. But as God's image is impressed upon increasingly distant entities, the image becomes more mixed with dissimilarity from God, making it more diverse and multiple, and less intelligible. This opinion, which runs through Dionysius,[151] is echoed by Beatrice and others in discussing the deterioration of the influence of God's guidance the farther one moves from God. The anagogical role of hierarchies, for Dionysius, is precisely to aid the human soul in moving from multiplicity and corporeality to simplicity and intelligibility.[152]

Thinking and willing are not distinct for God, though they are for angels and humans. If Dante encounters so multifarious and so complicated an array of places and persons, it is because in the realm of our lives, what is simple in God is distributed into a complex arrangement of distinguishable faculties operating in diverse circumstances. To reflect God's nature, to display the image of God in lower nature requires that God's simple properties be actualized in individual and diverse properties and entities. It is only in discovering the common underlying structure that Dante can begin to recover the simplicity of its source. The movement of passion with which Dante began the poem—and whether we call it a movement of desire toward God, or a movement of flight away from the terror of the dark wood, either is passionate—is completed in his ultimate understanding and enjoyment of God in the final lines of the poem. The journey is anagogy in Dionysius' terms, for it has brought Dante from the realm of multiplicity to that of simplicity. It is also a journey from error to knowledge. And it is a journey that completes an appetitive motion by coming to rest in the possession of its desired object. In the realm of multiplicity, all of these are separate issues. In God they are not.

In the first instant of Dante's direct knowledge of God, he sees characteristics that he can now see exist also in people, however mutilated the reproduction. And so, in that first instant, he believes he sees his own human image in God. But having come this close to God has also made Dante increasingly like God, at least within his own capacities. And as he accomplishes, through this divinization, that simplicity of understanding of which he is capable, in the second instant of Dante's direct knowledge of God he realizes that what he had recognized as human was what was always divine in him. And at the moment that he sees that it is not our image that appears in God but only God's, he becomes most like God and at that moment the movement of his intellect and will is made the same as God's in moving "il sole e l'altre stelle."

Conclusion:
Understanding, Desire, Poetry

Our investigations so far have aimed at discovering the doctrine of the *Divina Commedia*. But we cannot end with that, for the *Commedia* is not merely doctrine. It is not a speculative exercise but a practical one. The field of the poem, according to the *Letter to Can Grande*, is ethics, and ethics, Dante would know, and states explicitly, is not concerned with knowledge only but with action: "non ad speculandum, sed ad opus" (*Ep.* xiii, 16).[1] Dante's purpose is not merely to educate his readers, but to change their lives, to move them from misery to happiness: "finis totius et partis est, removere viventes in hac vita de statu miseriæ, et perducere ad statum felicitatis" (*Ep.* xiii, 15). If Dante had only addressed the intellect in the poem, he would have failed. But, as we consider the manner in which a reader comes upon the truths of the poem, we discover that Dante has already made provision to ensure that these truths find the readiest and most effective reception.

As we have seen, the three structures of the individual *cantiche* of the *Commedia* propose variations on a single theme. In those variations the meaning of the theme undergoes change and development, and the content of those changes is the content of the arresting new doctrine Dante expresses in the allegory of the poem. But the order in which these variations appear is itself significant. The principles of Dante's doctrine are found in the structure of the *Paradiso*. Yet we do not begin with the *Paradiso*; we begin farthest from it. This narrative decision embodies Dante's conviction regarding what is needed to ready the human intellect to understand such principles. When we look at the relation of the three *cantiche* to each other, we find that the sequence in which they are presented to us reflects two further structures. Those structures have been designed precisely to meet the demands of Dante's ethical intention, as, indeed, was his decision to express the doctrines of the *Commedia* in poetry rather than prose. Understanding the poem in its fullest sense requires that we recognize these structures and their meanings, and that we consider the special aptitude poetry has for Dante's purposes.

"VIRGIL, TO WHOM YOU GAVE ME FOR MY SALVATION"

In canto xxx of the *Purgatorio* occurs perhaps the most dramatic recognition scene in Western literature, certainly the most unexpected in its development. After not having seen one another in ten years, Dante and Beatrice meet across the river Lethe, at the border of the terrestrial paradise. Dante is overwhelmed by emotions he has not felt in ten years.

> E lo spirito mio, che già cotanto
>   tempo era stato che alla sua presenza
>   non era di stupor, tremando, affranto,
> sanza delli occhi aver più conoscenza,
>   per occulta virtù che da lei mosse,
>   d'antico amor sentì la gran potenza.
>   (*Purg.* xxx, 34–39)

Beatrice's response is not what either Dante or we expected. Her first words are a warning; her second express outrage; her third denounce Dante for having turned from her, and in doing so having turned from his salvation.

> Dante, perchè Virgilio se ne vada,
>   non pianger anco, non piangere ancora;
>   chè pianger ti conven per altra spada.
>   (*Purg.* xxx, 55–57)

"Non pianger anco, non piangere ancora." The tone of Beatrice's statement is immediately recognizable in its pattern: first with the endings of the words truncated as they would be in normal speech, then repeated with their full endings. The ominous slowing and emphasis of the full endings is an unmistakable signal of her anger. These are Beatrice's first words to Dante, who seems so taken aback as not to register either their meaning or their tone. And so her second statement is equally emphatic. She has recourse again to repetition; and the repetition again reveals the anger that drives it.

> Guardaci ben! Ben son, ben son Beatrice.
> Come degnasti d'accedere al monte?
> non sapei tu che qui è l'uom felice?
> (*Purg.* xxx, 73–75)

This is the whole of her second speech. "Ben son, ben son Beatrice"—
Look at me, Dante! This time he understands what she is saying and is
crushed by it. After ten years, all Beatrice has to say to Dante falls into six
angry verses. Then she is silent, and angels must come to Dante's defense
(*Purg.* xxx, 82–84). In the event, these six verses must have been said
connectedly, but Dante *poeta* chops them up into two fragments surrounded by thirty-some verses of his reaction, to give us time to measure the shock of her speech, and to ask ourselves what its explanation
can be. In chapter three we learned that there exists an angelic anger:
"not as a passion, but as the judgment of justice pronouncing judgment"
(*ST,* 2a2æ 162, 3). That must be what we are seeing here, for however
angelic Beatrice may now be, the marks of anger in her voice are unmistakable. What can have made her so angry that this is all she has to
say to Dante at this most emotionally charged moment?

When Beatrice does speak again, we find that she is outraged that
Dante could ever have been turned from his love of her. While she had
remained alive, and he could see her, his soul had remained focused on
her, and therefore on its right end; and his life followed the right path.
But when she died, he turned elsewhere.

> Alcun tempo il sostenni col mio volto:
> mostrando li occhi giovanetti a lui,
> meco il menava in dritta parte volto.
> Sì tosto come in su la soglia fui
> di mia seconda etade e mutai vita,
> questi si tolse a me, e diessi altrui.
> (*Purg.* xxx, 121–26)

Even beyond the grave Beatrice tried to return Dante to the *dritta
parte,* using other means to stand in for her. She tried visions *(ispirazion),* both in dreams and awake *(ed in sogno e altrimenti),* but these,
she says, had no effect:

> Nè l'impetrare ispirazion mi valse,
> con le quali ed in sogno e altrimenti
> lo rivocai; sì poco a lui ne calse!
> (*Purg.* xxx, 133–35)

Dante continued to follow the wrong road, pursuing false goods that could not deliver what they promised:

> E volse i passi suoi per via non vera,
> imagini di ben seguendo false,
> che nulla promission rendono intera.
>
> (*Purg.* xxx, 130–32)

It has been tempting to commentators to read this condemnation as referring to Dante's pursuit of philosophy, culminating in the *Convivio*, rather than theology or Christian doctrine, but such an interpretation cannot be long sustained. How can we say that while pursuing his philosophical studies Dante had abandoned Christian doctrine? The *Convivio* exhibits no conflict between philosophy and theology, or between philosophy and revelation.[2] And it would be equally absurd to say that in the *Commedia*, Dante had abandoned philosophy. The poem depends throughout on both Christian and pagan philosophical systems for its overall structure and for the explanation of many of its details. Not only is the philosophy of the *Convivio* thoroughly Christian, so is the Christian doctrine of the *Commedia* thoroughly philosophical.

What we know of the dates of Dante's life and of the dramatic date of the *Commedia* also prohibits us from seeing any condemnation of philosophy in Beatrice's angry remarks. If we are to take Beatrice's denunciation seriously, Dante's turning from her must precede the dramatic date of that denunciation, that is to say, must occur sometime *before* the Wednesday after Easter Sunday, 1300. She condemns Dante for what he has done before that date; any actions of his that follow that date are, from the standpoint of his salvation, irrelevant or benign. This is *Dante's* own judgment. Since the poem was written long after that date, had he wanted to include actions subsequent to it in Beatrice's condemnation, all he needed to do was change the dramatic dates of the poem. But with the date of Dante *personaggio*'s conversion set at 1300, however, neither the greater part of his study of philosophy nor its culmination in the writing of the *Convivio* (the latter, especially, years in the future)[3] can be the object of Beatrice's condemnation.

All that we can securely say, and it is very little, is that Dante's turning from Beatrice occurred sometime between her death and 1300. It is reasonable to assume that some of the episodes Beatrice condemns are those mentioned by Dante at the end of the *Vita Nuova* and in the *Convivio*, since in those places he speaks of visions—a *forte imaginazione* of Beatrice in glory (*Vita Nuova*, xxxix), and the *mirabile visione* of her (*Vita Nuova*, xlii) from which, we are to believe, arose the composition of the *Commedia* as fulfillment of his determination one day to write something worthy of her—that Beatrice's declaration in the *Purgatorio* seems to echo. But in the *Vita Nuova* Dante was convinced that Beatrice's intervention through these visions had been decisive and definitive in returning his attention to her.[4]

Nothing could be more fervent than Dante's insistence in the *Vita Nuova* that he rededicated himself wholly to Beatrice. But Beatrice could not condemn him in the *Purgatorio* had that remained so. We must conclude that even this passionate repentence came to be extinguished and superseded by another period of distraction from the pursuit of a divine truth. But it is fruitless to search for details of that event. That such a distraction occurred we know from Dante's confession that Beatrice's condemnation is just, and from this too we have the only explanation of what led him away from her. As it turns out, there was no dramatic upheaval. His error could not have been more banal. But at the same time, its very banality is what makes it so significant to us. What turned Dante from Beatrice? Things around him; nothing more.

> Piangendo dissi: «Le presenti cose
> col falso lor piacer volser miei passi,
> tosto che 'l vostro viso si nascose.»
> (*Purg.* xxxi, 34–36)

What were these things? Who can say? They might have been—probably were—almost anything. That is the banality of Dante's fall. Yet, however banal, these "present things" were powerful enough in their attraction to draw him from the memory of a woman he loved and from the heavenly goal she represented. Nor was it, we should remember, that their attraction went unopposed. Beatrice had sent visions and dreams, yet even they were not powerful enough to overcome the attraction of these "present things." And at that point, Beatrice realized, Dante was lost to every form of persuasion.

> Tanto giù cadde, che tutti argomenti
> alla salute sua eran già corti....
> (*Purg.* xxx, 136–37)

Argomenti may here mean nothing more specific than "any means to convince him." Yet I believe it would be wrong to ignore its associated technical meanings in favor of a merely generic meaning.[5] Rather, given the probable scholastic context of the years of Dante's life Beatrice is condemning, I think it likely that she is making a very pointed denunciation of Dante's state. Visions had no effect (or no lasting effect) on him; neither did *argument,* which here I believe should be taken in its standard philosophical sense of proof and logical reasoning. Every argument regarding what he should do for his salvation fell short of reaching him, we would say. But logical arguments and visions are no weak means, so much power did *le presenti cose* have.

The lesson of Dante's distraction is that the "presence" that gives *le presenti cose* their seductive power cannot be combated by abstractions that lack that presence: not by visions that lack Beatrice's substance, not by philosophy. The problem with philosophy is not that it is erroneous or leads away from religious truth and salvation. From a doctrinal point of view, philosophy is harmless. But it is also, from the standpoint of reaching the sinner in peril, useless.[6] This too is part of Beatrice's extended criticism of Dante's life. Late in the *Purgatorio* Dante asks Beatrice why she is speaking so obscurely to him. "To show you," she says, "how little the philosophy of the schools is capable of understanding."

> «Ma perchè tanto sovra mia veduta
> vostra parola disïata vola,
> che più la perde quanto più s'aiuta?»
> «Perchè conoschi» disse «quella scola
> c'hai seguitata, e veggi sua dottrina
> come può seguitar la mia parola;
> e veggi vostra via dalla divina
> distar cotanto, quanto si discorda
> da terra il ciel che più alto festina».
> (*Purg.* xxxiii, 82–90)

There is no reason to restrict Beatrice's use of the term *scola* merely to pagan philosophy (as we often use the phrase "schools of thought"). In the Middle Ages, *scola* would most naturally be used to refer to *scholastic* philosophy, as Dante uses the term *in propria persona* to describe his studies after Beatrice's death: "ne le scuole de li religiosi e a le disputazioni de li filosofanti" (*Conv.*, ii, xii, 7). (The word one would expect Dante to have used for "schools of thought," especially in Beatrice's mouth, would be *setta*—a word he uses in the *Convivio* of the Stoics [iv, vi, 10: "E costoro e la loro setta chiamati furono Stoici"].) Her disdain, therefore, extends beyond Aristotle and Cicero, let us say, to encompass Boethius, Thomas, and Bonaventure. No philosophy, not even scholastic theology, is capable of understanding the mysteries that Beatrice wishes to communicate to Dante.

Nor is it merely that philosophy's doctrines fall short of divine truth. Even more importantly, in the context of the danger in which Beatrice finds Dante, its instruments *(argomenti)* fall short of what is needed to move him to his salvation. And this makes all the more striking what it is to which Beatrice turns to save Dante, and all the more significant her confidence that this final resource will succeed where visions and argument did not. All that could reach Dante now, Beatrice asserts, was to show him the state of the damned after death, for what that example could—and apparently she is certain would—teach him.

> Tanto giù cadde, che tutti argomenti
>   alla salute sua eran già corti,
>   fuor che mostrarli le perdute genti.
>   (*Purg.* xxx, 136–38)

To accomplish this, to undertake the one action that could save Dante, Beatrice turns, as her last but most effective resort, to Virgil.

> Per questo visitai l'uscio de'morti,
>   e a colui che l'ha qua su condotto
>   li preghi miei, piangendo, furon porti.
>   (*Purg.* xxx, 139–41)

One of the oldest and most widely held pieces of conventional wisdom regarding the *Commedia* is that the figure of Virgil represents allegorically the power, and the limits, of the natural human intellect.[7] But considering the poetic possibilities open to Dante in the *Commedia*, and in the context of the present discussion, we must conclude that however widely held this belief may be, it cannot be what Dante intended. Had Dante wanted a symbol of the human intellect, there was a natural, and far more appropriate, choice than Virgil: Aristotle, a figure who was, above all others, *lo Filosofo* of the *Convivio* (*Conv.*, i, i, 1), and *'l maestro di color che sanno* (*Inf.* iv, 131) in the *Commedia*. If Dante's guide were to represent the intellect, what better representative could there be than the intellect's greatest glory? In the *Convivio*, Dante in fact calls Aristotle both master and *guide* of the human reason (*Conv.*, iv, vi, 8 and iv, vi, 16), and if the intellect can be a guide to salvation, surely the highest intellect would be the best guide. Nor had Dante revised his estimation of Aristotle. During their journey, it is in fact to Aristotle that Virgil himself must appeal again and again to explain phenomena the two travelers encounter. In matters of philosophy or science Aristotle reigns supreme even in the *Commedia*.

And yet it was not Aristotle to whom Beatrice turned to save Dante, and in that fundamental poetic choice we see Dante's conviction that the intellect is not in itself sufficient for salvation, not even as a guide toward it. When Beatrice declares that Dante, lost in sin, was deaf to reason and argument, we see why no philosopher could serve effectively as a guide. Intellect alone cannot save Dante. Hell is filled with souls who *knew* that their actions were sins, yet chose them anyway.[8] *Le presenti cose* can overpower the intellect. Beatrice needed a stronger force to move Dante: he must be shown the state of the lost souls—those lost souls must themselves become *presenti* to him, and we must read of that encounter in words that are not merely logical and true, but that could be effective because they were also affecting. And it is for this reason that she approaches Virgil—not as a representative of the intellect, but precisely because he was a poet.[9] Beatrice seeks out Virgil for his *parola ornata* (*Inf.* ii, 67) and his *parlare onesto* (*Inf.* ii, 113), believing that the profession Virgil practiced is precisely what could provide what Dante needed: "con ciò c'ha mestieri al suo campare / l'aiuta" (*Inf.* ii, 68–69).[10] Only someone who knows how in words to make events and persons present is capable of giving Dante the guidance his spiritual state demands.

She has chosen the right man. Dante, it turns out, is not the first person for whom Virgil could show the way to salvation. For Statius before Dante, Virgil had been not only a model for emulation as a poet, but also a guide in his spiritual journey:

> Ed elli a lui: «Tu prima m'invïasti
>   verso Parnaso a ber nelle sue grotte,
>   e prima appresso Dio m'alluminasti.
> Facesti come quei che va di notte,
>   che porta il lume dietro e sè non giova,
>   ma dopo sè fa le persone dotte,
> quando dicesti: 'Secol si rinova;
>   torna giustizia e primo tempo umano,
>   e progenïe scende da ciel nova'.
> Per te poeta fui, per te cristiano.»
>
>   (*Purg.* xxii, 64–73)

Dante recognizes that it is to Virgil that he owes his salvation: "Virgilio a cui per mia salute die'mi" (*Purg.* xxx, 51), and so his is the second soul that Virgil has saved, two more, it should be said, than Aristotle ever did, at least from what we know in the *Commedia*. By using Virgil, rather than Aristotle, as his guide, Dante *poeta* embodied his conviction that while philosophy was not, poetry could be capable of safely delivering a person from sin. For his safety he did not need doctrine; he needed a way to make doctrine effective. What stood in Dante's way were defects of two sorts: one on the part of the intellect, one on the part of the will; and it was to address both that Beatrice turned to Virgil and poetry to rescue Dante.

PART I
POETRY AS IT ADDRESSES THE INTELLECT

The Order of Human Understanding

Dante's state, for which Beatrice denounces him, is really the common state of mankind. He is connected to us, on the one hand, by the very banality of *le presenti cose*, so simple and common a cause for his failing as to present a far greater danger to spiritual health than the more flamboyant, but for that reason exceptional, vices and sins of the notable sinners he encounters in his voyage. On the other hand, when we ask why *le presenti cose* should be able to wield such power, we discover that their strength depends on a fundamental weakness in the human intellect and will, a weakness to which Dante has fallen victim, and a weakness that is common to all of humanity. Beatrice has a double reason for turning to poetry to rescue Dante: first, to adapt what he must know to the weakness of our intellect; second, to address his will, so that what is so painfully learned can then be made available to action.

It is poetry's concreteness that adapts it more perfectly than any other discourse to Beatrice's purposes. That the human mind depends on such concreteness in its reasoning (and that such dependence is a defect) is itself an explicit subject of the *Commedia*. Beatrice had pointed out to Dante that what he saw in the spheres in Heaven was not what was truly the case in Heaven, but only a sign of it. It was what that truth would look like when entitized in a way material enough for his weak, human intellect to absorb. The same principle governs the use of images in the Bible, otherwise divine truths could not be received by human intellects.

> Qui si mostraron, non perchè sortita
>   sia questa spera lor, ma per far segno
>   della celestïal c'ha men salita.
> Così parlar conviensi al vostro ingegno,
>   però che solo da sensato apprende
>   ciò che fa poscia d'intelletto degno.
> Per questo la Scrittura condescende
>   a vostra facultate, e piedi e mano
>   attribuisce a Dio, ed altro intende;
> e Santa Chiesa con aspetto umano
>   Gabrïel e Michel vi rappresenta,
>   e l'altro che Tobia rifece sano.
>   (*Par.* iv, 37–48)

For Dante, the explanation of this need would be found in a basic Aristotelian position (a commonplace among medieval Aristotelians, and cited by Dante himself) that human understanding begins with the material, particular effect, and only by stages progresses to the intelligible, universal cause.

> The natural way of proceeding is from things better known and more certain to us to those things more certain and better known in nature. For the same things are not known to us and known simply. Whence it is necessary that we proceed in this way, from things more uncertain in nature—though more certain to us—to things more certain and better known in nature. What are first manifest and certain to us are, rather, confused. Ultimately, by distinguishing them, their elements and principles may become known. And at that point we will proceed from universals to particulars. (*Phys.*, i, 1; 184a16–23a1)[11]

What is best known to us—and this must be taken in a double sense: best known in the sense of most familiar, but also best known in the sense of most easily comprehended by our intellects—is in an absolute sense least knowable. It is easiest to perceive precisely because it is particular and sensible, but for those same reasons it is farthest from the intelligible universals that are, of all things, best known in an absolute sense. Our understanding begins, therefore, with the least knowable, and attempts systematically to move toward what is best known to nature, though initially least known to us. Having said that, we are in a position to realize that the overall structure of the allegory of the

Commedia follows precisely this same inquisitorial itinerary, and, indeed, replicates in that process the psychological stages of an inquirer engaged in the process.

Because Dante *personaggio* manifestly did not understand, or did not effectively understand, what he needed to know, he must be led to that understanding. But he cannot begin with conclusions. He must start with the evidence of his senses, he has to be *shown* the souls lost in damnation. Then, and only in stages, can he be led to the principles that are embodied in, and that explain, the phenomena with which he began. The order of the narrative of the *Commedia* reflects these stages, and many of its narrative details are designed to make the transition from one stage to another possible and convincing. Indeed, many of the most common responses to the poem are the result of the reflection of the order of human knowing in the order of the *Commedia*. The apparently greater concreteness and vivacity of the *Inferno* and its events—and, on the other side, the apparent abstractness and poetic indistinctness of the *Paradiso* and its contents—are the result of our greater familiarity with embodiments of principle in flesh and mundane action than with the principles themselves, not to mention our greater familiarity with sin rather than blessedness. The greater popularity of the *Inferno* is referable to the same cause. Our difficulty in recognizing that Heaven and Hell share a common structure reflects, conversely, our incapacities when faced with moving from phenomena to cause. Dante is acutely conscious of this problem. In a sense, the problem is the central poetic problem of the *Commedia,* for which the doctrine of the poem provides an explanation and the order of the narrative of the poem attempts a solution. Far from demonstrating poetic weakness, the increasing tenuousness *we* feel as we move into the higher realms of the *Commedia* is itself a way for Dante to exemplify the problem, while the allegorical development of the poem is designed by Dante to enable us to reach its distant, and initially obscure, conclusion.

That the allegory, as well as the narrative, begins with Hell responds to a double appropriateness, or even necessity. First, of course, in the literal sense of the narrative, it is not only poetically more dramatic, but probably unavoidable. At the start of the poem, Dante *personaggio* is in a state of sin, and it seems reasonable and just that he first be confronted with the terrors that await him rather than be shown a blessedness to which he could not at that moment aspire. As he becomes increasingly pure and holy in the course of his pilgrimage, however, it is consistent with this initial judgment that he be shown as increasingly able to attain realms previously out of his reach, and to understand phenomena that earlier would have been incomprehensible to him. Dante *personaggio*'s expanding capacities for action and understanding are, indeed, explicit subjects of both the *Purgatorio* and the *Paradiso.*

But while the necessities of character and plot provide one justification, or even compulsion, to begin the epic with Hell, the most important reason for doing so lies in Dante's estimation of the capacities of *our* intellect. For we are, of course, in exactly the same situation as Dante *personaggio.* If it is consistent with the plot of the poem to say that Dante *personaggio* would not be capable of comprehending the blessedness of Heaven were he shown it at the beginning, it is also fair to say that neither would we, as readers, understand it so well were we shown it first, rather than last. As his character must be prepared in order to be capable of experiencing Heaven, so must we as readers be led from the comfortable concreteness of the poetry and appetites of the *Inferno* to the strangely abstract poetry and the unfamiliar motions with their obscure significances of the *Paradiso.* In Hell, and in the sins it contains, Dante shows us the most material, most earthly, most gross of human actions, knowing that it is in precisely this form, and perhaps only in this form, that we will be most able to recognize the appetitive powers from whose disorderly operations these sins result. Our comfort in recognizing the appetitive faculties in these base actions, and our discomfort, even incredulity, at being asked to recognize that the motions of souls in Heaven correspond to these appetites, and that the motions of the souls in Heaven are in fact the *origins* of these appetites, are proof that the poet must confront and deal with the incapacities of the human reason. They are the exact equivalents, among Dante *poeta*'s readers, of Dante *personaggio*'s moral and intellectual incapacities in the beginning of the *Commedia.* It is not that the poetry of the *Paradiso* is weaker or less moving than that of the *Inferno;* rather, it is that its poetic style is adapted to material of a vastly different nature, and seems tenuous to us only because of our distance from that material and its consequent initial alienness.

In the early cantos of the *Purgatorio,* souls again and again wonder at Dante's corporeality, at his ability to cast a shadow, which their aerial bodies cannot do:

Io era già da quell'ombre partito,
   e seguitava l'orme del mio duca,
   quando di retro a me, drizzando il dito,
una gridò: «Ve' che non par che luca
   lo raggio da sinistra a quel di sotto,
   e come vivo par che si conduca!»
                                                    (*Purg.* v, 1–6)[12]

The purpose of the repetition is not to remind us of Dante's materiality, something we are scarcely likely to forget, it is to remind us of the *immateriality* of the souls in Purgatory. Confronting us with their immateriality compels us to adjust our understanding of what we have seen, in two ways. On the one hand, we are forced to recognize that the souls in Hell too must actually be immaterial, despite their immateriality's being obscured by the circumstances of Hell. The grossness of the tortures undergone emphasized the bodily suffering of such torments; the vividness and concreteness of their descriptions served to reinforce our instinct that these tortures must be happening to bodies and to allay questions we might have asked regarding these souls' incorporeality. Even the darkness of Hell, reflecting not only the spiritual darkness surrounding the damned but also our ignorance of their souls' nature, conceals any easy proof of Dante's bodily difference from the damned souls.[13]

On the other hand, once we have finally recognized that all of the souls both of Purgatory and Hell must be immaterial, we are compelled to find an explanation of the paradox of these incorporeal souls' undergoing apparently corporeal suffering. This paradox, as we have seen in the second chapter, directs us to conclude that the passions being suffered must themselves be incorporeal "passions"—and, even more importantly, to conclude that the souls possess faculties for experiencing such "passions." These faculties must be incorporeal in their own right, yet somehow related to the sensitive passions with which we are familiar in this world. And it is at that point that we are capable of understanding Statius' explanation of the aerial bodies through which incorporeal souls suffer what appear to be corporeal pains as in fact a description of the origin of all appetites and passions in faculties that are in their original nature intellectual, of which corporeal faculties are only one embodiment. Recognizing the common organization of both the *Inferno* and the *Purgatorio,* then, forces us to reinterpret our understanding of the appetites that give them their organization. We are directed to consider that the incorporeal purgatorial passions appear identical to the corporeal passions of this life because both arise, ultimately, in spiritual faculties. For Dante, the primary purpose of purgation and the primary doctrine of the *Purgatorio* was to rehabilitate this intellectual soul so that, liberated at death from the body, it can then exercise its powers in ways that transcend the body and senses. Purgatory prepares the intellectual soul for the free operation of those powers, which is, after all, its destiny in Heaven.

As Purgatory prepares the souls of the *Commedia* for their operation in Heaven, so the *Purgatorio* prepares us to understand this operation. We are told that all operations in Purgatory, however they may appear, are in fact operations of a purely intellectual faculty. Though we are told that, what we *see* looks enough like what we know from our world that we find we can accept this new doctrine without struggle. It is, of course, when we move to the *Paradiso* that we are faced with a much more difficult step. The souls of Heaven no longer have any need of even marginally familiar instruments such as an "aerial body." Even the light by which they are cloaked is only for Dante's benefit. It is hard for us to see their operations as connected in any way to the appetitive operations of Hell. Had Dante not written the *Purgatorio* as an intermediate step, a step exhibiting to us the mundane appetites in what at that point appears a transformed state, I am convinced it would have been impossible for us to discern the connection. But insofar as we took seriously Statius' explanation of an intellectual origin for the sensitive appetites (indeed, all operations of the human soul), we actually also began our reflection on what the truly free operation of these faculties would be. To discover that the actions of the souls in Heaven ultimately do have a connection even to the appetitive operations of the body—indeed, are the origins of those operations, though, of course, of many others as well—is thus difficult but no longer impossible.

Even in the *Paradiso* Dante continues to deal explicitly with the liberation of our conceptions from the material. While at their ascent into Heaven Dante and Beatrice would seem to have left the material world behind, it becomes clear that Dante is not yet free of his human attachment to the evidence of the senses; nor will he be until almost the end of the poem. Souls manifest themselves to Dante encased in light. Of all phenomena, light is the least corporeal, but Dante nonetheless explicitly reminds us that however subtle, light remains phenomenal, and to that extent material. Dante asks Saint Benedict to reveal his face to him, uncovered by flame, but Benedict replies that such clarity of vision can be found only in the last sphere of Heaven (*Par.* xxii, 52–63). Even at so late a moment, light, though subtle matter, still obscures his vision of the intelligible realities of Heaven.[14] In calling attention to this Dante again indicates that his ascent from the material to the intelligible, the anagogy of the poem, is not complete simply with the entry to Heaven, but remains a subject and purpose of the poem right to the end. Even in the highest sphere, Beatrice warns Dante that what he first sees, even there, are only obscured versions of their actual existences:

> Anche soggiunse: «Il fiume e li topzaii
>   ch'entrano ed escono e 'l rider dell'erbe
>   son di lor vero umbriferi prefazii.
> Non che da sè sian queste cose acerbe;
>   ma è difetto dalla parte tua,
>   che non hai viste ancor tanto superbe.»
>   (*Par.* xxx, 76–81)

Her warning to Dante is his warning to us that the process of abstracting is not over until the very end of the inquiry. Until that time, though Dante, and we, may move through realms, and to concepts, increasingly divorced from matter, there remains some embodiment and particularization, and so, necessarily, some deficiency with respect to truth. When the souls appear to Dante veiled in flame, when rivers and topaz in the highest heaven are shown to him, these are figures adapted to his weaker intellect. That remains true of the narrative of the *Paradiso*. It can no more be taken as literal, rather than figurative, than any other of the *cantiche*.

The *Paradiso* also continues explicitly to remind us of the transition from material to intelligible by being the *cantica* in which take place the most serious discussions of the contingent relation of the material world to the intelligible causes from which it arises. Expanding on an image used earlier by Charles Martel to Dante (of the seal whose design is imprinted in wax: "suggello / alla cera mortal"; *Par.* viii, 127–28), Aquinas *personaggio* expresses the distance between divine causes and worldly effects as a successive obscuring of the divine nature by material more and more dissimilar to it:

Ciò che non more e ciò che può morire
non è se non splendor di quella idea
che partorisce, amando, il nostro sire:
. . . .
quasi specchiato, in nove sussistenze,
etternalmente rimanendosi una.
Quindi discende all'ultime potenze
giù d'atto in atto, tanto divenendo,
che più non fa che brevi contingenze;
e queste contingenze essere intendo
le cose generate.
. . . .
La cera di costoro e chi la duce
non sta d'un modo; e però sotto 'l segno
ideale poi più e men traluce.
(*Par.* xiii, 52–54, 59–65, 67–69)

Both Charles's and Aquinas' discussions echo, perhaps intention-ally, a similar discussion by Dionysius, which attributes the difference between God's simplicity and the multiplicity of other natures (as well as their diversity from the divine nature) to the different media in which the divine nature is reflected:

> Someone may say that the seal is not wholly the same in all its impres-sions. But the seal is not the cause of this. For the seal puts altogether the same and whole impression in everything. But it is the dissimilarity of things participating in difference that makes one single, whole, identical example appear discolored. So that, as some are soft and malleable, or are smooth and apt for receiving impressions, and are not hard with other impressions already in them, nor too soft and unstable, then they will take a pure, clear, and proper impression. But if it lacks this aforesaid capacity, this will be the cause of its failed participation [in its model] and of its obscurity. (*Div. nom.*, ii, 6; 1122d–1123a)

As has been the case throughout the *Commedia*, our understanding must be pushed to be spiritualized because it inevitably begins exactly backward. The operations we see in the *Paradiso*, which seem only dimly to remind us of human appetitive operations, are dim only to us. They are nearer to the original operations in their nature and ap-pearance; but we are unable to recognize the resemblance because we are so used to seeing these essential operations overlaid and obscured by the accidents of the contingent world in which we had first come to know them. The structure of the *Commedia* is designed to carry us from what is better known to us to what is better known to nature, or to God. In the end, what we discover is that what we recognize as corporeal appetites exist as corporeal appetites only for a time, and only under special circumstances. What we consider to be the "proper" appetites could not be less so. They are not the originals but the copies; not the proper operation, the true faculty, but the improper and muddied implementation of that faculty in the recalcitrant and distorting medium of the body. The essential discovery of the *Paradiso* is that every creature, including the universe as creature, reflects the Creator in its own appropriate way and in its own appropriated medium. As human beings, we reflect God in an array of faculties that, in their multiplicity, are the best we can do to reflect the simplicity of the divine nature. For us as human beings in this world, the image of God exists not only in the soul, but in the complex of soul and body as long as that complex endures. Our experience of the original faculties is not of them in their original form, but in the form adapted to the body. But what we recognize, then, as anger, for example, or the irascible appetite of which it is the passion, is not the original motion of a faculty, it is only a copy, indeed, among the basest copies, since a copy in the medium of flesh—the "outermost echo," as Dionysius says, of an original divine operation.

What is most remote from us is best known to nature; what is best known to us is furthest from the truth of nature. To be human is to begin inquiry and understanding with the evidence of the senses. For this reason too, then, it was inevitable that Dante begin the *Commedia* with Hell. But the evidence of the senses and our experience is also least like the truths to which we hope to come. Moreover, initially, those truths seem most obscure to us. Only at the end, when the initially obscure principle is understood, is it possible to turn round and understand the real nature of the sensory phenomena with which we began, seeing them as results of a cause we have finally understood.[15] At that last moment too the distance and disparity between the cause and its lowest effects becomes apparent. To use Dionysius' example, it is only when we understand what could be called the bravery of angels (which is in its nature an intellectual motion) that we would be able to understand anger by seeing it as the corporeal embodiment of that more spiritual motion. Indeed, we would understand that angelic bravery (or its equivalent among the motions of the human will) was the origin of that corporeal operation and passion, though in a profoundly mediated way. And at that moment, we would also recognize how little our anger actually resembled its ultimate source.

But it is not only as a dramatic device to reflect the spiritual development of Dante *personaggio* that Dante *poeta* organizes the narrative according to the order of human understanding. Doing so is also one of the most powerful sources of the *Commedia*'s poetic persuasiveness. Dante's journey is a convincing narrative of spiritual conversion and growth precisely because we recognize in it that very same intellectual movement that "converts" the intellect from ignorance to knowledge. What in the intellectual context is a movement from phenomena evident to the senses to the intelligible cause from which the phenomena descend is in the moral context an equivalent movement from sin to blessedness. As Beatrice turned to a poet to lead Dante *personaggio* into direct sight of the particulars with which he had to begin his understanding, so did Dante *poeta*, in turn, choose poetry to confront us with particulars of an equivalent concreteness with which to begin our own inquiry. And as these poetic details not only present us with particulars, but also establish for us a structure that mirrors the inquisitorial movement of Dante's narrative (complete with emotions appropriate to each of the stages of such a movement), we ourselves begin to participate with Dante in the intellectual discoveries to which he wished to lead us. As we make this intellectual progress, we become collaborators with Dante in convincing ourselves that the moral content of the allegory is itself grounded in, and therefore securely based upon, this philosophically guaranteed and humanly inescapable order of knowing. And insofar as we convince ourselves that the intellectual discovery of these moral truths follows a natural and proper human order, we also become convinced that the moral movement of the poem—not just the persuasion of the intellect but the conversion of the will—is equally well grounded and spiritually inescapable. The accuracy of Dante's reflection of the movement of the intellect acts as a rhetorical proof to compel the assent of the will.[16]

In any inquiry, the subject remains the same; it is our understanding of the subject that changes. The three *cantiche* of the *Commedia* have a common structure because all three pursue one single subject of inquiry. But each *cantica* brings us to new conclusions about that subject appropriate to each new stage of the inquiry, and all are aimed at our understanding the principle that creates and explains their phenomena. In any inquiry, the moment at which the principle is grasped alters everything about our previous understanding of the phenomena we have been studying. Not only do we now understand the phenomena properly, but phenomena that we earlier believed discrete or unconnected or chaotic now take their places within a larger and more meaningful order. Only when we suddenly recognized that the motions of the *Paradiso* are the cause of the motions of the *Inferno* did we understand the natural and significant connection between all of these images of God. In every inquiry, this moment happens quite suddenly, and the effect on the mind of the inquirer is dramatic. Even Aristotle attempted in the *Posterior Analytics* to capture the drama of that moment by employing a military simile to express it:

> From perception memory arises, as we say, and from memory . . . experience. From experience . . . may come a principle of art and science. . . . Therefore, art and science do not arise in us from any natural habit, nor from other better known habits, but from sense perception, and in a way that is like the turning point of a battle. For when one man takes a stand, then another does, and another, until they form a battle line. And the soul is of such a nature that it too can undergo this same process.[17]

Dante's description of his state of mind at the end of the *Commedia* is something very like this. We should take note of the shape of his experience. Having lived with the phenomena of the *Commedia* as they have changed in nature and developed throughout the poem, at the last moment of the poem those phenomena suddenly and instantaneously propose to him a principle that is both the goal for which he has been searching throughout the journey, and that also puts everything he has experienced into a single meaningful order. That, I take it, is the meaning of his description of the way the movements of his soul suddenly conform to the movements of the spheres and of the Creator who moves them.

> Ma non eran da ciò le proprie penne:
>   se non che la mia mente fu percossa
>   da un fulgore in che sua voglia venne.
> All'alta fantasia qui mancò possa;
>   ma già volgeva il mio disio e 'l velle,
>   sì come rota ch'igualmente è mossa,
> l'amor che move il sole e l'altre stelle.
>   (*Par.* xxxiii, 139–45)

The description has both a moral and an epistemological dimension. The harmonious motion of Dante's soul with the universe is, on the one hand, an image of the way in which his understanding of the nature and causes of things has been finally and definitively organized by his discovery of the one central mystery that is the principle of everything that exists. But at the same time, that harmonious motion is also the measure of Dante's accomplishment of the spiritual reconstruction for which he undertook his journey. That this moral conclusion should also come with the suddenness of the intellectual conclusion is both appropriate to the nature of the experience and fundamental to the poetic effectiveness of the poem. We should already have noticed how much the experience of discovering a principle can resemble, in the appropriate context, the experience of conversion. John Freccero has called attention to the way in which the completion of a conversion experience abruptly throws all past undergoing and understanding in a new light, reordering and clarifying what was previously inchoate and obscure, and he has pointed out how the narrative structure of the *Commedia* has been designed to secure for the reader (as it had for the poet) the psychological experience proper to it.

> The view from paradise is a spatial translation of what might be called a memory of universal history. The coherence of the whole poem may be grasped only with a view to its totality, a view from the ending, just as the coherence of the poet's life could be grasped only in retrospect, from the perspective of totality in death. . . . At the end of the poem, the dramatic convergence of pilgrim and poet is matched by the conceptual convergence of humanity and the divine.[18]

Insofar as our minds respond to an inquiry ordered in this way most natural to us, the journey has an innate verisimilitude, and the conclusion the inquiry reaches seems all the sounder to us for that. Moreover, since we are humans pursuing an inquiry, the successful conclusion of it is a matter not of speculation alone but of speculation mixed with emotion. The moment at which a principle emerges is not only intellectually satisfying, it is exhilarating as well. So too is the conclusion of the *Commedia*, and it is so because Dante has exploited the concreteness of poetry to fashion an inquiry that overcomes the natural defects of our intellects, and that makes it possible for us to reach so remote, yet exhilarating, a conclusion.

Power, Habit, Act

But given the particular principle at which Dante arrives, the epistemological order that the *Commedia* imitates can reach a successful conclusion only because the three *cantiche* of the poem also embody a second significant order in their relation to one another. This order too is Aristotelian, but ontological, rather than epistemological. In the three *cantiche* we not only witness three stages of Dante's understanding (and in a sense experience those same three stages ourselves), but are shown the subject about which his understanding develops in three progressive ontological states of its own. These three states are in fact what make Dante's epistemological development possible, and the way in which they confirm his conclusion, by imitating the natural relationship of subject matter and understanding, functions as another part of the rhetorical strategy that gives conviction to the experience of inquiry and conversion within this poem.

The principle toward which the *Commedia* develops is a principle about our human powers and their earthly and transcendent operation. Because of our familiarity with corporeal powers and their operation, we are comfortable recognizing the operation of three human appetitive powers in the sins presented in the *Inferno*. Indeed, the allegorical purpose of the *Inferno* is to direct our attention to these powers. Within that *cantica* taken by itself, our attention must be drawn to these powers because it is they that explain the diverse natures and gravities of specific sins. But the powers play an even more extensive and important role, for in the context of the entire poem, it is our progressive redefinition of these powers which provides the explanation of the nature of our ultimate blessedness. The *Inferno* makes us aware of the powers themselves; the *Purgatorio* exhibits to us the habits by which these powers are disposed to their best operation. But as Dante shifts his focus from the powers to their habits, he also begins the realignment of our conception of the appetites from their familiar corporeal forms to the intellectual powers that are the origins of these corporeal forms. For Dante, the Beatitudes that supplant the evil habits of the seven capital vices, we recall, are not habits of sensitive appetites, but of intellectual powers that are those appetites' sources.

We should, for a moment, consider Dante's strategy. In many, probably most, cases, the damned in Hell must also have possessed evil habits. But in the *Inferno*, Dante's focus is resolutely on the appetitive powers themselves, rather than on their habits. There are, I think, two reasons for this. One has already been considered in the first and second chapters: Dante's conviction that it was more appropriate to attribute sins to the powers from which they arose than to the habits that conditioned those powers. As we canvassed in chapter 2, a habit, especially a bad habit, can find expression in actions of quite different sorts. Classifying sins by the habits that disposed appetites to operation might then lead to mistakes in the evaluation of the seriousness of the actions that deserve punishment. The vice of avarice, for example, can easily result in acts of murder or fraud or betrayal, and when it does, the sinner should be punished with the severity appropriate to these worst of actions, even though, in the context of Purgatory, avarice is not among the worst of vices. Because we always act as unitary beings, vices in one appetite may call upon the operation of other appetites in fulfilling their ends. Only by focusing on the power in which the action begins did Dante believe it possible to judge sinful action fairly.

But in addition to this doctrinal reason for focusing on powers in the *Inferno*, Dante's focus on them is also the first step in establishing the second dynamic structure that is embodied in the *Commedia*. The *Purgatorio* is intended to perform a double transitional role: moving the reader's understanding of the appetitive powers from the corporeal to the intellectual (as is appropriate to the order of human knowing), but also redirecting the reader's attention from the powers themselves to their habits. At the same time that the Beatitudes force us to reconsider the nature of the powers of which they are the habits, their status as habits of powers of some sort, whatever their nature, also links them, ineluctably for an Aristotelian, to a third term that completes these two: act (*actus;* ἐνέργεια). If Dante used the incidents and structure of the *Inferno* to bring us to the discovery of *powers*, and the incidents and structure of the *Purgatorio* to bring us to a parallel discovery of *habits*, it is because he intended that the incidents and structure of the *Paradiso* would reveal to us the *acts* for which both power and habit had been ordained.

The relationship of power-habit-act is the most pregnant of Aristotelian relationships. It is only by their act that powers are truly known. Powers are said to be ordered to their act, because they become perfect and most truly what they are only in the completion of that act.[19] It is for this reason that the structure of the *Commedia* must also embody the ontological relations of power-habit-act in addition to the epistemological structure that we discussed in the previous section of this chapter. Since the principle that Dante finally understands is a principle regarding powers, he can reach that principle only when he can see those powers in their proper act. Powers, in themselves, are merely potential and therefore least properly real. Powers may operate or they may not; when they do operate, they may operate well or badly.[20] For Aristotelians, it is this contingency that makes powers most distant from actuality. When powers are not in operation, they can be said to exist only potentially, not actually. Since habits determine powers to act in one way rather than another, they bring powers closer to being "in act," thereby also making them less contingent and more nearly perfect. For this reason, habit was described in medieval Aristotelian ontology as "first act," and the proper act of a power was known as "second act."[21] But only to be in act is to be truly;[22] and only to be in act well with respect to the end of the power makes evident what the power was truly to be. Only when Dante (and we with him) sees the powers in their proper act can he understand what they truly are.

It is no accident, then, that Dante has Beatrice call explicit attention to the hierarchy of potency and act. The whole order of creation reflects this hierarchy, from the angels, whom Dante says are "pure act" (though only God would properly be said to be wholly and continuously *in* act), down to the most material creatures who exist more in potency than in act.

> Concreato fu ordine e costrutto
> alle sustanze; e quelle furon cima
> nel mondo in che puro atto fu produtto;
> pura potenza tenne la parte ima;
> nel mezzo strinse potenza con atto
> tal vime, che già mai non si divima.
> (*Par.* xxix, 31–36)[23]

As it must be if he is to come to understand truths of action, Dante's journey has been a journey from the realm of potency toward that of act. Paradoxically, while the souls we encounter in Hell are themselves fixed in their evil and the punishments they receive, their damnation calls our attention to the fundamental contingency of the powers that in their cases led to damnation. The embodied testimony of every damned soul (and sometimes also their very words) tells of the possibility of acting differently from the way they did, of bringing the potential of the appetitive powers into actuality in specific actions of natures quite different from the ones they had chosen. Since all damned themselves freely, all recognize, as do we, that their appetites could just as freely have aimed at sinless ends. Hell not only shows us the appetites in their most corporeal form, it also shows them to us in their most contingent form.

The habits we discover in the *Purgatorio* move us closer to act in a double sense. The intellectual powers to which Dante now directs our attention are, simply by being noncorporeal, less contingent and therefore less potential than the appetites of the corporeal world. But, in a second sense, powers determined by habit are also closer to act because they have been brought from the potency of indeterminacy (that they could be exercised in manifold operations) to the determinacy of the single end to which the habit orders them. Powers with the capital vices are nearer to act than powers without habits at all, though the act that will be completed will not be the act for which God intended the power. Powers rectified by the Beatitudes are closest to act because they are now determined to the single end for which they were intended. Throughout Purgatory the effort souls must make in their rehabilitation reminds us how significant and portentous is the process of moving from potency to act. Purgatory provides the souls the good habits their powers need for proper operation, but it is only when those powers are actually in act that they are finally unchangeable.

It is that state that we see in the *Paradiso*. Blessedness has nothing potential about it. Happiness is not a state; it is, according to Aristotle and medieval Aristotelians, an activity:

> There exists no constancy in human acts as constant as those activities which are in accordance with virtue.... If activities, as we have said, are the rulers of life ... happiness is a certain activity of the soul in accordance with perfect virtue. (*EN*, i, 10–13; 1100b20–02a5)

> Accordingly as a man's happiness is something created that exists in him, we must say that his happiness is an activity. For happiness is the final perfection of a man. To the extent that anything whatever is perfect, it is in act; for potency without act is imperfect. Therefore, it must be that happiness consists in man's ultimate act. Obviously, operation is the ultimate activity of one capable of operation. For this reason, too, it is called "second act" by the Philosopher; for whatever has a form may be operating only potentially, as one who knows may be thinking only potentially. And therefore even in these matters it is said that "anything whatever exists for its activity." Human happiness must therefore necessarily be an activity. (*ST*, 1a2æ 3, 2)

There is no point in having virtues if the powers of which they are the virtues are not used. While asleep, one can be said to be happy only metaphorically. To have the capacity to act in accord with virtue but not to be so acting is to be happy only potentially. One is truly and actually happy only while exercising one's perfect powers for the ends for which they were intended. *A fortiori* this must be true of blessedness as the most perfect form of happiness. It is the exercise of those powers that is blessed. Speaking of blessedness as it could be understood by an anagogical interpretation of Psalm 114, Dante in the *Convivio* had said, "When the soul has departed from sin, it has been made holy and free in its own powers" (*Conv.*, ii, i, 7).[24]

Dante organized the *Commedia* in such a way that the shared common structure of the three *cantiche* leads us to discover that, however different the subjects of the *cantiche* at first appear, one single subject is common to all three, though our understanding of the subject is appropriately different at each stage of the narrative. But, further, he arranged the three *cantiche* in such a way that we are also led to discover that their subject is exhibited to us in three progressive states: power, habit, and act. And by doing so, he made it possible to construct a figurative description of the nature of blessedness of a quite surprising concreteness.

Though they actually embody a more transcendent significance, as we initially understand them the structures of Hell, Purgatory, and even Heaven correspond to a set of powers that humans possess. Rectified by habits of the proper sort, freed from the corruptions and distortions of the flesh and senses, these powers are able to perfect themselves in their proper act in Heaven. Which is to say that the condition of the beatified soul is the perfect operation of powers we already know, though we know them initially only in their most attenuated form. We recognize these powers first as appetitive powers, but they are so only to us. To the extent that we can come to a suitable understanding of what the powers and their intended operations are in their original divinized forms, we can understand the actual nature of our blessedness. Since a power is only truly known by its proper act, it is only in the *Paradiso* that we can finally understand what these familiar powers really are. But, given our human failings, it is only because we can at least recognize them in the appetites—however remote that operation may be from their proper operation—that we are capable of understanding what operation, what act, in fact constitutes human blessedness in Heaven. If the *Paradiso* is necessary for us to understand the ultimate and real significance of faculties and habits to which we were introduced in the *Inferno* and *Purgatorio*, it is also the case that the two earlier *cantiche* are necessary so that we know to what the transformed meanings of the last *cantica* are to be applied.

Once the first two *cantiche* fulfill their purpose within the overall economy of the *Commedia* by moving the reader from the corporeal appetites we see in the *Inferno* to the paradoxical image of intellectual appetites operating in ways that mimic the corporeal which we see in the *Purgatorio*, the structure of the *Paradiso* can complete the transformation of our understanding of those powers. Dante's association of the souls encountered in different spheres with the activities of angels identified with those spheres, activities that we first regard as analogical to our own activities (though this, of course, is backward, as is inevitable with human understanding: it is our activities that are analogies of theirs, or, rather, imitations of theirs), leads us to conclude that our perfected operations would resemble theirs to the capacity that we can attain. In the angelic movements that we first understand as transfigured appetites are constituted the activities in which our blessedness consists. Moreover, since the angelic operations are ordered as they are to mirror divine operations, we are led to think—and how could we think otherwise?—that our blessedness must consist in our own mirroring of those divine operations in proportion to our ability.

That we would find the structure of our blessedness embodied in a structure of Heaven (and, for that matter of the other two realms, though in more obscure ways) which corresponds to the Trinity, of whose image all of creation bears some trace, is an easy conclusion to reach abstractly, but a difficult conclusion to understand concretely. But when the structure of the *Paradiso* associates the actions of the angels not only with the persons of the Trinity, but with properties of those persons in which we see precisely the transfigured, angelic or divine movements of which our natural appetites are merely material manifestations, we find that our human powers, and their blessed operation, can be reflected in the structures of Hell, Purgatory, and Heaven precisely because our powers in their turn reflect, in a suitably modest fashion, the divine characteristics expressed in the Trinity. The properties of the angels and the motions of their spheres are not merely *like* certain motions of ours, these angelic properties inform our characters and our powers at our birth, and therefore our vision of their properties provides an indication of what the native operation of our own faculties might be, were they freed from the distortions imposed upon them by flesh and bad habits.

A description of the state of the soul in blessedness is the special subject of one of the figurative meanings of a text, the anagogical meaning. Bonaventure had said the anagogical sense of a text was constructed "when by one fact another is understood, one that must be desired, to wit, the eternal happiness of the blessed" ("quando per unum factum intelligendum est aliud, quod desiderandum est, scilicet, æterna felicitas beatorum").[25] We recognize that we have discovered the nature of human beatitude precisely because we recognize that we have, with Dante, now seen that aspect of the divine nature which it is in our natures to imitate and actualize. Nothing other than this, we realize, could constitute beatitude. The *factum* that must be understood anagogically, and that provides us this vision of the ultimate beatitude is no single event within the *Commedia*, nor even the series of events that compose the *Paradiso*. Rather, it is the structure of the *Paradiso*, finally understood in its relation to, and as the fulfillment of, the structures of the two other *cantiche*. Just as within a *cantica* the meaning of an incident is completely understood only in relation to its location in the *cantica*, so the doctrines of the three *cantiche* are fully understood only in their location in the narrative as a whole. We are able to see our blessed activity in the structure of Heaven only because we can recognize that that structure is related to the structures of those realms more familiar to us, and, indeed, that that heavenly structure shows us what the source of our familiar nature has been; what our true nature is; what our activity in Heaven will be like.

At the last moment of the *Commedia*, Dante has an experience of the nature of God which simultaneously completes his understanding of the meaning of the journey he has undertaken and also completes the act of conversion for which he began that journey. There are two parts to this experience: a final vision that he cannot interpret, then a moment at which comprehension comes to him, and understanding and conversion are complete, though the content of that moment remains unexpressed.

> Quella circulazion che sì concetta
>   pareva in te come lume reflesso,
>   dalli occhi miei alquanto circunspetta,

dentro da sè, del suo colore stesso,
   mi parve pinta della nostra effige;
   per che 'l mio viso in lei tutto era messo.
Qual è 'l geomètra che tutto s'affige
   per misurar lo cerchio, e non ritrova,
   pensando, quel principio ond'elli indige,
tal era io a quella vista nova:
   veder volea come si convenne
   l'imago al cerchio e come vi s'indova;
ma non eran da ciò le proprie penne:
   se non che la mia mente fu percossa
   da un fulgore in che sua voglia venne.
All'alta fantasia qui mancò possa;
   ma già volgeva il mio disio e 'l velle,
   sì come rota ch'igualmente è mossa,
l'amor che move il sole e l'altre stelle.
                (*Par.* xxxiii, 127–45)

As we noted in an earlier section of this chapter, the character of
the experience that Dante describes, the sudden flash with which en-
lightenment comes, is recognizable as psychologically the same as the
experience of comprehending any principle at the end of an inquiry,
though here the principle is the highest principle, and here it is not
only apprehended but loved. The psychological verisimilitude of these
final lines of the poem, at the end of the long progress of Dante's voyage of discovery, is a crucial part of the conviction Dante *poeta* creates
of the success of his journey. Yet had this event not also been placed
within the context of the ontological process from potency to act, we
would find ourselves puzzled indeed, and perhaps disappointed. For, if
the content of this vision is taken as it most frequently is, we would be
disappointed that so well known a conclusion was the result of so long
and arduous an inquiry. Or, if we could not ourselves comprehend
what the principle is that Dante finally sees, while we would be certain
that Dante *personaggio* had found the solution to his inquiry, we
would be frustrated of the final goal. What of us? What would we have
found?

By far the most frequent interpretation of Dante's bewilderment
refers it to the ineffable mystery of the incarnation: Dante is asking, How
could God appear to humans in mortal flesh?[26] Yet however unfath-
omable that mystery may be, there is nothing especially appropriate in
it for this final moment of the *Commedia*. That mystery would have

stumped Dante at any moment in his journey. Since Dante himself has noted his increasing powers of discernment in the final cantos of the *Paradiso* (and once just before this vision: *Par.* xxxiii, 79–81), we are convinced, and probably demand, that what troubles him here be a question he could only ask, and answer, at this long-awaited moment. What puzzles Dante is not how what appears human—that is to say, Christ—could actually be divine. Indeed, Dante does not say that his confusion came from seeing Christ specifically in that circling light. At the moment of his incomprehension Dante is looking at the entire Trinity. What he cannot understand is how the whole of divinity could appear human. Why does he think he can see a *human* image in God in all three persons? That is a much more extensive and unexpected paradox, and it is only because of the knowledge he has gained by this final moment that he is able to grasp its solution. It is the acquisition of that very knowledge that Dante has painstakingly replicated for us so that, in its context, we too can understand the significance of his vision.

As we have said earlier, at the end of chapter 3, the epiphany that comes to Dante in the final lines of the poem is that he recognizes that once again he has interpreted precisely backward what he has seen. As he moved from Hell to Heaven, he thought at first he was seeing the progressive spiritualization of human faculties. At the end he recognized that it was the spiritual forms of these faculties which are prior. The corporeal versions of them were only later reflections of those spiritual originals. So here too, at the final moment, looking at the Trinity, Dante realizes that he is not staring at the mysterious appearance of the human image in God. He is staring, rather, at that aspect of God which he can recognize because its image is what defines human beings. He is not seeing our image in God; he is seeing the original that we know in the image that is in us.

But in context, that moment of seeing God's nature is no mere pious platitude, it is a solemn confirmation and solemn guarantee. It confirms that the faculties we first know as human are not human originally but divine; that the redefinition of those faculties that we have pursued in the *Commedia* is correct; that the carrying into act of those faculties as we have now come to know them is our blessedness; that it is our blessedness because it is what makes us like God, and in actualizing those faculties in their original form we become as much like God as we can be. Dante's initial error is also our guarantee that we are made for blessedness. We can be blessed only because we are made to the image of God; and our certainty that we are made to God's image is found in Dante's confusion as to whose image he is seeing. It was only because we are in God's image that it was possible for Dante, even for a moment, to think he saw a human image in God. When Dante understands and corrects this confusion, his faculties, which were being rehabilitated for perfect operation throughout the poem, become oriented to the proper order of original and image, of cause and effect. When that happens, not only have Dante's faculties been perfected for unimpeded operation, they are now aligned so that their operation harmonizes with the real order of creation. And it is for that reason that Dante says in the final image of the poem that his desire and will, his active faculties, are brought exactly into conformation with God's nature and love.

PART II
POETRY AS IT ADDRESSES THE WILL

Poetry, Truth, and Action

Everything that we have considered so far has examined poetry's special aptitude for presenting truths to the intellect. But there is another reason, perhaps even more important, for Beatrice's choice of a poet to guide Dante to salvation, and by extension, of course, for Dante's choosing poetry in which to present the doctrines we find in the *Commedia*. As we have said, Dante's purpose in the *Commedia* is not merely speculative, it is moral. But moral instruction is not completed simply by educating the intellect. Moral instruction that addresses only the intellect can be effective only for those whose intellect already commands the other faculties as it should. Had Dante addressed only the intellect in the *Commedia*, he would have been of use only to those who had no need of him. For the rest, and that means for any of the audience for whom Dante intended the *Commedia*, those "viventes in hac vita [in] statu miseriæ," instruction must alter their character. The moral direction of a person is known when we know in what the person takes pleasure and what the person finds painful.[27] Reforming character means substituting the right objects for the wrong as objects of desire and delight, and it means moving the will to the actions that will reform it. To fulfill Dante's purpose, the truths of the poem must become objects of desire attractive enough to overcome the otherwise greater attraction that will inevitably attach to *le presenti cose*. And for making truths objects of desire, poetry also has a special aptitude.

During his examination by Saint Peter in the *Paradiso* regarding faith, Dante expresses the critical importance of physical presence in human comprehension, for reasons that go beyond the limits of the human intellect which we have already considered. Having been asked by Peter about the origin of his faith, Dante answers that what he knows of the truths of faith he knows from the Old and New Testaments. When Peter asks him how he knows that what the Bible instructs is true, Dante replies that he is convinced of its truth by the miracles of which the Bible tells.

> . . . La prova che 'l ver mi dischiude
> son l'opere seguite, a che natura
> non scalda ferro mai nè batte ancude.
> (*Par.* xxiv, 100–02)

Peter challenges Dante: Is this not reasoning in a circle? Depending upon statements in the Bible to prove the truth of the Bible itself? Dante responds that it is not the content of the miracles that demonstrates the truth of the Bible, but their success as instruments of persuasion which convinces him that what occurred is true.

> «Se 'l mondo si rivolse al cristianesmo»
> diss'io «sanza miracoli, quest'uno
> è tal, che li altri non sono il centesmo;
> chè tu intrasti povero e digiuno
> in campo, a seminar la buona pianta
> che fu già vite e ora è fatta pruno.»
> (*Par.* xxiv, 106–11)

This is a strange, yet oddly moving proof. What Dante is saying in effect is that, knowing what he does about the nature of human understanding, it is inconceivable that human beings could ever have accepted the truths of the Bible without the manifest evidence that could only have been provided by the actual occurrence of these miracles. If people could come to believe such things, Dante is certain, they must have been convinced by miracles. Nothing else could have convinced them. Since the world did turn to Christianity, that conversion is proof of the veracity of the miracles, and from confirmation of their truth the truth of the Bible in general follows. For our purposes, the importance of this peculiar and indirect proof is what it tells us of Dante's understanding of how it is that people are persuaded to believe something. Even when it is Saint Peter and the other apostles doing the preaching, so Dante declares, doctrine alone will never convince the human intellect until the doctrine is revealed in incidents so palpable as to be perceivable by the senses.

Indeed we can go a step further. The early Christians about whom Dante is speaking to Peter did more than simply believe the doctrines of faith through the agency of miracles, they became active in pursuit of faith. The world not only believed what Peter preached; more importantly, it changed how it acted: it turned to Christianity ("si rivolse al cristianesmo"). It did so because the miracles, as events and therefore actions, could do more than teach people, they could move them. This, of course, is what Dante too needs to accomplish; it is not enough, for him, to convince people of his doctrines; he wants to get them to change how they act, to change what they love. And here we can see how poetry could be more effective than philosophy. Miracles have power, first, because of their actual, physical presence to their audience. This presence is sufficient, perhaps, with regard to the intellect's need for concrete particulars in which to begin its process of understanding. But the most important source of the power of miracles comes from their character as actions. Living people participated in these miracles, and because of their participation, those events, over and above the doctrinal content they were meant to communicate, were also inescapably charged with emotion. It is this emotional transfiguration that gave miracles their capacity not only to teach but to move. Since poetry too can embody doctrines and ideas in characters and actions, poetry can associate active qualities and attributes with these doctrines and, by clothing the doctrines in flesh, can clothe them also with emotion.[28]

Dante uses his own life as proof of the perilous evanescence of faith, when faith lacks such presence and affect. At the moment at which the action of the *Commedia* commences, as we noted at the beginning of this chapter, Dante had been lost to every intervention Beatrice had tried on his behalf. Every argument fell on deaf ears ("tutti argomenti / alla salute sua eran già corti" [*Purg.* xxx, 136–37]); even visions were without lasting effect ("Nè l'impetrare ispirazion mi valse" [*Purg.* xxx, 133]). "While I was alive," she says, "sight of me kept him on the right path; at my death, he turned away."

> Alcun tempo il sostenni col mio volto:
>> mostrando li occhi giovanetti a lui,
>> meco il menava in dritta parte volto.
> Sì tosto come in su la soglia fui
>> di mia seconda etade e mutai vita,
>> questi si tolse a me, e diessi altrui.
>>> (*Purg.* xxx, 121–26)

"What other object of desire could have attracted you more?" she asks.

> E quali agevolezze o quali avanzi
>> nella fronte delli altri si mostraro,
>> per che dovessi lor passeggiare anzi?
>>> (*Purg.* xxxi, 28–30)

And the confession that Dante is finally able to make, brief though it is, precisely corresponds to the origin of the danger in which he found himself, and from which Beatrice had no recourse but poetry, in the person of Virgil, in order to rescue him.

> Piangendo dissi: «Le presenti cose
>> col falso lor piacer volser miei passi,
>> tosto che 'l vostro viso si nascose.»
>>> (*Purg.* xxxi, 34–36)

We must recognize the very concrete sense that Dante attributes to the phrase *le presenti cose*. It does not mean merely "things that were present rather than absent." It means that, surely, but with the added emphasis that because these things were present, because they were being lived, and in being lived were colored with the emotions undergone in their experience, these *presenti cose* had, as we have been calling it, "presence"—they could exercise the attraction that concrete things always have for human apprehension and appetite, and they could in that way become the objects of desire that drew Dante away from Beatrice and the right road. Once Beatrice was dead, her face was no longer present to Dante. It remained with him in memory, but memory cannot compete with present apprehension. Even the visions that she sent to him in dreams and in other ways ("ed in sogno e altrimenti" [*Purg.* xxx, 134]), while present to Dante in time, lacked the concreteness that gives their presence to *le presenti cose*. Nor, though for different reasons, do arguments possess that presence. Their abstraction renders them pallid in relation to the material things of this world.

In the face of this incapacity to understand without sensible evidence, faith alone will always find itself at a disadvantage in moving the human will. Its deficiency (we should say, rather, our deficiency) is apparent from the definition Dante gives Saint Peter of its nature, citing Saint Paul:

> ... Come 'l verace stilo
> ne scrisse, padre, del tuo caro frate
> che mise teco Roma nel buon filo,
> fede è sustanza di cose sperate,
> ed argomento delle non parventi;
> e questa pare a me sua quiditate.
> (*Par.* xxiv, 61–66)[29]

Faith stands in for objects that cannot be seen. Were the things to be hoped for present, they would have their own substance. Faith substitutes for their substance. Faith is explicitly the argument for things that are not present. But how successfully do we believe *cose non parventi* can compete with *le presenti cose* even in regard to the intellect merely, let alone the will? Everything that we have considered regarding the process of human intellection and desire argues against that. If the lack of presence of the objects of faith renders belief in them difficult, how much more difficult must it be to make people love objects they cannot see. To Beatrice, it is outrageous that, having once loved her, Dante could love other goods, simply because she was no longer present to him. After his confession to her, it seems almost equally incomprehensible to him that he could have done so. But he did. For living human beings, however surely their unclouded judgment may know the absolute desirability of the true good, their contingent judgment and their desires are always prone to being overpowered by those goods that are actually present.

What rescued Dante were not arguments but examples (being shown the future state of souls [*Purg.* xxx, 136–38]), something concrete from which his mind could come to an understanding of the truth, and, even more importantly, *to which* his will could be drawn. As Dante describes his rescue to Saint John, he was saved by "arguments" that were truths embodied in concrete entities (the world's existence and his own) or in action (Christ's passion). These were not bloodless, merely intellectual proofs. These truths affected Dante so intensely that they could be said to have *bitten* him.

> ... Tutti quei morsi
>
> che posson far lo cor volgere a Dio,
>
> alla mia caritate son concorsi;
>
> chè l'essere del mondo e l'esser mio,
>
> la morte ch'el sostenne perch'io viva,
>
> e quel che spera ogni fedel com'io,
>
> con la predetta conoscenza viva,
>
> tratto m'hanno del mar dell'amor torto,
>
> e del diritto m'han posto alla riva.
>
> (*Par.* xxvi, 55–63)[30]

For Dante, poetry possesses a special moral capacity and appropriateness. Poetry—all art—is first of all embodiment. This is what distinguishes art from philosophy: art is concrete where philosophy is abstract. The degree of concreteness varies, obviously, depending on medium. Sculpture, painting, and drama are all more concrete, more completely embodied than narrative or lyric poetry. But all are embodiments of meaning when compared with the goal of abstraction to which all philosophy or science aspires. A poet does not merely report the truths of philosophy or theology; a poet embodies these truths in the characters and actions of the poem. In doing so, the poet takes one step beyond philosophy, investing those truths with emotion and passion insofar as we see the truths literally enacted in the events of the poem. And it is precisely because poetry is the embodiment of action, and is therefore suffused with emotion, that it is so perfectly adapted to moral instruction. The embodiment of poetry provides the emotional impetus that makes it possible not only to understand but also to act upon doctrine.

Further, the objects of inquiry of the *Commedia* and the truths of moral instruction are not abstract and immobile; they are themselves concrete, human, embodied. They are truths of action, truths that in their essence already include, and must take account of, the operation of emotion as well as intellection in the deliberation and choice that initiate action. Aristotle would frequently point out that the difference between the words *concave* and *snub* was that *concave* described a curve of a certain sort abstracted from matter, while *snub* was that same curve in relation to the flesh of a nose.[31] Though the principles Dante discovers through the *Commedia* are abstract *qua* principle, they too are resolutely connected, as cause to effect, to a certain matter, to the concrete actions that they explain.

We have already taken note that it is the nature of the human intellect always to begin its inquiries with the particular and material, and we have recognized that poetry is valuable to Dante for its capacity to supply particulars for our intellect to operate upon. But that our intellect begins with particulars is no less true in the speculative sciences than in practical fields. Yet inquiries with action as their end follow a very different trajectory than do speculative inquiries. While both begin in the concrete particulars, as practical inquiries move to more abstract and universal principles, they must nevertheless also remain connected to the concrete and particular. Practical inquiries are futile, indeed misguided, if their conclusions are not also recognizable in the world of action so that they can be applied back to that world. And here poetry, as an embodied medium, discovers a special fitness for these inquiries and their conclusions, for it can provide manifestations of the conclusions in precisely the forms in which they manifest themselves to us in the real world: as confusing and obscure embodiments at the outset of the inquiry, as clearer and more univocal embodiments—yet still embodiments, for truths of action are always embodied—at the successful conclusion of the inquiry.[32]

Reformation is substituting the right love for the wrong and requires the retraining of desire. This does not occur through argument; it is not complete when some principle is understood. New objects of desire must replace the old; and in real life rehabilitation additionally requires habituation to these new objects. For Dante's purposes, it was important that his audience undergo at least an attenuated, aesthetic experience of this process of reformation, for he wished to change their behavior from that which made them miserable to that which would make them blessed. Even such aesthetic reformation requires more than argument; it requires its own embodiments strong enough to bite, at least in art, in order to reorient the emotions and hence the desires, of the reader.[33] Poetry possesses its special moral capacity—the capacity that made Dante choose it rather than philosophy—because by being able to suffuse argument with emotion, it has the power not only to present arguments so they may be known, but to make the object of those arguments attractive enough to pursue. Philosophy can identify objects but cannot in itself make them lovable. The poet can be said to *make* the truths of faith objects of desire. Characters and actions of drama and poetry come to us, by virtue of their embodiment, in the trappings of circumstance and through both their concreteness and these circumstances compel us to react to them in emotional and aesthetic ways appropriate to them. Truths embodied are no longer abstract and dispassionate truths; they have now become objects of attraction or repugnance. As poetry makes those objects desirable, it has the capacity to direct human action.

Beatrice and the End of Poetry

One of the most satisfying, as well as convincing, characteristics of the *Commedia* is the perfect reflexivity by which poetic form matches doctrinal content from every perspective in the poem. The activity in which each individual's blessedness consists, as we have discovered in the third chapter, is the perfected operation of faculties that are the origin of our corporeal appetites. In their operation these faculties suitably reflect the divine nature in whose image they were created. Thus, the divine nature itself can quite properly be conceived of as displaying the form of appetition, bearing in mind, of course, that our understanding of "appetition" in this context must be translated so as to be accommodated to that nature. Everything that we discover as the doctrine of the *Commedia* is informed, in the end, by what we familiarly, if rather too materially, think of as appetition. Let us note, then, that Dante has created the most perfect image of this specific doctrinal content in the narrative of the *Commedia* itself. For, from start to finish the poem is a narrative of the perfect process of appetition. Action, base or blessed, begins in love and desire, and progresses toward its object until the moment at which it possesses it. Thus the very nature of action, animal, human, angelic, divine, has this progress at its core, but this progress toward a goal until it is reached is what we see in the story of the *Commedia:* that is, a journey. Now, any journey by its nature can be the image of appetition, but this journey most of all: for it begins explicitly with love, and follows through in pursuit of the object of its desire, until it culminates in the possession of that object and the delight that is consequent to that. As Aquinas says (*ST,* 1a2æ 31, 1 and 32, 2), in appetition, the soul moves outward toward the object of desire, until it is united to that object. This is the movement Dante has followed throughout the poem, and in this respect the narrative of the entire work is itself the image of the purpose of the work: to bring souls from a state of misery to blessedness.

At every stage of the poem we have been shown that desire is the explanation of the location of every soul encountered, and that in that location each soul continues to act by that desire. At each new stage of the poem, that is, with each new *cantica,* we see that the nature of the object of desire changes, such change being both cause and reflection of the improved condition of the souls we encounter. At the same time, at every moment we have seen that Dante *personaggio* too is acting from desire. The quality of Dante's desire (if not its object) changes too in harmony with the new locations in which he finds himself. At every stage, then, his desire is refined, and as it is, he is closer to blessedness. That is the moral content of the poem, and that is also its narrative. There is a perfect consonance and reflexivity between the content and the medium. And not only, we recognize at the end of the poem, in its moral dimension. Love does not only move Dante, it moves the stars. The original, immortal, and eternal creative force is love, and in the orientation of the protagonist of the poem to his true center, the narrative of the poem is the image not only of morality and piety, but also of the very nature of the created universe, and, by reflection, of its Creator.

But if it is desire in the guise of a journey that gives shape to the overall narrative of the *Commedia,* the terminus of that movement (at least as Dante *personaggio* originally intends it) is Beatrice. All desire begins with an object that is both beginning and end to the desire: the origin of the desire and the goal toward which the desirer moves. So too in this poem. It is Beatrice who is the object of Dante's desire; in being reunited with her, after ten years, Dante expects to complete his journey. His conviction is both true and not true. In being reunited with her he has, in fact, completed his journey of redemption. When Beatrice and Dante meet in Purgatory, he has finished his rehabilitation and can properly be said to have been saved. And that, indeed, was the object of both his journey and Beatrice's initiating embassy to Virgil to guide Dante through the journey. On the other hand, his journey does not end with his meeting with Beatrice. First, with Dante and Beatrice together, then with Dante apart from Beatrice, with Saint Bernard for a moment, and then with Dante alone the journey continues to its final end. The final object of desire is not Beatrice, we know, but God.

Yet Beatrice's role in the poem is unlike any other. She is not simply a guide to Dante. She is the very cause of his journey, since it is the object of desire that can most properly be said to be the cause of a movement.[34] It is not Dante's will that initiates the action of the *Commedia*, it is Beatrice who initiates it, through his love for her. Indeed, even when Beatrice leaves Dante to continue the journey on his own, it is only because of the role she had in his life that he is capable of completing the final stage of the journey. How she plays her role casts one final light on the role the medium of poetry plays in the *Commedia*.

Central to the single movement of desire that is the plot of the poem is the one irreducible biographical declaration in the *Commedia* that we must honor: that Dante was convinced that on Good Friday, 1300, Beatrice Portinari intervened, because of his love for her and hers for him, to save his soul from damnation. Whatever allegorical meanings we find in the poem, the literal narrative begins with this declaration. Within that literal narrative it is further notable that on two signal occasions it is only the love Dante has for her that makes it possible for him to continue and complete the journey of salvation, that is, to be able to receive the benefit of her intervention. Both at the very outset of Dante's rescue and virtually at its conclusion, Virgil is able to overcome Dante's otherwise insuperable resistance to the next frightening step he must take only by invoking the memory and image of Beatrice. Thus, she not only initiates the journey in persuading Virgil to act on her behalf, she remains an explicit cause of Dante's motion throughout the journey—indeed, the most effective cause—by being the loved object toward which he wishes to move.

In the psychological drama of the beginning of the *Commedia*, in the moments of terror, hope, and terror again which precede the entrance of Virgil, Dante laconically, but tellingly and concretely, shows us how crushing was the disappointment of his hope, and how intense the despair that convinced even as timid a traveler as he proves to be that he had no choice but to undertake this difficult journey. Yet no sooner are we shown this than, in the second canto, Dante demonstrates that no matter how powerful a motive this may have seemed to be, it was still not powerful enough to move him actually to set foot on his route. The impetus that fear and desperation had given him in canto i evaporated in its turn, in the face of the actual dangers of the voyage he had to begin. It is only when Virgil explains that he has appeared to him in response to *Beatrice's* intervention that Dante becomes resolute enough actually to begin the journey. Only love is powerful enough to overcome definitively such present fear.

Similarly, near the end of the ascent of Purgatory, when Dante is almost within sight of the goal for which the journey was undertaken, when all but one of his vices have been reformed, he again balks, this time at the final purifying fire through which he must pass. To encourage him to make this final step, Virgil first tries reasoning with Dante, recalling the more dangerous moments through which they have already passed. To no avail; and Dante's obduracy troubles Virgil. To move him Virgil has only one more argument, whose very brevity is proof of its efficacy: "Or vedi, figlio: / tra Beatrice e te è questo muro" (*Purg.* xxvii, 35–36). Dante is Pyramis to Beatrice's Thisbe, and at this argument his resistance melts. What the incident exhibits to us is also powerful: though Dante is almost completely reformed at this moment, he is still able to complete the process of his salvation only because of his love for Beatrice.

And so we must ask in our turn, What meanings does Dante intend to convey by making Beatrice so powerful a figure? What does Beatrice represent? It is not simply that we believe that all figures in the *Commedia* fulfill some allegorical purpose. Rather, what makes the question so important is Dante's continuing insistence that it is an actual, individual human being who plays so significant a role in the action of the poem. From what we have been considering of Beatrice, it should be clear to us that certain of the more frequent hypotheses regarding Beatrice's role as a symbol simply cannot be maintained. It is not possible to say that she represents theology, or even revealed truth, or even the truth in some more general sense.[35] We know, indeed, that Beatrice *personaggio* had no high opinion of theology as it is usually conceived. The doctrines of the *scuole de li religiosi* that Dante frequented after her death (*Conv.,* ii, xii, 7) are incapable, she says, of following her words (*Purg.* xxxiii, 85–87). But the problem is more general than that. Whatever Beatrice represents, she represents it as an object of desire. Dante does not just know Beatrice, he is drawn to her by love.[36] It is divine love that moves the stars (*Par.* xxxiii, 145), it is love for Beatrice that moves Dante until the moment, at the very end of the poem, when he too can be moved directly by divine love.

Theology and its doctrines are deficient, we have come to understand, because they are abstract and speculable rather than vivid and desirable. Their methods *(vostra via)*, Beatrice says, are as far removed from a properly divine method as the earth is from Heaven (*Purg.* xxxiii, 88–90). Until doctrine is loved and pursued, it cannot lead to Heaven; it cannot be a *via divina*. But the same problem attaches to any truth, even revealed truth. The truth is not loved because it is true. But until something be loved, there can be no movement toward it. Beatrice is pursued, and God through her, because of love, not truth. The three theological virtues by which the soul is prepared for blessedness are virtues that perfect the appetitive faculty of the soul, the will, or the intellect in relation to willing. Knowledge does not ready us for blessedness; properly desiring does. The sequential relation of faith, hope, and charity in fact replicates in regard to God the essential progression of appetition whatever its object: love, first of all (that is, the apprehension of an object that is an object of appetite, a good), then desire (the pursuit of that object), then delight (the result of union with the object). Faith provides not only a generic apprehension of the objects of belief, but specifically the apprehension of a desired object, God as an end. Hope pursues the object as future and to be attained. Charity perfects the will for the possession of the object.

For Aristotle, it is possible to determine someone's character by knowing what it is a person finds pleasant, that is, what is loved (*EN*, ii, 3; 1104b5–13). For Dante, it is likely that an even stronger statement might be made. People's fundamental moral nature is defined by what they love, for the object of desire informs the faculty of desire, and makes it of one nature or another.[37] As the will becomes determined by and to its objects, so the characteristic choices a person makes are determined by it. It would be possible to say that Dante could be saved precisely because he loved Beatrice. She certainly says that as long as his gaze remained fixed on her, his soul was safe (*Purg.* xxx, 121–23). As he was drawn by her again at *Inferno* ii and *Purgatorio* xxvii, he was again saved.

Of course, we ought to say that Dante was saved not because he loved Beatrice, but because he loved God. It is only insofar as God is his ultimate object of desire that Dante can be saved. But here too the literal story is quite clear: for most of his life until the final moments of the poem Dante is not capable of loving God directly. What he loves in Beatrice which saves him is, no doubt, God reflected in Beatrice as in a mirror. But it is significant that he indicates so clearly that he would have been incapable of even his journey were it not for the existence of this mirror. Thus, those who speak of Beatrice as the mediator between God and Dante accurately describe the role she plays,[38] and those who identify that role with grace are probably closest to Dante's intention, as long as we understand grace in the way it is explained to us in the *Paradiso*.

Dante himself has given us the frames of reference for defining Beatrice's role. Virgil speaks of her not only as a mediator in a general way between Dante and God, but in terms that in the context of the *Paradiso* take on an almost technical meaning:

> che lume fia tra 'l vero e lo 'ntelletto:
> non so se 'ntendi; io dico di Beatrice.
> <div align="right">(<i>Purg.</i> vi, 45–46)</div>

That is to say, Beatrice is the medium (light) between the faculty of understanding (intellect) and the object of understanding (truth). But it is precisely this role that is played by grace, in the explanation given Dante by Solomon in the fourth sphere of Heaven. The blessed shine in their ardor to the extent they can see God, and they have the capacity to see to the extent they have received the grace that makes sight possible.

> La sua chiarezza [di cotal vesta] seguita l'ardore;
> l'ardor la visïone, e quella è tanta,
> quant'ha di grazia sovra suo valore.
> . . . .
> per che s'accrescerà ciò che ne dona
> di gratuito lume il sommo bene,
> lume ch'a lui veder ne condiziona;
> onde la visïon crescer convene,
> crescer l'ardor che di quella s'accende,
> crescer lo raggio che da esso vene.
> <div align="right">(<i>Par.</i> xiv, 40–42, 46–51)</div>

Here too it is light that is the medium between the apprehending intellect and its object. If Beatrice is the light between the truth and Dante's intellect, then she is grace to him. But—and this is central both to Dante's notion of blessedness and to his understanding of the role of poetry—while the action of grace has been described altogether within the process of apprehension, as the medium for apprehending God, the acquisition of grace depends not on intellect or apprehension, but on love. Grace, we recall, is merited to the extent that appetite, will, is open to it.

> E non voglio che dubbi, ma sie certo
> che ricever la grazia è meritorio
> secondo che l'affetto l'è aperto.
> <div align="right">(<i>Par.</i> xxix, 64–66)</div>

Beatrice is grace to Dante, but she can be active as his grace only because he loves her. In a courtly address to his ancestor, Cacciaguida (*Par.* xv, 73–87), Dante distinguishes the state of the blessed from that of those still living. For the blessed, will and understanding are perfectly balanced. (This balance is, I think, identical to the state Dante announces at the very last instant of the poem, when he can say— using the same word of description—that his understanding of the final divine mystery came at the moment that his desire and will were moved "sì come rota ch'igualmente è mossa" [*Par.* xxxiii, 144].)

> Poi cominciai così: «L'affetto e 'l senno,
>   come la prima equalità v'apparse,
>   d'un peso per ciascun di voi si fenno,
> però che 'l sol che v'allumò e arse
>   col caldo e con la luce, è sì iguali,
>   che tutte simiglianze sono scarse.»
> (*Par.* xv, 73–78)

For those still alive, that is not yet so. Yet since both will and intellect must cooperate for the living to arrive at blessedness, in this world each of these must be addressed in its own right. Beatrice could not function as Dante's intermediary if she were only the medium of apprehension. It is because he *loves* her that he can be drawn to her as well as to the truth for which she is the medium. Beatrice can represent truth, but only insofar as she is loved truth; she can represent grace, but only insofar as we remember that for the living, grace too must be desired. And for the living, it is not inevitable that this be so. The truth is not necessarily loved because it is the truth; grace is not necessarily desired because it is grace. Both must be made lovable to the human soul. In this, as in every other object of knowledge and love in the poem, the human mind stands in need of embodiment in order to overcome its natural limitations.

Herein is the final reflexivity of the *Commedia*, the final appropriation of the medium of poetry to the doctrines it contains. For Dante, Beatrice could fulfill this office. Loving her, he would be drawn in the right direction, until he could finally be drawn to God directly. She could be the medium of the truth to his intellect because she was first the object of his love. This is the basis of the whole of the literal narrative of the poem: it is a journey whose movement begins in, and only because of, the attraction of the beloved for the lover, culminating first in the union of the lover with his beloved, and then with what the lover has loved in his beloved.

But we cannot all be in love with Beatrice Portinari. In fact, none of us can, except Dante. Yet for Dante every living human being stands in need of just such a figure. All need grace, in the sense of a medium that makes it possible for us to understand truths that would be naturally beyond our capabilities. And all need grace, in the sense of something that appeals to the will as well as to the intellect. Beatrice played this role for Dante. For us, the poem itself takes the place of Beatrice. Our wills must be engaged by something with the presence to overcome the attraction of *le presenti cose;* our wills must be engaged by something invested with the quality of desirability. While Beatrice had that presence and desirability to Dante, she is not concrete or real to us; we have no image of her face in our memories; she cannot engage our emotions and draw us to her. The *Commedia* will stand in for her. It is concrete and vivid to us; it engages our emotions; it can draw us, through its narrative, to the divine truths it too reflects as a mirror.

Is it possible for a mere book to fulfill such a role? Oh, indeed it is. The very first of the damned we met in the poem had been misled and destroyed by a book: "Galeotto fu il libro e chi lo scrisse" (*Inf.* v, 137). The power that the vividness of poetry can summon is thus apparent from the start of the *Commedia,* in the episode of Francesca and Paolo. But *this* poem will not be Galehault; it will be Beatrice, to lead us not to Hell but to Heaven.

Appendix 1:
Two Matters from the Inferno

Our discussion of the structure of Hell postponed two questions better treated in an afterword, inasmuch as their resolution in no way alters the structure we were discovering. Nonetheless, it would hardly be proper to complete our discussion without considering them. The first question concerns whether or where bestiality, a state of character defined in the *Ethics,* and to which Virgil refers in his explanation of the organization of Hell in canto xi, is represented in Hell. The second question concerns the location and nature of the ignoble *(gli ignavi),* those first souls Virgil and Dante encounter in the vestibule of Hell.

LA MATTA BESTIALITADE

When Virgil explains the justification for punishing the sins of concupiscence (which he calls sins of incontinence) less severely than those of malice, he refers to three states of character that Aristotle distinguishes at the beginning of book seven of the *Ethics:*

> Non ti rimembra di quelle parole
> con le quai la tua Etica pertratta
> le tre disposizion che 'l ciel non vole,
> incontinenza, malizia e la matta
> bestialitade?
>
> (*Inf.* xi, 79–83)

An old convention of interpreting this passage and the *Inferno* locates sins of bestiality in the seventh circle, the circle of the violent. I am inclined to agree with this interpretation, especially if we include the sixth circle in this category too, thus identifying the bestial sins with all those that we have come to call the sins of irascibility. In doing so, however, it is important to recognize that such an interpretation can

293

find no support in Aristotle's text. We must accept it as a purely Dantean usage of the term *bestiality*. The question is really of only minor importance, since whatever final determination we made regarding the term *bestiality* would be inconsequential as far as the structure of Hell is concerned.[1] The organization of Hell follows the order of the three human appetites, based on the evidence we have considered, whether one of the regions of Hell can also be qualified as bestial or not. Associating bestiality with the middle region of Hell would merely add one further description to the category of irascible sins.

It is not even altogether clear that Dante intends that Virgil's comment be taken as a directive to locate all three Aristotelian dispositions in the organization of Hell. Virgil's only explicit purpose in referring to Aristotle's distinction is to explain the lighter punishment of those he calls the incontinent. Doing so does not in itself imply his agreement that all three terms of the distinction are embodied in the structure of Hell. Moreover, given that the terms *incontinence* and *malice* are used with new, non-Aristotelian meanings in the context of the sins of Hell, it is difficult to know in what sense the term *bestiality* should be taken.

Indeed, if we intend to use *bestiality* to characterize the sins of irascibility, we cannot use the term in a strict Aristotelian sense. Bestiality, as a state of character, is initially defined by Aristotle as an extreme form of vice; it is the opposite of an equivalent virtue that he names "superhuman virtue" (*EN*, vii, 1; 1145a20).[2] In chapter 5 of book seven, he also speaks as if he recognized a bestial form of incontinence, which would be an extreme form of that state of character (*EN*, vii, 5; 1148b30–1149a5).[3] What distinguishes the bestial form of vice (or incontinence) from the more common human form is that the objects of the appetites of the bestially vicious person are unnatural and often appear savage. It is for this reason that the state of character receives its distinct name. Bestial individuals take pleasure in unnatural forms of sex, in eating materials that would normally be unpleasant, in actions that would normally be painful (*EN*, vii, 5; 1148b20–30). For the most part, therefore, Aristotle speaks of bestiality as coordinate to, and as an extreme version of, temperance/intemperance or continence/incontinence, sharing their forms of action and, in a certain sense, their objects but differing by having unnatural rather than natural objects. He does also, in a loose sense, characterize any excess of vice or incontinence as bestial (*EN*, vii, 5; 1149a6–10).

It is clear, therefore, that Aristotle makes no particular connection between bestiality and irascibility or violence. Indeed, the preponderant sort of object he describes is an object of what we would call the concupiscible appetite, not the irascible. What is more, to Aristotle bestiality is not an intermediate state of evil character (as the irascible appetite is intermediate between the concupiscible appetite and the will as an origin of sin); it is the extreme of vice.[4] On this basis, some recent commentators have argued that bestiality should not be identified with the middle region of Hell at all, and have looked to find examples of bestial behavior, rather, in many different circles in all three regions of Hell.[5] This latter course would in fact reflect a more orthodoxly Aristotelian interpretation of Virgil's words, but would undermine the utility of those same words for understanding the other regions of Hell. If bestiality is everywhere in Hell, why should we not find incontinence and vice everywhere too? That, actually, would be the most properly Aristotelian interpretation of all. The problem, however, is that it is manifestly not Dante's interpretation.

Though taking *bestiality* as describing the middle realm of Hell requires deviating from Aristotle's definition of the term, I believe the preponderance of evidence favors this familiar interpretation. And, of course, Dante's willingness to attribute new meanings to the two other terms of Aristotle's distinction makes it that much more likely that he would find a new meaning also for *bestiality*. Certainly, Dante's language and metaphors in the circle of the violent lean heavily on traits of bestiality to describe the individuals encountered there and the sins punished there. The Minotaur, whose own anger reflects that of the sins punished there, is described first as a *bestia* (*Inf.* xii, 19) and then as *quell'ira bestial* (*Inf.* xii, 33), and the half-animal nature of all of the guardians of the seventh circle, Minotaur, Centaurs, Harpies, would seem to emphasize the partly bestial nature of these sins, even as their partly human appearance recalls the participation of the irascible appetite in the reason.[6] Upon entering the seventh circle, Dante exclaims about the "cieca cupidigia e ira folle" (*Inf.* xii, 49) that has brought the souls there to their punishment. The soul of one who commits suicide is described by Pier della Vigna as *feroce* (*Inf.* xiii, 94); Capaneus' state and punishment are described as an almost animal madness (*rabbia; Inf.* xiv, 65). Insofar as we believe that the most authoritative evidence of Dante's interpretations of these sins is to be found in the imagery he uses to depict them, the imagery of the seventh circle must incline us to considering that he identified the sins of violence with the traits of bestiality.

Thus for the violent. The heretics, as we recall, are tied to the violent not only by geography, but by a common imagery, and here too Dante's comments about heresy (or at least the content of those doctrines that he considered heretical) support a common characterization of the sin as somehow bestial. In the *Convivio*, Dante contemptuously dismisses any belief in the mortality of the soul (the state of the Epicureans in circle six and, without too much exaggeration, that of all of the heretics) as the greatest of all bestialities: "intra tutte le bestialitadi quella è stoltissima, vilissima e dannosissima" (*Conv.*, ii, viii, 8).[7] The context does not allow us to read too much significance into this use of *bestialitade* (it may simply be abusive), but Dante does not commonly use the term to condemn other sorts of error, and so he may indeed mean it in a significant sense. In any case, the violent seem naturally, if nontechnically, bestial; we think of animals when we think of violence, and Dante's imagery supports that. The heretics could be bestial too, insofar as their sin's origin was tied, in Dante's mind, to irascibility. Heresy and violence would together be bestial because based on the irascible appetite, which, if in essence no more bestial than concupiscence, is linguistically more frequently associated with beasts because we more commonly associate bestiality with ferocity (consider the related term, *brutality*) than with mere desire.

On the basis of the imagery with which Dante depicts violence in the *Inferno*, and of the connection of heresy to violence in the *Inferno*, as well as Dante's characterization of heresy as bestial in the *Convivio*, my conviction is that Dante adapted the Aristotelian term *bestiality* to his own purposes in much the same manner that he adapted *incontinence* and *malice*. We would again be faced with a usage that clearly had origins in Aristotle, though could not be called properly Aristotelian. And while the strictly Aristotelian definition of *bestiality* places it as an extreme state, in one respect Aristotle's text would support Dante's usage of *bestiality* to characterize sins of the "middle" sort in the *Inferno*. Although Aristotle explicitly declares that bestiality is a worse disposition than vice, he also declares that it is less culpable than vice, insofar as it is a state of character that is diseased and consequently less rational than vice (*EN*, vii, 6; 1150a1–10 and vii, 5; 1149a18–25; also *In Ethica*, §§1401–3). Dante might then have believed that the middle position of bestiality in Hell also had an Aristotelian backing.

GLI IGNAVI

The very first souls Dante and Virgil encounter upon entering the gate of Hell, in what is generally called the "vestibule" of Hell, are the ignoble, souls who chose neither good nor evil. They cannot enter Heaven, and at the same time Hell refuses to have them. The paradoxes of their state and its justice multiply. They would not choose the good; why is that not in itself a sin, and why then are they not well and truly in Hell? If they have committed no sin, why are they tormented? And others who are in Hell itself, at least in its first circle, are lower in position than these, yet are not tormented. What is their state, and where in fact are they? Our conclusion that Hell is organized by the human appetites offers an explanation of its own concerning these anomalous figures.

When Dante has reached the absolute lowest point of Hell, and is ready to begin his transition to the realm of Purgatory, he describes his state with a sort of riddle:

> Io non mori', e non rimasi vivo:
> pensa oggimai per te, s'hai fior d'ingegno,
> qual io divenni, d'uno e d'altro privo.
> (*Inf.* xxxiv, 25–27)

Neither dead nor alive, he is about to pass from as close as it is possible to come to the absolute point of nonbeing into the world of life. He is, indeed, about to be born—so, I believe, is the answer to his riddle—as the events to follow are to demonstrate. Dante and Virgil leave Hell by means of a tortuous, hidden path (*Inf.* xxxiv, 127–36), and when they have emerged into Purgatory, Virgil will baptize Dante, as if he were newly born (*Purg.* i, 121–29). The path they follow to the Southern Hemisphere is nothing less than an allegorical birth canal, providing a narrative figure of Dante's spiritual rebirth.

For Aristotle, and Dante following him, the decisive characteristic of animal life (as distinct from that of plants) is movement, and in Aristotle the appetitive faculties are understood in relation to the capacity to move. Animals have appetites because appetites are the source of movement (*de An.*, iii, 10; 433a10–25). Not to move, not to be inclined by an appetitive choice to one object rather than another, is not to live (*SCG*, iv, 20). This is very much the state in which the souls of the ignoble have put themselves. They never exhibited any appetitive tendency, not even with regard to the most important, and therefore potentially most attractive or repulsive, objects. To that extent, they do not seem to have been alive, and that, indeed, is how Dante describes them:

> Questi sciaurati, che mai non fur vivi,
> erano ignudi, stimolati molto
> da mosconi e da vespe ch'eran ivi.
> (*Inf.* iii, 64–66)

As we would expect, the details of their torment reflect their state. Now of course these souls did move while on earth, but their aimless and indecipherable rushing about in the vestibule of Hell reiterates the purposelessness of their movement while alive. The insects that torment them, for their parts, were conventionally thought to grow spontaneously from rotting matter. In this respect, the souls of the *ignavi* seem not fully to be animal beings, but rather something closer to botanical life. If Dante travels away from death toward life by means of a birth canal at the end of Hell, the fact that the ignoble are stuck outside Hell without entering it figuratively suggests their inability to move from life to death. But in their case, they cannot move from life to death because they have never fully lived.

Appendix 2:
The Antepurgatory

Up to this point we have not considered the significance of the images and organization we encounter in what is conventionally called the antepurgatory—the area, divided poetically into discrete sections, that precedes the entrance to Purgatory itself. Obviously, insofar as these locations are explicitly outside Purgatory, they do not participate in the organization of Purgatory and the significance of that organization. Moreover, at the concrete and imagistic level, the sights with which we are presented in the antepurgatory seem to separate that region from Purgatory proper by their wide divergence from the sights we later see in Purgatory.

The most straightforward example of this difference is, perhaps, Dante's friend Belacqua, encountered among those who postponed their repentence to the last moments, in canto iv (*Purg.* iv, 97–135). For having waited so long to repent, Belacqua, and the other souls like him, must wait out a period as long as their lives before they can be admitted into Purgatory. But in this requirement, and even more forcibly in Belacqua's own demeanor, we see a poetic principle quite the opposite of that which we will encounter in Purgatory itself. Even before Dante recognizes Belacqua, he describes him to Virgil as "colui che mostra sè più negligente / che se pigrizia fosse sua serocchia" (*Purg.* iv, 110–11). Once Dante recognizes Belacqua, he questions his reason for sitting so:

> . . . Ma dimmi: perchè assiso
> quiritta se'? attendi tu iscorta,
> o pur lo modo usato t'ha' ripriso?
> (*Purg.* iv, 124–26)

We should notice two things: first, that the physical indolence Belacqua exhibits in his posture was already his habit, along with his spiritual

299

indolence, while living; second, that the spiritual indolence that has constrained him to tarry in this location finds its poetic embodiment in this physical indolence. When Belacqua eventually enters Purgatory, there can be no question that among whatever other vices he will purge, he will have to spend time in the fourth *girone*, among the slothful, purging this indolence. But how different will his behavior be then! Instead of this slumped inertia, he will be driven by zeal, rushing around the *girone* in a manner exactly the opposite of the one in which we see him.

What Belacqua shows us so conveniently is also true of the other souls in the antepurgatory. There, unlike the situation in Purgatory proper, the actions and attitudes of the souls reflect their actions and attitudes in life. That is, they repeat here the same defective behaviors and bad habits that damaged their souls such that they need rehabilitation. Those who repented late and were also excommunicated from the Church (demonstrating therein a compound reluctance in regard to their spiritual duties), whom Dante and Virgil encounter on the beach before the mountain, move more slowly than all other souls. Belacqua and his cohort repeat in their sluggish dispositions, though not slow movement, the indolence of their spiritual preparations. Theirs is only a simple indolence, not compounded by excommunication. Hence their slowness is not as extreme as that of the excommunicated. Among the souls in the antepurgatory only those who repented at the end of a life cut short by violence hurry in their movements. They come running up to inquire of Dante and Virgil who they are, and of them Dante says:

> Vapori accesi non vid'io sì tosto
> di prima notte mai fender sereno,
> nè, sol calando, nuvole d'agosto,
> che color non tornasser suso in meno;
> e, giunti là, con li altri a noi dier volta
> come schiera che scorre sanza freno.
> (*Purg.* v, 37–42)

In this impetuousness I believe we see repeated the violence of their lives, and the violence of their end. That violence is all that distinguishes them from the other late repentant souls, but that is the trait that Dante chooses to embody in this image.

What we see, then, in the souls of antepurgatory is very much the opposite of what we see in Purgatory itself, though very much like what we had already seen in Hell.[1] This is deliberate on Dante's part. Only in purging vices do we encounter remedies based on action the opposite of the vice. Until souls reach the point that they enter upon that course of rehabilitation, they, like the dead souls we encountered in Hell, are condemned to repeat the actions that reflect the state in which they died. Only in the antepurgatory do we encounter action that is consistent with the most conventional interpretation of Purgatory: that it is a place in which one passes time until one is allowed into a better place.[2] But this waiting does not purge them of their defects. Rather, the waiting is the price of justice before the souls can begin the rigorous path of rehabilitation on the mountain of Purgatory.

Entrapped as they are in their old sins, and suspended between this life and the preparation for the next life that they long to begin, these souls are like the souls in Hell in that they reflect their past actions, though without the torments of the damned. But why are they stalled here? What keeps them from passing through the gate of Purgatory? We must conclude that they lack something needed to begin on the path of rehabilitation. Now, necessary (though not in themselves sufficient) for the pursuit of beatitude are the theological virtues, faith, hope, and charity. These virtues do not in themselves perfect the soul for its life in Heaven. As Aquinas says, they merely direct us to God as our end.[3] But they are necessary for the very possibility of beatitude, for we must first be aimed at our goal before we can acquire the virtues that enable us to accomplish that end. I believe it is deficiencies in these virtues (though not, presumably, an absolute lack) that are restraining these souls. And although establishing firm correspondences between the four categories of souls in the antepurgatory and these three virtues is not completely straightforward, intuitive correspondences are surely there.

Those negligent of their spiritual duties (and this would include those whose lives were cut short by violence, for they were negligent to that moment too) can reasonably be said to have been deficient in hope. Among their purgatorial stops will be the fourth *girone*, precisely for their negligence, and as sloth as a vice can be said to be connected to the passion of hope (the most relevant of the passions of the irascible appetite to this vice of that appetite), so these negligent can be said to have lacked the habit, that is to say, the virtue, of hope. Those who died excommunicated may be said to have lacked faith, insofar, at least, as faith is a virtue of the intellect,[4] and their alienation from the Church can be said to be deliberate and based on judgment.

Symmetry suggests that the princes of cantos vii and viii are impeded from entering Purgatory for want of charity. And that, I believe, is correct. There are, in addition, significant details that make sense only in the light of this deficiency. First among them is the introductory scene between Virgil and Sordello that precedes the travelers' encounter with the princes themselves, along with Dante's invective against his contemporaries which interrupts the narrative of that scene. Stressed throughout this episode, at the end of canto vi (*Purg.* vi, 67–151), is the love that Virgil and Sordello show for one another based solely on their sharing a city of birth—that is, on being neighbors. In Dante's invective, what is stressed is the lack of such neighborly love in the Italy of his own time. Sordello is not perfect in charity; if he were, he would never have acted toward the travelers with the disdain and aloofness he shows them. This attitude reveals his defective charity and justifies his location outside the gate of Purgatory. Yet once the name *Mantova* has been pronounced, his disdain dissolves into love. Dante's invective against his Italy condemns Italians for lacking that love and condemns the Emperor Albert for failing to accept his responsibility for cultivating it.

Therein, I believe, is the significance of the episode of the princes, and of Dante's invective that makes such an odd introduction to it. It is conventional to say that the princes are becalmed outside Purgatory because they neglected spiritual duties in pursuit of worldly activities. It is not impossible that this interpretation is so, but there is certainly no warrant in any explicit statement in the poem to support it. As we encounter the princes in canto vii, they are not presented to us as those who regret their lost opportunities for performing spiritual duties. Rather, Sordello stresses unequivocally their regret for failures toward their subjects, failures to provide the leadership and peace upon which charity among their subjects could be based. Rudolf (*Purg.* vii, 91–96) regrets leaving undone what he should have done, and what would have cured the wounds of Italy. Ottokar, next to him (*Purg.* vii, 97–102), regrets leaving the dissolute Wenceslaus as his heir. Philip the Bold and Henry of Navarre also regret their heir, "France's evil" ("il mal di Francia"; *Purg.* vii, 103–11). About them, Sordello is explicit that that regret is the source of their pain. Other princes who are mentioned either never had the opportunity to provide the charity they should have (Alfonso or Pietro III of Aragon? *Purg.* vii, 115–18), or did not have the ability to make use of the opportunities they had. These are not failures of spiritual duties that are lamented, they are temporal and political failures. And if it is by their temporal failures that all these former rulers are pained, it is because those failures rendered them incapable of fulfilling a ruler's charitable obligations to his subjects.[5]

Now they are compelled to watch the same admonitory lesson night after night until they acquire the charity they lacked in life. The angels of the valley wield their swords to protect their charges from evil. That surely is the most plausible interpretation of the snake that enters the valley. The angels do not need to protect the princes from temptation specifically, since there are no temptations any longer in this place. The lesson attacks evil in its most general and nonspecific form. Protecting their charges is the angels' act of charity toward them, and it is protection for which the princes ask explicitly when they sing *"Te lucis ante."* But such protection was also specifically the act of charity that ought to have been their essential quality as rulers, who have responsibility to provide this protection, and with it peace, to their subjects. That is the lesson the princes must learn before they can enter Purgatory. Unlike souls in Purgatory, they do not enact this charity as a way of rehabilitation (consider, by contrast, the charitable remarks and actions of the envious in the second *girone*); they are merely shown this exemplary performance every night. And not only are they passive, they remain negligent of the lesson, as they were negligent—not of spiritual duties but of charitable action—in life. It is Dante who watches the show with rapt attention. The princes near him watch *him,* not the show. Ironically, the princes too repeat here the behavior they had showed in life, and thus confirm the principle of the antepurgatory.

Until the souls in antepurgatory acquire the theological virtues they lacked, which alone open the route to Heaven, they are compelled to remain outside Purgatory. Insofar as they are outside, their opportunity to change their natures is postponed, and so, still fixed in natures they already regret, they have no choice but to repeat the actions to which these natures disposed them. Their actions bear more resemblance to the actions of the damned than they do to those in Purgatory, though fortunately for them, only for a time, and with a suffering made up merely of their impatience to begin their cure. In this, however, we see the consistency of Dante's principles with respect to the role of the first two realms, and the actions appropriate to them.

Appendix 3:
Associating Persons of the Trinity
with the Angelic Orders

Any author who, like Dante, sought to articulate the associations of the orders of angels with the different persons of the Trinity throughout the whole of the angelic hierarchy faced, as was pointed out in chapter 3, two problems. First, there was no orthodox interpretation that could simply be followed for the entire hierarchy. There was, as we have already discussed, general agreement that the highest triad of angels should be associated with the Father, the middle with the Son, the lowest (the triad nearest to human beings) with the Holy Spirit. But there was no agreement regarding how to make the associations within the three triads. Indeed, and this is the second problem, immediately as one searched for a pattern by which to make associations within the triads, one discovered irresolvable conflicts and contradictions between principles. Not all commentators actually tried to explain the working out of the schematism for all nine orders; by not doing so, they avoided these dilemmas. For Dante, however, finding associations across the entire hierarchy compelled him to compromise. The solution that I asserted as Dante's in chapter 3 is the one that, on the one hand, he would have been convinced came closest to a consensus among his authorities as to how these associations should be made, and, on the other, most productively matched other principles he was attempting to embody in the *Paradiso*.

The notion that the hierarchy of angels should reflect the image of God in all of its parts would have been based on Dionysius' declaration (*CH*, x, 2–3; 1059a/b) that each triad contained within it highest, middle, and lowest locations, as did the hierarchy as a whole (and, indeed, every intelligent being or organization of intelligent beings). The simplest and most straightforward application of this axiom would be to associate the same persons within each triad with equivalent locations with which they were associated in the hierarchy as a whole. That is, if the Father is associated with the highest triad, so ought he to be associated with the highest individual order within a triad. Unfortunately, this most straightforward interpretation encountered an insuperable problem as soon as one considered the angelic orders in the highest triad.

In both Dionysius' and Gregory's arrangements of the angelic orders, the highest order of angels was the seraphim. If the highest triad of the hierarchy was to be associated with the Father, and if one applied an exactly parallel arrangement of associations with the individual orders within each triad, then the highest order of each triad should be associated with the Father too, and this would then assign to the seraphim a doubled association with the Father, as the highest order of the highest triad. Unfortunately, in Dionysius' text—and he was followed in this by almost every commentator on his text or writer on angels—the best-known attribute of the seraphim was their fiery warmth. Seraphim are properly called "heat-bearing" *(calefacientes)*, according to Dionysius (and his Latin translators), since that was the translation of their Hebrew name. But to Dionysius and his commentators, the names of the angelic orders signified their angelic natures,[1] and, indeed, would not only describe the angel's nature, but would also provide signs of the aspect of God's nature of which each angelic order was the image. With respect to the nature of the seraphim, their fiery heat was universally interpreted as signifying the superiority of these angels in charity.

> A multitude of celestial spirits is called an order when they resemble each other in their gift of grace, as is also the case in the possession of natural qualities. For example, they are called seraphim who more than all others burn with charity; for the name seraphim is translated as burning, or inflamed.[2]

But as a sign of divine qualities that pointed to the person of the Trinity from whom the quality was acquired, charity was more frequently seen as an attribute of the Holy Spirit than of the Father, and therein lies the problem for any simple application of the pattern of persons that appears among the triads to the orders within the triads. For if the charity of the seraphim ought to be associated with the Holy Spirit, either the seraphim are misplaced in an arrangement that has the highest positions (in the hierarchy as a whole or within triads) always associated with the Father, or, if the seraphim are properly placed in their triad, then the principle that places orders within the triads must be different from the one that orders triads within the hierarchy.

There is, in fact, no solution that does not compromise one of two important principles: either the straightforward application of Dionysius' axiom regarding highest, middle, and lowest ranks in hierarchies and orders, or the almost equally axiomatic conviction that the heat of the seraphim reflects their love, and thereby their association with the Holy Spirit. As an indication of just how problematic, and important, this conflict might seem to a theologian, we should note that Bonaventure went so far, in order to save both axioms, as to alter Dionysius' arrangements of the angelic orders, placing the seraphim in the lowest of the positions of the highest triad (*Collationes In Hexaëmeron*, xxi, 19–20).[3] That solution, in fact, was unique among commentators on the *Celestial Hierarchy*. No other medieval authority moved the seraphim out of the highest position in the highest triad of angels; and Bonaventure's unorthodox solution was manifestly made solely to make it possible to bring the seraphim into association with the Holy Spirit (in order to maintain their association with the quality of charity, and the Holy Spirit's association with charity), while yet maintaining the alignment of the Holy Spirit with the third position of every triad, as its association with the third triad of the hierarchy as a whole seemed to Bonaventure to require.[4]

For his part, it appears that Dante in the *Convivio* had tried to use the simplest application of Dionysius' axiom within the triads of the hierarchy. That is, he tried to maintain the principle that the highest locations would always be associated with the Father. Thus, the highest position in the first triad would give us a doubled association with the Father, as he claims, at least with respect to this triad: "The Father can be considered simply with respect to himself; this is the contemplation proper to the Seraphim" (*Conv.*, ii, v, 9). But Dante could manage to evade the problem of the association of the seraphim with the Holy Spirit only by staying silent regarding their association with charity. While other authorities (including authorities Dante would almost certainly have read by the time he wrote the *Convivio*) made much of the charity of the seraphim and the significance of their name, Dante speaks of them in terms of other attributes, and never mentions either the etymology of their name or their commonplace association with heat, or the further association of heat with charity.[5] Only by such an unconventional interpretation of the seraphim (not his only unconventional position with respect to the angels, as we shall see) could Dante avoid confronting the conflict of principles inherent in trying to apply a trinitarian system across all the angelic orders. (It should also be noted that Dante in the *Convivio* is inconsistent as to the alignment of orders with persons within any triad, assigning the Holy Spirit to the lowest order of the first triad but apparently to the highest order of the third [*Conv.*, ii, v, 10 and ii, v, 13].)

Most commentators on Dionysius, or writers on angelology, actually never encountered this problem at all, simply because they made no attempt to apply one consistent principle across all nine orders of the angelic hierarchy. If these writers associated angelic orders with persons of the Trinity, it was usually only within a single triad, in most discussions only the highest. And in these circumstances, they could simply declare that the seraphim were associated with the Holy Spirit, the cherubim with the Son, and the thrones (if they were following Dionysius' arrangement) with the Father, without worrying that this arrangement of associations with persons within a triad reversed the association of the triads of the overall hierarchy with the persons.[6] In effect, Aquinas had made this association for the first triad, following a principle that I believe Dante would have found not only congenial but fruitful for the exploitation of the angelic hierarchy for the interpretation of the degrees of grace represented in the order of the souls of the *Paradiso*.

In his *Commentary on the Sentences* (*In 2 Sent.*, ix, 1, 3), Aquinas had associated the order of thrones with the faculty of memory, the cherubim with the intellect, and the seraphim with the will, following associations whose origins were in more general theological discussions of the nature of the Trinity, especially Augustine's *de Trinitate*. In the *de Trinitate,* as was discussed in chapter 3, Augustine had likened the natures of the three persons to the three human intellectual faculties: the Father to the memory, the Son to the intellect, the Holy Spirit to the will. To a reader concerned with associating the angelic orders with the persons of the Trinity, Aquinas' association of the thrones with the memory would, translated through Augustine, also associate them with the Father; his association of the cherubim with the intellect would, in turn, associate them with the Son; and his association of the seraphim with the will, finally, with the Holy Spirit.

In the end, this is the solution I believe Dante settled upon for the *Commedia*, applying the order of this first triad to each of the three triads that make up the hierarchy. There was no "right" way to merge the two levels of order, and this solution at least did not conflict with the general thirteenth-century agreement regarding the way to associate the triads of angels with the divine persons. At the same time, it would also follow authority with regard to associating certain individual orders (such as the seraphim) with the persons of the Trinity believed to be most appropriate.[7] While it may not have implemented Dionysius' axiom regarding the parallel application of the principle of order in the simplest way, it at least saved the principle that there should be represented within each triad, in an orderly if not parallel way, the same organizing principle that existed at the level of the hierarchy as a whole. More than that, it seems, was not possible to do. Obviously, in trying to understand the appropriate alignment of angelic orders with the divine persons, Dante would not ignore more fundamental discussions of the Trinity, and between Augustine's association of the persons with the intellectual faculties and Aquinas' association of the angelic orders with these same faculties, Dante would have felt on secure ground in associating the orders with the persons in the way Aquinas had done.

This solution would have been especially welcome to Dante, for in his case there was a further complication to this already difficult problem. It was problematic enough associating angelic orders with persons of the Trinity, but Dante was also intent on associating the angelic orders with specific planets and spheres, so that any combination of theological attributes would also have to be somehow consonant with existing assumptions regarding the attributes of the planets and their influences. We have evidence of Dante's grappling with this problem in his discussion of one particular angelic order, the thrones, in the *Convivio*. Indeed, the stratagems he had to pursue in this discussion indicate compellingly how seriously he took associating angelic natures with persons of the Trinity, on the one hand, and with planetary spheres, on the other.

Dante's central intention, in the fifth chapter of the second book of the *Convivio*, was to provide an angelic explanation for the action of the third sphere of the heavens. He was interpreting the *canzone* "Voi che 'ntendendo il terzo ciel movete" and was claiming that it was addressed to the angelic intelligences who superintend this sphere—that is, the sphere of Venus. Inasmuch as he was at that moment using the

Gregorian arrangement of the angelic orders, that would associate the thrones with this sphere. And, indeed, Dante claimed it was the thrones that he was addressing in the *canzone* (*Conv.*, ii, v, 18), and he described them in a way that seemed especially appropriate to the action of "their" planet:

> ... Those who move Venus are the Thrones. These last, whose very nature it is to love the Holy Spirit, imbue with an abundance of love the activity which is proper to them and is of a kind with their nature, namely, the movement of that heaven. From this love the form of that heaven takes on a powerful ardor through which it enkindles love in souls here below, to the degree that they are disposed to receive it. (*Conv.*, ii, v, 13)

The problem that Dante ran into here, however, is that no matter how appropriate this description of the thrones may have been in relation to the love we associate with both the planet Venus and with the Holy Spirit, the description was altogether divergent from the most common understandings of the thrones' nature. Gregory, who is Dante's source for the arrangement of the orders in the *Convivio*, had made his interpretation of the thrones' nature based on the etymology of their name, and this interpretation, stressing their relation to judgment, rather than to love, was in fact consistently repeated by later commentators.

> This band [i.e., order] is called thrones, for God omnipotent presides in them when passing judgment. Since thrones are what we call seats in Latin, these are said to be the thrones of God, who are filled with such grace of divinity that God sits in them, and through them decides his judgment. Whence the Psalmist writes: You sit on your throne, you who judge fairly (Ps. 9:5 [Vulgate]).[8]

Indeed, by the time Dante wrote the *Paradiso*, he had brought his own interpretation of the thrones into line with the conventional interpretation of their nature, in part by adopting Dionysius' arrangement of the angelic orders, as we have already considered.

> Su sono specchi, voi dicete Troni,
> onde refulge a noi Dio giudicante.
> (*Par.* ix, 61–62)

The *su* of verse 61 refers to a celestial sphere far above that of Venus, a location to which Dionysius' arrangement would assign this order of angels. In making this assignment, though, as we have already noted, Dante would simultaneously be severing the connection of the order of thrones with the planet Venus, changing the nature of their function (from the movers of love to the bases of judgment), and, of course, revising his earlier views on this subject as expressed in the *Convivio*. In a passage that has already been cited, we can see him explicitly reminding the reader of his exegesis of the *canzone* about which he now has had second thoughts, and describing the replacement of the thrones in the third sphere by another order of angels, the principalities.

> Noi ci volgiam coi Principi celesti
> d'un giro e d'un girare e d'una sete,
> ai quali tu del mondo già dicesti:
> "Voi che 'ntendendo il terzo ciel movete."
> (*Par.* viii, 34–37)

The idiosyncratic description of the thrones that Dante had given in the *Convivio* (a description other commentators would more likely have given of the seraphim, among the angelic orders) was wholly driven by the association he was making at that time of the thrones with the planet Venus, and in that decision I believe we see confirmation of two important aspects of his angelology. First, his willingness to attribute an unconventional set of qualities to the thrones, essentially because of their location, as he then thought, in the sphere of Venus, is substantial evidence that his linkage of angelic orders to spheres (as the intelligences that move them and inform their influence) was no arbitrary figurative invention, but a serious conviction that there existed a concrete structural relationship between angelic natures, celestial bodies, and the human characters influenced by them. Second, in the linking of the thrones to the planet Venus and then to the Holy Spirit, I believe we have our first evidence of Dante's personal interpretation as to how to arrange the attribution of the persons of the Trinity within the triads of the angelic hierarchy. The planet Venus is third in its trio of planets—*highest*, not lowest, in its triad—and it is with this third location that Dante in the *Convivio* associates the Holy Spirit.[9] Insofar as it is possible to argue that in the *Convivio* Dante described the thrones as reflecting the Holy Spirit considered in itself,[10] one could say that Dante had, in effect, made just this combinatorial assignment—to the sphere, if not to the "right" order of angels. The sphere of Venus, as the highest sphere of the lowest triad would be the sphere with which the Holy Spirit was associated both for primary and secondary attributes. All that was necessary to reach the schematism of the *Commedia* was for Dante to apply this principle consistently across the nine spheres.

By the time of the writing of the *Paradiso,* Dante had come to rec-ognize the ardor of the seraphim as their fundamental property and would have noted that they too occupy a position third, or highest in their triad. The description given in the *Convivio* of the nature of the thrones (whom he believed at the time occupied the third position of the lowest triad) is equally appropriate for the seraphim, and to them too is appropriate the association with the Holy Spirit. What Dante came to recognize as important about the seraphim turned out to be most easily explicable by extending his earlier association of the Holy Spirit with the highest position of the first triad such that it applied to all triads of angelic orders. And so I believe we are on reasonably se-cure ground if we conclude that, in this intricate fabric of combinatory relations of the persons of the Trinity to the angelic orders, Dante wove the fabric as stated in chapter 3: for primary attributes, the highest triad of angels would be associated with the Father, the middle with the Son, the lowest with the Holy Spirit; for secondary attributes, how-ever, within any given triad, the highest order would be associated with the Holy Spirit, the middle again with the Son, the lowest with the Father. This solution was a compromise, but the nature of the problem did not admit of any solution that was not.

Notes

1. *INFERNO*

1. In the terms of Virgil's explanation, it is not altogether clear that Dante intends us to conclude that the sins of violence are equivalent to the disposition of bestiality. I believe that he does, and deal with the special question separately in Appendix 1. As far as understanding the nature of the division of Hell into three regions, however, it is not crucial that we here resolve this issue. I have also postponed until Appendix 1 a brief discussion of the *ignavi*, in the "vestibule" to Hell, a location that falls outside the structure Virgil describes.

2. The Greek term that *malitia* translates, κακία, is equally ambiguous in its origin, and is only given the technical sense of "vice" by Aristotle's treatment of it in the first six books of the *Ethics*. In almost all cases citations from the *Ethics* are from the Latin translation called the *versio antiqua* (usually attributed to William of Moerbeke), unless there is a compelling reason to consult the Greek text of Aristotle. William's text, or one rather closer to it than to the original Greek, would have been the text used by Dante, as well as by Thomas. Paradoxically, this Latin text is therefore more authoritative than the Greek when our purpose is tracing medieval continuities and divergences from Aristotle's doctrines.

3. *EN*, i, 11; 1100b20, and *EN*, vii, 9; 1151a15–20. This is an overstatement. Virtue is inherently more stable than vice, inasmuch as it is based on the real nature of human beings. The mean with respect to appetites, at which virtue aims, is overall a natural good for humans. Vicious actions not aimed at the mean are not only shameful, they are also naturally bad, that is to say, harmful, for people. Habitual bad behavior, while theoretically as durable as habitual good behavior, is not so in practice. The painful consequences of vicious activity, over time, should undermine bad habit. It is a commonplace to point out that it is rare to find someone perfectly and completely vicious. The practical necessities of life demand a certain measure of moderation. Nevertheless, within the argument of the *Ethics*, Aristotle intends that vice be seen as a permanent state of character equivalent to virtue.

4. *EN,* i, 9; 1099a12–15, and *In Ethica,* §156. See also *EN,* vii, 11; 1151b22–1152a7, and *In Ethica,* §§1446–54.

5. Cf. Aquinas' description of the knowledge the incontinent person has of the right principles—which are then ignored—compared with the vicious person's unconsciousness of the right principle, cleaving instead to a corrupt one: *Malo,* iii, 9 ad 7.

6. *EN,* i, 13; 1102b15–18, and *In Ethica,* §237. Also, *EN,* vii, 2; 1145b12–15, and *In Ethica,* §§1306–7.

7. The moral virtues are dispositions that perfect the appetites, and so in the technical language regarding such dispositions, they are said to have the appetites as their subject—i.e., the matter that they inform. This is lacking in the case of continence and incontinence, and so continence, as a desirable disposition, resides, for Aquinas, only in the intellectual appetite as the faculty of choice, not desire. The continent person lacks the habits that tame the appetites, and does well only through nonetheless persevering in the right choice. *ST,* 1a2æ 58, 3 ad 2, and 2a2æ 155, 3.

8. *EN,* iii, 13; 1118a1–32, esp. 25–32.

9. We certainly see the action of the intellect in Semiramis' legislation of her lust, and Virgil in fact speaks of her as corrupted by the "vice" of lust, not by incontinent lustful desires. An example of the problems the cases of both Semiramis and Cleopatra can give to someone trying to take *malizia* in its standard Aristotelian sense can be be seen in Alfred A. Triolo, "*Ira, Cupiditas, Libido:* The Dynamics of Human Passion in the *Inferno,*" *Dante Studies* 95 (1977): 1–37, esp. pp. 13–14 and 22.

10. His very nickname apparently reflects Florentine recognition of and contempt for a life spent in deliberate pursuit of gluttony, rather than in a painful struggle against unwanted gluttonous desires (see Vandelli at *Inf.* vi, 52: DDP).

11. Edward Moore, "The Classification of Sins in the *Inferno* and *Purgatorio,*" in *Studies in Dante, Second Series* (Oxford: The Clarendon Press, 1899), pp. 152–208 (see esp. p. 159), proposes that the sins of upper Hell are sins of "impulse," while those of lower Hell are sins of "habit." Moore's argument is an attempt to maintain the Aristotelian technical usage of *malizia* as "vice," but the examples here, as well as others, demonstrate the placement of habitual sinners (at least in Aristotle's terms) also in upper Hell.

12. Umberto Cosmo, "Il Canto XXIV dell'*Inferno,*" in *Letture dantesche,* ed. Giovanni Getto (Firenze: Sansoni, 1961), pp. 447–66, esp. p. 459, while recognizing Vanni's bestial character, makes the claim that he was always more a thief than a killer. Yet scarcely any of the early commentators refer to him as a *ladrone* (as he is apparently cited in the condemnation of 1295; see Bosco and Reggio [at *Inf.* xxiv, 122–39: DDP]). Far more speak of his *omicidi* and *violenze* (Anonimo Fiorentino, Serravalle, Guiniforto). The consensus is well captured by Longfellow (at *Inf.* xxiv, 122–39: DDP): "All the commentators paint him in the darkest colors. Dante had known him as 'a man of

blood and wrath,' and seems to wonder he is here, and not in the circle of the Violent, or of the Irascible."

13. *ST*, 1a2æ 71, 4. See also 1a2æ 63, 2 ad 2.

14. The example to which attention is often called is that of Buonconte da Montefeltro, saved for a single word, though among the "peccatori infino all'ultima ora" (*Purg.* v, 100–102). His father, Guido, by contrast, was damned for a single specific instance of evil counsel. That action, Guido admits, was not uncharacteristic. He had had a lifelong habit of slyness (*Inf.* xxvii, 74–75). But the slate had been wiped clean of these earlier acts at the time of the one piece of counsel for which he was damned. The relation between Guido's case and Buonconte's has been widely noted. See Patrick Boyde, *Dante, Philomythes and Philosopher, Man in the Cosmos* (Cambridge: Cambridge University Press, 1981), pp. 188–89.

15. *EN*, vi, 5; 1140b15–22, and *In Ethica*, §1170; *EN*, vi, 13; 1144a32–35, and *In Ethica*, §1274; *EN*, vii, 9; 1151a12–20. See esp. *In Ethica*, §1430: "There is a certain sort of person who pursues bodily pleasures excessively and beyond the order of right reason, but not because he is so disposed that he is convinced that such pleasures should be followed as if they were good. Such a person is incontinent. There is another sort of person, namely the intemperate, in whom the conviction has taken hold that such pleasures ought to be chosen, as if they were good. And this has occurred because of the disposition he has acquired by habit."

16. T. K. Seung, "The Metaphysics of the *Commedia*," in *The Divine Comedy and the Encyclopedia of Arts and Sciences*, Acta of the International Dante Symposium, 13–16 November 1983, Hunter College, New York, ed. Giuseppe di Scipio and Aldo Scaglione (Amsterdam/Philadelphia: John Benjamins, 1988), pp. 181–222, esp. p. 186, also notes Virgil's divergence from Aristotle, though he does not explore the divergence in the sense that we do. Busnelli, for his part, tries to resolve the problem by suggesting that in verses 22–23 Virgil is referring to a select set of *malizie* rather than all *malizia*, reading the verses as if they were distributive and saying, "Those *malizie* for which injury is the end are hated in heaven," as if there were other *malizie* that did not have injury as an end. But this is a misreading of the verses. They declare, simply, that injury is the end of every *malizia*. See Giovanni Busnelli, *L'Etica nicomachea e l'ordinamento morale dell'«Inferno» di Dante* (Bologna: Zanichelli, 1907), pp. 32, 39. The implication, moreover, that there might be some *malizie* that are not hated in heaven is itself, of course, untenable, though Boccaccio, indeed, tries to distinguish a *malizia* "from infirmity" from the deliberate intention to commit wrong (at *Inf.* xi, 22: DDP). Virgil's statement is clearly meant to apply to all *malizie*. Nor should one attempt to argue that the *malizia* of verse 22 is not the same as that of verse 82, as many modern commentators have done. (See the notes of Grabher, Steiner, and Casini/Barbi [at *Inf.* xi, 22: DDP] and of Porena and Chimenz [at *Inf.* xi, 82: DDP]. In most cases, these readers attempt to see the

malizia at verse 22 as a generic reference to bad action, and the *malizia* of verse 82 as a reference to fraud specifically.) The point of referring to book seven of the *Ethics* would be lost unless the two *malizie* are the same. The reference to Aristotle's distinction of *incontinenza* from *malizia* as a less blameworthy condition makes sense only if the *malizia* (than which *incontinenza* is less hated) of verse 82 is precisely the same as that of verse 22 (which is punished lower in Hell).

17. Cf. Gilles G. Meersseman, "Il Canto XI dell'«Inferno»," in *Nuove letture dantesche*, Casa di Dante in Roma, vol. 2, anno di studi 1966–67 (Firenze: Le Monnier, 1970): 1–16, esp. p. 5. Also, Allan H. Gilbert, *Dante's Conception of Justice* (Durham, N.C.: Duke University Press, 1925), p. 86.

18. *EN*, v, 3; 1129b25–1130a15, and *EN*, v, 4; 1130a30–1130b5.

19. *EN*, v, 4; 1130a30, and *In Ethica*, §§904 and 917–19. Also, *ST*, 1a2æ 60, 3, and 2a2æ 58, 2 and 58, 5.

20. *EN*, v, 4; 1130a24–30, and *In Ethica*, §§914–16.

21. *EN*, v, 3; 1130a1–15, and *In Ethica*, §910. In a slightly altered form, reflecting a medieval shift in the interpretation of the Aristotelian texts, Aquinas can say that the will is perfect with respect to strictly personal actions, but is in need of virtue for actions that go beyond the individual, whether social actions or actions that reflect the superhuman (and perforce transindividual) ends of human life. See *ST*, 1a2æ 56, 6, and 2a2æ 58, 2 ad 4.

22. It is not, however, Aristotelian. Its origin is apparently Cicero, *de Officiis*, i, 13, c. 41; see Antonino Pagliaro, "«Le tre disposizion . . .»," in *Ulisse, Ricerche semantiche sulla Divina Commedia* (Firenze: Casa Editrice G. D'Anna, 1967), vol. 1, pp. 225–52, esp. pp. 230–32, as well as a host of commentaries, such as those by Daniello, Lombardi, Siena, Scartazzini, and Tozer (DDP). Bruno Nardi, "Il Canto XI dell'*Inferno*," in Getto, *Letture dantesche*, pp. 191–207, mistakenly attributes it to Aristotle: "Perché i fraudolenti più giù dei violenti? Perché la *«frode è dell'uom proprio male»* e costituisce quella particolare specie di malizia che Aristotele distingue dall'incontinenza e dalla bestialità" (p. 198). As has been discussed earlier, Aristotle's distinction of vice from incontinence and bestiality is on quite other grounds. See Moore, "The Classification of Sins," pp. 157–58.

23. See, *ad loc.*, commentaries by Jacopo della Lana, Guido da Pisa, Benvenuto da Imola, Scartazzini, Torraca (DDP), as well as *Singleton* (citing Villani).

24. See, *ad loc.*, commentaries by Jacopo Alighieri, Jacopo della Lana, *L'Ottimo commento* (DDP), as well as *Singleton*.

25. For that matter, we might notice that some of the sins of the third *girone* of circle seven do not involve injury to others, and can be said to involve violence only in a certain, unusual sense. Here too, then, Virgil's distinction demands further interpretation.

26. *Ad loc.*, Jacopo Alighieri, Guido da Pisa, Benvenuto da Imola, Scartazzini, Torraca (DDP), and *Singleton*.

27. *Ad loc.,* Jacopo Alighieri, Jacopo della Lana, Guido da Pisa, Daniello (DDP), and *Singleton.*

28. Aristotle, indeed, includes many instances of violent action in his enumeration of injustices, but all such actions are committed for the sake of some other advantage. Justice and injustice are concerned with transactions between people. Any such transactions provide an opportunity for injustice, but Aristotle also specifically identifies what he calls "involuntary transactions," which by their nature would be unjust. Among them are theft, adultery, poisoning, procuring, enticement of a slave, assassination, false witness, beating, imprisonment, murder, robbery, despoiling parents of children, reproach, outrage (*EN,* v, 5; 1131a10).

29. Cf. how the distinction between *matta bestialità* and *malizia* proper is drawn in Vittorio Vaturi, *Il Canto XI dell'Inferno* (Firenze: Sansoni, 1925), p. 38.

30. *De An.,* iii, 9; 432b15.

31. Cf. *In Ethica,* §§291–92. Cf. Albert, in Albertus Magnus, *De Anima,* ed. C. Stroick, *Opera Omnia,* vol. 7, part 1 (Monasterii Westfalorum: Aschendorff, 1968), iii, iv, c. 3; iii, iv, c. 5; and iii, iv, c. 7.

32. *De An.,* iii, 10; 433a10–25. Cf. John of Damascus, *de Fide orthodoxa,* ii, xxii (*Burgundionis Versio,* c. 36, pp. 132–42).

33. Properly speaking, appetite implies inclination either toward or away from objects, depending on the nature of the objects apprehended. Objects apprehended as goods incline the appetite to pursuit. Objects apprehended as evils evoke the opposite movement of avoidance or flight.

34. The apprehensive and appetitive powers of the soul are distinguished from one another in *de An.,* iii, 3; 427a17, and iii, 9; 432a15. See *In de An.,* §§615–16 and 795–806.

35. Cf. *ST,* 1a 81, 1: "The act of the apprehensive power *[virtus]* is not so properly called a motion as is the action of appetite. For the operation of an apprehensive power is completed when the objects apprehended are *in* the apprehender. The operation of an appetitive power, however, is completed when a person inclines *to* the object of appetite." See also *In Ethica,* §291.

36. *De An.,* ii, 3; 414b3, and *In de An.,* §§286–87.

37. *In de An.,* §804. Although the distinction of simple desire from anger has its origin in Aristotle's text, the establishment of these as independent faculties with appropriately different objects, and the articulation of the nature of their objects, is not properly Aristotelian, but constitutes a medieval supplement to Aristotle's text. Cf. Albertus Magnus, *De Bono,* ed. H. Kühle, C. Feckes, B. Geyer, and W. Kübel, *Opera Omnia,* vol. 28 (Monasterii Westfalorum: Aschendorff, 1951), iii, Q. 5, A. 1, §357.

38. *In de An.,* §§288, 802–4, and 825, respectively. Cf. John of Damascus, *de Fide orthodoxa,* ii, xii (*Burgundionis Versio,* c. 26.15, pp. 118–19), and Albert, *De Anima,* iii, iv, c. 1. The classification, and much of the associated Aristotelian vocabulary for describing it, appears even in scholastic Augustinian

texts. Cf. Saint Bonaventure, *Breviloquium, Opera Omnia,* vol. 5, ed. P.P. Collegii a S. Bonaventura (Quaracchi: Collegii S. Bonaventuræ, 1891), iii, ii; iii, ix; and iii, xi. See Vittorio Russo, "«Ma dimmi: Quei della palude pingue . . . ?»," in *Sussidi di esegesi dantesca* (Napoli: Liguori editori, n.d.): 71–128, esp. pp. 71–75, and Patrick Boyde, *Perception and Passion in Dante's* Comedy (Cambridge: Cambridge University Press, 1993), pp. 54–55 and 253–54.

    39. *In de An.,* §805. See also *ST,* 1a2æ 25, 1.

    40. Cf. *In de An.,* §804. See also D. Odon Lottin, "La psychologie de l'acte humain chez Saint Jean Damascène et les théologiens du XIIIe siècle occidental," *Psychologie et morale aux XIIe and XIIIe siècles,* vol. 1, 2d ed. (Gembloux, Belgium: Duculot, 1957), pp. 393–424, and W. H. V. Reade, *The Moral System of Dante's* Inferno (Oxford: The Clarendon Press, 1909), pp. 96–123. Much of what Dante understood as Aristotle regarding psychological powers is, strictly speaking, not in Aristotle himself but is reinterpretation or expansion of Aristotelian doctrine by medieval commentators. For purposes of understanding Dante, therefore, Aquinas is frequently a more authoritative or more representative source than Aristotle himself. There is, for example, no *faculty* of will in Aristotle, though in Aquinas and other medieval Aristotelians, and in Dante, there is. In Aristotle, βούλησις, the Greek term for "wish" or "will" (in its medieval transformation), is a function of the reason, but not an independent faculty. For that matter, neither are the other appetitive *functions* mentioned by Aristotle in this location—desire (ἐπιθυμία) and anger (θυμός). At *de An.,* iii, 9; 432b7 he specifically denies these individual functions the status of parts or independent faculties in the soul. If they must be given separate location in the soul, Aristotle argues, they should be associated with one another in a common single appetitive power of the soul, distinct from the apprehensive and nutritive powers. By Dante's time, however, all three appetitive functions had been entitized: ἐπιθυμία and θυμός into the concupiscible and irascible appetites, βούλησις into the will. On the lateness of the invention of these faculties, see Charles H. Kahn, "Discovering the Will, from Aristotle to Augustine," in *The Question of "Eclecticism," Studies in Later Greek Philosophy,* ed. J. M. Dillon and A. A. Long (Berkeley: University of California Press, 1988), pp. 234–59; Pierre Michaud-Quantin, *La Psychologie de l'activité chez Albert le Grand* (Paris: Vrin, 1966), pp. 135–47; and Reade, *Moral System,* pp. 116–19. See also John Freccero, "The Firm Foot on a Journey without a Guide," in *Dante: The Poetics of Conversion* (Cambridge, Mass.: Harvard University Press, 1986), pp. 47–48.

    41. Aristotle and Aquinas come to the discrimination of the sensitive appetites and the will from two quite different directions. (In Aristotle's case, it may be more proper to say the discrimination of desire, spirit, and wish, since it is unclear that he entitizes these operations into faculties of the soul—*de An.,* iii, 10; 433b1–5, rejects a solution that in fact is the most common description of the nature of appetite throughout the Middle Ages.) For

Aristotle, appetite is a natural consequence of sensation. Animals with sensation will experience pleasure and pain. Desire (ἐπιθυμία) and spirit (θυμός) are merely tendencies in relation to objects that cause pleasure or pain. The appetites are the efficient cause of locomotion for animals that exhibit that function. Since some movements toward objects are the result of reason, there appears as well to be an equivalent tendency at the rational level, which Aristotle calls "wish," βούλησις (*de An.*, iii, 10; 433a15–25). Aquinas does not approach appetite either from the starting point of sensation, or from the terminus of explaining movement. The approach, rather, is from distinguishing appetition from apprehension. All animals have apprehensive faculties, whose operation renders the faculty like the object apprehended. (The apprehensive power, whether a sense or the intellect, is "assimilated" to the object [*ST,* 1a 80, 1].) Appetitive powers, on the other hand, do not become like the object apprehended; rather, they attempt to move toward this object. Insofar as the operation is different, the appetitive powers are distinct from the apprehensive (*ST,* 1a 81, 1). They are, however, related to the apprehensive powers. For every distinct mode of apprehension, Aquinas finds an equivalent appetitive power. Human beings possess apprehensive powers of sense in common with other animals, but also possess the intellect, itself an apprehensive power. Thus, Aquinas reasons, human beings have both sensitive and intellectual appetites. Since objects perceived by the senses may be perceived as good simply or as arduous goods, there are two sensitive appetitive powers. But since goods apprehended by the intellect are not distinguished as simply or arduously good, there is only a single intellectual appetite, the will (*ST,* 1a 81, 2 and 1a 82, 5).

42. Cf. *Malo,* viii, 2.

43. This distinction attributes a special meaning to a passage at the beginning of the fifth book of the *Ethics.* As rendered by William of Moerbeke, Aristotle states: "We must now turn to justice and injustice, to consider what actions they regard, what kind of mean justice is, and a mean between what extremes. Our intention is to follow the same method in regard to these as we used in our previous discussions" (*EN,* v, 1; 1129a1). To my mind, this introductory statement is entirely casual, but medieval commentators seized on the word *actions (operationes)* in order to distinguish justice and injustice from the moral virtues that had been the subjects of the preceding books. The distinction between virtues and vices concerned with passions and a different set concerned with actions can be found also in Albert's commentary on the *Ethics,* Albertus Magnus, *Super Ethica, commentum et quæstiones,* ed. W. Kübel, *Opera Omnia,* vol. 14 (Monasterii Westfalorum: Aschendorff, 1968), Book 5, Lectio 1, §361.

44. Cf. *In Ethica,* §§291–92; also *ST,* 1a 81, 2; 1a2æ 22, 2; 1a2æ 56, 4; and 1a2æ 59, 5.

45. *In Ethica,* §§292 and 889. All appetites are passive relative to their objects. *ST,* 1a2æ 22, 3; 1a2æ 59, 2 and 59, 5. But as an intellective function

rather than one tied to the body, as the sensitive faculties are, the will can operate without arousing physical and emotional changes.

46. This seems to be Thomas's own extension of the distinction between virtues and vices concerned with passion and those concerned with action. Cf. Aquinas, *de Virtutibus in communi,* ed. A. Odetto, in *Quæstiones disputatæ,* vol. 2, 9th ed. (Torino and Roma: Marietti, 1953), a. 5; also *ST,* 2a2æ 58, 1 and 58, 4. Such a claim is not found in Albert. Indeed, Albert is in every way much more faithful to the relevant Aristotelian texts in *de Anima* and the *Ethics* than Aquinas is. Albert speaks of temperance and courage as perfections with respect to anger and desire, not as virtues of specifically appetitive powers. See *Super Ethica,* Book 5, Lectio 3, §375. Justice he assigns as a perfection of the reason—not as the virtue of a specifically intellectual appetite. That Albert does indeed mean the reason, and not the will, is confirmed in his later need to distinguish between justice and prudence as two different perfections of the same faculty. See *Super Ethica,* Book 5, Lectio 4, §382. Here Albert describes justice as a perfection of the reason in the reason's capacity to cause action. Such a description is also much closer to Aristotle's formula in the *de Anima* than to Aquinas' formulation of justice as a virtue of the will.

47. The section of the *Ethics* on which Thomas is commenting when he makes this declaration contains no such assertions as that there needs to be a principle of action that is appetitive but not passionate, or that the will is such a principle. The will, per se, is never mentioned in the fifth book of the *Ethics.* It is my conviction that Aristotle's psychology does not in fact contain a faculty of will as the Middle Ages employed it. Βούλησις, the Aristotelian term that "became" the will in medieval psychology is frequently rendered as *wish* in English translations. Such a translation makes more sense in the dynamics of Aristotelian psychology than the use of a faculty-term such as *will* does. Βούλησις is appetitive, Aristotle says (*de An.,* iii, 10; 433a15–25), and is therefore a source of movement like other appetites. But the Aristotelian dynamic has no place for a final, authoritative faculty through which all decisions regarding action are passed. The actual initiation of action, choice (προαίρεσις), can be described either as appetite guided by reason or as reason ordered to appetite. Whichever alternative is taken, it is clearly the *result* of the operation of two faculties, not a faculty in its own right. The same combined but direct operation can be taken as occurring when wish is involved, without requiring that βούλησις exist as a general mediating faculty. Aquinas describes both βούλησις and προαίρεσις as aspects of the will (*In de An.,* §824; cf. *In Ethica,* §1133). Moreover, it seems to me that a simple but telling sign exists in Aristotle that βούλησις is not a faculty: were it a faculty, there would be one virtue or several to perfect its operation. Aquinas, of course, would reply: "There is. Justice is the will's virtue." But if Aristotle had meant book five of the *Ethics* to be the description of the virtue of a specific appetitive power different from the powers of desire and anger, would he

not have said it? Could he have meant us to understand that justice was the virtue of βούλησις without mentioning βούλησις (except in a nontechnical sense) in book five? For our purposes, though, it is enough that in the fifth book of the *Ethics* one does not find a single technical use of the Greek term βούλησις that was regularly rendered as *voluntas* in medieval translations of Aristotle. It appears only late in the fifth book, on three occasions where, in speaking about involuntary suffering, Aristotle's usage is loose and untechnical—equivalent simply to our use of the phrase "against someone's will" (*EN*, v, 11; 1136b5–25).

48. As mentioned above, the association of justice with the will is not a part of the earlier medieval Aristotelian tradition, not even in a writer close enough in time to Dante as Albert the Great. It is significant, then, that with Aquinas the first commentator definitively to assign justice as the virtue of the will, Dante's assertion of the same doctrine indicates his reliance either on Aquinas directly or on an immediate student of Aquinas for what are, in the *Commedia*, fundamental distinctions regarding the origin of moral action.

49. See also T. K. Seung, "The Metaphysics of the *Commedia*," p. 190.

50. Cf. *Malo*, viii, 3.

51. Cf. *EN*, vii, 8; 1150a30: "In general, the person who, without any desire or only a mild desire, does something shameful would seem worse than the one acting in the grip of vehement desire. Likewise, he who strikes another without anger is worse than one who does so after becoming angry."

52. *ST*, 1a2æ 73, 5 and ad 3 (citing *EN*, iii, 10); 1a2æ 66, 1 (citing *EN*, vii, 6); 1a2æ 56, 4 ad 1 and 1a2æ 66, 4.

53. *EN*, vii, 4; 1147b25. See also *ST*, 1a2æ 77, 5; 1a 81, 2; and 1a2æ 66, 4.

54. *ST*, 1a2æ 25, 1 and 23, 1 ad 1.

55. Aristotle describes these goods as not necessary, yet desirable in themselves: *EN*, vii, 4; 1147b28–30 (while denying in his discussion of temperance that one can properly speaking be called self-indulgent with respect to them: *EN*, iii, 10; 1117b25–1118a15). *ST*, 1a2æ 30, 3 (citing *EN*, iii, 11, and *Rhetoric*, i, 11).

56. One may also be said to be continent or incontinent with respect to other "unnecessary" goods, such as honor and wealth, and one may be said to be continent or incontinent with respect to an emotion such as anger, but such uses of the terms are analogical, rather than strict (*EN*, vii, 4; 1147b30–35, and *In Ethica*, §§1358–59).

57. *ST*, 1a 81, 2 and 1a2æ 23, 1. Cf. Aquinas, *Quæstiones de Anima*, ed. M. Calcaterra and T. S. Centi in *Quæstiones disputatæ*, vol. 2, 9th ed. (Torino and Roma: Marietti, 1953), a. 13: "Now, something is appetible either for the reason that it is pleasing to the senses and suited to them, and the concupiscible power is ordered to this; or for the reason that by means of it there is the possibility of enjoying things pleasing to the senses. And this latter sometimes occurs in conjunction with something painful to the senses, as when

by combat or by repelling obstacles an animal obtains the possibility of enjoying some pleasure appropriate to it. The irascible power is ordered to this."

58. In its Greek manifestations—θυμός—it does not appear so much as an appetite as a supporting or encouraging force. People with θυμός will undertake actions even where the good pursued or evil to be avoided is difficult; those without will not. Within medieval psychology this "tendency" toward objects of a certain sort qualified it as an appetite. See *In de An.*, §804. Also, *ST,* 1a2æ 58, 1.

59. *Rhetoric,* ii, 2; 1378a30–b10. *ST,* 1a2æ 48, 1. It is plausible that the other irascible passions also begin in sadness, at goods that must be postponed or evils that may not be averted. Also, *In de An.*, §805.

60. Cf. Nardi, "Il Canto XI dell'*Inferno,*" p. 200.

61. Cf. Russo, "«Ma dimmi,»" p. 76.

62. Cf. Nardi, "Il Canto XI dell'*Inferno,*" p. 198.

63. Vicious or sinful acts are the result of "inordinate" desire or anger or appetite generally—that is, appetite uncontrolled or improperly guided by the intellect. *In Ethica,* §1131. *ST,* 1a2æ 71, 1.

64. *EN,* i, 13; 1102b5–12. *ST,* 1a 78, 1 and 81, 3. Aquinas also points out that in humans, unlike animals, the sensitive desires participate in reason in a further way, since in humans a certain evaluative reason goes on even at the sensory level, while in animals this is directed solely by instinct. See also *ST,* 1a 78, 4 and 81, 3 ad 2.

65. Moreover, the order of this system corresponds (with some semantic modifications) quite closely to the order that Dante has Virgil enunciate as Aristotelian, and so Dante could use the structure of the appetites as the structure of Hell while feeling it appropriate to attribute this structure to Aristotle. Indeed, it is altogether likely that Dante, or any other medieval Aristotelian, would have believed that the three appetites that underlie the *Inferno* actually constituted an orthodox interpretation of Aristotle's *de Anima.* While a systematic Aristotelian would have had to disagree with Dante in maintaining Aristotle's distinction between vicious acts and other, similar, acts committed without vicious habits, no later medieval Aristotelian would have contested assigning the origin of unjust acts (whether properly of injustice or not) to the action of the will, or the origin of acts of incontinence to the concupiscible appetite. These would have been conclusions based on orthodox interpretations of the *Ethics,* and the eventual attribution of violent but passionate sins to the irascible appetite (in distinction from the will) would have been seen as a plausible conclusion to draw from these other readings of the *Ethics.*

66. *ST,* 1a2æ 73, 3. The same ordering and ordering principle can be seen—from the other end—in the value Aquinas gives to specific moral virtues. The virtues are more excellent as they have as their subjects more excellent appetites, that is, more rational appetites. "Among these [virtues],

one is better than another to the extent that it approaches reason more closely. Hence justice, which is in the will, stands ahead of all the other moral virtues; and fortitude, which is in the irascible appetite, stands ahead of temperance, which is in the concupiscible, an appetite which participates less in reason" (*ST*, 1a2æ 66, 1). Cf. *ST*, 1a2æ 66, 4.

67. *EN*, i, 9; 1099a10–15, and *In Ethica*, §§155–56. Also *ST*, 1a2æ 59, 2 and ad 3.

68. *EN*, vii, 9; 1150b30–37; also *EN*, iii, 8; 1114b30–1115a3. *ST*, 1a2æ 77, 2. Also 1a2æ 78, 4 and 10, 3; *Malo*, ii, 3 ad 9 and iii, 9.

69. *EN*, iii, 7; 1114a20–25. *ST*, 1a2æ 77, 7. For Aristotle, only the virtuous are truly capable of choice. All others have the range of free choice limited by their uncontrolled desires (*EN*, vi, 13; 1144a32–37, and *EN*, vii, 4; 1148a12–17). For Dante, of course, it would be inconceivable to say that most sinners did not exercise choice in their sins. There are no sins where we do not see the sinners aware of the evil choice they are making. But that is not to say that some choices are not freer (and therefore more blameworthy or praiseworthy) than others.

70. It should be said, however, that sins consequent on the concupiscent appetite were sins to which the greatest shame attached, since while it is most difficult to struggle with the least reasonable desires, it is the most shameful to yield to them. Cf. *ST*, 1a2æ 73, 5 ad 3; *EN*, vii, 7; 1149b1–5 and 1149b23–27.

71. Aristotle states that "anger is more natural and more difficult to resist than the desires for excessive and unnecessary pleasures" (*EN*, vii, 7; 1149b8).

72. *EN*, vii, 7; 1149a25. See also *EN*, iii, 11; 1116b32, and *In Ethica*, §573. Cf. *ST*, 1a2æ 46, 4.

73. *EN*, v, 3; 1130a5–10; *ST*, 1a2æ 73, 9.

74. *ST*, 1a 80, 2 and 82, 2. The generality of the operation of the will reflects an equivalent generality in Aristotle's description of the motives of those who commit injustice: "gain" (κέρδος), *EN*, v, 4; 1130a30–35.

75. We can find just this distinction in Aquinas, when, in discussing cupidity, he distinguishes between two kinds of avarice: "Covetousness implies a certain immoderation in regard to wealth in two senses: in one sense immediately, regarding the getting and keeping of wealth, insofar, that is to say, as someone acquires riches beyond what is due, by stealing or keeping what is someone else's. And this covetousness is contrary to justice. . . . In another sense it implies an immoderation in regard to one's interior passion for wealth; for example, if someone were to love or desire wealth too much, or took too much pleasure in it, even if he had no intention of stealing from others. In this sense, covetousness is contrary to liberality, which moderates passions of this sort" (*ST*, 2a2æ 118, 3). The second of these forms of avarice is the avarice we find in the fourth circle of Hell, where it is located as a sin of the concupiscible appetite. The avaricious, in this sense, have been

overwhelmed by passion (just as, in an opposite sense, have been the spend-thrifts with whom they share this circle). Their sin has as its opposed virtue temperance, a virtue of the concupiscible appetite. The first of the forms of avarice that Aquinas mentions, however, is that generalized desire for wealth which, with a similar desire for high position or honor or other general goods, constitutes the object of acts of injustice, or of the intellectual appetite we call will.

76. In *Malo*, iii, 13, Aquinas too associates sinning *ex malitia*, rather than *ex passione*, to the will. Staying within the bounds of Aristotelian orthodoxy, he argues that bad habits in the passions may constitute a form of choice in their own right, since our habits are within our election (*Malo*, iii, 12 ad 12). Thus, one can use the term *malitia* of vices of appetites other than the will. But it is clear that *malitia* in its most direct sense is an act of the will, as here in Dante. See also *ST*, 1a2æ 22, 3, *EN*, vii, 8; 1150a25–32, and *In Ethica*, 1412.

77. As also John Freccero, "The Firm Foot on a Journey without a Guide," pp. 47–49, though Freccero does not delve into the medieval redefinitions of Aristotelian terms on which this division depends. T. K. Seung, "The Metaphysics of the *Commedia*," p. 183 and *passim*, divides the sins of Hell by three powers, the vegetative, sensitive, and intellectual, apparently based on the (mis)identification of the concupiscible appetite with the vegetative power. The same mistaken interpretation of Aristotle mars his argument in T. K. Seung [Swing], *The Fragile Leaves of the Sibyl: Dante's Master Plan* (Westminster, Md.: The Newman Press, 1962). See pp. 29–32 and *passim*. C. A. Trypanis, "Dante and a Byzantine Treatise on Virtues and Vices," *Medium Ævum* 19 (1950): 43–49, argues for a neo-Platonic source of the divisions of sin. But Dante explicitly rejects the Platonic notion of three distinct souls. It is an Aristotelian tradition of distinct powers of a single, unified soul which provides the basis for our organization. See Agostino Pertusi, "Cultura greco-bizantina nel tardo medioevo nelle Venezie e suoi echi in Dante," in *Dante e la Cultura Veneta*, ed. Vittore Branca and Giorgio Padoan (Firenze: L. S. Olschki editore, 1966), pp. 157–95, esp. pp. 179–82.

78. Cf. Freccero, "Infernal Irony: The Gates of Hell," in *Dante, the Poetics of Conversion*, pp. 106–7: "If the bodies in hell are really souls, then it follows that their physical attitudes, contortions and punishments are really *spiritual* attitudes and states of mind, sins made manifest in the form of physical punishment. It is therefore correct to say that the punishments *are* the sins." Cf. also Anthony K. Cassell, *Dante's Fearful Art of Justice* (Toronto: University of Toronto Press, 1984), p. 9: "[The punishment] is, in all cases, . . . a strict manifestation of the sin as guilt. . . . The images of the damned figure symbolically, iconographically, and theologically the very mystery and complexity of their sins." See also Silvio Pasquazi, *Enciclopedia dantesca*, article "*Contrapasso*," 2:181–83, esp. p. 182, and Steno Vazzana, *Il Contrapasso nella Divina Commedia* (Roma: Ciranna, 1968). Also, Gilbert, *Dante's Conception of Justice*, p. 75.

79. Cf. Kenneth Gross, "Infernal Metamorphoses: An Interpretation of Dante's Counterpass," *MLN* 100 (1985): 42–69, esp. 48–49: "If nothing else, Bertran retains enough of his poetic insight to see that his punishment makes out of his sensible, corporeal form a symbol of the divisions he had formerly wrought within the body politic."

80. Two *gironi* in Purgatory, and their corrections—of the wrathful, and of the lustful—seem to exhibit the actions of the vices, rather than their opposites. We will discuss them again in the next chapter, but a comment is needed here too. Omberto's explanation of the *contrapasso* in Purgatory is unambiguous, and the new principle seems appropriate to Purgatory in both philosophical and poetic senses. In this context, it is perhaps worth considering that the dense and choking smoke of the third *girone* can represent the *extinguishing* of the flames of anger (flame being, in any case, a more common figure for anger than smoke), rather than the action of anger. With respect to the lustful, we should consider that lust would not be corrected by the absence or opposite of love, but by the presence of proper love. Both lust and love might reasonably be represented by fire. Here, as in the world, the two forms of love look confusingly similar. But the fires we see in the seventh *girone* are surely meant as refining fires of proper love. Cf. Gilbert, *Dante's Conception of Justice*, pp. 136–39 and 126–27, and Boyde, *Perception and Passion*, p. 289.

81. Vandelli, as do many other editors, glosses the following verses from Guido del Duca in Purgatory with the citation from Galatians:

> Fu il sangue mio d'invidia sì rïarso,
>   che se veduto avesse uom farsi lieto,
>   visto m'avresti di livore sparso.
> Di mia semente cotal paglia mieto.
>
>   (*Purg.* xiv, 82–85)

But the principle of Galatians is inappropriate here too. Having looked at others with envy, Guido now . . . cannot look at all. He does not continue to look with envy; he is not looked at with envy. He has reaped the opposite of his original action. I believe Trucchi is correct (*ad loc.*, DDP) in hearing, in Guido's statement, not the echo of Galatians but an echo from Proverbs: "Whoever sows iniquity shall reap vanity" (Prov. 22:8). Since Guido goes on to discuss the futility (one could say vanity) of desiring what cannot be possessed in common (*Purg.* xiv, 86–87), the echo of Proverbs would be appropriate.

82. Gross, "Infernal Metamorphoses," speaks of punishments as "sins converted to torturing images by what Dante would persuade us is the allegorizing eye of eternal Justice" (p. 42). "The pains of the damned are more revelation than retribution; they compose difficult moral emblems which shadow forth sin's inward nature" (p. 47). Cf. Giorgio Padoan, "Il Canto degli Epicurei," *Convivium* n.s. 27 (1959): 13–39, esp. p. 14.

83. Cf. Vazzana, *Il Contrapasso*, p. 10: "In altri termini, la pena che Dante attribuisce ad ogni peccato è la faccia e la forma del peccato stesso, che ora Dio, col suo giudizio ha rivelato nella sua vera fisionomia. Quindi mai un rapporto di contrasto tra peccato e pena, ma di analogia. Anzi, più che di analogia, si tratta di identità: la pena è il peccato visto nella sua natura maligna, la sua figurazione; gli attributi della pena sono gli attributi del peccato; insomma ogni atteggiamento della pena è un giudizio del poeta su quel peccato."

84. See *ST,* 1a2æ 22, 2 ad 3. Cf. *de An.,* i, 1; 403b1–3, and John of Damascus, *de Fide orthodoxa,* ii, xvi (*Burgundionis Versio,* c. 30, p. 122).

85. See, for example, Giovanni Busnelli, *L'Etica nicomachea e l'ordinamento morale dell'"Inferno" di Dante* (Bologna: Zanichelli, 1907), p. 152.

86. Even where the punishment seems unequivocally passive in respect of the action, Dante makes an effort to emphasize the sinners' recognition of and adherence to the action they now suffer. Richard Abrams, "Against the *Contrapasso:* Dante's Heretics, Schismatics, and Others," *Italian Quarterly* 27: 105 (1986): 5–19, points (p. 12) to an extraordinary instance of this in the same canto in which the term *contrapasso* itself appears for the only time in the *Commedia*. As Mohammed passes Dante, he shouts, "Or vedi com'io mi dilacco" (*Inf.* xxviii, 30), as if it were still he doing the dividing. See also Francesco d'Ovidio, "Il Canto XIX dell'*Inferno*," in Getto, *Letture dantesche,* pp. 345–76, esp. p. 352, on the passive representation of the sin of simony.

87. From this perspective one can scarcely speak of the damned as *condemned* to their punishments. They desired these actions while alive, and in a sense still do. Virgil explains that sinners rush to their punishment because their fear is turned to desire (*Inf.* iii, 126: "sì che la tema si volve in disio"), in regard to which Abrams, "Against the *Contrapasso*," p. 9, comments: "Each class of sinners embraces the divine judgment—fear turning to desire as the sinner fondly recognizes in his eternal fate, not an impersonal punishment, but a form of suffering reminiscent of his own inmost yearning." Cf. Karl Witte, "The Ethical Systems of the *Inferno* and the *Purgatorio*," in *Essays on Dante,* trans. C. M. Lawrence and P. H. Wicksteed (Boston: Houghton Mifflin, 1898), pp. 117–52, esp. p. 129. Also Vazzana, *Il Contrapasso*, p. 34: "Dio, che li ha giudicati in vita e che ha voluto che ciascuno da morto si avesse e fosse quello che volle e fu da vivo." From this perspective, Eleonore Stump, "Dante's Hell, Aquinas' Moral Theory, and the Love of God," *Canadian Journal of Philosophy* 16 (1986): 181–98, quite properly characterizes this as a manifestation not only of divine justice, but of God's *love* for the sinners (pp. 196–97). For a fuller discussion, see also Marc Cogan, "Delight, Punishment, and the Justice of God in the *Divina Commedia*," *Dante Studies* 111 (1993): 27–52.

88. *SCG,* iv, 93. Cf. 4 *Sent.,* 50, 1.

89. Abrams, "Against the *Contrapasso*," p. 9, provides a striking example of the fixity of damned character. The despair Cavalcante Cavalcanti experiences in misinterpreting Dante's remark about his son, Guido (*Inf.* x, 67–72),

depends on his continuing to act as if he believed that only life on earth mattered (as he had believed, insofar as an Epicurean, while alive), despite his now having the most vivid proof of a life beyond that one! See also Francesco de Sanctis, "Il Canto V dell'*Inferno*," in Getto, *Letture dantesche*, pp. 73–90, esp. pp. 88 and 86: "Nell'Inferno il terrestre rimane eterno ed immutato; perché i peccatori dell'Inferno dantesco servano le stesse passioni."

90. See also Stump, "Dante's Hell," pp. 196–97.

91. Cf. Gross, "Infernal Metamorphoses," p. 48.

92. Gross, "Infernal Metamorphoses," p. 50, states, "Only by dying into Eternity does the damned soul discover and become the emblematic form of its inward life." That is, while alive, that inward character is concealed by the circumstances of life. In death alone is the true nature of the action revealed, and only in the clarified posthumous state that Dante pictures does the action of the damned soul become didactic for us.

93. Cf. Vazzana, *Il Contrapasso*, p. 15.

94. Dante may even be going so far, with a sort of philosophic pun, as to indicate that he believed such sins share a common genus, in a strict philosophical sense of the term. For the physical connection of circles would have to be based on a common material substratum (figuratively, the continent beneath them in Hell), and it is the material cause that provides the genus of an entity.

95. Cf. Gross, "Infernal Metamorphoses," p. 45: "The phenomenological totality which one might call the 'state' of each of the damned in Dante's Hell—a condition embracing body, mind, language, landscape, and weather—is a complex reflection of and on the sinful disorder of his soul." Also, Christopher Kleinhenz, "Eternal Guardians Revisited: 'Cerbero, il gran vermo' (*Inf.* vi, 22)," *Dante Studies* 93 (1975): 185–99, esp. 186–88. See also Vazzana, *Il Contrapasso*, p. 64, regarding the *bolge* that characterize the landscape of the eighth circle: "La stessa struttura a fossati del campo maligno rende due qualità della frode: lo star nascosta e l'insidia. La violenza è aperta, visibile."

96. Cf. Vazzana, *Il Contrapasso*, p. 13.

97. At least he appears to use Aristotle as his source. There is a certain tone of condescension in Virgil's use of the adjective *tua* when he alludes to the distinction of incontinence-bestiality-malice in the *Ethics*:

> Non ti rimembra di quelle parole
> con le quai la tua Etica pertratta
> le tre disposizion che 'l ciel non vole. . . .
> (*Inf.* xi, 79–81)

In the distance from Aristotle that "*tua* Etica" implies, Dante may be suggesting that while Aristotle's terminology might be most familiar, and thus the most convenient way to describe the sins of upper Hell, these are not necessarily the most accurate terms to use. Dante might thus be signaling his own awareness of the distance between his interpretation and the orthodoxly Aristotelian.

98. Cf. Kleinhenz, "Eternal Guardians Revisited," pp. 188–90; also, Vazzana, *Il Contrapasso*, pp. 33–37.

99. Cf. *ST,* 1a2æ 77, 5.

100. See Giovanni Getto, "Il Canto VII dell'*Inferno*," in Getto, *Letture dantesche*, pp. 113–31, esp. p. 116.

101. Not that Dante does not have Virgil attribute *avarizia* to some of these sinners at *Inf.* vii, 48. Dante is aware of the ambiguity, but it is impossible in ordinary usage to escape it.

102. Pluto's abrupt collapse (*Inf.* vii, 13–15) perhaps suggests the insubstantiality of the objects of this sin. Though they seem imposing, they ought easily to be controlled, for once challenged, they simply and suddenly deflate.

103. Cf. Christopher Kleinhenz, "Inferno VIII," in *Lectura Dantis 6*, supp. (Spring 1990): 93–109, esp. 95.

104. Busnelli, *L'Etica nicomachea e l'ordinamento morale dell'«Inferno»*, pp. 68 and 79–80. See also the comments of Padoan, Castelvetro, and Berthier (at *Inf.* vii, 116: DDP).

105. Cf. Triolo, "*Ira, Cupiditas, Libido,*" p. 65.

106. *EN*, vii, 7; 1149b14–18 (the angry are "not plotters"), and *EN*, v, 10; 1135b20–28 ("whatever is done from anger must be regarded as done without premeditation"). Cf. *ST,* 1a2æ 48, 3: "Consequently, among all the passions, anger most manifestly impedes the reason's judgment, as is said in Ps. 30: 10: *My eye is troubled by anger.*"

107. What profit is there to Capaneus in his blasphemy, whether in this world or in Hell? His action is an act of pure anger, of pure passion (*Inf.* xiv, 49–66).

108. Cf. *EN,* vii, 7; 1149b20–23, where Aristotle distinguishes between acting from anger, which always involves pain, and acting "in wanton outrage" *(inurians)*, which is done for pleasure. Boccaccio's commentary on Dante's description of Filippo as "'l fiorentino spirito bizzarro" (at *Inf.* viii, 62: DDP) recognizes the peculiarity of the motivation of the wrathful, and suggests another dimension of it: "I think this word 'bizzarro' is used only by Florentines, and always has a bad sound to it, for we call those *bizzarri* who become angry suddenly and for the smallest reasons, nor can they be moved from their anger by any argument."

109. Cf. *ST,* 1a2æ 31, 7.

110. Triolo, "*Ira, Cupiditas, Libido,*" pp. 10 and 20, recognizes the existence of a sick concupiscence. At p. 20, discussing the sinners of circle seven, he speaks of motives of masochism (and, by implication, of sadism). While I do not believe it appropriate to speak of those sinners in this way, the notion of sadism and masochism seems absolutely apposite to the concupiscent responses to pain that we see in circle five.

111. Dante is explicit that these *accidiosi* are sullen in regard to worldly pleasures:

... Tristi fummo
　　nell'aere dolce che dal sol s'allegra,
　　portando dentro accidïoso fummo.
　　　　　　　　(*Inf.* vii, 121–23)

Cf. Moore, "Classification of Sins," p. 175.

112. We notice, in the journey through Hell, that Dante *personaggio* from time to time mirrors the character of the sinners with whom he is in contact at that moment. For the most part throughout Hell, Dante is moved to pity by the sight of the torments of the damned. In the case of Filippo Argenti, however, Dante experiences emotions almost on the order of glee at his punishment and added torment at the hands of his fellow sinners. It is the pleasure he takes here that shows him like the wrathful—that is to say, at this moment Dante takes pleasure in objects that he would normally find painful:

... «Maestro, molto sarei vago
　　di vederlo attuffare in questa broda
　　prima che noi uscissimo del lago».
. . . .
Dopo ciò poco vid'io quello strazio
　　far di costui alle fangose genti,
　　che Dio ancor ne lodo e ne ringrazio.
　　　　　　　　(*Inf.* viii, 52–54; 58–60)

113. *ST,* 1a2ae 82, 3. See also Augustine, *de Trin.,* xiii, 16 (21). Also *Malo,* ii, 3 ad 6.

114. 2 *Sent.,* 30, 8 and 30, 10.

115. *EN,* vii, 7; 1149a30–35; *ST,* 1a2æ 48, 2 and 48, 3.

116. Cf. Triolo, *"Ira, Cupiditas, Libido,"* p. 16. See also Kleinhenz, "Inferno VIII," pp. 101–4.

117. Cf. *ST,* 1a2æ 73, 5 ad 3: "The reason why it is more shameful to be incontinent in lust than in anger is that lust partakes less of reason."

118. The Minotaur is described once as wracked with anger, "e quando vide noi, sè stesso morse, / sì come quei cui l'ira dentro fiacca" (*Inf.* xii, 14–15), and once as anger itself, "quell'ira bestial ch'i' ora spensi" (*Inf.* xii, 33). Of the Centaurs, anger and impetuousness are stressed: "quell'altro è Folo, che fu sì pien d'ira" (*Inf.* xii, 72); "Chiron ... mal fu la voglia tua sempre sì tosta" (*Inf.* xii, 65–66). Nessus is said to have sought for revenge even in death: "fè di sè la vendetta" (*Inf.* xii, 69). Revenge is the pleasure aimed at by those suffering anger. Cf. *ST,* 1a2æ 48, 1. Cf. Umberto Bosco, "Il Canto XII dell'*Inferno,*" in Getto, *Letture dantesche,* pp. 209–19, esp. pp. 212–13; Aleardo Sacchetto, "Il Canto XII dell'*Inferno*" (Roma: Lectura Dantis Romana, Società Editrice Internazionale, 1959), p. 6; and Guido Favati, "Osservazioni sul canto XII dell'*Inferno* dantesco," in *Studi in onore di Italo Siciliano* (Firenze: Olschki, 1966): 423–36, esp. p. 426.

119. Other sinners in Hell are punished by fire, or by heated substances, but in none of these cases is it the quality of heat (that is, figuratively, the heated passion of anger) that is being appealed to, as it is here. Poetry's concreteness inevitably carries with it, and even creates, ambiguity; indeed, that is a characteristic that poets exploit. When the object used as an image is as potentially multivalent in significance as fire is, it is possible to use that object in such a way that at each use a different one of its qualities is designated as significant. In the eighth circle, for example, it is not the heat of the flames but the scriptural allusion that is significant about the flames that play on the feet of the simoniacs (*Inf.* xix, 33; d'Ovidio also suggests that the flame at their feet makes them grotesque parodies of sacramental candles, "Il Canto XIX dell'*Inferno*," p. 353); not the heat of the flames but the tonguelike appearance and brilliant instability of flame that is relevant to the fraudulent counselors (*Inf.* xxvi, 89; cf. Benvenuto Terracini, "Il Canto XXVII dell'*Inferno*," in Getto, *Letture dantesche*, pp. 515–45, esp. p. 519); not the heat of the pitch but its dense stickiness that is relevant to the barrators (*Inf.* xxi, 16–18); it is the smoke within which the transformation of the thieves takes place, more than the flame, that is relevant (*Inf.* xxv, 91–93; which Attilio Momigliano likens to the smoke that so frequently accompanies magic tricks, "Il Canto XXV dell'*Inferno*," in Getto, *Letture dantesche*, pp. 467–88, esp. p. 483). Here in circle seven, however, it is the heat of the boiling blood that is significant, just as the substance being heated, blood, is significant to the sins of violence it punishes. Likewise, it is the heat of the sand and burning snow that is important to the third *girone* of circle seven.

120. Cf. *de An.*, i, 1; 403b1–3, and John of Damascus, *de Fide orthodoxa*, ii 16 (*Burgundionis Versio*, c. 30, p. 122). Also, *ST*, 1a2æ 48, 2 and 1a2æ 22, 2 ad 3 (citing John of Damascus, 2.16).

121. Cf. Seung, *Fragile Leaves*, pp. 196–97.

122. The sense of pride involved in Pier's *sdegno* may also be a link to the irascible appetite. In commenting on 1 John 2: 16 ("All that is in the world is concupiscence of the flesh or concupiscence of the eyes or pride of life"), Aquinas associates "pride of life" to the irascible appetite: "The inordinate appetite for arduous good [i.e., excessive pursuit of objects of the irascible appetite] pertains to 'pride of life'" (*ST*, 1a2æ 77, 5).

123. Cf. Vazzana, *Il Contrapasso*, p. 55: "Il suicidio entra nel quadro della violenza. Morta ogni «cieca cupidigia», ci sono tuttavia i segni dell'«ira folle»: Pier de le Vigne dice di sé: «per disdegnoso gusto». È ancora l'ira che stimola il malvolere."

124. From Benvenuto's commentary on the *Commedia* (at *Inf.* xiii, 119–35: DDP).

125. *ST*, 2a2æ 78, 1.

126. Boccaccio, though recognizing the location of Epicureans in this circle, defines heresy strictly in terms of the falling away from Christian doctrine (at *Inf.* ix, 127: DDP; thus, one supposes that according to Boccaccio

Florentine Epicureans would be heretics, but Epicurus himself could not be—despite Dante's explicit statement that the leaders of every heretical sect are at the bottom of their tombs). See also the notes of Vellutello, Grabher, and Fallani (all at *Inf.* ix, 127: DDP) and Busnelli, *L'Etica nicomachea e l'ordinamento morale dell'«Inferno»*, pp. 6–9 and 16. Similarly, Raoul Manselli, in "Eresia," in *Enciclopedia dantesca*, 2d ed., vol. 2 (Roma: Istituto della Enciclopedia italiana, 1984), p. 720. However, Casini and Barbi (at *Inf.* ix, 127: DDP), citing Del Lungo, recognize the existence of "great heretics of paganism," as well as Christian heretics.

127. Nor is Virgil silent because heresy is not mentioned by Aristotle. There are other sins that Aristotle does not mention, for example usury, which Virgil does.

128. As, for example, Pagliaro, "Farinata e Cavalcante," p. 186, or "«Le tre disposizion . . .»," p. 228, or Moore, "Classification of Sins," pp. 177–78, though Moore restricts the error of heresy to a single wrong belief that at least matches Dante's doctrinal conviction, as does Padoan, "Il Canto degli Epicurei," pp. 17–18, 20, and 24.

129. *Inf.* iv, 129 and 143–44. Cf. Arsenio Frugoni, "Il Canto X dell'«Inferno»," in *Nuove letture dantesche*, Casa di Dante in Roma, vol. 1, anno di studi 1965–66 (Firenze: Le Monnier, 1968): 261–83, esp. 268. And this despite Averroism being, to a theologian like Aquinas, a serious heretical doctrine against which it was his duty to argue. We would do well, also, to remember that the sphere of theologians in Heaven contains among its named members theologians whose work had been condemned as heretical. The case of Siger de Brabant takes on a special significance in this context, for his glorification finds its place in the same sphere as Aquinas, though it was Aquinas who refuted and condemned the specifically Averroistic heresy of his views (*Par.* x, 133–38). And if heresy is not a sin of belief, neither is it a sin of the reason, as Vaturi, *Il Canto XI dell'Inferno*, pp. 8 and 11; or Ettore Paratore, "Il Canto X dell'«Inferno»," in *Inferno, Letture degli anni 1973–76* (Roma: Casa di Dante in Roma, Bonacci editore, 1977), pp. 241–81, esp. 247–48; or Meersseman, "Il Canto XI dell'«Inferno»," pp. 3–4.

130. *ST*, 2a2æ 39, 1.

131. Cf. Vaturi, *Il Canto XI dell'Inferno*, p. 11.

132. It is from this, after all, that Felice Tocco entitled his monograph *Quel che non c'è nella Divina Commedia, o Dante e l'eresia* (Bologna: Zanichelli, 1899). See esp. pp. 7–14 and 20; also Moore, "The Classification of Sins," pp. 177–78; Vaturi, *Il Canto XI dell'Inferno*, pp. 8–9; and notes by Trucchi (at *Inf.* ix, 124–31: DDP).

133. Augustine, *de Hæresibus ad Quodvultdeum liber unus*, ed. R. vander Plaetse and C. Beukers (Turnholt: Brepols, 1969); *SCG*, iv, 4–9, iv, 28–38.

134. Pietro Alighieri (at *Inf.* ix, 110–23: DDP) and Vellutello (at *Inf.* ix, 124–32: DDP) both compile lengthy lists of exemplary heresiarchs (including Arius and Sabellius), but neither mentions Photinus.

135. The charges were denied from a quite early date. See, for example, the *Vitæ et res gestæ pontificum romanorum*, vol. 1 (Romæ: De Rubeis, 1677), pp. 337–38. See also Tocco, *Dante e l'eresia*, pp. 20–21, and Vaturi, *Il Canto XI dell'Inferno*, pp. 7–8. Also Venturi, Tommaseo, Bianchi, and Berthier, *ad loc.* (DDP), and *Singleton.*

136. Cf. Guido Gonella, "Il Canto XI dell'«Inferno»," in *Inferno, Letture degli anni 1973–76*, pp. 283–92, esp. p. 284. Also Jacopo della Lana and *L'Ottimo commento* (DDP).

137. A similar calculation can be found in Richard of St. Victor's *Liber de Verbo incarnato*, c. 8; *PL*, 196, 1003c. Cf. *ST*, 3a, 1, 2.

138. Augustine points out that the first requirement of hope of blessedness is the conviction that the soul is immortal: "But the blessed life does not belong to this [life of] mortality, nor shall it exist until there is immortality. And if there were no way in which immortality could be given to men, then it were vain to search for blessedness, since it cannot exist without immortality" (*de Trin.*, xiii, 7 [10]).

139. See Moore, "The Classification of Sins," p. 177, and Padoan, "Il Canto degli Epicurei," pp. 17–18 and 20.

140. Cf. Abrams, "Against the *Contrapasso*," p. 9. Those who say they are punished in fire because heretics were burned at the stake (cf. Manselli, "Eresia," p. 722, or Meersseman, "Il Canto XI dell'«Inferno»," p. 13) have inverted the way Dante would have regarded both actions. For Dante, they receive an appropriate judicial punishment precisely because that punishment too is an image of the fundamentally passionate nature of their sin. Their eternal punishment replicates this eternally.

141. Cf. 1 *Sent.* 20, 2. Also Vaturi, *Il Canto XI dell'Inferno*, p. 8, and Frugoni, "Il Canto X dell'«Inferno»," p. 273. See also Seung, *Fragile Leaves*, pp. 40 and 222–23.

142. As also Dante *personaggio*'s irascible response to Farinata. See Paratore, "Il Canto X dell'«Inferno»," p. 262.

143. See also *SCG*, iv, 55, 14.

144. Cf. *Malo*, xi, 4. Cf. Padoan, "Il Canto degli Epicurei," pp. 20–21.

145. Benvenuto, at *Inf.* x, 22–24: DDP.

146. As Abrams, "Against the *Contrapasso*," p. 9, points out, Cavalcante's response reflects his sin in two distinct and equally important ways: in regard to his mistaken judgment—continuing (now against all reason) to regard terrestrial life as the only life, and in regard to the irascible passion, despair, that again both (mis)directs his judgment and comes as the consequence of it. His renunciation of hope is the despair that causes someone to seek after heresy and also the despair that follows the inevitable frustration of terrestrial hopes. Boyde, *Perception and Passion*, pp. 133–37, draws attention to a relevant incident recounted later in the *Inferno*. The eight days it takes Ugolino della Gherardesca and his sons to starve to death is usually stressed to point up the horror of their murder and to explain the rage with

which Ugolino attacks Archbishop Ruggieri degli Ubaldini in the ninth circle. But Boyde notes that those eight days also provided plenty of opportunity to pray for the forgiveness that could have kept Ugolino from damnation. Yet never once in those eight days did Ugolino think to pray. Boyde suggests that the horror of the dream Ugolino had at the beginning of his incarceration (*Inf.* xxxiii, 26–36) plunged him into so deep a despair that he was incapable of prayer. Ugolino's punishment (and its place) is for a sin worse than heresy, but this final incident in his life may show the power despair can exercise over the intellect and will.

147. Cf. *ST,* 2a2æ 5, 3; also *Malo,* viii, 1 ad 7. See also Padoan, "Storicismo critico e schematismo dogmatico," *Convivium* n.s. 28 (1960): 716–28, esp. p. 723.

148. Augustine, *de Trin.,* xiii, 16 (21): "And therefore, when it was said in the Gospel that Jesus gave 'the power of becoming sons of God to those who received him' . . . then lest this human weakness—which we see in others and carry ourselves—should despair of so great an excellence, it was there added: 'And the Word was made flesh, and dwelt among us,' so that, from its contrary, we might be persuaded of what appeared incredible" (*de Trin.,* xiii, 9 [12]).

149. 2 *Sent.,* 6, 2, and 2 *Sent.,* 3, 1. Cf. *ST,* 1a 59, 1, and esp. 1a 59, 4. See also *ST,* 1a2æ 22, 3. See also Boyde, *Dante, Philomythes and Philosopher,* p. 191. Boyde also notes that demons are restricted by Dante essentially to the eighth circle (and to the ninth, in the person of Satan), p. 188.

150. Dante's physical description of the demons is as relevant here as this theological doctrine regarding their natures. They are described as having distorted human shapes, and that, of course, is also what these sins are: most properly human (as Dante expresses in both the *Inferno* and the *Convivio*), yet a distortion of that most properly human appetite, the will. Moreover, the punishments of circle eight, specifically, more frequently depend on the distortion or degradation of the human shape than had been true of the punishments in earlier circles, reflecting the same characterization of these sins. Cf. Giovanni Getto, "Il Canto XVII dell'*Inferno,*" in Getto, *Letture dantesche,* pp. 313–29, esp. p. 317.

151. At *ST,* 2a2æ 118, 6, Aquinas argues that covetousness (always in the sense of a passionless acquisitiveness) is a spiritual sin, rather than a carnal one, and explains: "Those pleasures are called carnal which are completed in the bodily senses, such as the pleasures of food and sex. But those pleasures are called spiritual which are completed in the soul's apprehension alone. Therefore, those sins are called carnal which come to completion in carnal pleasures; those are called spiritual sins which come to completion in spiritual pleasures without any carnal pleasure. Covetousness is such a sin; for the covetous man takes pleasure in thinking of himself as the possessor of riches."

152. Cf. Pietrobono's commentary (at *Inf.* xviii, 37: DDP).

153. Cf. Vazzana, *Il Contrapasso*, p. 86. As the smoke that conceals them is also an image of their deceit. See Momigliano, "Il Canto XXV dell'*Inferno*," p. 483.

154. There is great self-irony in his characterizing the speech that so moved his companions as "that little talk" ("questa orazion picciola"; *Inf.* xxvi, 122). Teodolinda Barolini, *The Undivine Comedy, Detheologizing Dante* (Princeton: Princeton University Press, 1992), pp. 105–6, speaks of the flame as reflecting Ulysses' *"ardore*—burning desire." But this cannot be so. While it might be fair to speak of Ulysses as possessing such ardor, it is not for that that he is punished. He is punished within the same flame as Diomedes because they are punished for the same act of sin. But Diomedes did not accompany Ulysses on his last voyage, which is in this episode the signal instance of his undeniable ardor, nor, as far as we know, in any other of his arduous endeavors. Rather, they are both, according to Virgil, punished for an action they committed together, that is, for counseling the Greeks to commit fraud in the case of the Trojan horse ("l'agguato del caval"; *Inf.* xxvi, 59). Nor would it be easy, we should also note, to find any evidence of burning desire in the case of Guido da Montefeltro, the second example of fraudulent counselors, though he too is punished in a flame.

155. This is one piece of the sense of the *contrapasso* of the sorcerers and magicians. They do not so much look "backward," as "in the wrong direction." Some, of course, were simple frauds: they pretended to knowledge they did not have. But others, who could see the future, either by science or divine help (cp. *ST,* 1a 86, 4 and ad 2; 1a2æ 9, 5 ad 3, citing Augustine, *de Genesi ad litteram,* 2.17), are punished here for looking to fraudulent ends of their gifts—profit rather than charity. In Hell, then, they continue to look in the wrong direction. Cf. Richard Kay, "Astrology and Astronomy," in *The Divine Comedy and the Encyclopedia of Arts and Sciences,* pp. 147–62, esp. 158, and Vazzana, *Il Contrapasso,* p. 76. Teiresias is a particularly apposite example, in the Ovidian version Dante has Virgil cite (*Inf.* xx, 40–45): he had already been distorting his natural form while alive; damned, he merely continues this action.

156. Cf. Bosco, "Il Canto XII dell'*Inferno*," pp. 212–13, who points to the irrational and therein almost silly behavior of the Minotaur as exemplary of anger and violence uninformed by the intellect. The violence of the fraudulent of circles eight and nine is the more dangerous precisely because of the direct involvement of the intellect. It begins in calculation rather than rage.

157. Cf. Pietrobono's commentary at *Inf.* xxxi, 90.

158. In the need for assistance in moving from circle eight to circle nine, Dante makes the distinction between simple fraud and betrayal almost as poetically emphatic as the distinction between sins of violence and sins of fraud. There is, indeed, a major difference in the kind of fraud perpetrated in the two circles. All frauds of circle eight could be described as *verbal* frauds: something counterfeit is said to be genuine. All involve lying of a

sort, and the worst of the sins of the eighth circle is lying simply. In the ninth circle, the fraud has moved from words to actions: the betrayers should have *been* something other than they were. It was not in words only that they were fraudulent; they lied in their natures as well.

159. See *ST,* 1a2æ 18, 6; 18, 2; 12, 1; 71, 1; 72, 3.

160. Cf. Nardi, "Il Canto XIX dell'*Inferno,*" pp. 201–2 and 206–7. Nardi stresses three qualities of Dante's classification: (1) that the gravity of sins has to do with their degree of willfulness and consciousness, rather than their objects; (2) that this marks a significant departure from the principles of most theological discussions of the gravity of sin; and (3) that Dante's distinctions explain the nature and relative gravity of sins in a more directly human and affecting way: "Invece i peccati dell'Inferno dantesco sono i peccatori con la loro concreta e umana fisionomia, i peccatori che hanno peccato come peccano gli uomini sulla terra, sì da destare sdegno e compassione, pietà ed orrore, ma soprattutto quella umana commozione, che nessuno mai proverà leggendo gli aridi trattati dei moralisti" (p. 207).

161. As discussed above, the order of the *gironi* in the seventh circle: violence against others, against self, against God and nature, is not self-evident. Though few would dispute that violence against God should be considered to be worse than violence against any other object, why should violence against self be worse than violence against others, especially since it is unjust actions (that is, actions with others as victims) that are the subject of the circles of malicious sin? The answer, I believe, lies in the consideration that, while it is not the case that violence against self is more unjust than violence against others (Aristotle and Aquinas, in fact, say it is impossible, strictly speaking, to be unjust to oneself: *EN,* v, 15; 1138a4–b15, and *In Ethica,* §§1091–1108; *ST,* 2a2æ 59, 3; see also 1a2æ 29, 4), it is the case that violence against self is more *unnatural* than violence against others. It is, therefore, a more depraved operation of the irascible appetite.

162. Even Beatrice describes her flight to Virgil to enlist his aid in rescuing Dante in the standard terms of medieval discussions of the appetites (cf. *Inf.* ii, 109–11).

2. *PURGATORIO*

1. For Aquinas, the sufferings of Purgatory are the repayment of a debt incurred by sin. *ST,* Suppl. Appendix ii, 5. See also *ST,* 1a2æ 87, 6 ad 3. There is no notion of the soul's undergoing any specific rehabilitation. For Aquinas, no soul after death underwent alteration (*SCG,* iv, 95). But for Dante alteration is Purgatory's purpose.

2. We should note explicitly that Virgil's explanation relates to the organization of Purgatory proper. Our discussion in this chapter too will be similarly restricted to investigating the structure and significance of those

seven *gironi*. A brief discussion of the significance of the antepurgatory (whose narrative treatment, after all, takes up no fewer than eight cantos of the *Purgatorio*) is postponed to Appendix 2.

3. Our situation is pointedly expressed by Moore, "The Classification of Sins," pp. 162–63: "The problem may be stated thus:—(a) If (as many suppose) the two systems of Classification are meant to be the *same* (viz. the Seven Deadly Sins), why is there so much *divergence* in the results? (b) If they are (as we maintain) *different,* why is there so much *similarity*?" See also Russo, "«Ma dimmi»," p. 94.

4. Freccero has very cannily pointed out how one's experience of movement in the *Commedia* is filled with surprising reversals of expectation. Cf. "The Prologue Scene," and "Infernal Inversion and Christian Conversion: *Inferno* xxxiv," in *Dante: The Poetics of Conversion*, pp. 25–26 and 180–85. What seems to Dante (and to us) in the undergoing of the journey as a change in direction between Hell and Purgatory turns out, when viewed from the end of the experience, as all movement in one direction. Both aspects—the final, correct understanding *and* the earlier mistaken one—are equally significant to the experience of conversion generally, and to the moral and aesthetic properties of this poem.

5. Those of the first circle of Hell constitute a genuinely special case. Any baptized Christian figure who committed sin might appear either in Hell or Purgatory, depending on repentance or its absence. But the virtuous but unbaptized can have no parallel in Purgatory, since any figures who were both baptized and committed no sin would have no special place, if place at all, in Purgatory. Thus, the first circle of Hell cannot enter into the reciprocal structure of the two realms.

6. See Freccero, "The Prologue Scene," pp. 11–13. Also, Moore, "Unity and Symmetry of Design in the Purgatorio," in *Studies in Dante, Second Series*, pp. 246–68, esp. p. 265.

7. The earliest complete enumeration of these is found in Gregory the Great in the late sixth century A.D. (see below).

8. Cf. Witte, "The Ethical Systems of the *Inferno* and the *Purgatorio*," p. 129.

9. Cf. notes from Jacopo della Lana, Benvenuto, *L'Ottimo commento*, and *Singleton* (at *Purg.* xx, 66–69 and at *Purg.* xx, 103–17: DDP).

10. Cf. Busnelli, *L'Ordinamento morale del Purgatorio dantesco*, 2d ed. (Roma: Civiltà cattolica, 1908), who believes the two realms essentially identical in organization, and attributes their differences primarily to Dante's intention of avoiding a boring repetition of the same divisions (pp. 32–34). Many other earlier attempts to explain the parallels between the two realms look for occult appearances of pride, envy, and sloth in the *Inferno*. Moore, "The Classification of Sins," pp. 163–66, discusses these attempts. Cf. Triolo, *"Ira, Cupiditas, Libido,"* pp. 11–12 and 30. Moore is able to determine reasons for the difference between the two realms, but, by not noticing the

special relationship between sin and vice, is unable to explain the similarities. The same problem appears in Witte, "The Ethical Systems of the *Inferno* and the *Purgatorio*," p. 137.

11. For reasons we will consider shortly, *motive* is not the right term, within the neo-Aristotelian context in which Dante has cast his discussion, for the function avarice performs. We can use the term in its popular sense, since that is so convenient, as long as we remember that more general terms, such as saying that avarice provides the "reason" for a crime, or its "goal" or "purpose," would be safer and, ultimately, more philosophically sound. Cf. Moore, "The Classification of Sins," p. 165. Cf. Russo, "«Ma dimmi»," p. 95 (commenting on a statement in *ST,* 1a2æ 71, 6): "Il peccato è visto come «atto», che si concretizza in parole, in gesti o in desideri peccaminosi; l'altro per cui esso è visto nei suoi presupposti informativi, nelle «ragioni» che precedono l'atto e che dispongono l'anima ad allontanarsi dalla «legge eterna».... Queste «ragioni» del pecatto altro non sono che i vizi capitali."

12. Cf. *Malo,* ii, 2: sin is not deformity, but a deformed *act.*

13. Pagliaro, "Farinata e Cavalcante," p. 190, points out similarities between Farinata and Ulisse, though the two are punished in very different circles of Hell, and also dissimilarities in character between Farinata and Cavalcante, though they are punished together. Hell reflects the actions committed, not the characters of the souls being punished.

14. Dante himself contributes to such ambiguity by having the angel of Purgatory inscribe seven *P*s on his forehead to represent these vices. Nonetheless, his discussion of them in the *Purgatorio* treats them resolutely as vices, rather than as sins in the proper sense. Cf. *Malo, passim* in viii–xv.

15. The first complete description of these vices, in virtually the same form (and in the same order) as that in which they appear in the *Purgatorio,* is in Saint Gregory the Great's *Moralia in Job,* xxxi, 45 ff., *Corpus Christianorum Series Latina,* vol. 143b, ed. M. Adriaen (Turnholt: Brepols, 1985). Gregory speaks of them as "septem principalia vitia." As is relatively common, he separates pride out from the seven, replacing it among the seven with vainglory. These two vices were frequently exchanged for one another. See Reade, *Moral System,* pp. 243–47. Cf. Moore, "The Classification of Sins," pp. 184–204. In the *Purgatorio,* Dante himself has pride discussed in such a way as to combine characteristics of vainglory with it. Cf. *Purg.* xi, 91: "Oh vana gloria dell'umane posse!" in apposition to the *superbia* being purged in the first *girone.* E.g., *ST,* 1a2æ 84, 3 and 84, 4. Cf. *Malo,* viii, 1; also, 2 *Sent.,* 42, 6. See also Trucchi's interesting note (at *Purg.* xvii, 133–30: DDP).

16. Also, *EN,* ii, 4; 1105b25–35, and *EN,* ii, 5; 1106a15–23. Cf. Aquinas, *de Virtutibus in communi,* a. 3, and *ST,* 1a2æ 50, 5, esp. ad 1.

17. *ST,* 1a2æ 51, 3.

18. Cf. Russo, "«Ma dimmi»," p. 97.

19. It is action that acquires merit or demerit: *ST,* 1a2æ 21, 4. Cf. *Malo,* ii, 2 ad 9. Also *EN,* i, 12; 1101b10–1102a5.

20. Cf. Witte, "The Ethical Systems of the *Inferno* and the *Purgatorio*," pp. 129–32. Habits, as the passage from Aquinas cited above declares, may exist without being realized in action. Would unfulfilled bad habits need purging in Purgatory? That is, would the continent need to spend time in Purgatory to remove or reform the bad habits they repressed during their lives? As we have discussed, they do not deserve punishment, for they never acted on these bad habits. But as habits, they could still be improved by the corrections of Purgatory. My own conviction, given the purposes for which Dante believed Purgatory had been created, is that he would say that the continent do indeed need the corrections of Purgatory. He does not, however, provide any unequivocal poetic example of an individual in Purgatory for evil habits though he or she had committed no sinful action. See Witte, "The Ethical Systems of the *Inferno* and the *Purgatorio*," p. 132. (It may be that Sapia, at *Purg.* xiii, 106–32, does provide such an example. Her envy does not appear to have resulted in any action, beyond gloating, with regard to her fellow citizens. But might her one impulsive remark have been an instance of the sin of blasphemy? For that reason we cannot be sure that Dante would not have seen her as an active sinner as well as someone possessed of the vice of envy.)

21. Cf. the *Nota* to the *Inferno* in Bosco and Reggio's edition (DDP). They argue that the acts of the penitents have been canceled; what remains to be rehabilitated is the "inclination" to sin.

22. See also *ST,* 3a 86, 5. Cf. Russo, "«Ma dimmi»," p. 96: "Infatti nei peccatori del *Purgatorio* l'atto specifico del peccato è stato cancellato dal loro pentimento, che li ha resi degni della semplice espiazione, ma in essi è rimasto l'abito, (o gli abiti), la «ragione» (o le «ragioni») formali del peccato ... da cui devono purificarsi." Also Vazzana, *Il Contrapasso,* p. 111; Paul J. Wadell, C. P., *Friends of God, Virtues and Gifts in Aquinas* (New York: Peter Lang, 1991), p. 92; Pagliaro, "«Le tre disposizion ...»," p. 248; Moore, "Classification of Sins," pp. 165–66; and Witte, "The Ethical Systems of the *Inferno* and the *Purgatorio*," pp. 130–32.

23. *ST,* 1a 2æ 55, 1.

24. Cf. *In Ethica,* §375. Also *ST,* 1a2æ 87, 6 ad 3, and *EN,* ii, 3; 1104b18: "Medicines work naturally by contraries." Also, *In Ethica,* §249: "These virtues are perfected in us by application, so that, I mean, when we have acted many times according to reason, a new form is imprinted in the appetite by force of reason. And this impression is nothing other than a moral virtue." See also Gilbert, *Dante's Conception of Justice,* pp. 114–17.

25. Throughout his *Il Contrapasso,* Vazzana strives to discover a single principle of *contrapasso* in all three realms (see his declaration of this goal at pp. 6–7). As has already been mentioned, and will be further discussed below, there is indeed one single principle of justice at work in all the realms, as Vazzana also sees. All of the dead are given what they desire (see *Il Contrapasso,* p. 34). In trying to extend this consistency of justice even to what each

soul undergoes, however, Vazzana forces himself to interpret the corrections of Purgatory as images of the vices, rather than of their opposites. What should be remembered is that the souls of Purgatory desire these corrections by opposites as ardently as they had desired the vices while alive. Thus, they too receive what they are most desiring at the moment Dante encounters them.

26. *In Ethica*, §253. The same ethical principle is also a part of the explanation of the *contrapasso* in Hell, for the eternal reiteration by the damned of the actions that led to their damnation is a means of eternally reconfirming them in that sin, and thus justifying their damnation. Cf. *SCG*, iv, 93. The delight the damned take in these actions provides the remainder of the explanation of the *contrapasso* for Hell. Also, Cogan, "Delight, Punishment, and the Justice of God," pp. 38–40.

27. See also *ST*, 1a2æ 87, 6 ad 3.

28. The continuation of the citation from the *Ethics* makes its appropriateness clear: "Children are called happy as it were in hope, for they are still lacking—as we have discussed earlier—[the having acted] through perfect virtue during a complete life" (*EN*, i, 9; 1100a1–5).

29. See Moore, "Unity and Symmetry of Design," p. 263. An earlier use of the Beatitudes as virtues can be found in Conrad of Saxony, *Speculum Beatæ Mariæ Virginis* (previously attributed to Bonaventure), Lect. 15. Like Dante, Conrad proposes the Beatitudes as virtues that are the opposites of the seven capital vices (though he aligns the Beatitudes with different vices than Dante does), and, moreover, also like Dante, Conrad does this in the context of arguing that Mary is the exemplar of all of these virtues. See also Moore, "Classification of Sins," pp. 194–95, and Busnelli, *L'Ordinamento morale*, p. 97.

30. Cf. *ST*, 1a2æ 49, 1 (citing *Metaphys.*, v, 20; 1022b10–12): "A habit is a disposition by which what is disposed is disposed well or ill." See also *In Metaphys.*, §§1062–64.

31. Cf. *In Ethica*, §1125: "The virtue of anything whatever is determined to its characteristic operation, for it is to this that the thing is perfected by the virtue. That habit is said to be best by which any operation is most perfectly accomplished."

32. Cf. Aquinas, *de Virtutibus in communi*, a. 3.

33. Cf. *In Ethica*, §308.

34. *ST*, 1a 2æ 57, 1 and 58, 2.

35. Also *ST*, 1a2æ 50, 5, esp. ad 1.

36. For a fuller discussion of the structure of appetition and action as Dante would have most likely articulated it, see Cogan, "Delight, Punishment, and the Justice of God," pp. 32–35. Rocco Montano, *Il Canto XVII del «Purgatorio»* (Firenze: Le Monnier, 1964), pp. 30–31, explains Virgil's description of the appetitive nature of love as the understanding of a pagan who did not know charity. But, as discussed in Cogan, it is deeply significant

that Virgil's discussion exactly parallels Aquinas' idiosyncratic description of the process of appetition. Here is one of the signal instances in which we see Dante relying on Aquinas or on other Thomistic sources. Also Busnelli, *L'Ordinamento morale*, pp. 45–46.

37. Cf. Aquinas, *de Caritate*, ed. A. Odetto, in *Quæstiones disputatæ*, vol. 2, 9th ed. (Torino and Roma: Marietti, 1953), a. 2: "Love is the principle of all voluntary affections."

38. *In de An.*, §830. Cf. *In Ethica*, §§291–92. Cf. Albert, *De Anima*, iii, iv, c. 3, p. 231, iii, iv, c. 5, pp. 233–34, and iii, iv, c. 7, p. 236.

39. See Reade, *Moral System*, pp. 126–41 and 260–61.

40. The common underlying structure of the two realms also guarantees the propriety of Virgil's explanations to Dante regarding the purifications souls undergo in Purgatory. One might question the value of pagan comments on an essentially Christian activity. But in Dante's exposition of the capital vices, these vices too (just like the sins of Hell) have a natural origin that it is reasonable to expect even a pagan to understand.

41. Also, *de Caritate*, a. 12: "The habit of virtue inclines a man to right action according as by means of it the man has a right estimation of the end."

42. It is because vices propose the ends of action that I remarked earlier that it would not be strictly speaking correct to speak of them as the "motives" of action, except perhaps in a rather loose sense, which indeed we frequently use in ordinary conversation. But the motive, or "moving cause," is the efficient cause of action. It is as formal causes proposing ends that the vices are capable of disposing powers to later sins that may exhibit characteristics different from those of the vice. Cf. *ST*, 1a2æ 84, 3; also *Malo*, viii, 1, and Reade, *Moral System*, pp. 58–61 and 255–58. Also, *de Caritate*, a. 7, ad 17.

43. Cf. *ST*, 1a2æ 71, 1. Also *Malo*, xiii, 3, where Aquinas, citing Gregory (*Moralia in Job*, xxxi, 31), explains how the vice of avarice can result in acts of violence or fraud.

44. Moreover, the potential variability in the manner of pursuing goods would by nature be especially high when we are considering the actions of those suffering from vices—that is, those who pursue the wrong ends or react badly to certain passions, since vicious habits are by definition disorderly, and can therefore be expected to be less predictable with respect to the actions that might implement them.

45. Seung, *Fragile Leaves*, pp. 36–44, while matching *gironi* to circles of Hell in a way very similar to the one we will follow, fails to take account of this distinction, and forces his argument to make each vice of Purgatory appear in the parallel position in Hell. As we have seen, this is not possible—and now we can see is not desirable—to do.

46. Cf. *Malo*, viii, 3, and the individual discussions of each of the capital vices (ix–xv). Cf. Reade, *Moral System*, pp. 260–61 and 269. See also T. K. Seung, "The Metaphysics of the *Commedia*," though Seung does not

draw or exploit the distinction between sins (in the *Inferno*) and vices (in the *Purgatorio*).

47. Aquinas associated vices with appetites in two different ways. In *Malo*, viii–xv, pride (as a special case) was associated with both the will and the irascible appetite; anger (perhaps with vainglory) was associated with the irascible appetite; envy, sloth, avarice, gluttony, and lust were all associated with the concupiscible appetite. In *In 2 Sent.*, xlii, 2, 3, however, pride, vainglory, anger, and envy are all associated with the irascible appetite, sloth, avarice, gluttony, and lust with the concupiscible. It is essentially this latter order that Reade uses, *Moral System*, pp. 260–61 and 269, although he places pride in the will as a special form of vice, and later notes that sloth is concerned with the arduous goods more regularly associated with the irascible appetite (pp. 306 and 311).

48. Albert the Great had spoken of anger and desire (he uses a more properly Aristotelian way of referring to them than as appetitive faculties of irascibility and concupiscence) as naturally determined to their matter: *Super Ethica*, Book 5, Lectio 3, §375. Dante's own sense of these appetites sees them as considerably more malleable than that, but there can be no doubt that in their primary operations they are more closely attached to their natural matter than the will is to its objects. This is surely the foundation of the explanation of why the upper three *gironi* of Purgatory seem to resemble the upper three circles of Hell more closely than the lower *gironi* the lower circles. Both actions and habits of these appetites ought to resemble one another since both are, for the most part, determined by the same objects.

49. One other medieval source makes a very similar distribution, though I believe it very unlikely that Dante would have consulted this author. See Alcuin, *de Animæ ratione liber ad Eulaliam virginem, PL*, 101, 640c–d.

50. Envy: *Malo*, x, 3; cf. *ST*, 2a2æ 36, 3. Sloth: *Malo*, xi, 1; cf. *ST*, 2a2æ 35, 1.

51. *ST*, 2a2æ 118, 7, 118, 2, and 118, 3. Cf. *ST*, 2a2æ 117, 5, and *Malo*, xiii, 1.

52. *ST*, 1a2æ 36, 2. Aquinas derives all sins and vices from the passions of the concupiscible appetite solely—*Malo*, viii, 1 ad 20; also *ST*, 2a2æ 188, 7—though he associates the vices with all three appetites.

53. Cf. *ST*, 1a 2æ 46, 1.

54. Though Aquinas' attribution of vice to appetite is different from Dante's, he too distinguishes sadnesses of different origins and natures. Cf. *ST*, 2a2æ 158, 6 ad 1.

55. Cf. *ST*, 2a2æ 162, 3, ad 4, citing Prosper of Aquitaine, *Liber sententiarum*, sent. 294: "Pride is said to be 'love of one's own excellence' insofar as from this disordered love is caused that presumption of surpassing others; which properly pertains to pride." Also *ST*, 1a2æ 84, 2, and *Malo*, viii, 1; viii, 2; and viii, 3.

56. See Chimenz, Giacalone, and Bosco and Reggio (at *Purg.* xvii, 115–20:

DDP) and Porena (in his final *Nota* to canto xvii, "Nota finale: l'ordinamento morale del purgatorio": DDP). The standard definition is that cited by Porena: *stima esagerata di sé.*

57. Busnelli, *L'Ordinamento morale,* pp. 82–83, also stresses the interpersonal nature of Dante's conception of pride. See especially p. 83 on its association with injustice.

58. Cf. Busnelli, *L'Ordinamento morale,* p. 79.

59. Even Aquinas, though locating the pride of humans in the irascible appetite, locates the pride of demons in their will: *Malo,* viii, 3. See also *ST,* 2a2æ 162, 3 and 1a2æ 50, 6.

60. Cf. Tobia R. Toscano, "Canto X," in *Lectura Dantis neapolitana, Purgatorio,* ed. Pompeo Giannantonio (Napoli: Loffredo, 1989), pp. 205–25, esp. p. 209. Cf. Augustin Renaudet, *Dante humaniste* (Paris: "Les Belles Lettres," 1952), p. 203, and Busnelli, *L'Ordinamento morale,* p. 98.

61. Cf. *EN,* ii, 5; 1105b22–34, and *In Ethica,* §298. Also, *ST,* 1a2æ 59, 1 and 1a2æ 24, 1. *ST,* 2a2æ 158, 1 and 2 distinguish the passion, anger, from the vice.

62. See also *Par.* xii, 100–102; and *ST,* 2a2æ 123, 10: "the brave man employs moderate anger."

63. See the notes of Benvenuto, Scartazzini, and Giacalone (at *Purg.* xvi, 1–7: DDP). Also, Boyde, *Perception and Passion,* pp. 249–50, and Vincenzo Cioffari, "Canto XVI," in *Lectura Dantis neapolitana, Purgatorio,* pp. 337–47, esp. p. 338, who, following Benvenuto, sees in the smoke the mental confusion caused in the soul by anger. Cf. Vazzana, *Il Contrapasso,* pp. 125–27. But even this explanation makes the correction of this vice an image of the vice itself, not of its opposed virtue. (In Vazzana's case, this is consistent with his general interpretation that all of the corrections of Purgatory are images of the vices.)

64. Though Vazzana believes the trials of those undergoing purgation reflect the nature of their vices, he gives a description of the smoke in which the angry are purged which would seem more appropriate to its opposite, or at least to its restraint: "Qui non c'è più la passione, ma un ricordo di essa, il fumo" (*Il Contrapasso,* p. 125).

65. Cf. *ST,* 2a2æ 162, 3: "And it is in this way that we attribute anger to God and the angels: not as a passion, but as the judgment of justice pronouncing judgment." See Boyde, *Perception and Passion,* pp. 268–70.

66. Moore, "The Classification of Sins," p. 198, cites Brunetto Latini's attributing the origin of sloth to anger.

67. *ST,* 2a2æ 35, 1; cf. *Malo,* xi, 1 ad 6.

68. *Malo,* xi, 2.

69. *ST,* 1a2æ 62, 3 and ad 2; also *ST,* 2a2æ 17, 1. As we will see below, Dante did see a connection between the virtue, hope, and irascibility. Even here, Dante's use of an example of the lack of martial zeal (the fainthearted Trojans) and of examples of simple cowardice (Statius' explanation of the

reason for his need to purge this vice, *Purg.* xxii, 89–90) as explanations of the lack of active pursuit of spiritual duties in this world inescapably associates the vice here purged with concrete, indeed corporeal, failures that we recognize in terms of this world. Dante thus links this vice to the normal operation of the irascible appetite.

70. Cf. Montano, *Il Canto XVII del «Purgatorio»*, p. 31.

71. Aquinas links heresy and sloth at *Malo,* viii, 1 ad 7, in respect of their flight from spiritual goods—a description much closer to Dante's understanding of the sin of heresy.

72. Dante's dream before moving from the fourth to the fifth *girone* (that is, from the last *girone* of irascibility to the first of concupiscence, *Purg.* xix, 7–33) is appropriate to the moment of the narrative. The emotional content of the dream is clearly concupiscent, and refers to the appetite whose vices we will next see purged. Dante is saved in the dream by two figures, Virgil and the *donna santa,* who in different ways represent reason, for the vices of this appetite develop when the reason does not control it, and virtue is restored by application of the reason. Finally, the female figure who represents these vices or their objects is ugly or beautiful by operation of Dante's imagination, and this detail is especially appropriate as Dante enters the *girone* of avarice, where the imagination has transformed objects not naturally desirable in themselves (that is, money) into objects of concupiscence.

73. Cf. Gilbert, *Dante's Conception of Justice,* p. 132.

74. Cf. Fernando Figurelli, "Il Canto XXV del «Purgatorio»," in Casa di Dante in Roma, *Nuove letture dantesche,* vol. 5, 1969–70 (Firenze: Le Monnier, 1972): 33–67, esp. p. 66. Also, Gilbert, *Dante's Conception of Justice,* pp. 136–38; Boyde, *Perception and Passion,* p. 289; and Busnelli, *L'Ordinamento morale,* pp. 21–24.

75. With Dante substituting pride for vainglory in Gregory. Gregory writes: "There are seven principal vices: . . . vainglory, envy, anger, sadness [sloth], avarice, gluttony, lust" (*Moralia in Job,* xxxi, 45). Hugh of St. Victor, *Summa sententiarum septem tractatibus distincta,* iii, 16; *PL,* 176, 113d, follows Gregory's order but substitutes pride for vainglory. Aquinas treats the vices in a common variant of Gregory's order (*Malo,* ix–xv): vainglory, envy, acedia [sloth], anger, avarice, gluttony, lust (pride is dealt with separately and earlier; *Malo,* viii). See Moore, "Classification of Sins," pp. 184–201, for alternate orders and sets of these vices.

76. By contrast, Dante alters the scriptural order of the Beatitudes. The nature of that alteration is determined by the affinity of a given Beatitude to a given capital vice, and thus Dante's reordering of the Beatitudes is itself another indication of his adaptation of the Beatitudes for use as the virtues (or the acts of the virtues) of the appetites.

77. *ST,* 1a 95, 1 and 95, 3.

78. As Montano has rightly pointed out, *Il Canto XVII del «Purgatorio»,* pp. 32 and 37, Dante has two guides for his transit through Purgatory. As

Statius takes over more and more of the explanation, it is not that we deny what we have already learned from Virgil, but, rather, that we reinterpret it from a new perspective. Indeed, the very moment at which the need for such reinterpretation arises is also the moment at which Dante *poeta* has Virgil pass the explanatory role to Statius.

79. The pseudo-Augustinian *de Spiritu et anima* did maintain that these powers continued their operation in the separated soul. It is possible that Franciscan circles may have given this work more authority than Aquinas did, and possible that Dante may have felt influenced by them. Aquinas explicitly cites the work in this article of the *Summa theologica*, and explicitly denies it authority on the question. My inclination is to believe that Dante followed Aquinas' rejection of the text; nor does the doctrine that Dante articulates require this text for its basis. See also Aquinas, *Quæstiones de Anima*, a. 19, and *de Virtutibus in communi*, a. 4 ad 3; *ST*, 1a2æ 67, 1 ad 3.

80. Indeed, this is very much the interpretation that Busnelli follows, *L'Ordinamento morale*, p. 4. Recognizing that the rehabilitations of Purgatory must be of faculties that endure after death, yet believing that only memory, intellect, and will endure as faculties, Busnelli tries to attribute all of the defects corrected in Purgatory to these three faculties.

81. In the *Convivio*, Dante makes a tripartite distinction, based on the treatise *de Causis*, between an animating power, the intellectual power, and a divine power, which he there associates with the possible intellect (*Conv.*, iv, xxi, 4–10). It may be that that distinction underlies Statius' statement, in which case the "human" faculties would be memory, will, intellect; the "divine" the possible intellect. In this case too the sensitive powers would here seem to have fallen away. Cf. Bruno Nardi, "Le Citazioni dantesche del «Liber de Causis»," in *Saggi di filosofia dantesca* (Firenze: «La Nuova Italia», 1967), pp. 81–109, esp. pp. 91–92 and 94.

82. See Boyde, *Dante, Philomythes and Philosopher*, p. 280.

83. This is the most likely reason for saying that both the human and the divine powers exist in the separated soul *in virtute*: they leave the material body to which they had been originally adapted as separated powers now capable of informing other substances (here air).

84. On human life having two standards, one of this world, one of the next, see *ST*, 2a2æ 17, 1. Also, Mario Trovato, "Dante and the Tradition of the 'Two Beatitudes,'" in *Lectura Dantis Newberryana*, ed. Paolo Cherchi and Antonio C. Mastrobuono, vol. 1 (Evanston, Ill.: Northwestern University Press, 1988), pp. 19–36. On the cardinal virtues of this world, Aquinas, *de Virtutibus cardinalibus*, ed. A. Odetto, in *Quæstiones disputatæ*, vol. 2, 9th ed. (Torino and Roma: Marietti, 1953), a. 1; *ST*, 1a2æ 62, 1.

85. See Toscano, "Canto X," in *Lectura Dantis neapolitana, Purgatorio*, p. 208, and Hermann Gmelin, "Il Canto X del Purgatorio," in Getto, *Letture dantesche*, pp. 869–80, esp. pp. 874–75, who both find the source of using the

Beatitudes as virtues in the *Speculum Beatæ Mariæ Virginis*. Gmelin finds there also the source for some of the images of the *exempla*.

86. To have used the seven capital vices to organize Hell would thus have been unjust, not only because the source and date of their articulation is definitively Christian, such that one could not fairly expect pagans to know them, but also, as we now realize, because they describe the origins of sin from the standpoint of it as an obstacle to salvation, which is closed to pagans in any case. Using the capital vices in Purgatory is appropriate, however, insofar as only Christians would pursue this route, and also because by conjoining them to the Beatitudes, it would be possible to reveal virtues that, in replacing these vices, aim at perfect operation beyond merely human action.

87. A similar adaptation of new virtues to new purposes is used as the explanation of the relation between the cardinal virtues and the three theological virtues, faith, hope, and charity. Aquinas distinguishes these different sets of virtues by the different ends for which they are intended. The moral virtues are ordered to a natural human end, and therefore are also within human power to acquire. By contrast, the theological virtues aim at an end beyond nature, and, indeed, are for this reason beyond human power to acquire: "Man is perfected by virtue in those activities by which he is ordered to happiness, as was explained above [*ST,* 1a2æ 5, 7]. Now, there is a double happiness or blessedness for humans, as was also stated above [a. 5]. One is proportionate to human nature; a happiness, that is, which man can achieve by natural principles. But the other is a blessedness exceeding human nature, which man can achieve by divine virtue alone, in accordance with a certain participation in divinity, about which it is written (2 Pet. 1: 4) that through Christ we are made *partakers of the divine nature*. Since blessedness of this sort exceeds the proportion of human nature, the natural human principles by which men come to act well according to their own measure no longer suffice for ordering men to this blessedness. Hence it is necessary that there be, divinely added, certain other principles by which a man may be ordered to supernatural blessedness, just as by natural principles he is ordered to his connatural end, not, however, without divine assistance. Such principles are those virtues which are called 'theological'" (*ST,* 1a2æ 62, 1). I should hasten to add that Dante is neither equating the Beatitudes with the theological virtues, nor replacing the theological virtues with them. Dante certainly accepts that the theological virtues must be acquired in order for a soul to achieve a life in Heaven. But as far as the narrative of the *Commedia* is concerned, the standard theological virtues have presumably already been acquired before a soul is allowed to enter Purgatory proper. Dante's use of the Beatitudes is for an end beyond that of the theological virtues.

88. It should be noted that this problem would not disappear simply by choosing an association of capital vices with appetitive faculties different from the one we have made. Aquinas, as we have mentioned, associated sloth

to the concupiscible appetite, rather than the irascible. Even Aquinas' assignment encounters the same problem. Insofar as *any* vice is assigned to one of the sensitive appetites, if there is a Beatitude or some other virtue that replaces that vice as a virtue enduring into the next life, the fact of replacement carries the implication that the power for which there is such a virtue also endures in the separated soul.

89. Boyde, *Dante, Philomythes and Philosopher,* p. 270, points out that the issue could have been far more poignantly raised as Dante and Casella vainly try to embrace one another at almost the exact beginning of the *Purgatorio* (*Purg.* ii, 76–84). See also Elvio Guagnini, "Canto XXV," in *Lectura Dantis neapolitana, Purgatorio,* pp. 487–502, esp. pp. 488–89.

90. Cf. Figurelli, "Il Canto XXV del «Purgatorio»," esp. pp. 59–60.

91. The attempt to identify Dante's sources has often led readers to lose track of the way in which Dante has adapted the account of the origin of the soul to the needs of the explanation of aerial bodies. Dante's theory of the origin of the soul cannot be attributed to any single authority, as we will explore during this discussion. The most magisterial survey of possible sources is that by Bruno Nardi, "L'Origine dell'anima umana secondo Dante," in *Studi di filosofia medievale* (Roma: Edizioni di storia e letteratura, 1960), pp. 9–68. It is Nardi's contention that Dante's doctrine in the *Commedia* follows that of Albert the Great. As will be clear, I disagree with this identification, which depends on Nardi himself attributing to the *Commedia* assertions that are never made in the passages under consideration.

92. In two important essays, Bruno Nardi makes a serious and significant error in regard to this specific operation. Relying on a statement by Dante in the *Convivio* (iv, 21, 4) and on similar statements in Albert the Great, whose doctrine Nardi sees as the source of Dante's position, Nardi concludes that the formative function is actually performed by a *virtù formativa* found in the sperm, which operates before the creation of the soul. See Nardi, "Il Canto XXV del *Purgatorio,*" in *Letture dantesche,* ed. Getto, pp. 1173–91, esp. pp. 1182 and 1189, and "L'Origine dell'anima umana secondo Dante," pp. 42 and 50–52. Such, indeed, is the position of Albert, and of Dante in the *Convivio.* But here in the *Commedia,* Dante is explicit that these operations are operations of a soul that is already in existence: it is of the *anima fatta* that the formative powers operate. The significance of Dante's revision between the *Convivio* and the *Commedia* will become clear as we consider the nature of the soul whose formative power conducts these operations.

93. This perfect animal development includes even the articulation of the embryo's brain, for it is only following the completion of that stage that God intervenes. See Guagnini, "Canto XXV," p. 491. See also Boyde, *Dante, Philomythes and Philosopher,* p. 275.

94. Cf. *In de An.,* §§224–25: "The substantial form is what causes something to exist in actuality simply. An accidental form, therefore, is present only in a subject already existing in actuality. . . . It is clear from this that it is

impossible that there be multiple substantial forms of any single thing, since the first would cause the thing actually to exist (simply), and all the rest would come to be present in a subject that already exists in actuality, and thus would only be present accidentally in this already existing subject." Also, *SCG*, ii, 58.

95. For an indication of how important this issue had been in the generation preceding Dante, see Bruno Nardi, "Anima e corpo nel pensiero di San Tommaso," in *Studi di filosofia medievale*, pp. 163–91, esp. pp. 166–71.

96. Nardi, "Il Canto XXV del Purgatorio," in Getto, *Letture dantesche*, pp. 1173–91, mistakenly expresses the relation (p. 1185) as one in which the animal soul develops through being a vegetable soul to its final animal form. That is not the distinction Dante is having Statius make. The animal soul has always been an animal soul, distinguished from a vegetable soul both by being able to perform animal functions (which the vegetable soul cannot) and also by being able to perform vegetable functions as well. The animal soul will not "outgrow" its vegetable functions. As a superior soul it possesses the capacity for those functions too.

97. Aquinas, *de Unitate intellectus contra Averroistas*, in *Opuscula philosophica*, ed. R. M. Spiazzi, O.P. (Torino and Roma: Marietti, 1954), c. 1 (§205, in this edition).

98. See Boyde, *Dante, Philomythes and Philosopher*, p. 274.

99. See also Ingrid Craemer-Ruegenberg, "The Priority of Soul as Form and Its Proximity to the First Mover," in *Albert the Great, Commemorative Essays*, ed. Francis J. Kovach and Robert W. Shahan (Norman: University of Oklahoma Press, 1980), pp. 49–62, esp. p. 60, and Nardi, "Anima e corpo," p. 180.

100. See Nardi, "L'Origine dell'anima umana secondo Dante," pp. 10–12 and *passim* throughout section two of the essay.

101. Aquinas, *de Unitate intellectus*, c. 1 (§205).

102. Cf. *ST*, 1a 76, 3 ad 3; and 118, 2 ad 2.

103. See Bruno Nardi, "Alberto Magno e San Tommaso," in *Studi di filosofia medievale*, pp. 103–17, esp. p. 106. But neither does Dante subscribe to Albert's notion that the human soul is intellectual *in potento*, in the sense that Albert had also said that the sensitive soul is first merely vegetative, though sensitive *in potento*.

104. It is precisely on the issue of development that Dante diverges markedly from Albert, and it is for this reason that Nardi is in error in attributing Dante's doctrine to Albert. There is no notion in Dante of the human soul's having a specific potential to accept God's implanting of its intellectual nature. Cf. Nardi, "Alberto Magno e San Tommaso," p. 107. (See also Bruno Nardi, "L'anima umana secondo Sigieri," in *Studi di filosofia medievale*, pp. 151–61, esp. pp. 153–55 and 160.) As Dante describes it, that moment marks a complete transformation of the nature the soul had up to that intervention (a position that Nardi seems to accept in "Il Canto XXV del

Purgatorio," p. 1187). Similarly, there is nothing in Statius' discussion of the earlier stages of the embryo's development to suggest that Dante believed an animal soul was first vegetative in act, though animal in potential. According to Statius in passages already cited, even as it performs the vegetative functions, that animal soul is already an animal soul in act—it is acting vegetatively in a way that only an animal soul can.

105. As mentioned earlier, Dante shows no evidence of believing that the human soul had a potential for the receipt of the new spirit. Statius' description, rather, describes a fundamental, miraculous, and completely unnatural transformation. While Nardi is right in saying that this doctrine is not Aquinas' supersession, it is closer in one important sense to Aquinas than to Albert. In Aquinas' theory of supersession, a soul of a wholly new (intellectual) character replaces the earlier animal soul. That is what Statius too describes, though Statius' account does not say that a new soul is implanted to replace the old, but rather that the old soul is transformed into the new. Boyde, *Dante, Philomythes and Philosopher,* p. 279, likens the act to that of God's breathing life into Adam, to an individual recreation of the origin of the species. In the context of discussions we will pursue in the third chapter, however, perhaps Dante's allusion is rather to the incarnation.

106. Cf. James A. Weisheipl, "The Celestial Movers in Medieval Physics," *The Thomist* 24 (1961): 286–326, esp. p. 311. Did Dante have in mind the mysterious tag from Aristotle's *Physics* (cited by Albert), "homo ex materia generat hominem et sol" (*Phys.*, ii, 2; 194b13: materially, man generates man, with the sun too)?

107. Cf. Nardi, "Anima e corpo," p. 169. Nor is it one sort of soul atop another. Earlier in the *Purgatorio* Dante made an explicit reference to the error of believing the human soul was constituted of multiple souls:

> Quando per dilettanze o ver per doglie
> che alcuna virtù nostra comprenda
> l'anima bene ad essa si raccoglie,
> par ch'a nulla potenza più intenda;
> e questo è contra quello error che crede
> ch'un anima sovr'altra in noi s'accenda.
> (*Purg.* iv, 1–6)

108. Aquinas, *de Unitate intellectus,* c. 1 (§198).

109. Even Aquinas had stated that both separated souls and demons could suffer from corporeal fire: *ST,* Suppl. 70, 3 and Suppl. 97, 5; *SCG,* iv, 90. But this is a reversal of Dante's intention: the suffering is spiritual; the aerial bodies merely reflect that spiritual suffering.

110. Bruno Nardi, "La filosofia di Dante," in *Grande antologia filosofica,* ed. Umberto Antonio Padovano and Andrea Mario Moschetti, vol. 4, *Il Pensiero cristiano (la scolastica)* (Milano: Marzorati, 1954), pp. 1149–1253, esp. p. 1186, fn. 1, mistakes the role of the aerial body. See also Guelfo

Cavanna, *Il Canto XXV del Purgatorio* (Firenze: Sansoni, 1908), p. 29. That body is not the occasion of the soul's suffering; rather, it merely reflects spiritual desires and sufferings the soul is already undergoing. The same was true in Hell, of course, but the greater permanence of the state in which the damned appear to us, as well as the physical darkness of Hell, obscured that for us. Since matter is informed by the soul, the damned in Hell will always resemble their sins and their sins' disorders. The damned will never change, and what will not change about them are precisely the soul's disorders that brought them to Hell. Thus, their aerial bodies will always bear the impression of these disorders, and the permanence of that state created an illusion of corporality for their bodies. The saved in Purgatory will exhibit their disorderly states until their vices are corrected. Cf. *ST,* 3a 86, 5, and Waddell, *Friends of God,* p. 92. Their aerial bodies also bear the impression of their disordered faculties, but only for a time. And if the blessed we encounter in Heaven in the next *cantica* do not look like the souls we have seen in the first two *cantiche,* it is for the same reason. For their surroundings bear the impression of their orderly souls, and that impression looks very different from the appearances with which we are most familiar.

111. *ST,* 1a 77, 5 and 76, 5 ad 2.

112. Guagnini, "Canto XXV," pp. 500–501, also stresses the spiritual transformation of Dante's subject which occurs with Statius' explanation of the origin of the human soul, an explanation that, as Guagnini puts it, shows "le ragioni della spiritualità umana, di un'anima improntata dall'influenza della virtù divina e—al tempo stesso—capace di sussumere (sia pure transformandoli e trasfigurandoli) i tratti della materialità e della sensibilità naturale."

113. Any single power may be perfected in its operation by multiple virtues insofar as it has multiple functions to perform: *ST,* 1a2æ 54, 1. We know the virtues of these faculties adapted to their worldly functions; the *Purgatorio* shows us a new set of virtues adapted to otherworldly functions.

114. Aquinas speaks in other places of the habits of even the cardinal virtues remaining after death, though adapted to completely new acts: *de Virtutibus cardinalibus,* a. 4. Cf. 3 *Sent.,* 33, 3.

115. *Malo,* viii, 3: "Any object to which the irascible or concupiscible appetite can be drawn the will may also be drawn to.... But the will is drawn to its object without passion, since it uses no corporeal organ, but the irascible and concupiscible are drawn with passion. Hence, all motions which occur in the irascible and concupiscible with passion (such as love, joy, hope, and so forth) can also occur in the will without passion."

116. E.g., of envy, *Malo,* x, 2 ad 2; of sloth, *Malo,* xi, 3; of anger, *Malo,* xii, 3 and ad 6. Cf. *ST,* 2a2æ 36, 3.

117. Cf. Aquinas, *Quæstiones de Anima,* 19 ad 7: "In the separated soul there is neither joy nor anger insofar as these are irascible and concupiscible acts, for these are in the sensitive part; but, rather, insofar as by these are

designated movements of the will, which is in the intellectual part." Also *Quæstiones de Anima,* 19 ad 8, and *ST,* 1a 77, 8 ad 5.

118. Cf. *ST,* 1a2æ 67, 1 ad 3: "In the state before the resurrection, the irrational parts will not be in the soul actually, but only in their roots in its essence, as stated in the First Part [1a 77, 8]. For this reason neither will virtues of this sort [fortitude and temperance] exist actually, except in their roots, namely in the reason and will in which are certain 'nurseries' of these virtues, as stated above [1a2æ 63, 1]."

119. Also *ST,* 2a2æ 162, 3: "But the irascible faculty can be understood more broadly, namely as it pertains to the intellectual appetite, to which anger is also sometimes attributed. And it is in this way that we attribute anger to God and the angels: not as a passion, but as the judgment of justice pronouncing judgment." Cf. Aquinas, *Quæstiones de Anima,* 19 ad 17: "The virtues and vices which are of the irrational parts will not remain in the separated soul unless in their principles; for of all the virtues, the seeds are in the will and the reason." See also Aquinas, *de Virtutibus cardinalibus,* a. 4, and *de Virtutibus in communi,* a. 4, ad 3. Cf. 3 *Sent.,* 33, 3.

120. Cf. *ST,* 1a2æ 114, 1: "Therefore, a man's merit with God cannot exist except according to a presupposition of the divine ordering; namely, so that from God—as if as a reward—a man attains to, by his own operation, that for which God delegated to him the power of operating; just as natural things by their own proper motions and operations attain to those things for which God ordained them."

3. *PARADISO*

1. See, for example,

> O voi ch'avete li 'ntelletti sani,
>   mirate la dottrina che s'asconde
>   sotto 'l velame de li versi strani.
> (*Inf.* ix, 61–63)

And

> Aguzza qui, lettor, ben li occhi al vero,
>   chè 'l velo è ora ben tanto sottile,
>   certo che 'l trapassar dentro è leggero.
> (*Purg.* viii, 19–21)

2. Cf. Freccero, "*Paradiso* X: The Dance of the Stars," *Dante Studies* 86 (1968): 85–111, esp. p. 86: "Unlike any other part of the poem, the *Paradiso* at this point [*Par.* iv, 40–42] can claim no more than a purely *ad hoc* reality." See also Giuseppe Mazzotta, "Teologia ed Esegesi Biblica (*Par.* III–V)," in *Dante e la Bibbia* (Firenza: Olschki, 1988), pp. 95–112.

3. Cf. Francis X. Newman, "St. Augustine's Three Visions and the Structure of the *Commedia*," *MLN* 82 (1967): 56–78, esp. pp. 73–74.

4. Given the literal story, we might be tempted to consider that the nature of the rewards of the blessed can be seen in their literal actions in the narrative. However, not only do the declarations of Beatrice and Benedict render such a notion impossible, but we should also recall that in the *Letter to Can Grande* Dante continues to speak of both a literal and an allegorical level to the *Paradiso*. What the narrative shows literally, according to the letter, is the *status* of the blessed souls after death, but it is in the allegory that Dante says he describes their rewards as the just reflection of the merit of their free choices (*Ep. xiii*, 25).

5. Cf. 4 *Sent.*, 49, 1.

6. See also Bruno Nardi, "I Bambini nella candida rosa dei beati," in *Nel Mondo di Dante* (Roma: Edizioni "Storia e Letteratura," 1944), pp. 317–34 (originally published in *Studi danteschi*, vol. 20).

7. Cf. *SCG*, iii, 58: "Since the mode of operation follows the form which is the principle of operation, and since the principle of that vision by which the created intellect sees the divine substance is that certain light which was spoken of before . . . [and since] it is possible for there to be different degrees of participation in this light, so [it is possible] that one intellect be more perfectly illuminated than another. Therefore it is possible that one of those who see God may see Him more perfectly than another, although both see His substance." Also, Singleton, "The Three Lights," in *Journey to Beatrice* (originally published as *Dante Studies 2*) (Cambridge: Harvard University Press, 1958), pp. 15–38.

8. *ST*, Suppl. 93, 2. But see 4 *Sent.*, 49, 3.

9. Vazzana, *Il Contrapasso*, pp. 6–7, argues for the artistic need for a single principle of the *contrapasso*. The proper principle, however, is not so much in the figure, as it were, of the treatment of souls in the afterlife (because he looks for such a figure he runs into the error of trying to take the corrections of Purgatory as the image of their vices, rather than of their opposed virtues), but in the content: to each what he or she most wished. Vazzana himself enunciates this principle of not only justice but love in a passage previously quoted, *Il Contrapasso*, p. 34.

10. Cf. Waddell, *Friends of God*, pp. 58–59.

11. See also *de Trin.*, xiii, 14 (18); and *ST*, 3a 1, 2 and ad 2; 3a 46, 1 ad 3. See also Richard of St. Victor, *Liber de Verbo incarnato*, c. 8.

12. Their cases, however, although striking in their unexpectedness—and especially dramatic in Siger's case, given the fierce condemnation of him by Thomas Aquinas while both were alive—may not be altogether clear cut, since the relatively short period of time between their deaths and Dante's sight of them in the *Paradiso* (especially true of Siger, though Joachim's death is not long in the purgatorial terms we have encountered in the second

cantica, even if he had spent all of the time in Purgatory, which we have no reason to believe) apparently indicates that Dante largely absolves them of sin despite their heterodox writings. See also Renaudet, *Dante humaniste*, pp. 262–68 and 272. Kenelm Foster, "The Celebration of Order: *Paradiso* X," *Dante Studies* 90 (1972): 109–24, esp. pp. 120–21, argues that Siger represents a certain kind of wisdom worth representing in Heaven. More attractive, I believe, is the conclusion that the principle of judgment is not a human one. We know from the placement of Saladin, Averroës, and Avicenna in Limbo that Dante did not see believing in the wrong doctrines itself a sin. The heterodoxy of Siger's writings, therefore, would be irrelevant from such a perspective. Siger is rewarded for his capacities, not his conclusions.

13. Of Constantine, Dante unsparingly says that from his gift "avvegna che sia 'l mondo indi distrutto" (*Par.* xx, 60), though the gift itself is described as "il suo bene operar" (verse 59). Hezekiah's final action as king would lead Isaiah to say: "Behold, the days come, that all that is in thine house, and that which thy fathers have laid up in store until this day, shall be carried to Babylon: nothing shall be left, saith the Lord. And of thy sons that shall issue from thee, which thou shalt beget, shall they take away; and they shall be eunuchs in the palace of the king of Babylon" (Isa. 39:6–7, KJV). To which Hezekiah replied: "Good is the word of the Lord which thou hast spoken. He said moreover, For there shall be peace and truth in my days" (Isa. 39:8). Cf. 2 Kings 20:16–19 and 2 Chron. 32:31. But in his rule Hezekiah "did that which was right in the sight of the Lord, according to all that David his father did" (2 Kings 18:3; cf. 2 Chron. 29:2). Richard Kay points to Hezekiah's need for repentance to prolong his life, indicating thereby the commission of actions that demanded repentance, *Dante's Christian Astrology* (Philadelphia: University of Pennsylvania Press, 1994), p. 214. Cf. Renaudet, *Dante humaniste*, p. 206.

14. Renaudet, *Dante humaniste*, p. 203, cites Trajan as a persecutor of Christians, and we should note that even this does not disqualify him from Heaven.

15. See *Singleton* at *Par.* xx, 46–48, 49–54, 61–66, and 67–72.

16. Ironically—from a human perspective—Nathan, the prophet who denounced David's adultery and murder (2 Kings 12: 1–10), is rewarded in a sphere of Heaven lower than David is (*Par.* xii, 136). Cf. Renaudet, *Dante humaniste*, p. 271.

17. See the commentaries of the Anonimo Fiorentino, Vandelli (citing Fra Giordano), and Chimenz (at *Par.* iv, 49–54: DDP).

18. See the comments of Sapegno (at *Par.* iv, 58–60: DDP).

19. Dante attributed his own genius to the action of the stars and, from the direct tone in which he expressed it, did not expect that this would appear strange to his readers.

O glorïose stelle, o lume pregno
di gran virtù, dal quale io riconosco
tutto, qual che si sia, il mio ingegno.
(*Par.* xxii, 112–14)

See also *Purg.* xvi, 73, and *Par.* ii, 67. Cf. Paolo Pecoraro, *Le Stelle di Dante, saggio d'interpretazione di riferimenti astronomici e cosmografici della* Divina Commedia (Roma: Bulzoni editore, 1987), pp. 21 and 299, and *passim.* Also M. A. Orr, *Dante and the Early Astronomers,* rev. ed. (London: Allan Wingate, 1956), pp. 144–48 and 318–24; and G. Buti and R. Bertagni, *Commento astronomico della Divina Commedia* (Firenze: Remo Sandron, 1966), pp. 78 and 218.

20. Cf. *ST,* 1a 115, 4; also *SCG,* iii, 85–92. See Thomas Litt, *Les Corps célestes dans l'univers de Saint Thomas d'Aquin* (Louvain: Publications universitaires, 1963), esp. pp. 201–14. The question is of importance to us, for Aquinas' interpretation did not allow to stars or their spheres any direct influence over the intellect or will, or any other faculty that by being incorporeal could endure in Heaven. On this issue, there is no way to avoid concluding that at the literal level of the *Commedia* Dante appears to be in disagreement with Aquinas, insofar as he attributes far more extensive powers to the stars. (It is important to stress that the disagreement may exist only at the *literal* level of the poem. The underlying allegorical principle of the *Commedia* is that physical manifestations are used to exhibit spiritual states, and that is especially true for the *Paradiso,* where everything Dante sees is explicitly stated to be manifested as it is for didactic purposes. It is possible that Dante's allocation of characters to spheres is simply another such poetic embodiment. Dante might actually agree with Aquinas that the stars influence only the materially linked parts of the soul, yet still use this physical influence and the order of the celestial spheres as an image of corresponding incorporeal dispositions of the spiritual capacities of the soul which we discovered in the *Purgatorio,* and their order of merit.) Moreover, Aquinas was willing to attribute some considerable indirect influence: "However much celestial bodies act directly on inferior bodies and change them by their own power, nevertheless they act only accidentally on powers associated to organs; not acting by way of necessitating anything, but only of inclining. We may say that a certain man is irascible (that is, prone to anger) because of celestial causes; but he is irascible directly because of the free choice made by his will" (*In Matthæum Evangelistam Expositio,* in *Opera Omnia,* ed. S. E. Fretté [Paris: Vivès, 1876], vol. 19, c. 2). See also *ST,* 1a2æ 9, 5, and Tullio Gregory, "Astrologia e teologia nella cultura medievale," in *Mundana sapientia: Forme di conoscenza nella cultura medievale* (Roma: Storia e letteratura, 1992), pp. 291–328, p. 314 fn. 63.

21. Cf. Richard Kay, "Astrology and Astronomy," pp. 148 and 150–51. Also, Marie-Thérèse d'Alverny, "Dante et les astrologues de son temps,"

Bulletin de la Société d'études dantesques du Centre universitaire mediter-ranéen (Nice) 19 (1970): 3–15, esp. p. 5.

22. The simile of the spheres' imprinting their properties on the charac-ter of humans born under their influence like a seal's impressing its design on wax can be found repeatedly in Retoro d'Arezzo, *La Composizione del mondo colle sue cascioni,* ed. Alberto Morino (Firenze: L'Accademia della Crusca, 1976), for example, ii, 6.1.2, and ii, 6.3.1. On the imprint of the stars' overcoming heredity, see Orr, *Dante and the Early Astronomers,* p. 323. Cf. Edward Moore, "The Astronomy of Dante," in *Studies in Dante, Third Series* (Oxford: The Clarendon Press, 1903), pp. 1–108, esp. pp. 20–21.

23. Cf. *Conv.,* iii, ii, 4: "Every substantial form proceeds from its first cause, which is God, as is written in the *de Causis.* Nor does a substantial form receive any diversity from its first cause, which is most simple. It receives its diversity from its secondary causes, and from the matter in which it descends." The action of the spheres is essential for Dante, for the divine origin of every human soul is again something all human souls have in common. What distinguishes them must be attributed to secondary causes, as the passage from the *Convivio* states. In the context of the *Commedia,* it can only be the spheres that account for the different characters of humans. See Nardi, "Le Citazioni dantesche del «Liber de Causis»," p. 107. Also, Stephen Bemrose, *Dante's Angelic Intelligences* (Roma: Edizioni di Storia e Letteratura, 1983), p. 91: "Dante certainly believed the heavens to be in-volved in the *generation* of men (as opposed to the creation of their rational souls, which is a direct act of God)."

24. Richard Kay, "Astrology and Astronomy," pp. 150–51, argues that Charles Martel's two paired examples at *Paradiso* viii, 124–26 (Solon and Xerxes, Melchisidek and Dædalus), show the relation of stars and free will, and the room left to the will. The stars give people their talents, which they, in turn, are free to use well or badly.

25. Cf. Bruno Nardi, "Il Canto XXIX del 'Paradiso,'" *Convivium* n.s. 3 (1956): 294–302, esp. p. 294: ". . . gli spiriti beati cominciano a rivelarsi a Dante, dal cielo della Luna fino a quel di Saturno, nel pianeta dalla cui virtù sono stati piú fortemente impressi."

26. When God by action of the stars imprints or forms a person's char-acter, that imprint in effect determines the individual's ultimate location in Heaven, if the person reaches Heaven, since the location of souls in Heaven reflects the characteristic influences of their stars. But the determination of character does not guarantee that a person will attain Heaven: that remains for the operation of the individual's free will. The destiny of infants and young children in Heaven is a special case that confirms this principle. Such children *(questa festinata gente),* according to Dante, are granted greater and lesser grace, just as adults are, but, given that they never had the opportunity to perform any meaningful actions in the world (having died before reach-ing an age at which they could be said freely to have chosen their actions),

their differential rewards cannot reflect any actual actions they took while alive. Rather, Dante says, their rewards were fixed by the natures they had at their birth *(nel primiero acume)*—that is, their rewards correspond to their capacities for action, or character. It is that innate capacity that reflects, better or worse, God's image *(suo lieto aspetto)*. See Nardi, "Bambini," pp. 328–29: "Ma se questa infusione di grazia è «sanza merzè di lor costume», cioè senza il merito delle buone opere, non è senza proporzione alle disposizioni naturali onde l'anima di ciascuno è più o meno «apparecchiata a riceverne». Insomma la grazia rispetta la diversa fisionomia psicologica di ogno bambino e la diversa personalità che potenzialmente si cela in ciascuno di essi."

> E però questa festinata gente
> a vera vita non è sine causa
> intra sè qui più e meno eccellente.
> . . . .
> [L]e menti tutte nel suo lieto aspetto
> creando, a suo piacer di grazia dota
> diversamente; e qui basti l'effetto.
> . . . .
> Dunque, sanza merzè di lor costume,
> locati son per gradi differenti,
> sol differendo nel primiero acume.
> (*Par.* xxxii, 58–60, 64–66, 73–75)

See also Nardi, "Il Canto XXIX del *Paradiso*," esp. pp. 294–95.

27. Cf. Bruno Nardi, "«Sì come rota ch'igualmente è mossa»," in *Nel Mondo di Dante*, pp. 337–50 (originally published in *Studi danteschi*, vol. 19), esp. p. 348: "Nel concetto cristiano e dantesco della beatitudine eterna, v'è la preoccupazione costante di mantenere intatta la personalità individuale di ogni spirito creato."

28. Cf. Luigi Mario Capelli, "Le «Gerarchie angeliche» e la struttura morale del «Paradiso» dantesco," *Giornale dantesco* 6 (n.s. 3) (1898): 241–59, esp. p. 248, citing Ronchetti: "I beati non soggiornano già nei diversi pianeti, ma vi fanno solo una breve apparizione, allo scopo esclusivo di mostrarsi al Poeta, significando in pari tempo la tendenza prevalente del loro spirito in vita *(tendenza che la loro beatitudine ha ora spogliata di ogni colpabilità)*" (emphasis added).

29. Cf. 4 *Sent.*, 49, 2.

30. Cf. Maria Corti, *Percorsi dell'invenzione, il linguaggio poetico e Dante* (Torino: Einaudi, 1993), chap. 6, "Metafisica della luce come poesia," esp. pp. 154–59. Also *Singleton* at *Par.* ii, 148; and Steiner and Grabher (at *Par.* ii, 148: DDP).

31. Cf. Nardi, "Le Citazioni dantesche del «Liber de Causis»," pp. 97, 103, and *Ep. xiii*, 53–61. Cf. Weisheipl, "Celestial Movers," p. 319, and Orr, *Dante and the Early Astronomers*, p. 321.

32. Cf. Seung, *Fragile Leaves,* pp. 102–5.

33. See Nardi, "Il Canto XXIX del 'Paradiso,'" p. 294. Cf. *Conv.,* iv, xxi, 4–10.

34. Again, the diverse grades of grace awarded children—who had no opportunity to act well or badly—demonstrate that grace follows character rather than action. See Nardi, "Bambini," p. 328: "Ogni fanciullo possiede, sia pure allo stato latente, una sua propria individualità e personalità, chè è il fondamento, posta da natura, di tutte le disuguaglianze sociali. Alla naturale disuguaglianza nel grado di nobiltà, egli [Dante] inoltre fa corrispondere una differente elargizione di grazia."

35. *Conv.,* ii, iii, 7–8, *Ep. xiii,* 68, and *Par.* xxx, 39. Cf. Buti and Bertagni, *Commento astronomico,* p. 51, and Moore, "The Astronomy of Dante," pp. 12–13.

36. Cf. Orr, *Dante and the Early Astronomers,* p. 161, and Buti and Bertagni, *Commento astronomico,* pp. 78 and 218. See also Vasoli's commentary at *Conv.,* ii, iv, 3. Also, Moore, "The Astronomy of Dante," p. 26.

37. Kay, *Dante's Christian Astrology,* p. 141, confirms this after assiduously consulting all of Dante's likely sources. He explains that medieval astrologers tended largely to repackage and transmit their own pagan sources, authors who, of course, would have no reason to associate angels with their doctrines. Cf. Bemrose, *Dante's Angelic Intelligences,* pp. 79 ff., esp. fn. 20 (p. 85), and p. 89; Boyde, *Dante, Philomythes and Philosopher,* p. 198; A. Vacant, in "Ange" in *Dictionnaire de théologie catholique,* ed. Vacant and Mangenot, vol. 1 (Paris: Letouzey et Ané, 1909), pp. 1211–12; and Vasoli at *Conv.,* ii, iv, 10. Buti and Bertagni, *Commento astronomico,* pp. 78 and 218, assert that Dante was following a medieval tradition in his assignment, but cite no source other than Dante himself. Orr, *Dante and the Early Astronomers,* p. 161, suggests that the concept can be found in Restoro d'Arezzo's *Composizione,* but in fact it is not there. Restoro speaks of the different spheres' being moved by intelligences of greater and lesser dignity, but never identifies the intelligences as angels, let alone with the nine orders of angels found in Gregory or Dionysius. See Restoro d'Arezzo, *La Composizione del mondo,* ii, 8.2–3. Some authors, in fact, never identified the intelligences with angels at all, among them Albert the Great. See Weisheipl, "Celestial Movers," pp. 298 and 307–8; Vacant, "Ange," p. 1226; and Gregory, "Astrologia e teologia," pp. 309–11. Aquinas identifies all the spheres with a single order among the nine orders of angels (though without reference to any authority for the identification), writing that the intelligences that were the movers of all nine spheres were to be found in the angelic order (in Latin) virtues: "[It is evident that] the source of universal operation belongs to this order. Hence it appears that pertinent to this order is the motion of the celestial bodies, from which bodies as universal causes, the particular effects in nature follow" (*SCG,* iii, 80).

38. Speaking about the first three of the angelic orders (in the arrange-

ment of Gregory the Great, which Dante was following at the time of writing the *Convivio*), Dante indicates that each order of angels is to be associated with each of the planets and its sphere: "It is, then, reasonable to hold that those who move the heaven of the Moon are the order of Angels, and those who move Mercury are the Archangels, and those who move Venus are the Thrones" (*Conv.*, ii, iii, 13).

39. Cf. Bemrose, *Dante's Angelic Intelligences*, pp. 95–96, and Nardi, "Il Canto XXIX del *Paradiso,*" pp. 295–96. Dante's continuing association of individual orders of angels with planetary spheres in the *Commedia* is confirmed by Beatrice at *Paradiso* xxviii, 67–78. See also Pertusi, "Cultura greco-bizantina," p. 191.

40. Cf. Pecoraro, *Le Stelle di Dante*, esp. p. 299, in which he emphasizes together the potency of the intelligences, their association with specific orders of angels, and thereby their possession and transmission of properties diverse in quality: "Orbene, gli influssi di un pianeta non possono non risalire, in ultima istanza, alle Intelligenze che lo governano ... e il suo movimento è effetto delle Intelligenze celesti, le quali muovono l'astro in correlazione con le proprie particolari qualità o doti. Di più: le medesime Intelligenze hanno conferito specifica virtù al corpo celeste loro affidato, in analogia con il particolare carattere di ciascuna di esse. Infatti, le «virtute» e la conseguente «salute» (ovvero influenza benefica) appartengono al corpo celeste, il quale a sua volta corrisponde a un determinato coro angelico e dunque ne ripete in qualche modo le caratteristiche."

41. Cf. Litt, *Les Corps célestes*, p. 188, citing Aquinas, *de Potentia*, iii, 11 ad 14. See also Weisheipl, "Celestial Movers," p. 310.

42. The source of the simile is Albert the Great, *de Cælo et mundo*, in *Opera omnia*, vol. 5, part 1, ed. Paul Hossfeld (Monasterii Westfalorum: Aschendorff, 1971), Book 2, Tract. 3, c. 5: "But if we take [the primary qualities of stars] as instruments of the motions toward every form, then they possess in themselves the capacities *[virtutes]* of many forms, just as the blacksmith's hammer and anvil possess all the forms which take shape in the iron." See Gregory, "Astrologia e teologia," pp. 309–11. Cf. *Conv.*, iii, vi, 5–6: "Consequently, all the Intelligences know the human form in its mode of existence as an ideal norm in the divine mind. It is known especially by the Intelligences that cause movement, since they are the highest particular causes of the human form and of every generated form. ... So when I say: *Every Intellect there on high gazes on her*, what I wish to convey is that she has been thus formed as the ideal exemplar of the human essence which exists in the divine mind, and, through it, in all other minds, especially in those angelic minds which by means of the heavens fashion things down here." See also Cesare Vasoli, "Intelligenza," in *Enciclopedia dantesca*, vol. 3, p. 473, and Litt, *Les Corps célestes*, pp. 104–7, 126, 129, and 179–85; and *SCG*, iii, 103: "When ... angels ... employ natural things for the sake of any determinate effects, they make use of them as if they were instruments. ... However,

there proceeds from the instrument not only the effect corresponding to its own capacity, but also an effect beyond its own capacity, to the extent that it acts through the power of its principal agent. . . . Therefore it is appropriate that certain higher effects are produced from these same natural things precisely because they are used as instruments by spiritual substances." Earlier in this chapter we had noted what appeared to be a significant divergence—at least at the literal level of the poem—between Dante's and Aquinas' views regarding the power of celestial bodies or their spheres over human character. Given that the stars would, according to this description by Beatrice, be used as instruments by angels (and angels who, according to Aquinas *personaggio* himself, at *Paradiso* xiii, 52–66, are specifically acting to implement in multiplicity the simplicity of God, such that their instruments might well also display powers that result from God as their ultimate mover), perhaps Dante might have believed that there was actually little divergence between his views and Aquinas'. Stars that had acquired powers either directly from God or from God's agents could well be thought to have the capacity to influence even the immaterial parts of the human soul.

43. See also Kay, "Astrology and Astronomy," p. 149; Boyde, *Dante, Philomythes and Philosopher,* p. 253; Pertusi, "Cultura greco-bizantina," pp. 186–88; and Nardi, "Il Canto XXIX del *Paradiso*," p. 298. Beatrice had earlier, in fact, explicitly called the planets and spheres "instruments" or "organs" for the articulation of the diverse properties to be expressed in the physical world:

> Li altri giron per varie differenze
> le distinzion che dentro da sè hanno
> dispongono a lor fini e lor semenze.
> Questi *organi* del mondo così vanno,
> come tu vedi omai, di grado in grado,
> che di su prendono e di sotto fanno.
> (*Par.* ii, 118–23)

Thinking of the spheres as organs would itself be a form of confirmation of the essential qualitative differences in the nature of the spheres. With respect to bodily powers, the existence of a corresponding organ can be used to prove the existence of a distinct power, since organs come into existence for the sake of powers and are adapted to the exercise of the power. Since an organ is adapted to the operation it is intended to perform, the nature of an organ can itself provide clues as to the nature of the power of which it is the organ. Thus, when Beatrice states that the stars are organs for the powers of the intelligences that are their motors, and that their motion and powers resemble their intelligences as the purposeful movement of the hammer (*l'arte del martello*) does its wielder, she is arguing as well that the very existence of distinct spheres proves the existence of distinct powers that operate through these spheres, and that the action of the spheres is determined by, and is evidence of, the natures of the celestial intelligences that move them. In this regard, the descriptions of the stars, as Dante travels through their spheres, can be used as figures of the powers the stars distribute, and of the angels who superintend them. In fact, Dante works poetically in both directions: using descriptions of the stars to figure truths about the angels, and using what he believes of the angels to discover the powers expressed by the spheres.

44. The names I am using for the orders of angels are those used by Dante and other writers who, like him, depended on a Latin translation of the pseudo-Dionysius' *Celestial Hierarchy*. Cf. *CH*, vi, 2; 1049d–1050b, and, for example, Hugh of St. Victor's commentary, *In Hierarchiam cœlestem S. Dionysii Areopagitæ libri x*, *PL*, 175, 1021b–1026d. The Greek names used by the pseudo-Dionysius would nowadays, anyway, be translated quite differently from the way they were by the medieval translators. A more accurate translation of the Greek text would at this stage, therefore, actually obscure the relation of Dante and other late medieval authors to the pseudo-Dionysius. Maurice de Gandillac, ed. and trans., *Denys l'Aréopagite, La Hiérarchie Céleste* (Paris: Éditions du Cerf, 1958), pp. 65–66, points to the irony that for both Dionysius and his medieval commentators the names of the angelic orders were filled with significance. To Dionysius, the names to be examined were Greek; as for his Latin commentators, they searched for significances as much in the conventional Latin translations of the names (even if inaccurate) as in the Hebrew or Greek names. See also René Roques, *L'Univers dionysien: Structure hiérarchique du monde selon le pseudo-Denys* (Paris: Aubier, Éditions Montaigne, 1954), pp. 138–39 and 142 n. 6.

45. *Conv.*, ii, v, 6. In Gregory's writings one can find two somewhat different hierarchies. The hierarchy used by Dante in the *Convivio* is that of the *Moralia in Job*, xxxiii, 48, *PL*, 76, 665: angels, archangels, thrones, dominations, virtues, principalities, powers, cherubim, seraphim. In his *XL Homiliarum in Evangelia*, ii, 34, *PL*, 76, 1249, Gregory alters this order to: angels, archangels, virtues, powers, principalities, dominations, thrones, cherubim, seraphim. Peter Lombard, 2 *Sent.*, 9, 1–2, uses this second Gregorian list. Dionysius' order was: angels, archangels, principalities, powers, virtues, dominations, thrones, cherubim, seraphim. According to Vacant, "Ange," pp. 1192 and 1209, there had been even earlier references to all nine orders of angels in writings by Cyril of Jerusalem and Saint John Chrysostom, but the several competing lists of angels were not regularized until pseudo-Dionysius and Gregory. See Boyde, *Dante, Philomythes and Philosopher*, pp. 184–87.

46. Aquinas found the differences so minor as to make it easy work to reconcile the two systems (*ST*, 1a 108, 5 and 108, 6); Peter Lombard first presents Dionysius' order, and immediately after attributes the order used by Gregory in the *Homilies* to Dionysius, as if he saw no difference (2 *Sent.*, 9, 1). Similarly, Hugh of St. Victor uses Gregory's order in the *Summa*

sententiarum, ii, 5; *PL,* 176, 85d, but Dionysius' in the *de Sacramentis,* i, v, 30; *PL,* 176, 260c/d.

47. In her description of the angelic hierarchy in canto xxviii, Beatrice remarks on Gregory's amused surprise to discover that Dionysius had been correct about the angelic hierarchy, implying that Dante too ought to experience the same surprise, since up to this moment he had subscribed to Gregory's erroneous interpretation (*Par.* xxviii, 133–35). On two earlier occasions in the *Paradiso,* Dante drew even more pointed attention to the alteration in his opinions, by having interlocutors in the third sphere, the sphere of Venus, remind him of his earlier incorrect assignment of a particular order of angels, the thrones, to this sphere (following Gregory). Charles Martel makes a specific reference to the *canzone, Voi che 'ntendendo,* and Dante's discussion of it in the *Convivio* (*Par.* viii, 34–37). Later, Cunizza speaks of the thrones as occupying a higher sphere (thrones being the seventh order from below in Dionysius' hierarchy), thereby reminding Dante that, in following Gregory, he had initially placed the thrones too low in Heaven (*Par.* ix, 61–62). Cf. Vasoli, p. 165, and Bemrose, *Dante's Angelic Intelligences,* p. 85, fn. 21.

48. See Pertusi, "Cultura greco-bizantina," pp. 186–89.

49. Cf. *SCG,* iii, 19. Also Waddell, *Friends of God,* p. 39; Roques, *L'Univers dionysien,* pp. 92–93.

50. Both Peter Lombard and Hugh of St. Victor sometimes follow Gregory's arrangement of the angelic orders while yet dividing the nine orders into three triads (which Gregory did not do) and explaining the division as exhibiting the image of the Trinity (which Gregory did not claim). Cf. *2 Sent.,* ix, 1, and *Summa sententiarum,* ii, 5; *PL,* 176, 85d: "Three triads are discovered in these orders, so that the likeness of the Trinity that has been impressed on them before all other creatures may be evident." Moreover, as Mellone, "Gerarchia angelica," in *Enciclopedia dantesca,* vol. 3, p. 123, argues, Dante's statement that the fallen angels fell from all nine orders (*Conv.,* ii, v, 12), by indicating that this order had existed from the very creation of the angels, implies that it was created as a hierarchy as an image of God.

51. *ST,* 1a 93, 2, esp. ad 4; also *SCG,* iii, 80.

52. Cf. *In 2 Sent.,* xvi, 1, 3, and Gregory, *Moralia,* xxxii, 23. On medieval interpretations of angels, humans, and lesser parts of creation embodying the image of God in various degrees, see Étienne Gilson, *La Philosophie de Saint Bonaventure,* 2d ed., rev. (Paris: J. Vrin, 1943), pp. 165–91.

53. Roques, *L'Univers dionysien,* pp. 171–74.

54. Cf. Aquinas, *de Spiritualibus creaturis,* ed. M. Calcaterra and T. S. Centi, in *Quæstiones disputatæ,* vol. 2, 9th ed. (Torino and Roma: Marietti, 1953), a. 8 ad 17: "Any created nature whatever, since it is finite, does not represent the divine goodness as perfectly as does a multitude of natures; for what is contained in many natures in multiplicity is comprehended in God

unitarily. Therefore was it necessary that there be many natures in the universe, and even among the angelic substances." Also, Nardi, "Le Citazioni dantesche del «Liber de Causis»," p. 103.

55. See Boyde, *Dante, Philomythes and Philosopher*, pp. 265–66. Also Roques, *L'Univers dionysien*, p. 325, and Nardi, "Il Canto XXIX del 'Paradiso,'" p. 294.

56. Cf. 1 *Sent.*, 3, 3–5.

57. Cf. *CH*, xv.1; 1064d–65a: "And now, resting the eye of our intellect, as it were, from the angelic rigor of sublime contemplations, and returning to the divided and manifold expanse of the multiform variety of angelic figurations, let us return, by analytically considering such inconsequential things, toward the simplicity of celestial souls." Also, *EH*, i, 5; 1073d: "Nor did our highest holy priests deal with these things in open observances, nor as unveiled intelligibles, but with holy symbols. For not everyone is pure; nor, as Scripture says, does everyone possess knowledge. . . . So necessarily the highest leaders of our hierarchy . . . transmitted supercelestial things to us in sensible images, mixed with variety and multiplicity, the divine in human form, the immaterial in material guise."

58. Cf. *CH*, ii, 3; 1041d–1042b, and especially 1040a/b: "The Bible has used most holy artful fictions, applying them to intellectual beings who have no forms, revealing them thereby, as it is said, to our soul, taking account of the proper nature of our soul, and shaping the upliftings of holy Scripture to it." It is this same defect in our intellects that demanded that the Bible be written in embodied stories; it is that deficiency that demands that the souls of the blessed manifest themselves to Dante in discrete locations, so that he be capable of recognizing distinctions that unaided he would not be able to make. (We might add, it is that deficiency that demands the *Commedia* be written as poetry, as we will discuss in the concluding chapter.)

> Così parlar conviensi al vostro ingegno,
> però che solo da sensato apprende
> ciò che fa poscia d'intelletto degno.
> Per questo la Scrittura condescende
> a vostra facultate, e piedi e mano
> attribuisce a Dio, ed altro intende;
> e Santa Chiesa con aspetto umano
> Gabrïel e Michel vi rappresenta,
> e l'altro che Tobia rifece sano.
>
> (*Par.* iv, 40–48)

59. Peter Lombard had even used the trinitarian interpretation with Gregory's arrangement of the individual angelic orders, 2 *Sent.*, 9, 1. Peter uses the arrangement that appears in the *XL Homiliarum in Evangelia*. In his commentary on the *Celestial Hierarchy*, Hugh of St. Victor acknowledges the existence of this same arrangement as an alternate. He too divides it into

triads though Gregory had not. See Vacant, "Anges," p. 1211. Cf. Hugh of St. Victor, *In Hierarchiam cœlestem, PL,* 175, 1025a; also Hugh of St. Victor, *Summa sententiarum,* ii, 5, *PL,* 176, 85c.

60. By contrast, since Gregory did not distribute his nine orders into triads at all, his text could not offer support for any argument regarding a schematic parallel between the angelic hierarchy and the Trinity. In this regard, Dante had already absorbed certain fundamentally Dionysian interpretations into his angelology, even while making use, in the *Convivio,* of Gregory's sequence of the angelic orders. It may not, then, have been a difficult step for him to take, in the *Commedia,* to abandon the Gregorian sequence in favor of the Dionysian.

61. Agreement on this principle can be found in both Dominican and Franciscan texts, and this concurrence indicates that it was not even a matter of controversy but simply formed part of the received wisdom. Cf. 2 *Sent.,* 9: "It now remains to consider what Scripture teaches regarding the orders of angels. It declares in many places that there are nine orders of angels, to wit, angels, archangels, principalities, powers, virtues, dominations, thrones, cherubim, and seraphim. And three triads can be found in these orders, with three orders in each, so that the resemblance to the Trinity that has been impressed on them may be understood." Cf. *In 2 Sent.,* ix, 1, 1: "The term hierarchy means, as it were, a holy kingdom, from 'hieron,' holy, and 'archon,' king. Now, in every kingdom there must be distinctions of power and purpose, and so in a holy kingdom these distinctions must be holy and divine. And so, as in a worldly kingdom the purpose is that the multitude of subjects be peacefully disposed to the good intended by their king (as is clear in the case of an army which, as the Philosopher says in *Metaphys.,* xi, is ordered to its leader as to a final end), so it must be that in a holy kingdom the end must be similarity to God. Nor could the angels pursue this end except through ordered activity, and for this there must be an ordered power and directing knowledge. And therefore order is a part of the definition of hierarchy, in which is articulated the distinctions of power *(potestas),* the directing knowledge *(scientia),* and the activity *(actio)* leading to the end, with similarity to God being the intended end." Also, *ST,* 1a 108, 1. The division into triads was, under the influence of Dionysius, used also by Scotus Eriugena and Hugh of St. Victor. See also Gilson, *La Philosophie de Saint Bonaventure,* pp. 214–16.

62. See Acts 2: 38, where the Holy Spirit is described as a gift to humans. Augustine's argument, at *Confessions,* 13.9 (10), that this gift is what makes possible the reversal of our "weight"—such that we are drawn toward God, and not toward the earth—seems strikingly similar to comments in Dionysius, as well as to the fundamental poetic image of the journey of the *Commedia.* It is a principle of Dionysius' celestial hierarchy that those orders nearest to others below them help them to ascend. Thus, those angelic orders closest to humans have special obligations to help humans ascend toward God. Cf.

CH, ix, 2; 1057a. This would be a further reason to associate these orders, then, with the Holy Spirit.

63. See Boyde, *Dante, Philomythes and Philosopher,* p. 187.

64. Pseudo-Dionysius does in a general sense attribute the *ecclesiastical* hierarchy to the Trinity (and, since for him all hierarchies share the same origin and principle, this would then also apply to the celestial hierarchy), but without specifically identifying each member of the hierarchy with a specific person. Cf. *EH,* i, 3; 1073a, and Scotus' commentary to the *Celestial Hierarchy,* Iohannis Scoti Eriugenæ, *Expositiones super Ierarchiam cœlestem,* vii, 4, *PL,* 122 193b/c (the text being interpreted is at *PL,* 122 1053c).

65. Roques, *L'Univers dionysien,* pp. 171–74.

66. Dionysius refers to this consistent application even at the human level in the *Celestial Hierarchy.* Cf. *CH,* i, 3; 1038d–1039a, ix, 2; 1056b, and x, 3; 1065a/b (cited above), and *EH,* i, 3–i, 4; 1073a–c, which articulates the application of these principles, begins with reference back to the *Celestial Hierarchy.* Also, *EH,* i, 2; 1072b.

67. Cf. the statement by Bonaventure, *Collationes in Hexaëmeron,* in *Opera Omnia,* vol. 5, ed. P.P. Collegii a S. Bonaventura (Quaracchi: Collegii S. Bonaventuræ, 1891), xxi, 17–18. "According to Dionysius, hierarchy is defined: 'Hierarchy is a sacred order, a science, an activity that assimilates itself, as much as possible, to deiformity, and, proportionally to the illuminations which God has given it, raises itself—to the extent of its capacity—to the imitation of God.' The order of power corresponds to the Father, the sacred knowledge to the Son, the action to the Holy Spirit. . . . It is necessary that any hierarchy whatever have three orders; that the first hierarchy be appropriated to the Father, the second to the Son, and the third to the Holy Spirit. And the first hierarchy must be assimilated to the Father in all three [persons]; the second to the Son in all three; the third to the Holy Spirit in all three, as shall be made clear." Also, Gilson, *La Philosophie de Saint Bonaventure,* pp. 214–16.

68. Bonaventure worked out the combinations for all of the persons, *Collationes in Hexaëmeron,* xxi, 19. While both Hugh of St. Victor, *In Hierarchiam cœlestem, PL,* 175, 1062c–1063a, and Aquinas, *In 2 Sent.,* ix, 1, 3, state explicitly that the division of the nine orders into three triads of three orders each is in order best to reflect the image of the Trinity, each works out the combinations of persons to orders only for the highest triad. (In *ST,* 1a 108, 6, Aquinas does only a fragment of that first triad.) Peter Lombard, 2 *Sent.,* 9, 1, likewise declares that the three triads of three orders reflects the persons of the Trinity but does not actually enumerate how. (Hugh of St. Victor, *Summa sententiarum,* ii, 5, *PL,* 176, 85c–d, follows this practice.) Dante worked out the combinations for only the first triad at *Conv.,* ii, v, 7–11, but declared that this principle can and should be applied to all three triads.

69. Insofar as it is possible to argue that in the *Convivio* Dante described the thrones as reflecting the Holy Spirit considered in itself (see Vasoli,

Conv., p. 165, commenting upon *Conv.*, ii, v, 13), one could say that Dante had, in effect, made just this combinatorial assignment—to the sphere, if not to the "right" order of angels. The sphere of Venus, as the highest sphere of the lowest triad would be the sphere with which the Holy Spirit was associated both for primary and secondary attributes. All that was necessary to reach the schematism of the *Commedia* was for Dante to apply this principle consistently across the nine spheres.

70. On the use of our knowledge of medieval notions of the characteristics of planets as a means of specifying the characters that are rewarded in each of the spheres, see Kay, "Astrology and Astronomy," pp. 159–62. In my view, however, known planetary qualities ought still to be reconciled to properties of the persons of the Trinity.

71. Cf. *Div. nom.*, ii, 6; 1122d and vii, 3; 1155b.

72. Cf. Capelli, "Le «Gerarchie angeliche»," pp. 257–59. We do not even have to make a final determination whether Dante believed the angelic intelligences could influence the human soul in some way that bypassed the body, or whether (following *ST,* 1a 115, 4, and *SCG*, iii, 78–82) the influence they and the planets exerted on human character was always mediated by an initial corporeal influence. (Cp. Pecoraro, *Le Stelle di Dante*, p. 299; Buti and Bertagni, *Commento astronomico*, pp. 235–36; and Orr, *Dante and the Early Astronomers*, p. 323.) It could simply be that souls manifest themselves to Dante where they do because he was convinced that in a poetic sense, and adapted to the limits of the human intelligence, it was easiest to assert this connection without even knowing precisely how the influence was effected.

73. *ST,* 1a 108, 6; also *In 2 Sent.*, ix, 1, 3.

74. Aquinas associated thrones with memory, cherubim with intellect, and seraphim with the will: *In 2 Sent.*, ix, 1, 3.

75. See, for example, Alain de Lille, *Expositio prosae de angelis*, in *Textes inédits*, ed. M.-T. d'Alverny (Paris: Vrin, 1965), p. 213.

76. With a possible reference to Paul's statement about martyrs in Romans 8:36. Vazzana, *Il Contrapasso*, p. 157, speaks of the militants and martyrs of the fifth sphere as sharing Christ's "combative virtue": "Costoro hanno del Cristo la virtù combattiva."

77. Roques, *L'Univers Dionysien*, pp. 142–43, points out the close linkage between Dionysius' description of order and the virtue courage, and argues that this gives a certain appropriateness to the medieval translation of the name of the order by the word *virtue*.

78. Cf. *CH*, ii, 4; 1042c: "A courageous rationality and an unmovable coming to rest in the divine and unchanging foundations." Cf. Kay, *Dante's Christian Astrology*, pp. 142–49, and Georg Rabuse, "Les paysages astrologiques de la 'Divine comedie,'" *Bulletin de la Société d'études dantesques du Centre universitaire mediterranéen* (Nice) 21 (1973–74): 57–68, esp. p. 62.

79. *XL Hom. in Evang.*, xxxiv, 10, *PL,* 76, 1251c/d.

80. *In 2 Sent.*, 9, 1, 3; see also *SCG*, iii, 80.

81. This would argue against Foster's order for the middle triad (sphere 4, Son in relation to Holy Spirit; sphere 5, Son in relation to Father; sphere 6, Son in relation to self) in "The Celebration of Order: *Paradiso* X," p. 110. It would also argue against other schemes that, as Foster does, always associate the highest order of a triad with a specific person of the Trinity "in relation to himself." See, for example, Capelli, "Le «Gerarchie angeliche»," pp. 255–58.

82. Aquinas' distribution of the three triads according to modes of understanding, *In 2 Sent.*, ix, 1, 3, also stresses these active qualities. The entire middle triad of the celestial hierarchy is associated by Aquinas with government and ordering (indeed, it is the ordering of *peace*): that is, with making the results of contemplation active and effective, with obvious relevance to the human characters we meet in its three spheres.

83. Augustine, *de Trin.*, xv, 21 (41); see also xiv, 6 (8), xv, 7 (12), and xv, 17 (27–31).

84. Cf. Renaudet, *Dante humaniste*, pp. 192–94.

85. Dionysius' description of the order of dominations, with whom this sphere is associated, stresses their abhorrence of tyranny and subjugation, associating them strongly with justice, and therefore with the will, as its cardinal virtue (*CH*, viii, 1; 1053d–1054a). Scotus, in his commentary, says the dominations act humbly and modestly, rather than proudly, and these too, as we know from the *Purgatorio*, are virtues of the will. Scotus Eriugena, *Expositiones super Ierarchiam cœlestem*, PL, 122, 195a/b: "The heavenly dominations rule not tyrannically, not proudly, but modestly in their love of God and their subjects."

86. Cf. *de Monarchia*, i, xi, 13–14, in Dante Alighieri, *Opere minori*, vol. 2, ed. B. Nardi, (Milano and Napoli: Ricciardi, 1979). Also, Renaudet, *Dante humaniste*, p. 226. Also, Étienne Gilson, *Dante and Philosophy* (1949; reprint, New York: Harper & Row, 1963), p. 177: "Now just as the slightest trace of greed is enough to obscure justice, so too charity, that is to say integrity in love *(recto dilectio)*, refines and clarifies justice."

87. Several souls named to Dante are not theologians at all. A more generally applicable description would be to call these souls—given the distinctions Dante is making in the order of souls in Heaven—"discursive thinkers," but the greater number of them are theologians too, and it is convenient to continue to identify them in that way.

88. Cf. Hugh of St. Victor, *In Hierarchiam cœlestem*, PL, 175, 1078a/b: "I consider that this very name, powers, declares their orderliness, that is, an ultramundane—and an intellectual—ordering." Dionysius further describes the powers as exercising an "exusiarchia": "Powerfully, yet in good order, they raise themselves, and the orders beneath them, toward the divine, assimilating themselves, as much as is right, to that authority which is the source of all power" (*CH*, viii, 1; *PL*, 122 1054b). Scotus Eriugena leaves the Greek word *exusiarchia* untranslated in his version of the text. Would Dante have known that this Greek term meant that they exercised a special

"authority," with obvious appropriateness to the role of the theologians as *auctoritates*?

89. *XL Hom. in Evang.*, xxxiv, 10; *PL*, 76, 1251d. Peter Lombard, 2 *Sent.*, 9, 2; and Hugh of St. Victor, *Summa sententiarum*, ii, 5; *PL*, 176, 85d–86a paraphrase Gregory's statement. Also Gilson, *La Philosophie de Saint Bonaventure*, pp. 215.

90. Cf. Renaudet, *Dante humaniste*, pp. 257–59.

91. Cf. Bosco and Reggio (at *Par.* Nota/Canti xi–xii: DDP). Not only do they call attention to the military terms in which the two saints are described, they specifically indicate Dante's deliberate selectivity in describing the saints in this way: "L'eroico non è invenzione di Dante, è anche in Bonaventura [i.e., in Bonaventura's life of Francis, the *Legenda maior*] perché era in Francesco: solo che l'accento del poeta batte quasi esclusivamente su esso, lasciando in ombra quel molto altro che c'era nel santo e quindi anche nella biografia di Bonaventura." See also the note at *Par.* xi, 58–59 (DDP).

92. Cf. *In 2 Sent.*, ix, 1, 3: "The number of and distinctions between the orders of the first hierarchy [i.e., triad] can be understood in the following way. There are three acts by which the soul may enjoy God. One of these is to comprehend or to retain God in the mind, and it is memory that accomplishes this. The order of thrones must be understood in this mode, since God takes his seat in them, and comes to rest in them, and makes them come to rest in themselves." Aquinas also speaks of the thrones as providing a ground to the actions of the two higher orders in its triad. The same relationship could also be said to exist between the theologians and the two higher orders in their triad. They too provide the intellectual products that the other two members of their triad make active and bring to fulfillment in the pursuit of their own characteristic activities.

93. It should be remembered that Dante was convinced, and states explicitly in the *Paradiso* (*Par.* xxix, 76–81), that angels do not themselves possess the faculty of memory, having no need for it. But Augustine's original likening of the persons of the Trinity to the human intellectual faculties did not assert that God possessed these faculties. The association was merely for the sake of providing a comparison accessible to the human understanding. Similarly, angelic operations could also be described in terms of human faculties, simply to make their operation comprehensible to human intellects, without such a description's implying that angels themselves possessed these faculties. But even while the expression of the qualities of these operations in terms of human faculties was analogical, Dante could still apply these descriptions within the matrix of the combinations of divine attributes as a way of elucidating not only the operation of angels, but, more importantly, the significant qualities of the human characters informed by the angels. Indeed, since it is ultimately the human characters that are the subject of the *Paradiso*, analogies to human faculties are particularly appropriate and relevant.

94. Cf. Vazzana, *Il Contrapasso*, p. 144.

95. According to *Singleton*, at *Par.* iv, 100–102, a *voluntas secundum quid*. Cf. *ST*, 1a2æ 6, 4–6, and Boyde, *Perception and Passion*, pp. 197–202.

96. Aquinas' way of distinguishing angelic triads from one another is again germane. With respect to the lowest triad of angels, Aquinas stresses the particularity of the knowledge they possess (as distinct from the more universal knowledge of the higher orders of angels), and the limits placed on it by its particularity. Cf. *SCG*, iii, 80. It is the particularity of practical choice that was also the limiting factor in the characters of the humans under these angels' influence.

97. *CH*, vii, 2; 1051a; viii, 2; 1054d–1055a; and xiii, 3; 1062a–b. Cf. *SCG*, iii, 80.

98. According to Dionysius, it is angels and archangels alone who communicate with humans; scriptural statements that appear to say that higher orders communicated directly with humans must be interpreted metaphorically. It was not a seraph who communicated with Isaiah, but an angel, though either the source of the illumination or the august nature of the illumination could make it possible to call the illumination "seraphic" (*CH*, xiii, 4; 1063d–1064b). In commentaries on Dionysius, an effort is made to identify the specific responsibilities of the three orders of the lowest triad. For Aquinas, the angels communicate with individual humans; the archangels with individual humans for the good of a multitude; the principalities with nations (*In 2 Sent.*, ix, 1, 3. Cf. *SCG*, iii, 80). Other commentators provide slightly different interpretations. All, however, agree on the special relation between the lowest triad and the human hierarchy and humanity.

99. Other special connections between the Holy Spirit and this world were also enunciated: it was the Spirit through whom the physical universe was created (*SCG*, iv, 20); God was said to operate on the hearts of people especially through the Spirit (*SCG*, iv, 21); and, in regard to the special communion between God and humanity, it is by the Spirit that the incarnation is physically prepared (*SCG*, iv, 46). Also Gilson, *La Philosophie de Saint Bonaventure*, p. 215.

100. See *SCG*, iv, 19. Aquinas' argument specifically distinguishes the way in which the beloved is in the will from the way an object may be in the intellect as a means of distinguishing spiration from generation—that is, as distinguishing the Son from the Holy Spirit. The association of Spirit with will, then, is meant to be revelatory of a critical aspect of the relation of the three persons. Cf. Augustine, *de Trin.*, xv, 21 (41).

101. *In Ethica*, §1129. Cf. *ST*, 1a 83, 3 and 1a2æ 13, 1.

102. The medieval consensus was that angels had received grace, and were distributed into the orders that composed the celestial hierarchy and indicated greater degrees of dignity, according to their natures, rather than specific actions. 2 *Sent.*, 3, 2. See *ST*, 1a 108, 4 and 108, 8. Also, *ST*, 1a 62, 6. Aquinas explicitly denied that grace was bestowed on humans in accord

with their natural capacities. See *ST,* 1a 62, 6 and 1a 108, 4. Yet insofar as Dante's principle of human reward depends on character rather than on historical action, its similarity to the angelic principle must be noted, and this similarity might well have provided Dante a further reason for using the celestial hierarchy as the structure by which to organize Heaven in the *Paradiso,* and thus provide a figure for the rewards of human souls. It might be noted, moreover, that the very argument Aquinas uses to account for the diversity of grace among humans might have suggested to Dante that different characters among people could be the grounds for differential awards of grace. Aquinas argues, "It is reasonable that the angels, since they had a better nature, were turned more strongly and efficaciously to God. This happens, too, among men: that greater grace and glory is given proportionate to the intensity of their turning toward God. Whence it seems that the angels, who had better natures, had more of grace and glory" (*ST,* 1a 62, 6). In this argument, angelic nature and human earnestness are made parallel to one another as a determinant of grace. If Dante were to interpret this earnestness as the result of character—especially if that character were informed by a certain relation to the Trinity, something common, though in different ways, to both angels and humans—there would turn out to be little ultimate difference between his position and Aquinas'.

103. Cf. Roques, *L'Univers dionysien,* pp. 136 and 319–20.

104. A further indication of the consistency with which Dante uses this strategy to figure the greater immediacy of the knowledge of God of the souls of the eighth sphere is his exclusion of Saint Paul from the encounters in this sphere. Despite the importance (either direct or indirect) of Paul's words to the answers Dante gives in his examination by Saints Peter, James, and John regarding faith, hope, and charity, Paul himself does not appear at any moment in this sphere, for Paul had not seen Christ during his life.

105. Bernard of Clairvaux stresses the serenity and settledness of the thrones' judgment: *Five Books on Consideration,* in the *Works of Bernard of Clairvaux,* vol. 13 (Kalamazoo, Mich.: Cistercian Publications, 1976), pp. 148–49. Also Gilson, *La Philosophie de Saint Bonaventure,* p. 215.

106. *CH,* iii, 2; 1044c/d; *EH,* i, 4–i, 5; 1073a–c.

107. The examination is likened to a scholastic disputation (*Par.* xxiv, 46–48), and terms from scholastic logic are used to characterize Dante's responses (*Par.* xxiv, 66, 69, 77, 81, 94, 96, 97–98 [in these latter verses the Old and New Testaments are called "l'antica e la novella proposizion," as if they were the premises of a syllogism]). It even seems to progress from one professional level to another. At first, Dante is bachelor to Saint Peter's *maestro* (*Par.* xxiv, 46–47). Having successfully completed the first part of the examination, Dante describes his relation to James, who asks the second question, as that of student to doctor (*dottor, Par.* xxv, 64), which must imply that Dante has by now himself become a master. And in his answers to Saint John, Dante's effort is dignified as itself *ragionando* (*Par.* xxvi, 6), surpassed only by the authori-

ties (*autore, Par.* xxvi, 40; *autoritadi, Par.* xxvi, 47) from which it draws arguments. (And when Dante calls both Peter and James *baroni* [*Par.* xxiv, 115, xxv, 17], is it possible that the word is meant in its academic sense?) Certainly, the questions for which Dante wants answers from Adam might themselves perhaps best be described as academic (*Par.* xxvi, 109–42).

108. For Aquinas, certainly, one of the prime characteristics of the middle triad of the angelic orders is its role in active mediation. The three middle orders are all, for him, assigned roles involving the execution of divine mandates coming from above, thus stressing both the active or operative nature of their role, as well as its mediated and mediating nature. See *ST,* 1a 108, 6, and *In 2 Sent.,* ix, 1, 3. Inasmuch as Adam and the apostles are the intermediaries through whom divine intentions are communicated to humanity, they may be, in their appropriate way, reflecting this active attribute of the Son.

109. Cf. Kay, "Astrology and Astronomy," pp. 150–51.

110. The same principle lies at the heart of the *de Monarchia,* i, viii, 2–i, ix, 1: "The human race does well—does best, even—when, to the extent it can, it likens itself to God. . . . The human race does best when—insofar as its own nature allows—it imitates the traces of the heavens."

111. See *CH,* iv, 2; 1047a: "Their life [i.e., the angels'] is entirely intellectual." Also Aquinas, *de Spiritualibus creaturis,* a. 6. Cf. Aquinas, *de Substantiis separatis,* in *Opuscula philosophica,* ed. R. M. Spiazzi, O.P, (Torino and Roma: Marietti, 1954): c. 18 (§101 in this edition).

112. The one early writer who seemed to argue for the endurance of the sensitive appetites after death, the pseudo-Augustinian author of *de Spiritu et Anima,* is explicitly denied authority on this issue by Aquinas (*ST,* 1a 77, 8 ad 1).

113. See also *ST,* 1a 59, 4 ad 3, and Hugh of St. Victor, *In Hierarchiam cœlestem, PL,* 175, 976c–978d.

114. Cf. *Div. nom.,* iv, 23; 1142c. Cf. Roques, *L'Univers dionysien,* pp. 85 and 99.

115. Scotus Eriugena, *Expositiones super Ierarchiam cœlestem,* ii, 4; *PL,* 122 160b–d (the text commented on is from *PL,* 122 1042b–c) and xv, p. 211 (= *PL,* 122 1069b).

116. Ibid., ii, 4; *PL,* 122 162b–c. (The passage being interpreted is from *CH,* ii, 4; 1042c–d).

117. The words Dionysius uses are the words of the appetites: *furor* and *concupiscentia* literally, with *phantasia* standing in for the intellectual appetite. Cf. Aquinas, *Quæstiones de Anima,* a. 19 ad 8. Aquinas believed that in speaking so forcefully Dionysius was only employing a humanly recognizable simile in this passage, though it depends, for its appropriateness, on the existence of some proportionate demonic faculties. With respect to demons, Aquinas could also admit the existence of faculties that, if not identical to the faculties of human appetite, stood in a certain proportion to them: "Let it not be thought that there is an imagination in demons, or an irascible or

concupiscible appetite, all of which belong to the sensitive part; rather, there is something equivalent to these, but proportioned to an intellectual nature." Cf. also *ST*, 1a 82, 5 ad 1.

118. Cf. Augustine, *de Trin.*, xv, 21 (41).

119. Scotus Eriugena, *Expositiones super Ierarchiam cœlestem*, viii, 1; *PL*, 122, 196c–197a (the text being interpreted is *PL*, 122, 1054a). Cf. Roques, *L'Univers dionysien*, pp. 142–43.

120. See also *SCG*, iii, 80.

121. Scotus Eriugena, *Expositiones super Ierarchiam cœlestem*, viii, 1; *PL*, 122, 194c–195a (the text being interpreted is *PL*, 122 1053d).

122. *ST*, 1a 108, 5 ad 2.

123. See *CH*, viii, 1; 1053d–1054a; also Scotus Eriugena, *Expositiones super Ierarchiam cœlestem*, viii, 1; *PL*, 122 195a/b.

124. Cf. Hugh of St. Victor, *In Hierarchiam cœlestem*, *PL*, 175, 1078a/b.

125. *XL Hom. in Evang.*, xxxiv, 10; *PL*, 76, 1251d.

126. Cf. *SCG*, iii, 80, cited above, which stresses the relation of the three lowest orders of angels (associated with the will, as we have concluded) to contingency and contingent knowledge.

127. Cf. Roques, *L'Univers dionysien*, p. 160.

128. Cf. Bosco and Reggio's note to cantos xi and xii (DDP): "Il primo atto della santità di Francesco è un atto di guerra, . . . e questa guerra è per una donna tale, che, come la morte, non piace a nessuno [citing *Par.* xi, 58–60]. . . . Ma si noti la violenza di «guerra», l'energia di «corse»: la biografia di Francesco sarà tenuta da Dante costantemente su questo registro." Indeed, all of the souls of this middle triad had an appetite—nothing less can be said—for arduous goods. The description of Dominic in relation to the heretics shows this irascibility most clearly: the more resistance he encountered, the stronger his own response to overcome it. Kay, *Dante's Christian Astrology*, pp. 198–102, 150–51, and 187, points out that medieval astrological sources would associate all three of the planets of the middle triad, the sun, Mars, and Jupiter, with heat and with heated passions, and thus, in conventional metaphors as well as the specific emblems of the *Commedia*, with irascibility. Rabuse, "Les paysages astrologiques de la 'Divine comedie,' " p. 62, speaks of astrologers who associated Mars with the *ardor* of sacrifice.

129. Cf. Aquinas, *Quæstiones de Anima*, a. 19 ad 7: "In the separated soul there is neither joy nor anger insofar as these are irascible and concupiscible acts, for these are in the sensitive part; but, rather, insofar as by these are designated movements of the will, which is in the intellectual part." Using neo-Platonic distinctions, Roques, *L'Univers dionysien*, pp. 85 and 99, argues that Dionysius believed all intelligent creatures (and this would include the angels) possessed νοῦς, θυμός, and ἐπιθυμία.

130. See Cogan, "Delight, Punishment, and the Justice of God," pp. 32–35.

131. The relation of the three theological virtues to faculties of appetition may also play a part in Dante's ordering of the appetitive faculties in

Heaven. The order, we notice, is in a certain sense the opposite of that of the previous two *cantiche*. In Heaven, what had been the "lowest" of appetites, concupiscence, is placed highest. In *ST,* 2a2æ 17, 8, Aquinas argues that perfect love (charity), though last attained, is the best relation to God. Hope, associated with the irascible appetite, is a form of imperfect love, and precedes it. Faith, associated with the will because it is an intellectual virtue, precedes even hope, since it merely supplies the object to be loved.

132. Cf. 2 *Sent.*, 26, 6, and 2 *Sent.*, 11, 2.

133. Dante repeats this fusion of apprehension and appetite in the mouth of Bernard of Clairvaux:

> Lume è là su che visibile face
>> lo creatore a quella creatura
>> che solo in lui vedere ha la sua pace.
>> (*Par.* xxx, 100–102)

This restlessness of the soul is essentially an appetitive condition, although here, paradoxically, it can only be satisfied by an act of apprehension. See Nardi, "«Sì come rota»," p. 337.

134. Cf. *ST,* 1a2æ 22, 2: "The soul is drawn to a thing by the appetitive faculty rather than by the apprehensive faculty. . . . Indeed, the apprehensive power is not by its own nature drawn to anything, but knows it according to the intention of the thing which it has in itself." Also, *ST,* 1a 16, 1.

135. Cf. Roques, *L'Univers dionysien,* p. 60.

136. Cf. Roques, *L'Univers dionysien,* pp. 235–40.

137. Cf. Nardi, "«Sì come rota»," p. 347: "Cagione del loro [i.e., the nine angelic orders'] moto è l'affocato amore che li punge."

138. Cf. *ST,* Suppl. 93, 2. In canto xxix, it should be noted, Beatrice speaks as if *l'affetto* itself followed apprehension.

> Onde, però che all'atto che concepe
>> segue l'affetto, d'amar la dolcezza
>> diversamente in essa ferve e tepe.
>> (*Par.* xxix, 139–41)

In this passage, however, she is clearly not speaking of the same *affetto* as in canto xxviii. *L'affetto* cannot follow apprehension, as here, and yet be the condition of apprehension, as in canto xxviii. The term must be used in two different senses in the two passages. In the earlier citation, *l'affetto* is a capacity for appetition; here, it is the process, or result of appetition, as its association with *amar* shows. It is scarcely surprising that a word like *l'affetto* could be used to describe power, process, or result. It is ambiguity, rather than contradiction, that we see between these two passages.

139. Such would also seem to be implied by Aquinas' unexpected distinction with regard to Saint Paul's rapture: "It was for this reason that the Apostle said he was rapt—not only to the third heaven, which pertains to the

contemplation of the intellect—but even to Paradise, which pertains to the emotions [*affectum:* in context, this might better be translated by 'will']" (*ST,* 2a2æ 175, 2). Cf. *ST,* 1a2æ 3, 4; also *ST,* Suppl. 95, 5. The quotation from Gregory is from the *Homiliarum in Ezechielem prophetam libri duo,* 14, *PL,* 76, 786a–1072c. The passage cited is at 954a.

140. Cf. *ST,* 2a2æ 180, 1: "And since everyone experiences delight when they attain what they love, therefore the contemplative life ends in delight—which is in the appetite—since love is its goal."

141. Cf. Waddell, *Friends of God,* pp. 24–25. Cf. Pecoraro, *Le Stelle di Dante,* pp. 314–17, on Dante's avoidance of any sterile dichotomy between contemplation and love.

142. Cf. Roques, *L'Univers dionysien,* pp. 235–40.

143. On the confounding or conflating of apprehension and desire, see also Cacciaguida's statement to Dante at *Paradiso* xv, 64–65, and Dante's explanation, not contradicted by either Cacciaguida or Beatrice, that for the blessed, *l'affetto e 'l senno* are the same, though they are not for the living (*Par.* xv, 73–83).

144. Aquinas is not much given to figurative language, but even he, paraphrasing Gregory (*Homiliarum in Ezechielem,* 14, properly cited in *ST,* 2a2æ 180, 7 ad 1), addresses this appetitive dimension of contemplation: "And for this reason Gregory sets the contemplative life in the love of God, insofar as because of the love of God someone is set aflame to gaze on His beauty" (*ST,* 2a2æ 180, 1).

145. This was not only poetry to the Middle Ages and especially to Aristotelians. For Aristotle, the only things that can be said to cause motion without being moved are objects of desire and objects of thought. And he further asserts that "the primary objects of desire and thought are the same" (*Metaphys.,* xii, 8.2; 1072a25–30). The primary good causes motion by being an object of love (*Metaphys.,* xii, 8.4; 1072b4). Cf. Albert the Great's commentary, in Albertus Magnus, *Metaphysica,* ed. B. Geyer, *Opera Omnia,* vol. 16 (Monasterii Westfalorum: Aschendorff, 1964), Book 11, tract. 1, c. 13. See Weisheipl, "Celestial Movers," pp. 305–6 and 309; Beniamino Andriani, *La forma del paradiso dantesco* (Padova: CEDAM, 1961), pp. 114–17; and Howard P. Kainz, *"Active and Passive Potency" in Thomistic Angelology* (The Hague: Martinus Nijhoff, 1972), p. 52.

146. Cf. Mellone, "Gerarchia angelica," in *Enciclopedia dantesca,* vol. 3, p. 123, on the cause of the fallen angels' damnation. We could argue that the angels could fall precisely and only because they would not open themselves to the grace that was offered. Thus, the blessedness of the angels depended (and of humans, subsequently, depends) on having *l'affetto* in the proper condition to receive grace. Cf. *ST,* 1a2æ 21, 2.

147. In the *Convivio,* Dante had attributed a greater infusion of the possible intellect, a gratuitous gift, to a greater capacity for receiving it, and that capacity to greater purity of soul (*Conv.,* iv, xxi, 7–8). It marks a significant

change that here in the *Paradiso* it is *l'affetto* that determines a soul's capacity to receive divine gifts.

148. See the resonant statement from Aquinas: "So that from God—as if as a reward—a man attains to, by his own operation, that for which God delegated to him the power of operating; just as natural things by their own proper motions and operations attain to those things for which God ordained them" (*ST,* 1a2æ 114, 1).

149. The "appetitive" image of God is given further credibility by a doctrine concerning the angels to which Dante uses Beatrice to call specific, and emphatic attention. Contrary to the teachings of the "schools" (*le vostre scole*), Dante has Beatrice insist (*Par.* xxix, 70–81) that angels do not possess the faculty of memory because they have no need of it, never being divided from their object of apprehension, God. Nardi, "Il Canto XXIX del *Paradiso,*" pp. 301–2, emphasizes the seriousness of Dante's break from more conventional doctrines, including those of Aquinas. Yet angels too are made in the image of God, indeed show a more perfect image of God than people do. For Augustine, the image of God in the intellectual soul was reflected in the three faculties, memory, reason, and will. But if angels, whose image of God is better than ours, have no memory, Dante must here be insisting that the Augustinian model of the human image of the Trinity is not necessarily the best model. Angels do have three *affetti,* as do people in a more material and lesser manifestation, and it is those *affetti,* properly understood, that to Dante constitute the image of the Trinity in angels. Insofar as the goal of the *Paradiso* is to bring the human intellect to the recognition of superhuman origins for human faculties and to an understanding of their perfected operation, these *affetti* would seem to provide a more appropriate model of the image of the Trinity not only for angels but also for the beatified souls of Heaven.

150. Dionysius makes an equivalent point about God and images of God: "This is the power of the divine likeness: that it returns all created things to their cause. These things must then be said to resemble God, according to the divine image and likeness. But God does not resemble them, just as no man 'resembles' his own portrait" (*Div. nom.,* ix, 6; 1162a). Dante *personaggio* had placed himself in the position of the portrait: he was amazed that the original looked so much like him, when in fact he appeared as he did because he was the image of that original.

151. Cf. *CH,* i, 3; 1038d–1039b; ii, 3; 1058c/d; x, 1; 1065a; xv, 1, 328a. See also, *EH,* i, 5; 1073d.

152. *CH,* iii, 2; 1044c–45b.

CONCLUSION

1. Cf. *EN,* ii, 2; 1103b27–30, and *In Ethica,* §256.

2. Cf. "As yet, our immortality is ascertained only by that truest

doctrine of Christ, which is the way, the truth, and the light. Way, because by means of it we come without impediment to the happiness of that immortality; truth, because it suffers no error; light, because it illuminates us in the darkness of worldly ignorance. This doctrine, I say, makes us certain beyond all other reasoning, because He has given it who sees and measures our immortality. Nor can we see that immortality perfectly as long as our immortal nature is mixed with our mortal. But we see it perfectly by faith, and by reason we see it shaded in obscurity, which is the result of the mixture of mortal with immortal" (*Conv.*, ii, viii, 14–15). See also Gilson, *Dante and Philosophy*, pp. 158–59 and 215.

3. Gilson, *Dante and Philosophy*, pp. 9–12, claims in fact that at the dramatic date of this scene, Dante had yet to begin to study philosophy, and therefore could scarcely be accused of having deserted theology for it (Gilson goes on to suggest other, more personal sins, p. 64).

4. In the *Convivio* Dante speaks also of a vision, and of the certainty he has of Beatrice's residence in Heaven—a *graziosa revelazione* that Beatrice herself had sent him of it (*Conv.*, ii, vii, 6; the *revelazione* is "hers"—*sua*). Without the *Purgatorio*, we would read this as confirmation of the visions of the *Vita Nuova;* in the context of the *Purgatorio*, however, we must read this as a reference to the journey of the *Commedia* itself, since this *revelazione* does not suffer the deficiencies of the earlier visions of the *Vita Nuova*. For what should be fascinating to us is that however convinced Dante had been at the end of the *Vita Nuova* of his rededication to Beatrice, he was wrong. In the *Convivio*, an older and wiser Dante recognizes the impetuousness of his younger self: "And if the present work, which is entitled the *Convivio* [the *Banquet*]—and I hope it is one, treats the subject of the *Vita Nuova* more maturely, yet I do not intend to denigrate that earlier work, but rather to value that one higher because of this one, seeing how reasonably both that early and passionate work agrees with this moderate and mature one" (*Conv.*, i, i, 16). See also Scartazzini's lengthy note on the problems inherent in reconciling the dates of these events (at *Purg.* xxx, 133–34: DDP).

5. As so many commentators have done, taking *argomenti* simply as "means." See, as examples, Benvenuto da Imola, Lombardi, Tommaseo, and Scartazzini (at *Purg.* xxx, 136: DDP).

6. This, I believe, is why the project of the *Convivio* was abandoned. Boyde, *Dante, Philomythes and Philosopher*, pp. 28–29, argues that Dante turned to poetry in order to reach a broader and less philosophically proficient audience. In a certain sense that is true, but Beatrice here makes it clear that the first member of that audience is Dante himself. As we will examine below, for the purposes Dante intends, every audience would stand in need of poetry, no matter how technically proficient in philosophy or theology.

7. Of "reason," or "the reason of *Romanitas*" (Triolo, "Ira, Cupiditas, Libido," p. 17); or of "reason illuminated [or moved] by faith" (Casini/Barbi at *Inf.* x, 61, and Giacalone at *Inf.* x, 61–63: DDP); or of "human reason

educated by wisdom and conscious of divine things" (Steiner at *Inf.* x, 62: DDP); or of human philosophy (Nardi, "La Filosofia di Dante," p. 1171); or of natural and political philosophy (Tommaseo at *Inf.* x, 61–63: DDP); or of pagan wisdom (Montano, "Il Canto XVII del «Purgatorio»," p. 28). Robert Hollander, "Dante's *Commedia* and the Classical Tradition: The Case of Virgil," in *The Divine Comedy and the Encyclopedia of Arts and Sciences,* pp. 15–26, esp. p. 17, derides this interpretation and cites many who have taken it.

8. Cf. Freccero, "The Firm Foot on a Journey without a Guide," p. 29.

9. Cf. Erich Auerbach, "Figura," in *Scenes from the Drama of European Literature* (New York: Meridian Books, 1959), pp. 11–76, esp. pp. 70–71.

10. Cf. Steiner (at *Purg.* xxx, 85: DDP): "Beatrice intende mostrargli quanto corra dal sillogismo, dalla scienza umana, al divino linguaggio della sapienza nelle Sacre Scritture. Nella loro ardua eloquenza così ricca di simboli, il concetto espresso con immagini ardite e il calore del sentimento constituiscono un linguaggio intenso e suggestivo che molto dice, molto fa intravedere e fantasticare. La differenza che corre tra una pagine di Aristotle e un salmo di Davide, o una profezia di Ezechiele è intuitiva."

11. Cited by Dante at *Conv.,* ii, i, 13: "Whence it is, as the Philosopher says in the Physics, that nature intends that our understanding proceed in an ordered way, that is, advancing from what we know better to what we know less well. I say nature intends it, insofar as this route of understanding is innate and natural in us." See also Aquinas' commentary to *Phys.,* i, 1: "The Philosopher says, in the first book of the *Posterior Analytics,* that particulars are better known to us, but universals are better known to nature, or simply. It should be understood that what are there taken as particulars are individual objects of sense, which are better known to us because sense perception, which is of particulars, precedes the understanding of the intellect, which is of universals" (in *Opera Omnia,* ed. S. E. Fretté [Paris: Vivès, 1875], v. 22, pp. 294–95). See also *Posterior Analytics* in Aquinas, *Expositio libri posteriorum,* in *Opera omnia,* vol. 1, part 2 (Roma: Commissio Leonina, and Paris: Vrin, 1989), i, 18; 81b5 and i, 2; 72a1, and *ST,* 1a 85, 3. Cf. Jean Pépin, *La Tradition de l'Allégorie de Philon d'Alexandrie à Dante* (Paris: Études augustiniennes, 1987), p. 272, and *Conv.,* ii, i, 8–14. Nor is this only an Aristotelian doctrine. The same doctrine is maintained, from a neo-Platonic perspective, by Dionysius: "He modeled our most pious hierarchy on the hierarchies of heaven, and clothed these immaterial hierarchies in numerous material figures and forms so that, in a way appropriate to our nature, we might be uplifted from these most venerable images to interpretations [anagogies] and assimilations which are simple and inexpressible. For it is quite impossible that we humans should, in any immaterial way, rise up to imitate and contemplate the heavenly hierarchies without the aid of those material means capable of guiding us as our nature requires" (*CH,* i, 3; 1038d–1039a).

12. See also Virgil's preparation of this trope at *Purg.* iii, 22–30, and *Purg.* iii, 88–96.

13. Some indication of Dante's distinction as a live human being is given by means of his weight. He makes a boat on which he travels ride lower in the water after he has boarded it (*Inf.* viii, 27); it is remarked that his feet move what he walks on, unlike those of the dead (*Inf.* xii, 80–82). On another occasion, it is noticed that his Adam's apple moves as he breathes and speaks (*Inf.* xxiii, 88). But for the most part, the material comparison of Dante's state to that of other souls is left obscure. Moreover, when in the Antenora section of the ninth circle he inadvertently kicks the head of Bocca degli Abati (*Inf.* xxxii, 77–79), the head seems to have a convincing solidity, as apparently do his neck and hair, by which Dante grabs him (*Inf.* xxxii, 97, 103–5).

14. Cf. Charles Martel's declaration that the light that clothes him *conceals* him from Dante:

> La mia letizia mi ti tien celato
> che mi raggia dintorno e mi *nasconde*
> quasi animal di sua seta fasciato.
> (*Par.* viii, 52–54)

15. The narrative of the *Commedia* in its totality corresponds to the earliest uses of the term *anagogy,* a crucial term in dealing with Dante's allegorical intentions. The term appears insistently and portentously throughout Dionysius' *Celestial Hierarchy.* The primary purpose of any hierarchy, pseudo-Dionysius asserts, whether celestial or human, is to make possible the movement of its members from the corporeal to the intelligible: "Nor is it possible for the divine ray to shine to us except by being anagogically veiled in a variety of holy veils, and by means of these, which are adapted to our natures, are the paternal providences naturally and properly prepared. It was for this reason that even our most holy Hierarchy was established by those perfected leaders in sacred things, judging it worthy in ultramundane imitation of the celestial hierarchies. It introduced variety into these immaterial (as we have said) hierarchies, conveying them to us in material figures and in composed forms. It did so in proportion to our understandings, so that we might ascend from most holy forms to those simple, and not figurative, highnesses and similarities" (*CH,* i, 2–3; 1038d–1039a). See also *EH,* i; ii; 1072b: "We see hierarchy proportionate to our ability, multiplied into the variety of perceptible symbols, but even from these we are hierarchically raised toward divine uniformity, as far as we can be, and we are raised to God and to divine virtue.... For us, it is by means of the perceptible images that our understandings are raised as far as they can be to the divine."

16. Cf. Boyde, *Perception and Passion,* pp. 76 and 95.

17. *Posterior Analytics,* ii, 19; 100a5. While it is not likely that Dante would have known the text of Plato's Seventh Letter, Plato's description is

remarkably similar, at least from a psychological perspective, to Aristotle's description of this moment. "But after the effort of turning these things over, and confronting them with one another—words and propositions, appearances and perceptions—scrutinizing them in friendly examinations, engaging in question and answer without any jealousy, straining one's powers to their human limit, suddenly the intelligence, and the mind, flash with illumination about each of these things" (Letter vii, 344b/c).

18. Freccero, "The Prologue Scene," pp. 25–27. In a similar vein, see also Christopher Kleinhenz, "Virgil, Statius, and Dante: An Unusual Trinity," in *Lectura Dantis Newberryana,* vol. 1, pp. 37–55.

19. *Metaphys.,* ix, 8; 1050a10–15, and *In Metaphys.,* §§1857–60; *ST,* 1a 77, 3 and 77, 7; 1a2æ 49, 3; see also *ST,* 1a2æ 3, 2.

20. *In de An.,* §§304 and 308; and *ST,* 1a2æ 24, 1; 49, 2; 49, 4 ad 1; 50, 5; also *Metaphys.,* ix, 6; 1048a32–35, and *In Metaphys.,* §1825.

21. *ST,* 1a2æ 49, 3 ad 1; also 50, 2 ad 3. See also *In de An.,* §216.

22. *ST,* 1a 77, 3; 4, 1; 1a2æ 49, 4. And in a theological context, one says that God most truly is because God is most truly and uninterruptedly in act. Even angels, insofar as they are not completely in act, are not pure act, and stand in need of habits to dispose their operations: *ST,* 1a2æ 50, 6.

23. Cf. Kainz, *"Active and Passive Potency,"* pp. 35 and 69.

24. We see evidence of the progress from potency to act in a crucial change in the immutability of purpose among the blessed. Though it might seem inconceivable to us, at the gate of Purgatory the angel warns Dante that even there it is possible to turn from God and be damned (*Purg.* ix, 130–32). Though Dante does not turn away, nor are we ever shown any other who did, the warning remains as proof that in Purgatory, though the soul has turned itself toward its proper end, it is nonetheless still in potency to that end until wholly determined to that end by its liberation from all vices that might pull it in the opposite direction. Only something in potency could change its ordering to its end—that is, could act either one way or another (in the angel's terms, could turn away from its goal). Powers, until they are actually in act, are always in potency to some degree, even when habituated to one end more than another. In Heaven, by contrast, it is clear that it would be absolutely impossible that a soul turn away from God, and this fixity is our proof that the progress from potency to act is completed, and that the souls in Heaven have now reached the perfection for which they were intended. For it is not merely that souls in Heaven could not turn away from God because the direct sight of God would exercise so strong a pull of desire on them that they could not bear to turn away. It is also that that unwavering looking at God is itself the very act (the *actus*) for which the souls' powers were created. In looking at God every soul is as perfectly in act as it can be, and being in act it *is* most completely, and could not be other than it is.

25. Bonaventure, *Breviloquium prooem.,* §4 (cf. *Collationes in Hexaëmeron,* xiii, 10–13).

26. See, for example, the commentaries of Scartazzini, Grabher, Trucchi, Momigliano, and Sapegno (at *Par.* xxxiii, 127–32: DDP)

27. *EN*, ii, 3; 1104b5–13; also 1104b30–1105a16.

28. Cf. Nardi, "Il Canto XIX dell'*Inferno*," p. 207: "I peccati dell'Inferno dantesco sono i peccatori con la loro concreta e umana fisionomia, i peccatori che hanno peccato come peccano gli uomini sulla terra, sì da destare sdegno e compassione, pietà ed orrore, ma soprattutto quella umana commozione, che nessuno mai proverà leggendo gli aridi trattati dei moralisti."

29. Hebrews 11:1: "Faith is the substance of things to be hoped for, the argument of things not seen" ("Est fides sperandarum substantia rerum, argumentum non apparentium").

30. Cf. Trucchi's comment (at *Par.* xxvi, 46–51: DDP): "Va bene, replica San Giovanni: io vede bene che il sovrano dei tuoi amori *guarda*, è diretto a Dio per filosofici argomenti che parlano all'intelletto, e per l'autorità della Santa Scrittura, in ciò a quelli concorde. Ma guardar con la mente non basta, non bastano argomentazioni e dottrina; *sentire* bisogna: dimmi dunque gli impulsi d'ordine sentimentale che ti elevano a Dio e ti stringono a Lui! e l'Apostolo chiede ciò mostrando tutto l'ardore suo proprio con quelle frasi tanto potenti delle *corde* che tirano a Dio, dei *denti* con cui morde l'amore di Dio, che sono convenientissime in lui, Aquila di Cristo!"

31. *Metaphys.*, xi, 7; 1064a19–29.

32. As a personal aside, I might point out that in this regard, Dante's convictions about his subject matter and the capacities of his audience drive him to poetry as a medium for reasons equivalent to those directing Thucydides in the manner of writing his history of the Peloponnesian War. For Thucydides too the causes of historical events could be learned in a useful manner only if a history of those events represented the causes in a way that reproduced their action in the world. Thucydides, therefore, never draws abstract conclusions about the factors that initiate and shape events; he reproduces the moments of public deliberation in which all factors— material, intellectual, emotional—find their active nexus. Cf. Marc Cogan, *The Human Thing: The Speeches and Principles of Thucydides' History* (Chicago: University of Chicago Press, 1981).

33. Cf. Augustine, *de Doctrina christiana*, iv, 12 (27): "And just as a hearer is delighted if you speak sweetly, so he is moved if he loves what you promise, fears what you threaten, hates what you denounce; if what you commend is embraced, if that at which you pour out grief, he grieves, if what you preach should be rejoiced, he rejoices at; if he pities those whom in speech you put before his eyes to be pitied; if he flees those whom you showed, terrifyingly, he should beware of. In general, anything is of the grand style of eloquence which can be put to moving the souls of the hearers not so that they know what should be done, but that they do what they already know should be done." See also iv, 13 (29).

34. *De An.*, iii, 10; 433a18–20; also *In de An.*, §§821–24.

35. Revealed truth: Busnelli, *L'Ordinamento morale*, p. 63, Auerbach, "Figura," p. 75 (though Auerbach, at least, recognizes the importance that Beatrice be an *incarnate* truth); or divine philosophy (Nardi, "La Filosofia di Dante," p. 1171); or "reasoned faith" (Meersseman, "Il Canto XI dell'«Inferno»," p. 3).

36. Thus, while Singleton's notion of dividing the duties of Virgil and Beatrice as guides between correction of the will (Virgil) and of the intellect (Beatrice) is appealing (*Journey to Beatrice*, pp. 11–12), in the end it is contradicted by just this quality. Beatrice's attraction is not to Dante's mind, but to his heart, and her appearance—at both the outset of the poem in coming to Virgil, and also at the end of the *Purgatorio* in taking over from him—serves to correct the end to which Dante is trying to move.

37. Cf. *In de An.*, §305.

38. Gilson, *Dante and Philosophy*, p. 79: "On the strength of the love that he bore her, Beatrice is exclusively marked out to be his intercessor with God. If God can win him back, it will be through her, and it is surely because Dante loves her still that God sends her to him. This man Dante will undoubtedly follow her, though he will follow no one else! And, in fact, he does follow her, in the character that she has now assumed—that of the mediator between his soul and God." But what is especially interesting in the nature of the poem, however, is that Beatrice as mediator stands in need herself of a mediator to Dante: Virgil. That Virgil too is truly a mediator can be seen from the way in which he was twice called on to remind Dante of Beatrice in order to move Dante to action he would otherwise avoid undertaking. The narrative itself, then, provides us a figure of the primacy of poetry in the process of salvation. It is poetry that mediates, and apparently must mediate, between lover and beloved.

APPENDIX 1

1. See Boccaccio (at *Inf.* ix, 110–33: DDP), and Sapegno and Fallani (at *Inf.* xi, 81: DDP). Boccaccio and Fallani both link circle six (heresy) to circle seven as sins of bestiality. Sapegno points out that whether we call the sins of irascibility bestial or not does not alter our understanding of them.

2. See also Moore, "The Classification of Sins" pp. 160–61.

3. It does not seem theoretically possible that there be a "superhuman" form of continence, but Aristotle is silent on this matter.

4. Giovanni Ferretti, "La «matta bestialità»," in *Saggi danteschi* (Firenze: Le Monnier, 1950), pp. 77–112, esp. pp. 84–87.

5. Triolo, "*Ira, Cupiditas, Libido*," pp. 21–23, recognizes that for Aristotle bestiality is an extreme, rather than an intermediate, evil disposition, but in trying to attribute Dante's use of the term to the sins of the ninth circle of Hell does serious violence, I believe, to Virgil's statement. See,

much earlier, Witte, "The Ethical Systems of the *Inferno* and the *Purgatorio*," p. 128.

6. Cf. Nardi, "Il Canto XI dell'*Inferno*," p. 200; Bosco, "Il Canto XII dell'*Inferno*," p. 211; Sacchetto, "Il Canto XII dell'*Inferno*," p. 6; and Favati, "Osservazioni sul canto XII dell'*Inferno* dantesco," p. 426.

7. Cf. Pagliaro, "«Le tre disposizion . . .»," p. 226; also Ferretti, "La «matta bestialità»," who goes too far, however, in restricting bestiality to heresy alone.

APPENDIX 2

1. Vazzana, *Il Contrapasso*, p. 114, also comments on the souls of the antepurgatory re-enacting their evil disposition. Since it is his general conviction that all of the souls in Purgatory also re-enact their vices, the distinction between the activities of the antepurgatory and of Purgatory proper becomes blurred.

2. *ST*, App. 1, 2, 5, and App. 2, 1.

3. *ST*, 1a2æ, 62, 3: "The theological virtues order man to supernatural blessedness just as man is ordered by natural inclination to the end natural to him."

4. *ST*, 2a2æ 4, 2.

5. Cf. *de Monarchia*, i, xi, 13–14.

APPENDIX 3

1. *CH*, vii, 1; 1050b–c: "We say that this must be understood in the order of holy hierarchies: that the names given these heavenly intelligences declare the property each has that conforms it to God." Cf. 2 *Sent.*, 9, 2; *ST*, 1a 108, 5. The same assumption is also held by Gregory, whose descriptions of angelic orders are for the most part consistent with those of Dionysius and his commentators, despite his use of a different arrangement of the orders. Cf. *XL Hom. in Evang.*, xxxiv, 13, PL 76, 1255b–d.

2. *Sent.*, 9, 2. Cf. *In 2 Sent.*, ix, 1, 3.

3. The pattern Bonaventure (*Collationes in Hexaëmeron*, xxi, 18–20) uses makes the highest order in a triad correspond to an association with the Father and the lowest to the Holy Spirit. This is the pattern he uses for the second and third triads. But in the first triad, this arrangement would associate the seraphim only with the Father (and not at all with the Holy Spirit) as long as Dionysius' enumeration of the orders is followed. Rather than give up the consistent pattern, Bonaventure alters Dionysius' enumeration for the first triad (and only for that triad): "In the first hierarchy, these are the names [of the orders]: thrones, cherubim, seraphim; in the second, dominations, virtues, powers; in the third, principalities, archangels, angels. . . . The

order corresponding to the Father, according as he exists in himself, is the order of thrones; the order corresponding to the Father, according as he exists in the Son, is the order of cherubim; the order corresponding to the Father, according as he exists in the Holy Spirit, is the order of seraphim."

4. "The order corresponding to the Father, according as he exists in himself, is the order of thrones; the order corresponding to the Father, according as he exists in the Son, is the order of cherubim; the order corresponding to the Father, according as he exists in the Holy Spirit, is the order of seraphim. The order corresponding to the Son, according as he exists in the Father, is the order of dominations, to whom it belongs to rule; according as the Son exists in Himself, the order of virtues; according as the Son exists in the Holy Spirit, the order of powers. The order corresponding to the Holy Spirit, according as he exists in the Father, is the order of principalities; according as he exists in the Son, the order of archangels, to whom it belongs to reveal secrets; according as he exists in himself, the order of angels" (*Collationes in Hexaëmeron*, xxi, 20). See also Gilson, *La Philosophie de Saint Bonaventure*, pp. 214–16.

5. When later, in the *Paradiso*, Dante adjusts his interpretation of the angelic hierarchy to match Dionysius' arrangement, he brings his interpretation of the seraphim (and of the cherubim, whose common medieval association with wisdom was also ignored in the *Convivio*) into agreement with the common medieval views of their nature. In Aquinas *personaggio*'s metaphorical association of the ardor of seraphim with Saint Francis and the cherubim's plenitude of knowledge with Saint Dominic, Dante makes an easily recognizable reference to the standard etymological interpretations of the names of these angelic orders.

> L'un fu tutto serafico in ardore;
> l'altro per sapïenza in terra fue
> di cherubica luce uno splendore.
> (*Par.* xi, 37–39)

6. Cf. Hugh of St. Victor, *In Hierarchiam cœlestem*, *PL*, 175, 1023b–1025c; also *ST*, 1a 108, 6. Foster, "The Celebration of Order: *Paradiso* X," pp. 109–24, pursues a different strategy, which would end, it seems, with a somewhat different order of persons for each of the triads. In each triad, the person "in relation to itself" would occupy the highest position. This would run into problems in both the middle triad (as I will mention below) and the highest triad.

7. Cf. Vasoli, *Conv.*, p. 152, Attilio Mellone, in "Angelo," in *Enciclopedia dantesca*, vol. 1, p. 269, and Nardi, *Dal Convivio alla Commedia*, pp. 55 ff., on Dante's eclecticism in the principles of his angelology.

8. *XL Hom. in Evang.*, xxxiv, 10, *PL*, 76, 1252a. Cf. Hugh of St. Victor, *In Hierarchiam cœlestem*, *PL*, 175, 1023c and 1048c–1049d; 2 *Sent.*, 9, 2; also *ST*, 1a 108, 6.

9. Pecoraro, *Le Stelle di Dante,* p. 298, argues from the location *to which* Dante moved the thrones that it should be the first, or lowest, position in a triad that is associated with the Holy Spirit. Pecoraro takes the description Dante gave of the thrones in the *Convivio* as a fixed point of reference, and believes that they would carry the association there made with the Holy Spirit with them wherever they moved in the hierarchy. I do not think that that is the most satisfactory interpretation. Rather, as stated above, I think the earlier description of the thrones was conditioned by their being then associated with the planet Venus. To claim, as Pecoraro does, that the lowest position in a triad should be associated with the Holy Spirit would rob the seraphim, on the one hand, and the planet Venus, on the other, of any association with the Holy Spirit. But both conclusions would be highly unconventional and unnatural. It is far easier to imagine that when Dante moved the thrones in the hierarchy, he also revised his understanding of their character.

10. See Vasoli, *Conv.,* p. 165, commenting upon *Conv.,* ii, 5, 13.

General Index

accidiosi (sinners), 52, 328
acedia. *See* sloth
act: operation of a power, 269; perfection of a power, 270–71, 377; "second act," 271
activity. *See* act
Adam, 118, 155, 208, 211, 215, 369
Æneas, 113
aerial body, 123, 129, 348–49; as poetic device, 260–61
affections: and grace, 237, 290, 371; in aerial body, 123, 261; in *Commedia,* actually spiritual, 141–42
affetti. See affections, passion
Alain de Lille, 364
Alberigo (Frate), 15
Albert I of Austria, 302
Albert the Great, Saint (Albertus Magnus), 317, 319–20, 346, 347, 357, 372; on angelic hierarchy and intelligences, 356–57; on seven capital vices, 341
Alcuin, 341
Aldobrandesco, Omberto, 38, 90, 92, 108
Ali, 61
allegory, 149, 153, 188, 249, 351; one single allegory, 244–45; structure replicates order of understanding, 258–59; structure replicates passage from potency to act, 273–74; structure

replicates process of appetition, 285–87
Amore, 189
anagogy, 246, 263, 274, 375–76
Anastasius II, Pope, 61–63
angel: and appetites, 222–28, 229, 242–43, 244, 369; and memory, 190, 366, 373; coincidence of knowledge and love, 239; degrees of merit, 155, 367; intelligences, 176–77, 356–59, and human character, 186–87, 217, 274; will only appetite, 69, 108, 223. *See also* angelic hierarchy, angels, *and individual orders of angels*
angelic (celestial) hierarchy: and blessedness, 179–80; and multiplicity, 180–81, 246, 360–61; Dante's arrangement in *Convivio,* 176–77, 307–8, 309, 356–57; Gregory's arrangements, 177, 359–60; in Peter Lombard, 359–60; order of Paradise, 175–78, 187, 368; pseudo-Dionysius' arrangement, 177–78, 359; reflects Trinity, 182–85, 217, 220, 305–12, 360. *See also indivdual orders of angels*
angelology. *See* angelic hierarchy
angels (angelic order), 177, 357, 367; association with persons of

280, 282, 301, 378; and
appetition, 289, 371
Farinata degli Uberti, 67–68, 337
Father (person of the Trinity): and
highest triad of angelic
hierarchy, 183, 212, 305, 307;
and lowest locations in triads,
215–16; and memory, 189, 199,
308; and order, 189, 212; and
power, 189, 199, 207; secondary
associations, 186, 199, 206–7
fear (passion), 30, 53
fire: as refining fire in Purgatory,
116; with heat as primary image
of irascibility, 53–54, 330; without heat as image of passionless
sins, 71–72, 330, 334
fixed stars, sphere of (8th), 211, 213
flatterers, 71; relative seriousness of
sin, 74
Folquet of Marseilles, 168, 201, 204
fortitude (virtue), 23; angelic,
145–46, 193, 226–27, 265; in
irascible appetite, 23
Francesca da Rimini, 28, 292
Francis, Saint, 197–98, 212, 366,
370, 381
fraud, 2, 14, 18, 100, 270, 316; and
injustice, 24–26; and profit, 25,
70; and will, 25–26, 70; most
hated, 24; proper to humans, 24
freedom, 92–93, 118
free will, 168, 354
Fucci, Vanni, 9, 72, 85, 314

Galeotto, 292
geography: as principle of
structure, xix, xxi, 1, 42–43, 48,
73, 80–81, 103, 118, 190, 327
Geryon, 69
gluttons (and gluttony): act and
habit distinguished, 104; in Hell
(sin), 8, punishment, 44–45; in

Purgatory (vice), 82, 99, 100,
127, and concupiscible appetite,
102, 114–16
Gorgons, 54
grace: and Beatrice, 290; and merit,
169–70, 174–75, 354–55; and vision, 156–58, 170, 235–36, 290,
351, 372
Gregory the Great (Pope and
Saint): and angelic hierarchy,
177, 193, 197, 227, 310, 359–60;
and seven capital vices, 117, 337,
343
Guido da Montefeltro, 15, 315, 334
Guido del Duca, 107, 325

habit, 6, 86–88, 95, 324; between
power and act, 88, 269; distinguished from actions and passions, 103–4; "first act," 271;
reformed by contraries, 338;
structure of Purgatory, 272
Harpies, 295
health, 91, 118
Heaven: order of, 175–78, 214–18,
220–21; significance of order,
214
Hell: lower Hell, 8, circles of fraud
and will, 25–26, 35, 68–72, of
heresy, 60–68, of violent sins,
30–31, 35, 53–68; order of
regions, 34–36, 322; structured
by powers, 270; upper Hell, 2,
29, 327, and concupiscible appetite, 29, 34, 44–53; symmetry
with Purgatory, 78–84, 99–102,
119–20
Henry of Navarre, 302
heretics (and heresy), 26, 60–68,
109, 330–33; and bestiality, 65,
296, 379; and despair, 65, 332;
and fire, 64; and irascibility, 65,
114; and passion, 64–65; and

Index of Authors of Works on the Commedia

Page references are to first citation of a work.